The
Simon & Schuster
SHORT
PROSE
READER

Third Edition

ROBERT W. FUNK
Eastern Illinois University

SUSAN X DAY
Iowa State University

ELIZABETH McMAHAN
Illinois State University

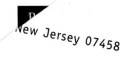

New Jersey 07458

Library of Congress Cataloging-in-Publication Data

The Simon & Schuster short prose reader / [compiled by] Robert Funk, Susan X Day,
Elizabeth McMahan.—3rd ed.
    p.   cm.
Includes index.
ISBN 0-13-097410-2
1. College readers.   2. English language—Rhetoric—Problems, exercises, etc.   3. Report
writing—Problems, exercises, etc.   I. Title: Simon and Schuster short prose reader.

PE1417.S453   2003
808'.0427—dc21   2002019028

VP/Editor in Chief: Leah Jewell
Acquisitions Editor: Craig Campanella
Editorial Assistant: Joan Polk
VP, Director of Production
    and Manufacturing: Barbara Kittle
Executive Managing Editor: Ann Marie McCarthy
Production Liaison: Fran Russello
Project Manager: Linda B. Pawelchak
Manufacturing Manager: Nick Sklitsis
Prepress and Manufacturing Buyer: Benjamin Smith
Cover Director: Jayne Conte
Cover Art: "Flowers below a Window in Greece," Getty Images, Inc./
    PhotoDisc, Inc.
Marketing Manager: Rachel Falk
Copy Editing: Katherine Evancie
Proofreading: Cheryl Rivard

Acknowledgments begin on page 371, which constitutes
a continuation of this copyright page.

This book was set in 11/13 Bembo by TSI Graphics
and was printed and bound by Von Hoffman Press, Inc.
The cover was printed by Phoenix Color Corp.

© 2003, 2000, 1997 by Pearson Education, Inc.
Upper Saddle River, New Jersey 07458

10 ┤ in the United States of America
    ⟍ 7   6   5   4   3

ISBN
ISBN 'ᑈ-097410-2 (student text)
      097421-8 (annotated instructor's
               edition)

Pearson Education
Pearson Education ╷
Pearson Education Sin ╷
Pearson Education Nort Limited, *Sydney*
Pearson Education Canada
Pearson Educación de Mexicl
Pearson Education—Japan, *Tok Kong*
Pearson Education Malaysia, Pte. ╷
Pearson Education, *Upper Saddle Ri*

In loving memory of

Ray Lewis White

CONTENTS

2

THE READING–WRITING CONNECTION   15

3

STRATEGIES FOR CONVEYING IDEAS: 29
NARRATION AND DESCRIPTION

4

STRATEGIES FOR MAKING A POINT: 67
EXAMPLE AND ILLUSTRATION

5

STRATEGIES FOR CLARIFYING MEANING: 100
DEFINITION AND EXPLANATION

6

STRATEGIES FOR SORTING IDEAS: CLASSIFICATION AND DIVISION   **136**

"The best of friends, I still believe, totally love and support and trust each other, and bare to each other the secrets of their souls, and run—no questions asked—to help each other, and tell harsh truths to each other when they must be told."

"A sadist and a masochist may work out a mutually rewarding relationship, but does that make them healthy?"

"The major task of psychological stress management is to find ways to balance and coordinate the demands that come from within with those that come from without."

"What all the world really loves is not a lover. It's a love story. People can't get enough of love stories."

"Some people are so obsessive about not missing one episode that all other activities cease while *ER* is on."

7

STRATEGIES FOR EXAMINING TWO SUBJECTS: COMPARISON AND CONTRAST   **175**

8

STRATEGIES FOR EXPLAINING HOW THINGS WORK: 214
PROCESS AND DIRECTIONS

9

STRATEGIES FOR ANALYZING WHY THINGS HAPPEN: 248
CAUSE AND EFFECT

10

STRATEGIES FOR INFLUENCING OTHERS: 284
ARGUMENT AND PERSUASION

11

FURTHER READINGS   340

THEMATIC CONTENTS

MORALS AND ETHICS

EDUCATION AND LEARNING

LANGUAGE AND WRITING

MINORITY PERSPECTIVES

GENDER

HUMAN BEHAVIOR

SOCIAL ISSUES

EDITING SKILLS CONTENTS

C h a p t e r

ACTIVE READING

Most people who write well also read well—and vice versa. The two skills are so intertwined that they are often taught together, as we do in this textbook. Reading gives you not only information and amusement but also a sense of how sentences and paragraphs work. Most of the time, you get this sense without really paying attention: it just seeps into your mind with the rest of the material. In this textbook, we ask you to make the reading–writing connection more consciously than you may have done before. By looking carefully at good writing, you will better understand the content as well as the techniques the writers use.

LEARNING TO BE AN ACTIVE READER

Did you ever finish reading something, look up from the page, and realize that you didn't take in anything at all? That you passed your eyes over the print, but you might as well have stared out the window? At such times, you know that you have been an extremely passive reader. On the opposite end of the spectrum, you've probably had the experience of being swept away from reality while reading, so involved in the printed word that the rest of your world fades. Much of your college reading won't be able to carry you off that completely. By learning to be an **active reader,** though, you will be able to handle your reading assignments competently. The main idea is to stay involved with the reading through interaction—bringing mental and emotional energy to the task.

KEEPING A JOURNAL

One good way to become an interactive reader is to keep a journal about what you read. In a journal, you can experiment with ideas and express your responses with greater freedom than you can in formal writing assignments. Before each reading selection in most chapters of this book, we ask you a Preparing to Read question that you may answer in your journal as well as in class discussions. This activity starts you thinking about the ideas you will find in the essay that follows. After each selection, we give you a Responding to Reading suggestion to consider in your journal, encouraging you to write about your personal reactions. You will see as this chapter goes along how your two journal entries fit into your role as an active reader.

PREVIEWING THE READING

If you're the type who simply plunges into a reading assignment, you're missing something. Study skills experts emphasize the value of previewing the reading, getting your mind ready for full comprehension. **Previewing** involves more than merely counting the number of pages you have to go: no one needs to remind you to do that! The trick is to develop a mental set that makes your brain most receptive to the material.

Title

Try stopping after you read the **title** and asking yourself what it suggests to you. The sample essay we will use in this chapter is named "Handled with Care." Where have you heard such a phrase before? What image does it bring to your mind? The title often gives you a clue about what's ahead.

Author and Other Publication Facts

With some assignments, you will recognize the author's name. Bob Greene is the writer of "Handled with Care," and you may know that he is a columnist for the *Chicago Tribune.* You may also know that his columns often comment on culture and politics and the connections between them. Again, the author's name provides clues about the essay that follows. You may know something about the time period when it was written (as you would if the byline read "Mark Twain"). If the byline read "Erma Bombeck," you'd expect something humorous about modern domestic life.

Even when you don't recognize the author, you can take note of other publication facts. The date of publication, if you have it, gives you an idea of how current the information is. If the reading is reprinted, as the ones in this textbook are, consider where it originally appeared and whether that means anything to you. If an essay first showed up in *U.S. News & World Report,* you can assume it will have a conservative political slant; if it came from *The Nation,* it will probably have a leftist slant. If it came from a city newspaper, such as the *Chicago Tribune,* you can't be so sure about the political slant, since most big newspapers attempt to cover the spectrum.

Visual Features and Supplements

Page through the reading, looking at parts that stand out from the ordinary print, such as headnotes, headings, photos, diagrams, boxed material, summaries, and questions after the reading. Your textbooks are specially designed to include lots of these helpful materials. Unfortunately, many students skip them, thinking they're not as important as the rest. Actually, they are there to focus attention on what *is* important in the reading. Or they may give you information that assists you in understanding the reading; for example, the headnote paragraphs before essays in this textbook give a little biographical information about the writer. The Terms to Recognize section lists some difficult words from the essay and their definitions, so you won't have to look them up in the dictionary right away. In this list, we provide only the definition that fits the way the term is used in the reading; the term probably has other meanings as well.

Some reading material doesn't include any obvious helps. It's just straight print. But you can benefit from the only visual clue: paragraph indentations. Read the first sentence of each paragraph. This survey will probably give you ideas about the content and organization of the reading.

Responses and Predictions

"This preview stuff just slows me down," you may be thinking. "I don't have time for it." Let us assure you, the first stage does seem slow, but it makes later stages faster and more efficient. It also markedly increases your memory for what you read.

The main thing you're doing as you preview is responding to clues and making predictions about what the reading contains. It may seem like a guessing game, but actually you are clearing the brush from pathways in your brain, making the way easy for the information to get through. Through guessing what to expect, you are directing your attention, focusing on the material so that it won't be fighting through a tangle of thoughts about why you squabble with your roommate and what you'll have for lunch.

Instead, let your mind wander through the associations and experiences you already have with the material suggested by your preview. What people, events, and feelings in your own life did you stumble across in your preview? If you are from Chicago, you are able to visualize the setting of the essay and may even be able to predict Bob Greene's overall style. Or the title, "Handled with Care," may have reminded you of a delicate package that happened to reach you intact, miraculously, through the mail.

A FIRST READING

Now is the time to plunge in. Try to place yourself in a setting that aids concentration. This setting varies from person to person, and you probably know your ideal situation. You can't always get it, but at least don't undermine yourself by choosing a spot where you know you'll be distracted or where you know you'll be lulled to sleep. Sitting up at a table or desk is a good idea because the position suggests that you are going to work.

You'll need a pencil or pen to read interactively. Make it a habit. Mark words and terms that you need to look up later. Write questions—or just question marks—in the margins near material you don't quite understand. Write your spontaneous responses *(Yes! No! Reminds me of Aunt Selma! What!? Prejudiced crap!)* in the margins. Underline sentences that you think may contain the main ideas and phrases that impress you with the way they are worded. We provide one reader's markings of "Handled with Care" in this chapter.

STAYING AWARE OF CONVENTIONS

Conventions are the traditional ways of doing things: for example, we have conventional ways of beginning and ending telephone conversations, and we expect everyone to follow them. If a friend closed a phone conversation by saying, "Pick me up at 9:15," and immediately hung up, you would think it strange not to have any of the usual sign-off words. The same type of expectation goes for writing **conventions,** some of which we outline here. Stories and poems don't have to follow these conventions, but nonfiction works like **essays,** textbooks, and manuals do. You can enhance your reading by looking for conventional features as you go along.

Subject

Each piece of writing is expected to deal with one subject or topic. This should be fairly clear to you near the beginning, perhaps even from the title ("Why We Crave Horror Movies," in Chap. 9, is about exactly that). Once you identify the subject, you can be pretty sure the whole reading will stay on that topic.

Main Idea or Thesis

We expect a reading not only to have a subject but also to say something *about* the subject. That is the **thesis** or main idea. Frequently, the main idea comes up early in the reading, clearly expressed in one sentence. At other times, you must put together the main point piece by piece as you read. It may finally be stated in a sentence at the end, or it may not be stated directly at all. As you read, underline sentences that seem to add to your understanding of the author's main point.

Supporting Material

Writers must prove their main points by providing convincing **supporting material.** This can be in the form of logical reasoning, emotional appeal, examples, evidence from experts, specific details, facts, and statistics. Different main points lend themselves to different types of supporting material: for example, your math textbook uses mostly logical reasoning and examples, while an essay about capital punishment might use all the forms we listed. While you read an assignment, ask yourself: "What forms of supporting material does this author use?"

Patterns of Organization

The conventions of subject, thesis, and supporting material deal with the content of the reading. You also need to look at *how* the content is presented. After each selection in the following chapters, you will see questions called Considering Content and Considering Method. The method questions ask you to consider the techniques the author used to present material, including organization.

We organize the chapters in this book according to **patterns of development** that are the most conventional ways to organize writing: patterns such as comparison and contrast, cause and effect, and narration. Each chapter explains one basic pattern. As you read an essay, notice how the writer uses a pattern (usually, a combination of patterns) to arrange ideas.

Paragraphs

As a reader, you will also notice how writers package their meaning in units of thought called **paragraphs.** Paragraph indention usually signals the introduction of a new topic or a new aspect of a current topic. In other words, writers start new paragraphs to show that they are moving on to another topic or subtopic. Paragraphs in prose essays tend to be longer than paragraphs in newspapers and magazines, where journalists break their paragraphs frequently to make narrow columns of type easier to read.

Transitions

Another element of a writer's method involves how he or she makes connections between ideas. These connections are called **transitions.** A common place for a transition is between two paragraphs (at the end of one and/or at the beginning of the next one), where the author shows the logical relationship between them. Recognizing transitions helps you direct your thought process in the way the author wants you to. For example, a paragraph that begins "Furthermore, . . . " lets you know that you should expect material that adds to and agrees with the material before it. A paragraph that begins "On the other hand, . . . " lets you know that you should expect material that contradicts or shows the opposite of the material before it. By noticing transitions, you prepare the appropriate mindset for understanding what comes next.

A SAMPLE ESSAY

Handled with Care

BOB GREENE

the day the lady took her clothes off on Michigan Avenue, people were leaving downtown as usual. The workday had come to an end; men and women were heading for bus and train stations, in a hurry to get home.   1

She walked south on Michigan; she was wearing a white robe, as if she had been to the beach. She was blond and in her thirties. As she passed the Radisson Hotel, Roosevelt Williams, a doorman, was opening the door of a cab for one of the hotel's guests. The woman did not really pause while she walked; she merely shrugged the robe off, and it fell to the sidewalk. She was wearing what appeared to be the bottom of a blue bikini bathing suit, although one woman who was directly next to her said it was just underwear. She wore nothing else.   2

Williams at first did not believe what he was seeing. If you hang around long enough, you will see everything: robberies, muggings, street fights, murders. But a naked woman on North Michigan Avenue? Williams had not seen that before and neither, apparently, had the other people on the street.   3

It was strange; her white robe lay on the sidewalk, and by all accounts   4
she was smiling. But no one spoke to her. A report in the newspaper the
next day quoted someone: "The cars were stopping, the people on the
buses were staring, people were shouting, and people were taking pictures."
But that is not what other people who were there that afternoon said. The
atmosphere was not carnival-like, they said. Rather, they said, it was as if
something very sad was taking place. It took only a moment for people to
realize that this was not some stunt designed to promote a product or a
movie. Without anything telling them, they understood that the woman was
troubled, and that what she was doing had nothing to do with sexual titil-
lation; it was more of a cry for help.

The cry for help came in a way that such cries often come. The woman   5
was violating one of the basic premises of the social fabric. She was doing
something that is not done. She was not shooting anyone, or breaking a
window, or shouting in anger. Rather, in a way that everyone understood,
she was signaling that things were not right.

The line is so thin between matters being manageable and being out of   6
hand. One day a person may be barely all right; the next the same person
may have crossed over. Here is something from the author John Barth:

She paused amid the kitchen to drink a glass of water; at that instant,   7
losing a grip of fifty years, the next-room-ceiling plaster crashed. Or he
merely sat in an empty study, in March-day glare, listening to the
universe rustle in his head, when suddenly a five-foot shelf let go. For
ages the fault creeps secret through the rock; in a second, ledge and railings, tourists and turbines all thunder over Niagara. Which snowflake
triggers the avalanche? A house explodes; a star. In your spouse, so apparently resigned, murder twitches like a fetus. At some trifling new assessment, all the colonies rebel.

The woman continued to walk past Tribune Tower. People who saw her   8
said that the look on her face was almost peaceful. She did not seem to
think she was doing anything unusual; she was described as appearing "blissful." Whatever the reaction on the street was, she seemed calm, as if she
believed herself to be in control.

She walked over the Michigan Avenue bridge. Again, people who were   9
there report that no one harassed her; no one jeered at her or attempted
to touch her. At some point on the bridge, she removed her bikini bottom.
Now she was completely undressed, and still she walked. "It was as if people

knew not to bother her," said one woman who was there. "To tell it, it sounds like something very lewd and sensational was going on. But it wasn't like that at all. It was as if people knew that something very . . . fragile . . . was taking place. I was impressed with the maturity with which people were handling it. No one spoke to her, but you could tell that they wished someone would help her."

Back in front of the Radisson, a police officer had picked up the woman's   10 robe. He was on his portable radio, advising his colleagues that the woman was walking over the bridge. When the police caught up with the woman, she was just standing there, naked in downtown Chicago, still smiling. The first thing the police did was hand her some covering and ask her to put it on; the show was over.

People who were there said that there was no reaction from the people   11 who were watching. They said that the juvenile behavior you might expect in such a situation just didn't happen. After all, when a man walks out on a ledge in a suicide attempt, there are always people down below who call for him to jump. But this day, by all accounts, nothing like that took place. No one called for her to stay undressed; no one cursed the police officers for stopping her. "It was as if everyone was relieved," said a woman who saw it. "They were embarrassed by it; it made them feel bad. They were glad that someone had stopped her. And she was still smiling. She seemed to be off somewhere."

The police charged her with no crime; they took her to Read Mental   12 Health Center, where she was reported to have signed herself in voluntarily. Within minutes things were back to as they always are on Michigan Avenue; there was no reminder of the naked lady who had reminded people how fragile is the everyday world in which we live.

MARKING THE TEXT

Here is an example of how a student reader marked the Bob Greene essay.

Handled with Care

like a package with breakables in it

Chi.
Tribune

BOB GREENE

—*Emotion*—
shock value!
The day the lady took her clothes off on   1
Michigan Avenue, people were leaving downtown
as usual. The workday had come to an end; men

Time of day important?

and women were heading for bus and train stations, in a hurry to get home.

2

She walked south on Michigan; she was wearing a white robe, as if she had been to the beach. She was blond and in her thirties. As she passed the Radisson Hotel, Roosevelt Williams, a doorman, was opening the door of a cab for one of the hotel's guests. The woman did not really pause *Why?* while she walked; she merely shrugged the robe off, and it fell to the sidewalk. She was wearing what appeared to be the bottom of a blue bikini bathing suit, although one woman who was directly next to her said it was just underwear. She *What* wore nothing else. *difference*

would that   3
Williams at first did not believe what he was *make??* seeing. If you hang around long enough, you will see everything: robberies, muggings, street fights, *Contrast with* murders. But a naked woman on North Michi- *other outrageous* gan Avenue? Williams had not seen that before *events* and neither, apparently, had the other people on *Subject—an* the street. *unusual*

event   4
It was strange; her white robe lay on the sidewalk, and by all accounts she was smiling. But no one spoke to her. A report in the newspaper the *Papers were* next day quoted someone: "The cars were stop- *wrong—* ping, the people on the buses were staring, people *misreported* were shouting, and people were taking pictures." *event* But that is not what other people who were there that afternoon said. The atmosphere was not carnival-like, they said. Rather, they said, it was as if some- *Main point?* thing very sad was taking place. It took only a moment for people to realize that this was not some stunt designed to promote a product or a movie. Without anything telling them, they understood that the woman was troubled, and that what she was doing had nothing to do with sexual titil- *People* lation; it was more of a cry for help. *had*

↺   *sympathy*   5
The cry for help came in a way that such cries *Transition:* often come. The woman was violating one of the *expand on* basic premises of the social fabric. [She was doing *"cry for help"* something that is not done. She was not shooting

anyone, or breaking a window, or shouting in *other* anger.] Rather, in a way that everyone understood, *violations* she was signaling that things were not right.

The line is so thin between matters being *Thesis?*   6 manageable and being out of hand. One day a person may be barely all right; the next the same person may have crossed over. Here is something from the author John Barth:

Supporting material from expert— more examples

She paused amid the kitchen to drink a glass of   7 water; at that instant, losing a grip of fifty years, the next-room-ceiling plaster crashed. Or he merely sat in an empty study, in March-day glare, listening to the universe rustle in his head, **?** when suddenly a five-foot shelf let go. For ages the fault creeps secret through the rock; in a second, ledge and railings, tourists and turbines **?** all thunder over Niagara. Which snowflake triggers the avalanche? A house explodes; a star. In your spouse, so apparently resigned, murder twitches like a fetus. At some trifling new assessment, all the colonies rebel.

Because she was acting out her cry for help?

The woman continued to walk past Tribune   8 Tower. People who saw her said that the look on her face was almost peaceful. She did not seem to think she was doing anything unusual; she was described as appearing "blissful." Whatever the reaction on the street was, she seemed calm, as if she believed herself to be in control.

She walked over the Michigan Avenue bridge.   9 Again, people who were there report that no one harassed her; no one jeered at her or attempted to touch her. At some point on the bridge, she removed her bikini bottom. Now she was completely undressed, and still she walked. "It was as if people knew not to bother her," said one woman who was there. "To tell it, it sounds like something very lewd and sensational was going on. But it wasn't like that at all. It was as if people knew that something very . . . . fragile . . . . was

taking place. I was impressed with the maturity
with which people were handling it. No one *Def. of*
spoke to her, but you could tell that they wished *maturity*
someone would help her."

Back in front of the Radisson, a police officer   10
had picked up the woman's robe. He was on his
portable radio, advising his colleagues that the
woman was walking over the bridge. When the
police caught up with the woman, she was just
standing there, naked in downtown Chicago, still
smiling. The first thing the police did was hand
her some covering and ask her to put it on; the
show was over.

Contrast   People who were there said that there was no   11
w/what   reaction from the people who were watching.
was   They said that the juvenile behavior you might
expected   expect in such a situation just didn't happen.
After all, when a man walks out on a ledge in a
suicide attempt, there are always people down
below who call for him to jump. But this day, by
all accounts, nothing like that took place. No one
called for her to stay undressed; no one cursed
the police officers for stopping her. "It was as if *People*
everyone was relieved," said a woman who saw *identified*
it. "They were embarrassed by it; it made them *with*
feel bad. They were glad that someone had *her—*
stopped her. And she was still smiling. She *thesis?*
seemed to be off somewhere."

The police charged her with no crime; they   12
took her to Read Mental Health Center, where
she was reported to have signed herself in voluntarily. Within minutes things were back to as they
always are on Michigan Avenue; there was <u>no</u> *People are*
<u>reminder</u> of the naked lady who had reminded *shallow?*
people <u>how fragile is the everyday world in which *Main*
we live.</u> *point? see*
¶ 6.

CLARIFYING MEANING

Put yourself in the student reader's place to see what happens next after
reading and marking the text.

Using the Dictionary

First, look up terms and words you marked as unfamiliar on the first reading. In this textbook, some will be defined right before the selection. Be sure to look up even words you *think* you know but are a bit fuzzy on. What exactly does *assessment* mean in paragraph 7? Though we often use the word to mean *evaluation,* in this case it means *taxation,* which makes more sense in the context.

You may use specialized dictionaries to look up unfamiliar references in the selection. For example, Greene writes that John Barth is an author. If you looked in a biographical or literary dictionary, you would find that Barth is a contemporary author who sees the world as absurd, as making no real sense. This detail helps you understand the quotation. Many writers make references to names from mythology, philosophy, and literature that you will need to look up. The reference librarian will show you where the specialized dictionaries are kept.

Reading Aloud

Return to the spots where you drew a question mark, and read those passages slowly aloud. Hearing your voice find the proper way to read a sentence may shed the necessary light on its meaning.

Discussing

Having a conversation about your reading will usually help you understand it. Another person who has read the same selection will probably have different reactions and may be able to clarify points that stumped you. Even someone who has not read the selection may be a good sounding board to discuss the ideas with.

Rereading

At some point, you will need to go back and reread the whole assignment, especially if you are going to be tested on it or intend to write a formal essay about it. With difficult material, the second read through will be more comfortable and will allow you to notice things you missed the first time.

MAKING INFERENCES AND ASSOCIATIONS

Bob Greene's essay is a good example of one that isn't completely spelled out for you. You have to make judgments about what he writes, inferences or conclusions about the meaning.

Reading between the Lines

You can train yourself to infer knowledge that lies below the surface meaning of the words. To *infer* means to arrive at an idea or a conclusion through reasoning. When you infer, you balance what the writer says with your own ideas and hunches about what is left unsaid. This process may sound difficult, but making **inferences** is a skill that can be learned.

Developing Inference Skills

Here are some suggestions for improving your ability to read between the lines:

Read beyond the words. Fill in details and information to complete the writer's suggestions. Use the writer's hints to discover the meanings that often lie beneath the surface. But don't go too far: you should be able to point to words and phrases that support what you have inferred.

Question yourself as you read and after you finish. You might use questions like these: Why did the author include these details? What does this example mean? How am I supposed to react to this sentence?

Draw conclusions and speculate on outcomes. In reflecting on Bob Greene's essay, for example, you might ask yourself these questions: Is the article saying that people are more sensitive than we usually assume—or less sensitive? Is the message of the selection positive or negative? Would people have reacted differently if the woman had not been young, blond, and attractive? What truths about our society does this incident suggest?

Make associations between the reading and your own experience. For instance: Have you ever witnessed a "cry for help"? Was it like the one Greene describes, or different? How did you and other people respond?

Your own observations and reflections add richness to the selection's meaning. Our Responding to Reading exercises will assist you in developing your personal reaction.

WRITING TO UNDERSTAND AND RESPOND

If you write out your Responding to Reading assignment, you have already begun the interactive process that will set the selection firmly in your memory. Study skills experts point out that we have four modes of verbal communication: we listen, we read, we speak, and we write. Different people learn best through different modes, but college learning often emphasizes only the first two: listening to course lectures and reading textbooks. When you add the other two modes to your study habits, you more than double your learning potential. Speaking in class and discussing the material with friends and class-mates are important. Writing about what you have heard and read is equally important. Here are some ways to write about a reading assignment:

1. Without looking at the reading, write a summary, 100 to 200 words long, of the selection. As you write, you will develop a sense of which parts of the selection are unclear in your mind. These will be the parts you find hard to express. Compare your summary to the original, and revise your summary to make it as accurate as possible. This summary will be a fine study aid if you are going to be tested.

2. You can make another study aid by constructing an outline of the important points. This outline can be a simple list of key thoughts in the order they appeared in the essay, like this:

A. A woman removed her clothes while walking down Michigan Avenue.
B. The witnesses say the crowd reacted in a sad way, not in the excited, noisy way one might expect.
C. The woman was crying out for help by violating conventional behavior.
D. The episode reflected the thin line between ordinary and shocking events.
E. The crowd identified with the woman instead of looking at her as a freak.
F. After the woman was taken away, Michigan Avenue quickly went back to its usual state.

3. In your journal, write a letter to the author of your selection. What would you say to him or her if you could? Do you have any questions? These might be brought up in class discussion if you have them on hand.

4. You will also benefit from writing out answers to the Considering Content and Considering Method questions, which are designed to help you focus on meaning and technique.

The writing you have done so far will be of great help to you when you need to draft an assigned essay of your own based on your reading. This process is the subject of the next chapter.

WEB SITE

http://chicagotribune.com/news/columnists/chi-bobgreene.columnist
Read some of Bob Greene's recent columns; find out more about him and his writing.

C h a p t e r

THE READING–WRITING CONNECTION

The connections between reading and writing are strong: in both activities you use language to create meaning. In Chapter 1, you learned how writing can help you to understand and remember what you read; in this chapter, you will learn how reading and responding to essays can help you to improve your writing.

WRITING IN RESPONSE TO READING

The basic principle of this book is that reading and writing go together. Each chapter follows a four-part pattern that you will discover works well in many of your college classes: (1) read a selection, (2) examine the content, (3) analyze the techniques, and (4) write something of your own that relates to the reading.

When you read, you get ideas for your own writing. Reading can supply you with topics to write about and show you how to write about them. Even when you already have a topic, reading can help you to come up with material to develop that topic. Reading will also provide you with models to follow. By studying the strategies and techniques that professional writers use, you can learn methods and procedures for writing effectively on many different subjects and in many different writing situations.

BUILDING AN ESSAY

Writing an essay is a lot like building a house. A writer fits separate pieces of meaning together to make an understandable statement. If you want to write well, you need to learn the basic skills of constructing an essay.

Despite differences in education and personality, most writers follow a remarkably similar process of *prewriting, planning, writing, revising,* and *editing.* Whether building a single paragraph or a ten-page article, successful writers usually follow a series of steps that go roughly like this:

1. Find a subject; gather information. (Prewriting)
2. Focus on a main idea; map out an approach. (Planning)
3. Prepare a rough draft. (Writing)
4. Rework and improve the draft. (Revising)
5. Correct errors. (Editing)

If you follow these steps, you will learn to write more productively and more easily. But keep in mind that this sequence is only a general guide. The steps often overlap and loop around. The important point to remember is that writing is done in stages; successful writers take the time to build their essays step by step and to polish and finish their work the way a good carpenter sands rough surfaces.

Finding Ideas

One of the most difficult challenges of writing is coming up with a topic. Even when you are responding to a reading, you still have to decide what to say about it. In this textbook and in most classes, you will be given some direction toward a topic; the job from there is up to you. Rather than wait for inspiration to strike, you can go after the ideas you need by doing some **prewriting.** Here are three methods that experienced writers use to generate material for writing.

1. **Freewriting.** Write without stopping for five or ten minutes. Don't pause to consider whether your ideas are any good or not; just get down as many thoughts as you can within the time limit. If you're freewriting on a computer, turn down the contrast to write without seeing the screen, or turn the monitor off. After the time is up, read through your freewriting and highlight anything that strikes you as interesting or important. Then do some more freewriting on one or two of these points. Here is an example of freewriting done by student Tara Coburn in response to "Handled with Care," the article by Bob Greene that you read in Chapter 1:

```
Basic themes of Greene's essay. People watched a
break in normalcy with maturity, saw the fragility of
life, a lesson with tones of sadness, embarrassment,
```

```
sympathy, but then forgot it. Compared with the
lesson of the fragility of life when the situation is
personal. The reaction of the people on Michigan
avenue was formed by their detachment from the woman.
If they'd known her, someone would have spoken to
her, helped her, the world would not have gone back
to normal, the incident would not have been
forgotten. Their lesson was fleeting but when there
is a tear in the social normalcy of your daily life
and someone you love shows you the fragility of life,
it is more real.
```

At this point, Tara stopped and looked at what she had written. She liked the idea that surfaced in the last sentence and decided that she had a topic she could develop into an essay. She put the freewriting aside for a while—to let the ideas work around in her mind before she moved on to the next stage in the process.

2. **Brainstorming.** As an alternative to freewriting, you can ask yourself a question and list as many answers as you can. For example: *What have I done that's unexpected or out of the ordinary?* or *When is it all right to get involved with someone in trouble?* Challenge yourself to make the list as long as you can. If necessary, ask yourself a new question: *When is it a bad idea to help someone in trouble?* In making this list, you have already started writing. Think of it as a bank of raw material on which you can draw.

In order to develop ideas for her topic, Tara Coburn posed this question to herself: When did the fabric of my life begin to tear? And then she brainstormed a list of responses to that question:

```
part of my world, my fabric, was belief in my dad
thought he could do anything
helped us build a snowman
finished the ice cream
fix anything
even our cat brought him things
build anything—bed, chairs, room
not a book smart guy
tear happened gradually
getting older, tired, looking older
can't fix everything—computer
as strong as everything seemed, it was fragile
```

```
not a cry for help, more a sign that he can't help anymore
like the people on Mich. Ave., it's a sign it's my turn
to come forward
```

3. **Questioning.** Write a broad topic—such as *Helping People in Trouble*—at the top of a sheet of paper. Then write the headings *Who? What? When? Where? Why? How?* down the page. Fill in any thoughts about the topic that occur to you under these headings. If you can't think of anything for one heading, go to the next, but try to write something under each heading. The goal is to think creatively about the topic as you try to come up with material to use in writing.

Devising a Working Thesis

At this stage, you need to collect the ideas that you came up with in prewriting and organize them. One way to focus your material is to ask yourself, "What point do I want to make?" The answer to that question will lead you to your main idea, or working **thesis.** Once you decide what point you want to make, then you can go through your prewriting material and decide which details to use and which ones to toss.

As you learned in Chapter 1, a thesis says something *about* the subject of a reading. As a reader, your job is to discover the writer's thesis; as a writer, your job is to provide a clear thesis for your readers. Look at the difference between a **subject** and a thesis in these examples:

Subject: Helping strangers
Thesis: I think we are responsible for helping people in trouble.

Subject: Doing something socially unacceptable
Thesis: As soon as I got to college, I set out to prove that I was an adult
and beyond the control of my parents.

Here is an example of the thesis statement that Tara Coburn devised from her freewriting and her brainstorming list:

```
When I saw that my dad's strength was limited, I
began to realize that life was fragile and fleeting
and that I would have to learn to be strong and do
things for him and for myself.
```

You may change or refine your thesis as the paper develops, but having an idea of what you want to say makes the actual writing considerably easier.

Making a Plan

Having a plan to follow makes you less likely to wander from your main point. An outline of your major points will provide you with a framework for your first draft; it can help you shape and arrange your thoughts and keep you from making organizational missteps. There is no need for complete sentences or balanced headings in your outline. Just make a list of your main points in the order that you plan to cover them. The following brief plan is based on the thesis you just read:

```
SOMEONE TO HELP

1. Opening
     Yarn ankle bracelet—first clue that life is fragile
     My social fabric—my belief in my dad
2. Always thought Dad could do anything
     Helped us with the giant snow bunny
     Lifted its head—not as easy as it looked then
3. Dad always did the hard work
     Cranked the ice cream
     Even the cat came to him
     Built furniture, almost everything around me
4. Realized he was getting older
     Hair and beard turned white
     Couldn't fix the computer—but I could
     I became the fixer—my chance to grow stronger
5. Closing
     People on Michigan Ave.—strangers didn't know what
     to do
     I love my dad—I can step forward to help him
     Helping makes me grow and become stronger
```

Composing a Draft

If you have an outline or plan to work from, you shouldn't have any trouble producing the first draft of your paper. Don't fret about trying to write a brilliant **introduction**. Skip it if you can't come up with anything inspired, and start right in on the first main point. You can always come back and add an introduction when you revise.

Some people write the first draft from start to finish without bothering to search for the best word or the right phrase. If that's your method, fine. But many successful writers stop frequently to reread what they have written; they consider such rereading an important part of the drafting process. The main goal is to get your ideas down on paper in a reasonably complete form. Then you are ready for the important next step: revising.

Improving the Draft

Set your first draft aside, at least overnight, so you can look at it in a new light. This process of looking at your draft *again* is called **revising,** and it literally means "re-seeing." In fact, you want to try to see your work now with different eyes—the eyes of a reader.

When revising your draft, concentrate on making major improvements in content and organization. Such improvements might include enlarging or narrowing the thesis, adding more examples or cutting irrelevant ones, and reorganizing points to improve logic or gain emphasis. Tackling the simple problems first may seem reasonable, but you will find that dealing with a major difficulty may eliminate some minor problems at the same time—or change the way you approach them. If you try to do the fine-tuning and polishing first, you may burn up valuable time and energy and never get around to the main problems.

Getting Feedback

Writers routinely seek the help of potential readers to find out what is working and what is not working in their drafts. Someone else can often see places where you *thought* you were being clear but were actually filling in details in your head, not on the page.

The ideal people to help you evaluate your first draft are the members of your own writing class. They will be familiar with the assignment and will understand why you are writing the paper and for whom. In many writing classes, students work together on their papers. Meeting in small groups, they read photocopies of each other's drafts and respond to them; sometimes they post their drafts on a class Web site or submit them electronically on a computer bulletin board. If your instructor doesn't set up a peer review system, try to get several readers' reactions to your drafts. You can meet together outside of class or use an Internet mailing list. Here are some questions to use in asking for feedback:

Have I made my thesis clear to the reader?

Does the introduction get the reader's attention?

Are there any points that the reader might not understand?

Do I need to give the reader more reasons and examples?

Have I shown the reader how every point relates to the thesis?

Does the **conclusion** tie everything together for the reader?

Polishing the Final Draft

When you are satisfied with the changes you've made to improve content and organization, you can move on to matters of spelling, word choice, punctuation, capitalization, and mechanics. This is the **editing** stage, and you cannot skip it. Readers become quickly annoyed by writing that is full of errors.

For Better or For Worse®   **by Lynn Johnston**

Source: Copyright © 1995 by Lynn Johnston Productions Inc./Dist. by United Media/United Features Syndicate Inc. Reprinted with the permission of Universal Press Syndicate, United Media

Here are some additional tips that will help you polish and correct your final draft:

1. Let your work sit for a day to clear your head and increase your chances of spotting errors.
2. Read your draft out loud, listening for anything that sounds unclear or incomplete or awkward.
3. Don't try to do everything at once; save time to take a break when you need one.
4. Slow down when you edit: look at each word and punctuation mark individually, and watch for mistakes that you know you usually make.
5. Ask a reliable reader to check over your draft one more time before you turn it in.

SAMPLE STUDENT ESSAY

The essay that follows was written by Tara Coburn, a first-year student at Eastern Illinois University. She was responding to some of the ideas expressed in "Handled with Care" by Bob Greene. The comments in the margin call your attention to important features of organization and development.

Someone to Help

When I was eight, I had a favorite red yarn ankle bracelet that I wore for an entire year. I tugged on it one day to show that it was strong enough to last another year, and it broke. It was a clue that the things we count on in life are fragile. In his essay "Handled with Care," Bob Greene describes how the sudden appearance of a naked woman on busy Michigan Avenue taught the people walking in the street a similar lesson--that "the line is so thin between matters being manageable and being out of hand." Part of my world--my "social fabric"-- was based on my childhood belief that my father could do anything. When I began to see that my dad's strength was limited, his weakness reminded me that life is fragile and fleeting and that I would have to learn to be strong on my own.

Introductory paragraph: opens with a specific example; relates main idea to the reading; leads into thesis.   1

Thesis: last sentence of first paragraph.

As a child, no matter how big the problem, I always thought, "Dad can do it." One winter, the other neighborhood children and I had a grand plan to build a giant snow bunny. We somehow managed to lift the bottom and middle balls into place, but the head was far too heavy for us to boost up six feet onto a half-finished snow bunny. My very first thought was to ask my dad, and he tramped out into the snow to check the situation. At the time, he seemed to lob the snow bunny's head effortlessly into place, but thinking back I realize how heavy that big ball of snow must have been.

First body paragraph: begins with topic sentence and develops it with an extended example.   2

Dad was always the one we called on to do the hard work. When the homemade ice cream was getting to the final stages of freezing, we called Dad to kneel down and crank the final turns that no one else could manage. His reputation as a Mr. Fix-it was renowned, even to our cat, Mousie. When she had played too roughly with the mouse or snake from the backyard, she'd drop the dead animal at his feet with a look that said, "Daddy, I broke my toy. Will you make it play again?" My dad built much of the world I lived in, from the chairs in the living room to the bed I slept in. Being surrounded by things he built is probably the reason my ideas about him were so important to me.

The tears in my social fabric appeared gradually as I realized that my dad was getting older. When I came home from college for the first time, I noticed that his beard had started to turn from red to white; he was becoming an old man. Not only was his appearance changing, but the arrival of our household's first computer also revealed that my dad cannot fix everything. Now when he says to me, "The computer's little doodad is spinning and I can't make it stop!" his frustration is obvious. But his inability has given me the chance, for once, to be the fixer. I always relied on him, but as he gets older and I learn more, I can let him rely on me. The fragility I now see in my dad has given me the chance to be stronger.

Margin notes:

Second body paragraph: begins with a topic sentence and develops it with specific examples. [3]

Ends paragraph by summing up the significance of the examples.

Third body paragraph: begins with topic sentence and develops it with two specific examples. [4]

Ends paragraph by summing up the point and relating it to the paper's thesis.

Conclusion returns to the reading to make a point through contrast.	The people on Michigan Avenue did

5

The people on Michigan Avenue did not step forward to help the naked woman. One passerby remarked, "No one spoke to her, but you could tell that they wished someone would help her." The crowd felt sorry for the woman, but they were strangers and didn't know how to respond. My dad's turn from strong to fragile was not a cry for help; it was just a sign that he cannot always help me as he once did. But because I know and love my father, I can step forward to help him. And by helping him I have grown strong and have learned to help myself.

Closing sentences reinforce thesis.

RESOURCES FOR WRITERS ON THE INTERNET

You can find a lot of advice on the writing process at Web sites and online services. They vary widely in quality, presentation, and amount of detail. The following are some of the most helpful and usable:

- **http://web.uvic.ca/wguide/**
  The University of Victoria's Hypertext Writer's Guide will help you through the basics of the writing process and answer questions about essays, paragraphs, sentences, words, and documentation.

- **www.powa.org/**
  Paradigm Online Writing Assistant offers useful advice on writing various types of papers. It contains sections on discovery, organization, editing, and other topics.

- **http://owl.english.purdue.edu/**
  Purdue University's Online Writing Lab has more than seventy-five handouts about the process and mechanics of writing—one of the most extensive collections of advice about writing on the Web.

RESPONDING TO A READING

Now that you have seen samples of close reading and of writing in response to reading, it's time to try these skills yourself. Use the advice in Chapters 1 and 2 as you practice.

PREPARING TO READ

Are you a good writer? Do you like to write? Did you have any experiences in English class that affected your attitude toward writing? What were they?

Learning to Write

RUSSELL BAKER

The winner of a Pulitzer prize for journalism, Russell Baker began his career as a writer for the *Baltimore Sun* and moved to the *New York Times* in the 1950s, where he wrote the "Observer" column from 1962 to 1998. He currently hosts the *Masterpiece Theater* series on PBS. Baker is known for his humorous observations of everyday life, but in this excerpt from his autobiography *Growing Up* (1982), his lighthearted tone gives way to a serious description of an important personal event.

TERMS TO RECOGNIZE

notorious *(para. 1)*	known widely and usually unfavorably, disreputable
prim *(para. 1)*	formal and neat, lacking humor
listless *(para. 2)*	without energy, boring
ferocity *(para. 2)*	fierce intensity, savagery
irrepressible *(para. 2)*	impossible to control or hold back
essence *(para. 3)*	the most important ingredient or element, fundamental nature
antecedent *(para. 4)*	the word that a pronoun refers to
exotic *(para. 6)*	rare and unusual
reminiscence *(para. 8)*	a thing remembered, a memory
contempt *(para. 10)*	scorn, disrespect
ridicule *(para. 10)*	mockery, teasing
ecstasy *(para. 11)*	bliss, delight, joy

When our class was assigned to Mr. Fleagle for third-year English I   1
anticipated another grim year in that dreariest of subjects. Mr. Fleagle was notorious among City students for dullness and inability to inspire. He was said to be stuffy, dull, and hopelessly out of date. To me he looked

to be sixty or seventy and prim to a fault. He wore primly severe eyeglasses, his wavy hair was primly cut and primly combed. He wore prim vested suits with neckties blocked primly against the collar buttons of his primly starched white shirts. He had a primly pointed jaw, primly straight nose, and a prim manner of speaking that was so correct, so gentlemanly, that he seemed a comic antique.

I anticipated a listless, unfruitful year with Mr. Fleagle and for a long time   2 was not disappointed. We read *Macbeth*. Mr. Fleagle loved *Macbeth* and wanted us to love it too, but he lacked the gift of infecting others with his own passion. He tried to convey the murderous ferocity of Lady Macbeth one day by reading aloud the passage that concludes

> . . . I have given suck, and know
> How tender 'tis to love the babe that milks me.
> I would have, while it was smiling in my face,
> Have plucked my nipple from his boneless gums. . . .

The idea of prim Mr. Fleagle plucking his nipple from boneless gums was too much for the class. We burst into gasps of irrepressible snickering. Mr. Fleagle stopped.

"There is nothing funny, boys, about giving suck to a babe. It is the—   3 the very essence of motherhood, don't you see."

He constantly sprinkled his sentences with "don't you see." It wasn't a   4 question but an exclamation of mild surprise at our ignorance. "Your pronoun needs an antecedent, don't you see," he would say, very primly. "The purpose of the Porter's scene, boys, is to provide comic relief from the horror, don't you see."

Later in the year we tackled the informal essay. "The essay, don't you see,   5 is the. . . ." My mind went numb. Of all forms of writing, none seemed so boring as the essay. Naturally we would have to write informal essays. Mr. Fleagle distributed a homework sheet offering us a choice of topics. None was quite so simpleminded as "What I Did on My Summer Vacation," but most seemed to be almost as dull. I took the list home and dawdled until the night before the essay was due. Sprawled on the sofa, I finally faced up to the grim task, took the list out of my notebook, and scanned it. The topic on which my eye stopped was "The Art of Eating Spaghetti."

This title produced an extraordinary sequence of mental images. Surg-   6 ing up out of the depths of memory came a vivid recollection of a night in Belleville when all of us were seated around the supper table—Uncle Allen, my mother, Uncle Charlie, Doris, Uncle Hal—and Aunt Pat served spaghetti for supper. Spaghetti was an exotic treat in those days. Neither

Doris nor I had ever eaten spaghetti, and none of the adults had enough experience to be good at it. All the good humor of Uncle Allen's house reawoke in my mind as I recalled the laughing arguments we had that night about the socially respectable method for moving spaghetti from plate to mouth.

Suddenly I wanted to write about that, about the warmth and good 7 feeling of it, but I wanted to put it down simply for my own joy, not for Mr. Fleagle. It was a moment I wanted to recapture and hold for myself. I wanted to relive the pleasure of an evening at New Street. To write it as I wanted, however, would violate all the rules of formal composition I'd learned in school, and Mr. Fleagle would surely give it a failing grade. Never mind. I would write something else for Mr. Fleagle after I had written this thing for myself.

When I finished it the night was half gone, and there was no time left 8 to compose a proper, respectable essay for Mr. Fleagle. There was no choice next morning but to turn in my private reminiscence of Belleville. Two days passed before Mr. Fleagle returned the graded papers, and he returned everyone's but mine. I was bracing myself for a command to report to Mr. Fleagle immediately after school for discipline when I saw him lift my paper from his desk and rap for the class's attention.

"Now, boys," he said, "I want to read you an essay. This is titled 'The Art 9 of Eating Spaghetti.'"

And he started to read. My words! He was reading *my words* out loud 10 to the entire class. What's more, the entire class was listening. Listening attentively. Then somebody laughed, then the entire class was laughing, and not in contempt and ridicule, but with openhearted enjoyment. Even Mr. Fleagle stopped two or three times to repress a small prim smile.

I did my best to avoid showing pleasure, but what I was feeling was 11 pure ecstasy at this startling demonstration that my words had the power to make people laugh. In the eleventh grade, at the eleventh hour as it were, I had discovered a calling. It was the happiest moment of my entire school career. When Mr. Fleagle finished he put the final seal on my happiness by saying, "Now that, boys, is an essay, don't you see. It's—don't you see—it's of the very essence of the essay, don't you see. Congratulations, Mr. Baker."

WEB SITE

www.nytimes.com/books/99/05/02/specials/just-baker.html

Read a review of *The Good Times,* Baker's sequel to *Growing Up.*

Suggestions for Writing

1. Baker's experience in eleventh-grade English changed the way he thought about himself. Have you ever had such an eye-opening experience—some event you really want to write about, some incident you want to "recapture and hold" for yourself? Write an essay in which you describe what happened.

2. Write an essay about the most important thing that happened to you in school. It could be either a positive or negative experience—one that taught you something about yourself or about school or about the subject you were studying.

3. Get together with a small group of classmates and talk about how each of you feels about writing. Compare notes on what you like and don't like about writing. Discuss the kinds of writing that you have done, and tell each other about previous writing experiences. Then write an essay explaining your thoughts and feelings about writing. If you changed your attitude (as Baker did), tell about that change.

4. Write an essay describing your writing process: how you get started, how you go about getting ideas, what you like to write about, where you like to write, whether you like background music or need quiet, whether you make an outline or plunge right in, how long it takes to complete an assignment, whether you work in stages, how many drafts you write, whether you write by hand or use a computer, how much correcting and recopying you do, and so on. Think carefully about the way you write, and describe it in as much detail as you can. Conclude your essay by explaining what you think you could do to make your writing process more efficient.

C h a p t e r

STRATEGIES FOR CONVEYING IDEAS

Narration and Description

> *He falls back upon the bed awkwardly. His stumps, unweighted by legs and feet, rise in the air, presenting themselves. I unwrap the bandages from the stumps, and begin to cut away the black scabs and the dead, glazed fat with scissors and forceps. A shard of white bone comes loose. I pick it away. I wash the wounds with disinfectant and redress the stumps.*
>
> —Richard Selzer, "The Discus Thrower"

That powerful paragraph, written by a surgeon good with words as well as with scalpels, combines description and narration. Dr. Selzer, narrating an experience in treating a terminally ill patient, uses **description** to make his account of this brief event vividly, compellingly real. Simply put, a narrative is a story; **narration** is the telling of a story. The preceding passage is taken from a longer narrative (with a beginning, a middle, and an end) that makes a point. As you can see, the strength of narrative and descriptive writing lies in the use of vivid language and in the selection of precise details.

THE POINT OF NARRATION AND DESCRIPTION

Most of the selections in this chapter are complete narratives that make a point using descriptive details to add clarity, zest, and interest. But as is true of most of the readings in this text, the writers use both narration and description to help them develop all kinds of essays.

Using Narratives

Consider how often we use narrative in everyday speech. If you want to convince your daughter to avoid becoming pregnant as a teenager, you'll probably tell her the story of your high school friend who made that mistake and missed her chance to become the architect she always wanted to be. We tell stories because they are convincing—they have the ring of truth to them—and most people are able to learn from the experience of others. So, narrative is a good strategy to consider if you are writing to persuade, to make a point.

If you are going to write a narrative essay, be sure your story has a point. You wouldn't tell a joke without a punch line, and only mothers and close friends will hold still for stories without a purpose.

Much more frequently, you will use short narratives as part of a longer essay. Notice in your reading how often writers begin essays with a brief narrative to catch our interest and lead us into the topic. Once the writers have our attention, they may move to other methods to develop their ideas and present the material, but a good story makes an effective lure.

Using Description

Essays of pure description are rare, but descriptive details provide one of the most common ways of adding interest and clarity to your writing. Description can put a picture in the minds of readers, helping them to see what you mean. Most writing would seem dull and lifeless without descriptive details, like this sentence:

The firefighter rescued a child.

Although the action referred to is exciting, the sentence is blah. But add some descriptive details, and the sentence gains meaning and interest:

The exhausted firefighter, a rookie on the force, staggered from the flames with the limp body of an unconscious child cradled in his arms.

You can, of course, use too much description. But use any details that come to you while writing your first draft. Then, when you revise, decide whether you've gone too far, and eliminate any that seem overdone or unnecessary. Of course, add more if you think you have too few.

THE PRINCIPLES OF NARRATION AND DESCRIPTION

Good narrative and descriptive writing depends, as does most writing, on making choices. In narratives, the main choices involve deciding which events to include and which ones to leave out. In descriptions, the choices involve selecting words that appeal to the senses—usually to sight, but also to touch, taste, hearing, and smell.

Organizing the Events

If you've ever listened to a boring storyteller, you know how important a concise and effective framework is to a narrative. Organizing a narrative seems easy because the story almost always proceeds in **chronological order** (according to the time in which events happened). But a poor storyteller (or a writer who fails to revise) will get things out of order and interrupt the tale with "Oh, I forgot to mention that Marvin got fired just before his cat got lost and his dog was run over." Or the storyteller will get hung up on a totally unimportant detail: "The moment I saw him—I think it was at the senior prom—or was it at the homecoming dance—or it could have been the party at Yolanda's—oh, wait, I don't think it was at a party at all, it was at a football game—or no, a basketball game. . . ." when the point of the story has nothing to do with where or when it happened.

Get your story straight in your mind before you begin, or straighten it out when you revise. Eliminate any dull or unnecessary material, and then go to work on making it interesting.

Including Specific Details

All good writing is full of specific **details,** but a narrative will simply fall flat without them. Recall the paragraph we quoted by Dr. Richard Selzer. We could summarize that paragraph in a single sentence:

After the patient fell back awkwardly in bed, I removed the bandages, cleaned, disinfected, and rebandaged the ends of his amputated legs.

What did we leave out? The details—in this case mostly descriptive details—and what a difference they make in allowing us to visualize the doctor's performance.

Selecting Descriptive Words

Effective description depends heavily on the use of specific details, but also crucial are the words you choose in presenting those details. Consider this sentence quoted from Dr. Selzer's paragraph:

I unwrap the bandages from the stumps, and begin to cut away the black scabs and the dead, glazed fat with scissors and forceps.

Look at what happens when we substitute less specific, less descriptive words in that same sentence:

> I take the bandages off the amputated legs, and begin to remove the dead tissue with my instruments.

The meaning is the same, and most of us would probably have written it that way, but it's clear that the force of Dr. Selzer's sentence lies in his word choice: *unwrap, stumps, cut away, black scabs, glazed fat, scissors, forceps.*

Good description stems from close observation, paying close attention to the sights, sounds, textures, tastes, or smells around you. Then you must search for exactly the right words to convey what you experience to your readers. Try to think of words that go beyond the general to the specific:

GENERAL	⟵————————⟶		SPECIFIC
a drink	a soft drink	a diet cola	a cold diet Coke
move	run	run hard	race headlong
weather	rain	cold rain	cold, blowing rain

You get the idea. As you read, be alert for words that convey **images,** that let you know how something looks or feels or moves or tastes or smells or sounds.

When you revise, try to replace the following useful but run-of-the-mill verbs with words that are more specific and more interesting:

is (are, was, were, etc.)	go	get	has
come	move	do	make

Notice the difference a livelier word choice makes:

> O'Malley moved on to second base.
> O'Malley slid into second base.

> I'm going to do my homework.
> I'm going to wrestle with my homework.

> Jessie made a luscious chocolate mousse.
> Jessie whipped up a luscious chocolate mousse.

Keep a vocabulary list and try to use the new words in speaking and writing. The theory is that if you use a word three times, it enters your vocabulary. Part of becoming a good writer (as well as a good speaker) depends on increasing the number of words you have at your command, so get to work on it.

THE PITFALLS OF NARRATION AND DESCRIPTION

The narratives included in this chapter, written by experienced authors, will not show you the many things that can go wrong in this kind of writing. Descriptions and narratives are among the easiest kinds of writing to do, but they are probably the most difficult to do well. You need to find someone who will read your draft, not only for enjoyment but also with the promise of helping you improve it. It's always hard to see the flaws in our own writing. It's especially hard with narratives and descriptions. But you can do a good job if you are willing to work at it and can find a reliable person to help you.

As you revise, ask yourself—and ask your helper to answer—the following questions:

1. Is the point of my narrative clear? It may not be stated directly, but readers should be able to see *why* I'm telling this story.
2. Are the events in order? Are there any gaps? Any backtracking?
3. Are there enough details to be clear and interesting?
4. Are there any details that I should take out?
5. Do the descriptions provide an image (a picture, a sound, a smell, a taste, an atmosphere, an action)?

Respond to the questions as honestly as you can—and have your helper do the same. Then keep revising until you are both happy with the results.

WHAT TO LOOK FOR IN NARRATION AND DESCRIPTION

As you read the essays in this chapter, pay attention to these characteristics:

1. *Look at the way the essay is put together.* Probably the events are told chronologically, as they happened, but if not, try to figure out why the writer departed from the usual method of organization.
2. *Decide what point the narrative makes.* Its purpose may be simply to entertain the readers, but more often it will illustrate or make a point. Look for an underlying meaning that you discover as you think about the story and the author's reasons for telling it.
3. *Consider the elements of the narrative.* Think about why these particular events, people, and descriptions are included. If they are not crucial, try to decide what they add to the story and what would be lost if they were left out.
4. *Notice the descriptive details.* Underline any sentences or phrases that appeal to your senses or put a picture in your mind.
5. *Pick out good descriptive words.* Most of these you will already have underlined. Add them to your vocabulary list.

THE FAR SIDE® BY GARY LARSON

The Arnolds feign death until the Wagners, sensing the sudden awkwardness, are compelled to leave.

Why do the Arnolds pretend to be dead? What happened during the visit?

What advice would you give the Wagners to help them avoid repeating this situation?

PREPARING TO READ

Have you ever been through a tornado, a hurricane, or a severe thunderstorm? Describe how you felt at the time. Were you frightened, excited—or did everything happen too fast? Record the thoughts and feelings you had once the incident was over.

Wind!

WILLIAM LEAST HEAT-MOON

William Least Heat-Moon began his career as a professor of English at the University of Missouri but decided to quit teaching and become a writer instead. This brief selection, taken from a much longer essay in the September 1991 *Atlantic Monthly,* uses vivid description to make the narrative come to life. The author records a story told to him by a couple who were actually carried aloft by a rip-roarin' Kansas tornado.

TERMS TO RECOGNIZE

animated *(para. 1)*	lively
tinder *(para. 1)*	material that burns easily
seersucker *(para. 3)*	a light, thin fabric with a crinkled surface
ballast *(para. 4)*	weight carried to steady a balloon
veered *(para. 7)*	shifted and went in another direction
aloft *(para. 10)*	off the ground, into a high place

P aul and Leola Evans are in their early seventies but appear a decade   1
younger, their faces shaped by the prairie wind into strong and pleasing lines. They have no children. Paul speaks softly and to the point, and Leola is animated, the kind of woman who can take a small smoldering story and breathe it into bright flame. Paul listens to her in barely noticeable amusement and from time to time tosses tinder to her.

Leola says: "It was 1949, May. Paul was home from the Pacific. We'd   2
made it through the war, then this. We were living just across the county line, near Americus, on a little farm by the Neosho River. One Friday night I came upstairs to bed, and Paul gawked at me. He said, '*What* are you doing?' I was wearing my good rabbit-fur coat and wedding rings, and I had a handful of wooden matches. It wasn't cold at all. I said I

didn't know but that something wasn't right, and he said, 'What's not right?' and I didn't know.

"We went to bed and just after dark it began to rain, and then the wind 3
came on and blew harder, and we went downstairs and tried to open the door, but the air pressure was so strong Paul couldn't even turn the knob. The wind had us locked in. We hunkered in the corner of the living room in just our pajamas—mine were new seersucker—and me in my fur coat. The wind got louder, then the windows blew out, and we realized we were in trouble when the heat stove went around the corner and out a wall that had just come down.

"We clamped on to each other like ticks, and then we were six feet in 4
the air, and Paul was hanging on to my fur coat—for ballast, he says now— and we went up and out where the wall had been, and then we came down, and then we went up again, longer this time, and then came down in a heap of animals: a cow and one of our dogs with a two-by-four through it. The cow lived, but we lost the dog.

"We were out in the wheat field, sixty yards from the house, and Paul 5
had a knot above his eye that made him look like the Two-Headed Wonder Boy. Splintered wood and glass and metal all over, and the electric lines down and sparking, and here we were barefoot. Paul said to walk only when the lightning flashed to see what we were stepping on. We were more afraid of getting electrocuted than cut. We could see in the flashes that the second story was gone except for one room, and we saw the car was an accordion, and our big truck was upside down.

"The old hog was so terrified she got between us and wouldn't leave 6
all the way up to the neighbors'. Their place wasn't touched. They came to the door and saw a scared hog and two things in rags covered with black mud sucked up out of the river and coated with plaster dust and blood, and one of them was growing a second head. The neighbors didn't know who we were until they heard our voices."

Paul says, "That tornado was on a path to miss our house until it hit the 7
Cottonwood and veered back on us. The Indians believe a twister will change course when it crosses a river."

Leola: "The next morning we walked back home—the electric clock 8
was stopped at nine-forty, and I went upstairs to the room that was left, and there on the chest my glasses were just like I left them, but our bedroom was gone, and our mattress, all torn up, was in a tree where we'd have been."

Paul: "We spit plaster for weeks. It was just plain imbedded in us." 9

I'm thinking, What truer children of Kansas than those taken aloft by 10
the South Wind?

RESPONDING TO READING

Did you notice that Leola and Paul never mentioned their feelings in describing their adventure? What feelings do you think they had? How would you have felt? Would their account have been more interesting if they had included their feelings? Why or why not?

GAINING WORD POWER

Leola and Paul use some lively, descriptive verbs in telling their story:

Paul *gawked* at me. (para. 2)
We *hunkered* in the corner. . . (para. 3)
We *clamped* on to each other. . . . (para. 4)
It was just plain *imbedded* in us. (para. 9)

We repeat the sentences below, minus the verbs. Fill in each blank with your definition of the missing word.

Paul _____ at me.
We _____ in the corner.
We _____ on to each other.
It was just plain _____ in us.

What specific meanings are lost or changed in the second set of sentences? Which sentences do you prefer?

CONSIDERING CONTENT

1. What was unusual about Leola's appearance when she came upstairs to bed on the night of the tornado?
2. After they went downstairs, why was Paul unable to open the door?
3. Where, exactly, did the tornado set the couple down?
4. What two hazards made walking to the neighbors' house in the dark dangerous?
5. Why did the neighbors not recognize Paul and Leola?
6. Paul says the tornado was "on a path to miss our house," but "it veered back on us." What does he think might have caused the twister to change course?
7. What happened to Leola's glasses?

CONSIDERING METHOD

1. Why do you think William Least Heat-Moon chose to let Leola and Paul tell the story in their own voices?
2. Leola begins her tale by saying, "We'd made it through the war, then this." Does that strike you as a good way to introduce the episode—or do you think she should have left out that detail? Explain your response.
3. Leola's description is fascinating largely because she uses details that bring a picture to your mind. For instance, she says that she and Paul "came down in a heap of animals" (para. 4). Find three more "pictures" that you can see in your mind's eye.
4. This selection also contains a few **metaphors**—imaginative comparisons that put pictures in the readers' minds. Here, for example, is a metaphor:

   The tornado was a twisted black ribbon in the sky.

   And here is a **simile** (a metaphor introduced by *like* or *as*):

   The tornado looked like a twisted black ribbon in the sky.

   Now, find a simile in paragraph 4 and a metaphor in paragraph 5.
5. Does this selection have a thesis sentence? If not, why not?

WRITING STEP BY STEP

Think about a catastrophe—a flood, a fire, an auto wreck, a boating accident, a plane crash, an earthquake, a tornado or hurricane—that you witnessed or were involved in. Jot down as many specific details as you can remember. Then write a short narrative describing the experience.

A. Begin by describing the people who were involved.
B. Give a brief statement of the background information: where and when did this story take place?
C. Then recount the story as it happened, from beginning to end. Describe the events as specifically as you can, but do not include a thesis sentence. If your narrative has a point, let your readers guess what it is from what you imply.
D. Use "I" in referring to yourself and "we" if others join you in the action. If you speak directly to the readers, address them as "you."
E. Use direct quotations to report interesting remarks that people made.
F. Keep your feelings out of your account. Instead, let the readers experience your emotions through your forceful description.

G. Use plenty of specific details, and make them as descriptive as possible. Put pictures in your readers' minds. Lively verbs can create striking images—words like *tosses, gawked, hunkered,* and *clamped.*

H. Experiment with a couple of metaphors (or similes).

I. Write a final sentence that brings the story to a definite close. Don't let your narrative just trail off at the end.

OTHER WRITING IDEAS

1. Write an essay describing a solitary experience you once had— going to the movies alone for the first time; taking a relaxing, long, soaking bath; hiking alone on your favorite trail. Include your feelings; in fact, try to recapture your sensuous responses and convey whether the occasion was positive or negative.

2. Tell the story of the first time you were punished, either at school or at home. Explain briefly what you were being punished for, but focus on specific details about how the person doing the punishing looked to you and how you reacted. Try to remember what words were spoken—or invent them. Conclude by telling how you felt about the punishment at the time and how you feel about it looking back on it today.

3. Write a narrative to support or disprove some familiar proverb or saying, such as "A winner never quits," "Home is where the heart is," "Crime doesn't pay," or "Virtue is its own reward." Get together with several classmates before you begin writing to help one another decide what saying would make a good choice and what story might provide a convincing illustration.

EDITING SKILLS: ELIMINATING EXCESSIVE *ANDS*

Because William Least Heat-Moon is reproducing Leola and Paul's speech throughout most of the reading selection, he uses far more *and*s than would usually appear in an edited essay—thirty-seven, to be exact, in just ten paragraphs. Because people do, indeed, talk that way, the *and*s are effective in making the narrative sound authentic.

Most of the time, you would not want to use that many *and*s in writing. So, for practice, try editing a few of them out.

EXERCISE

First, underline all the *and*s in paragraphs 2, 3, and 4 of "Wind!" Then, rewrite the sentences to eliminate all the *and*s that have commas in front of them. Try to give the sentences more variety as you decide how to change them. In other words, make them sound like written text, rather than spoken.

As an example, here are several ways to go about eliminating the second *and* from the following sentence:

Paul speaks softly and to the point, and Leola is animated.

1. Replace the *and* with a period:
   Paul speaks softly and to the point. Leola is animated.
2. Replace the *and* with a semicolon:
   Paul speaks softly and to the point; Leola is animated.
3. Replace the *and* with another connecting word:
   Paul speaks softly and to the point, while Leola is animated.
4. Begin the sentence a different way:
   Although Paul speaks softly, Leola is animated.

Write several versions of each sentence you find with an *and* in paragraphs 2, 3, and 4.

Now examine the essay you just wrote to see how many *and*s you used. Rewrite any sentences that can be improved by eliminating unnecessary *and*s.

WEB SITE

www.tornadoproject.com/

The Tornado Project Online contains all kinds of information about tornadoes, including facts about recent and past tornadoes, safety advice, myths, oddities, stories, and "other neat stuff about tornadoes."

PREPARING TO READ

Did you ever have an experience that changed the way you look at the world—perhaps while traveling, or getting to know a stranger, or suffering a serious illness, or being inspired by a teacher?

Jackie's Debut: A Unique Day

MIKE ROYKO

Born in Chicago, Mike Royko (1932–1997) attended Wright Junior College there. He wrote a syndicated column for the *Chicago Tribune* and was awarded the Pulitzer prize. His columns often ridicule human greed, vanity, and stupidity. The piece reprinted here is perhaps not typical, since it focuses on an uplifting event—a step toward reversing the usual pattern of ignorant prejudice. This column appeared in the *Chicago Daily News* on Wednesday, October 15, 1972, the day after Jackie Robinson died.

If you enjoy this article about Jackie Robinson, you might want to read Robinson's autobiography, *I Never Had It Made*.

TERMS TO RECOGNIZE

scalpers *(para. 3)*	people selling tickets at higher than regular prices
Ls *(para. 4)*	elevated trains
caromed *(para. 11)*	hit and bounced
chortling *(para. 12)*	chuckling and snorting with laughter

all that Saturday, the wise men of the neighborhood, who sat in chairs on the sidewalk outside the tavern, had talked about what it would do to baseball. I hung around and listened because baseball was about the most important thing in the world, and if anything was going to ruin it, I was worried. 1

Most of the things they said, I didn't understand, although it sounded terrible. But could one man bring such ruin? They said he could and would. And the next day he was going to be in Wrigley Field for the first time, on the same diamond as Hack, Nicholson, Cavarretta, Schmidt, Pafko, and all my other idols. I had to see Jackie Robinson, the man who was going to somehow wreck everything. So the next day, another kid and I started walking to the ball park early. 2

We always walked to save the streetcar fare. It was five or six miles, but   3
I felt about baseball the way Abe Lincoln felt about education. Usually, we
could get there just at noon, find a seat in the grandstands and watch some
batting practice. But not that Sunday, May 18, 1947. By noon, Wrigley
Field was almost filled. The crowd outside spilled off the sidewalk and into
the streets. Scalpers were asking top dollar for box seats and getting it.

I had never seen anything like it. Not just the size, although it was a new   4
record, more than 47,000. But this was 25 years ago, and in 1947 few blacks
were seen in the Loop, much less up on the white North Side at a Cub
game. That day, they came by the thousands, pouring off the northbound
Ls and out of their cars. They didn't wear baseball-game clothes. They had
on church clothes and funeral clothes—suits, white shirts, ties, gleaming
shoes, and straw hats. I've never seen so many straw hats. Big as it was, the
crowd was orderly. Almost unnaturally so. People didn't jostle each other.

The whites tried to look as if nothing unusual was happening, while the   5
blacks tried to look casual and dignified. So everybody looked slightly ill
at ease. For most, it was probably the first time they had been that close to
each other in such great numbers.

We managed to get in, scramble up a ramp and find a place to stand   6
behind the last row of grandstand seats. Then they shut the gates. No place
remained to stand.

Robinson came up in the first inning. I remember the sound. It wasn't   7
the shrill, teen-age cry you now hear, or an excited gut roar. They
applauded, long, rolling applause. A tall middle-aged black man stood next
to me, a smile of almost painful joy on his face, beating his palms together
so hard they must have hurt.

When Robinson stepped into the batter's box, it was as if someone had   8
flicked a switch. The place went silent. He swung at the first pitch and they
erupted as if he had knocked it over the wall. But it was only a high foul
that dropped into the box seats. I remember thinking it was strange that a
foul could make that many people happy. When he struck out, the low
moan was genuine.

I've forgotten most of the details of the game, other than that the   9
Dodgers won and Robinson didn't get a hit or do anything special,
although he was cheered on every swing and every routine play. But two
things happened I'll never forget. Robinson played first, and early in the
game a Cub star hit a grounder and it was a close play. Just before the Cub
reached first, he swerved to his left. And as he got to the bag, he seemed
to slam his foot down hard at Robinson's foot. It was obvious to everyone
that he was trying to run into him or spike him. Robinson took the throw
and got clear at the last instant.

I was shocked. That Cub, a home-town boy, was my biggest hero. It was   10
not only an unheroic stunt, but it seemed a rude thing to do in front of
people who would cheer for a foul ball. I didn't understand why he had
done it. It wasn't at all big league. I didn't know that while the white fans
were relatively polite, the Cubs and most other teams kept up a steady
stream of racial abuse from the dugout. I thought all they did down there
was talk about how good Wheaties are.

Later in the game, Robinson was up again and he hit another foul ball.   11
This time it came into the stands low and fast, in our direction. Somebody
in the seats grabbed for it, but it caromed off his hand and kept coming.
There was a flurry of arms as the ball kept bouncing, and suddenly it was
between me and my pal. We both grabbed. I had a baseball.

The two of us stood there examining it and chortling. A genuine, major-   12
league baseball that had actually been gripped and thrown by a Cub pitcher,
hit by a Dodger batter. What a possession! Then I heard a voice say: "Would
you consider selling that?" It was the black man who had applauded so
fiercely. I mumbled something. I didn't want to sell it.

"I'll give you $10 for it," he said.   13

Ten dollars. I couldn't believe it. I didn't know what $10 could buy   14
because I'd never had that much money. But I knew that a lot of men in
the neighborhood considered $60 a week to be good pay. I handed it to
him, and he paid me with ten $1 bills. When I left the ball park, with that
much money in my pocket, I was sure that Jackie Robinson wasn't bad for
the game.

Since then, I've regretted a few times that I didn't keep the ball. Or that   15
I hadn't given it to him free. I didn't know, then, how hard he probably
had to work for that $10. But Tuesday I was glad I had sold it to him. And
if that man is still around, and has that baseball, I'm sure he thinks it was
worth every cent.

RESPONDING TO READING

Read again Royko's last paragraph. Explain in your journal why he
wishes, as an adult, that he had given the baseball to the man who bought
it from him. Do you think you would feel the same way?

GAINING WORD POWER

Following is the vocabulary entry for the word *unique,* which appears in
Mike Royko's title. It comes from the *Webster's New World Dictionary,* third
college edition, published by Simon & Schuster. Can you make sense of it?

u|nique (yo͞o nēk´) *adj.* [[Fr < L *unicus,* single < *unus,* ONE]] 1 one and only; sole *[a unique* specimen*]* 2 having no like or equal; unparalleled *[a unique* achievement*]* 3 highly unusual, extraordinary, rare, etc.: a common usage still objected to by some—**u|nique´ly** *adv.*—**u|nique´ness** *n.*

All dictionaries are unique, but here's how to read this entry from the *New World.*

1. The boldfaced word itself tells you how to spell it, and the thin line (between the *u* and the *n*) shows where it divides into syllables. Some dictionaries use centered dots instead.
2. The syllables inside the parentheses (some dictionaries use slash marks) let you know how to pronounce the word. If you don't understand the symbols, check inside the front or back cover or at the bottom of the page.
3. The boldfaced abbreviation tells you the part of speech. Notice that further down in the entry you'll see other forms of the same word that are different parts of speech (*uniquely* adv. and *uniqueness* n.). Sometimes those other parts of speech have different meanings listed.
4. Those weird notations inside the double brackets give the *etymology* of the word—that is, they tell us how it came into our language. The entry reads this way: "The word *unique* comes to us from the French, derived from the Latin *unicus,* meaning *single,* derived from *unus,* meaning *one.*" Check the explanatory notes in your dictionary to learn how to figure out the etymologies.
5. Various meanings are numbered. Some dictionaries list the most common meaning first; others begin with the oldest meaning, which would often be the least common. So, again, check your dictionary's explanatory notes. The *New World* lists meanings from oldest to newest.
6. All dictionaries give warnings about usage. If you look up the word *ain't,* you will find it labeled *slang* or *nonstandard,* perhaps even with a warning that some people have strong objections to it. In the entry for *unique,* the third meaning of "highly unusual, extraordinary, rare, etc." is followed by a caution that this is "a common usage still objected to by some." Those *some* often include English teachers, so avoid writing *most unique* or *quite unique* or *very unique.* Remember the etymology.

Now, to practice what you just learned, look up the word *debut* from Royko's title, and answer the following questions:

1. How many syllables does it have?
2. What different ways can it be correctly pronounced?
3. What parts of speech can it be?
4. What language did it come from?
5. What are two meanings of the word?
6. Are there any usage labels or warnings?

CONSIDERING CONTENT

1. What made the old men of the neighborhood say that Jackie Robinson would ruin the game of baseball?
2. How did young Royko and his friend get to Wrigley Field, and why did he choose that way to get there?
3. What does he mean when he says, "I felt about baseball the way Abe Lincoln felt about education" (para. 3)?
4. Why was he surprised to see so many black people at the game?
5. Why were the black people wearing their good clothes?
6. When the young narrator says, "It wasn't at all big league" (para. 10), what does he mean?

CONSIDERING METHOD

1. How does Royko get the readers' attention in the opening paragraph?
2. How does he let us know that the "wise men of the neighborhood" are not truly wise—that he is being sarcastic? What small detail in the sentence gives us the clue?
3. Why does Royko tell most of the narrative through the thoughts of himself as a young boy?
4. In paragraph 3, why does he give the exact date—Sunday, May 18, 1947?
5. When you think about all the details he could have included in describing the crowd at the baseball game, why do you think he chose to relate how the black people were dressed?
6. The **point of view** shifts briefly in paragraph 10, as Royko tells us something he learned later. How does he handle this shift so that we scarcely notice it?
7. In paragraphs 12 and 13, why does he give us the exact words of the man who wants to buy the baseball?
8. Explain why the final paragraph makes a good conclusion.

WRITING STEP BY STEP

Using Mike Royko's column as an example, write a narrative essay about a childhood experience that suddenly let you see some less than admirable aspect of the adult world. Royko, after making it clear that he grew up in a white section of the city, lets us see how the vicious action of his former hero on the Cubs team opened his eyes to racial prejudice.

Think of a similar experience in your own past that will allow you to show the unfairness of some human behavior or the pain caused by some human weakness. Perhaps you could tell about your accidental discovery of disloyalty or cheating by someone you admired and trusted. Or you could tell the story of the first time you observed adult violence or adult cruelty.

A. Think about the story and the insight you gained from it. Write out the meaning of the incident as a thesis statement, but do not include it in the essay. Just keep it in mind as a guide in selecting details.

B. Jot down the events you want to cover, leaving lots of space between them. Next, go over the events, and fill in the spaces with all the details you can think of about each event. Then, go through the whole sheet again, and carefully decide just which events and which details you want to use in your narrative. Select only the most descriptive details that will allow your readers to experience the event as you did.

C. Use *I* in telling your story. Consider narrating it from the point of view of yourself as a child, as Royko does. Try to remember how you actually saw things when you were young and innocent and tell the story that way. See Royko's paragraphs 1, 10, and 14 for good examples.

D. Begin, as Royko does, by briefly setting the scene. Be sure to work in the time, either here or later (as Royko does in para. 3).

E. Don't give away the point of your story, but try to work in a teaser (or a *delay*) as he does in his opening. The men are talking about what "it" would do to baseball, but we readers have no clue what "it" means and read on to find out.

F. In your conclusion, try to let your readers understand what you learned from the incident, but don't tell them straight out. See Royko's last three paragraphs, in which he tells us how he felt as a child and how he feels now as a man—and both are positive feelings. He lets us see how wrong racial prejudice is and at the same time reminds us of how proud blacks could feel about Jackie Robinson's success.

G. If exactly what people say is important to the story, put the speech in direct quotations, as Royko does in paragraphs 12 and 13.

OTHER WRITING IDEAS

1. Did you ever do something quite wrong in response to peer pressure? Tell the story of how this happened and how you felt about it at the time—and how you feel about it now.
2. Write a narrative to illustrate one of the following:

   Mother was right.

   Winning is not all.

   Nice guys finish last.

   I learned _____ the hard way.
3. With a group of classmates, discuss difficult ethical and moral decisions you have faced and how you responded. For many, deciding whether to cheat, steal, or tattle creates their first moral crisis. Then, tell the story of a tough decision you had to make and what happened as a result.

EDITING SKILLS: PUNCTUATING CONVERSATION

When adding conversation to your narrative, you know, of course, to use quotation marks around other people's words. But you also need to notice how other marks are used with those quotation marks. Look at the punctuation in these sentences from Royko's essay:

Then I heard a voice say: "Would you consider selling that?"
"I'll give you $10 for it," he said.

The words telling who is talking—called a tag—need to be separated from the quotation. When the tag comes *before* the quotation, you can use either a comma or a colon to separate. When the tag comes *after* the quoted words, use a comma.

Sometimes you may want to put the tag in the middle:

"I don't want to sell it," I mumbled; "it's mine!
"Go away!" I yelled, "or I'll call a cop."
"I'm going home," I told Joe, "before I lose this ball."

If you start a new sentence after the tag, you need a semicolon or a period, just as you would in any other writing.

And don't stack up punctuation. If you use an exclamation mark or a question mark, omit the comma or period.

Notice that periods and commas go before the ending quotation marks. But with question marks (and exclamation marks), you have to decide whether the tag is a question (or an exclamation) or whether the quoted words are.

"Oh, well," Jamal said, "it takes all kinds!"
Can you believe Jamal said, "It takes all kinds"?

Finally, whenever you change speakers, begin a new paragraph.
As you read your way through the selections in this text, pay attention to the way quoted material is punctuated.

EXERCISE

Now, for practice, put the necessary punctuation in the following sentences.

Oh, heaven help us Marvin exclaimed I forgot to do our income taxes
We'd better get started on them fast then responded Rosa
Marvin groaned You get the receipts together while I try to find the calculator
How am I supposed to know where to find the receipts asked Rosa
Surely roared Marvin you've been keeping them all together some place
Rosa was silent during a long pause, then asked Was I supposed to
Marvin slapped his palm against his forehead and yelled We're doomed
Don't worry, honey soothed Rosa they never send you to Leavenworth on a first offense

Go back and look at the essay you just wrote: did you punctuate the conversations accurately? Check all your quotations carefully, and make any necessary corrections.

WEB SITES
www.nc5.infi.net/moxie/nlb/nlb.html
The Negro League Baseball Online Archives
www.blackbaseball.com/
The Negro League's Web Site

Both sites provide historical background and perspectives that relate to the topic of Royko's essay.

PREPARING TO READ

How do you picture a typical prison guard? Have your ideas been shaped by movies and television? In your journal, write a brief description of how you think a prison guard would look, talk, and act.

A Guard's First Night on the Job

WILLIAM RECKTENWALD

William Recktenwald is a journalist who once served as a guard in a maximum-security prison in Pontiac, Illinois. The following firsthand account first appeared in the *St. Louis Globe Democrat* in 1978.

TERMS TO RECOGNIZE

orientation *(para. 1)*	an introduction to and explanation of an activity or a job
contraband *(para. 2)*	smuggled goods
cursory *(para. 2)*	hasty, not complete or thorough
apprehensive *(para. 9)*	worried, anxious, uneasy
virtually *(para. 9)*	for all practical purposes
ruckus *(para. 9)*	noisy disturbance
din *(para. 10)*	loud, continuous noise
equivalent *(para. 15)*	the equal of, the same as

When I arrived for my first shift, 3 to 11 P.M., I had not had a minute   1
of training except for a one-hour orientation lecture the previous day. I was a "fish," a rookie guard, and very much out of my depth. A veteran officer welcomed the "fish" and told us: "Remember, these guys don't have anything to do all day, 24 hours a day, but think of ways to make you mad. No matter what happens, don't lose your cool. Don't lose your cool!"

I had been assigned to the segregation unit, containing 215 inmates who   2
are the most trouble. It was an assignment nobody wanted. To get there, I passed through seven sets of bars. My uniform was my only ticket through each of them. Even on my first day, I was not asked for any identification, searched, or sent through a metal detector. I could have been carrying weapons, drugs, or any other contraband. I couldn't believe this was what's

meant by a maximum-security institution. In the week I worked at Pontiac, I was subjected to only one check, and that one was cursory.

The segregation unit consists of five tiers, or galleries. Each is about 300   3 feet long and has 44 cells. The walkways are about 3½ feet wide, with the cells on one side and a rail and cyclone fencing on the other. As I walked along one gallery, I noticed that my elbows could touch cell bars and fencing at the same time. That made me easy pickings for anybody reaching out of a cell.

The first thing they told me was that a guard must never go out on a   4 gallery by himself. You've got no weapons with which to defend yourself, not even a radio to summon help. All you've got is the man with whom you're working. My partner that first night was Bill Hill, a soft-spoken six-year veteran who immediately told me to take the cigarettes out of my shirt pocket because the inmates would steal them. Same for my pen, he said— or "They'll grab it and stab you."

We were told to serve dinner on the third tier, and Hill quickly tried to   5 fill me in on the facts of prison life. That's when I learned about cookies and the importance they have to the inmates. "They're going to try and grab them, they're going to try and steal them any way they can," he said. "Remember, you only have enough cookies for the gallery, and if you let them get away, you'll have to explain to the guys at the end why there weren't any for them."

Hill then checked out the meal, groaning when he saw the drippy ravi-   6 oli and stewed tomatoes. "We're going to be wearing this," he remarked, before deciding to simply discard the tomatoes. We served nothing to drink. In my first six days at Pontiac, I never saw an inmate served a beverage.

Hill instructed me to put on plastic gloves before we served the meal.   7 In view of the trash and waste through which we'd be wheeling the food cart, I thought he was joking. He wasn't. "Some inmates don't like white hands touching their food," he explained.

Everything went routinely as we served the first 20 cells, and I wasn't   8 surprised when every inmate asked for extra cookies. Suddenly, a huge arm shot through the bars of one cell and began swinging a metal rod at Hill. As he ducked away, the inmate snared the cookie box. From the other side of the cart, I lunged to grab the cookies—and was grabbed in turn. A powerful hand from the cell behind me was pulling my arm. As I jerked away, objects began crashing about, and a metal can struck me in the back.

Until that moment I had been apprehensive. Now I was scared. The   9 food cart virtually trapped me, blocking my retreat. Whirling around, I noticed that mirrors were being held out of every cell so the inmates could watch the ruckus. I didn't realize the mirrors were plastic and became terri-fied that the inmates would start smashing them to cut me up.

The ordinary din of the cell house had turned into a deafening roar. For the length of the tier, arms stretched into the walkway, making grabbing motions. Some of the inmates swung brooms about. "Let's get out of here— now!" Hill barked. Wheeling the food cart between us, we made a hasty retreat. [10]

Downstairs, we reported what had happened. My heart was thumping, my legs felt weak. Inside the plastic gloves, my hands were soaked with sweat. Yet the attack on us wasn't considered unusual by the other guards, especially in segregation. That was strictly routine, and we didn't even file a report. [11]

What was more shocking was to be sent immediately back to the same tier to pass out medication. But as I passed the cells from which we'd been attacked, the men in them simply requested their medicine. It was as if what had happened minutes before was already ancient history. From another cell, however, an inmate began raging at us. "Get my medication," he said. "Get it now, or I'm going to kill you." I was learning that whatever you're handing out, everybody wants it, and those who don't get it frequently respond by threatening to kill or maim you. Another fact of prison life. [12]

Passing cell no. 632, I saw that a prisoner I had helped take to the hospital before dinner was back in his cell. When we took him out, he had been disabled by mace and was very wobbly. Hill and I had been extremely gentle, handcuffing him carefully, then practically carrying him down the stairs. As we went by his cell this time, he tossed a cup of liquid on us. [13]

Back downstairs, I learned I would be going back to that tier for a third time, to finish serving dinner. This time, we planned to slip in the other side of the tier so we wouldn't have to pass the trouble cells. The plates were already prepared. "Just get in there and give them their food and get out," Hill said. I could see he was nervous, which made me even more so. "Don't stop for anything. If you get hit, just back off, 'cause if they snare you or hook you some way and get you against the bars, they'll hurt you real bad." [14]

Everything went smoothly. Inmates in the three most troublesome cells were not getting dinner, so they hurled some garbage at us. But that's something else I had learned; getting no worse than garbage thrown at you is the prison equivalent of everything going smoothly. [15]

RESPONDING TO READING

After reading the essay, write a paragraph in your journal describing what kind of person you think William Recktenwald is and how he responds to his new job. In another paragraph, note any ways in which he is different from your expectations of a typical prison guard.

GAINING WORD POWER

Since our brief definitions are sometimes cursory, look up in a college-size dictionary the following words from the Terms to Recognize list. Then write a sentence using each word.

orientation   apprehensive
contraband   equivalent
cursory

CONSIDERING CONTENT

1. What was the only piece of advice the author got during his orientation as a rookie guard?
2. What can you tell about race relations in the Pontiac prison? Are the guards white and the prisoners black?
3. What qualities would a prison guard need in order to work in the segregation unit?
4. Why is the width of the galleries an important detail?
5. What kind of weapons does a guard carry?
6. At the end of the essay, why are the guards not much bothered by having food thrown at them?

CONSIDERING METHOD

1. Why does the writer quote directly the "welcoming" advice given by the veteran officer?
2. The descriptive details in paragraph 2 have no vivid appeal to the senses. Why, then, are they included?
3. Look at the action verbs in paragraph 8: *shot, ducked, snared, lunged,* and *jerked.* Why are they more effective than *came, moved, took, stepped forward,* and *pulled*? What extra feeling do Recktenwald's verbs add? Find five more examples of verbs that you think add color and feeling.
4. In paragraphs 7 and 9, the writer uses short-short sentences: "He wasn't" and "Now I was scared." Why do you think he uses such short statements?
5. How is the essay organized?
6. What sentence serves as a thesis statement to tell readers what the essay is about?
7. What is the author's purpose?
8. Do you think the conclusion is effective? Can you explain why?

WRITING STEP BY STEP

Did you ever hold a difficult job? If so, write an essay describing a bad day. Use specific details that will let your readers share your experience. Follow the form of "A Guard's First Night on the Job." If you don't have a job, describe a bad day at home or at school.

A. Begin by giving your readers a brief orientation—that is, explaining where you work, what you do, maybe what time you begin, if you have a shift job.

B. At the end of your introduction, let your readers know that the essay will be about a bad day on the job. Your purpose may be to entertain, if you have some humorous incidents to relate, or you may write simply to inform your readers about how trying your job is, as William Recktenwald does, or maybe you want to make the point that your line of work is pitifully underpaid for the stress it causes you.

C. Use the informal "you" to speak directly to your readers.

D. Think of one particularly troublesome detail of your job that bothers you repeatedly (like Recktenwald's problems with the cookies) and focus on that. Or jot down a number of incidents that drive you crazy and relate those in the order in which they typically occur.

E. Include specific details (like the cigarettes, pen, plastic gloves, plastic mirrors) as you describe incidents.

F. Use action verbs whenever possible (like Recktenwald's *shot, snared, lunged, grabbed, jerked, barked, hooked,* and *hurled*) to give your readers a picture of what happened.

G. If you include people, briefly identify them ("Bill Hill, a soft-spoken six-year veteran").

H. Write a closing that reinforces how bad your day can be without actually saying so, as Recktenwald does when he concludes that merely having garbage thrown at him means his shift is "going smoothly."

OTHER WRITING IDEAS

1. Write an essay explaining how you think prisons should be run. Try to offer concrete ideas for improving them.

2. Describe the most stressful vacation you ever took (or the most stressful picnic or wedding or trip to the zoo or any activity that you would expect to be pleasurable).

3. Get together with classmates or friends and talk about memorable "firsts," like your first day of school, your first date, your first rock concert, or your first family reunion. See how many "firsts" the group can come up with. Then choose the experience from your own life that will make the most interesting story and write about it.

EDITING SKILLS:
COMMAS AFTER DEPENDENT ELEMENTS

Copy these sentences from the reading exactly. As you write, look for a pattern they all follow.

As he ducked away, the inmate snared the cookie box.
When we took him out, he had been disabled by mace and was very wobbly.
As we went by his cell this time, he tossed a cup of liquid on us.

Each of these sentences has two parts. Notice that the second part, after the comma, can stand alone as a sentence; it's called an **independent clause.** If you read the first part alone, it does not sound complete. The first part is called a **dependent clause** for this reason. When you write a sentence in which the *independent* part comes after a *dependent* part, you need to put in a comma to separate the two.

EXERCISE

Put commas in the following sentences:

While planning is important do not overschedule your time.
Since the best courses fill up early plan at least a term or two in advance.
If you cannot write well you will be at a disadvantage.

Now fill in the blanks to make complete sentences below:

Although studying is the major task of college life, _____
_____.

Because grades are important to some employers, _____
_____.

_____, Henry
went to the basketball game.

Next, write three sentences that follow this dependent-comma-independent pattern.

Finally, check your essay to be sure that you have included the commas in sentences like these.

🌐 WEB SITE

www.prisonexp.org/

The Stanford Prison Experiment gives details about the controversial simulation study of the psychology of imprisonment that was conducted at Stanford in 1971.

Did you ever think of houses as having tales to tell about the lives of the people who live in them? In your journal, write the story that a house you are familiar with might tell—if it could.

More Room

JUDITH ORTIZ COFER

Born in Puerto Rico, Judith Ortiz Cofer moved with her family to the United States in 1955 and settled in Paterson, New Jersey. Besides essays, she writes poetry and fiction. The following piece appeared in *Silent Dancing: A Partial Remembrance of a Puerto Rican Childhood*, published in 1990.

TERMS TO RECOGNIZE

geneology *(para. 2)*	family history
acrid *(para. 4)*	harsh, bitter
malingering *(para. 4)*	pretending to be ill
inviolate *(para. 5)*	pure, virginal (never entered)
obligatory *(para. 6)*	required
purgatives *(para. 6)*	medicines to cleanse the body
animosity *(para. 9)*	hostility, resentment
coup *(para. 9)*	brilliant, surprising tactic that overcomes an opponent
vortex *(para. 9)*	whirlpool
fecund *(para. 9)*	fruitful in offspring
acceded *(para. 10)*	gave in to, went along with
emanate *(para. 12)*	to emit, to give off

my grandmother's house is like a chambered nautilus; it has many rooms, yet it is not a mansion. Its proportions are small and its design simple. It is a house that has grown organically, according to the needs of its inhabitants. To all of us in the family it is known as *la casa de Mamá*. It is the place of our origin; the stage for our memories and dreams of Island life. 1

I remember how in my childhood it sat on stilts; this was before it had a downstairs—it rested on its perch like a great blue bird—not a flying sort of bird, more like a nesting hen, but with spread wings. Grandfather 2 had built it soon after their marriage. He was a painter and housebuilder by trade—a poet and meditative man by nature. As each of their eight children were born, new rooms were added. After a few years, the paint didn't exactly match, nor the materials, so that there was a chronology to it, like the rings of a tree, and Mamá could tell you the history of each room in her *casa,* and thus the geneology of the family along with it.

Her own room is the heart of the house. Though I have seen it recently— and both woman and room have diminished in size, changed by the new perspective of my eyes, now capable of looking over countertops and tall beds—it is not this picture I carry in my memory of Mamá's *casa.* Instead, I see her room as a queen's chamber where a small woman loomed large, a throne room with a massive four-poster bed in its center, which stood taller than a child's head. It was on this bed, where her own children had been born, that the smallest grandchildren were allowed to take naps in the afternoons; here too was where Mamá secluded herself to dispense private advice to her daughters, sitting on the edge of the bed, looking down at whoever sat on the rocker where generations of babies had been sung to sleep. To me she looked like a wise empress right out of the fairy tales I was addicted to reading. 3

Though the room was dominated by the mahogany four-poster, it also contained all of Mamá's symbols of power. On her dresser there were not cosmetics but jars filled with herbs: *yerba* we were all subjected to during childhood crises. She had a steaming cup for anyone who could not, or would not, get up to face life on any given day. If the acrid aftertaste of her cures for malingering did not get you out of bed, then it was time to call *el doctor.* 4

And there was the monstrous chifforobe she kept locked with a little golden key she did not hide. This was a test of her dominion over us; though my cousins and I wanted a look inside that massive wardrobe more than anything, we never reached for that little key lying on top of her Bible on the dresser. This was also where she placed her earrings and rosary when she took them off at night. God's word was her security system. This chifforobe was the place where I imagined she kept jewels, satin slippers, and elegant silk, sequined gowns of heartbreaking fineness. I lusted after those imaginary costumes. I had heard that Mamá had been a great beauty in her youth, and the belle of many balls. My cousins had ideas as to what she kept in that wooden vault: its secret could he money (Mamá did not hand cash to strangers, banks were out of the question, so there were stories that her mattress was stuffed with dollar bills, and that she buried coins in jars in her garden under rose-bushes, or kept them in her inviolate chifforobe); there might be that legendary gun salvaged from the Spanish-American conflict over the Island. We went wild over suspected treasures that we made up simply because children have to fill locked trunks with something wonderful. 5

On the wall above the bed hung a heavy silver crucifix. Christ's agonized   6
head hung directly over Mamá's pillow. I avoided looking at this weapon
suspended over where her head would have lain; and on the rare occasions
when I was allowed to sleep on that bed, I scooted down to the safe middle
of the mattress, where her body's impression took me in like a mother's lap.
Having taken care of the obligatory religious decoration with the crucifix,
Mamá covered the other walls with objects sent to her over the years by her
children in the States. *Los Nueva Yores* was represented by, among other things,
a postcard of Niagara Falls from her son Heman, postmarked, Buffalo, N.Y.
In a conspicuous gold frame hung a large color photograph of her daughter Nena, her husband and their five children at the entrance to Disneyland
in California. From us she had gotten a black lace fan. Father had brought
it to her from a tour of duty with the Navy in Europe. (On Sundays she
would remove it from its hook on the wall to fan herself at Sunday mass.)
Each year more items were added as the family grew and dispersed, and
every object in the room had a story attached to it, a *cuento,* which Mamá
would bestow on anyone who received the privilege of a day alone with her.
It was almost worth pretending to be sick, though the bitter herb purgatives
of the body were a big price to pay for the spirit revivals of her storytelling.

Except for the times when a sick grandchild warranted the privilege, or   7
when a heartbroken daughter came home in need of more than herbal
teas, Mamá slept alone on her large bed.

In the family there is a story about how this came to be.   8

When one of the daughters, my mother or one of her sisters, tells the   9
cuento of how Mamá came to own her nights, it is usually preceded by the
qualification that Papá's exile from his wife's room was not a result of animos-
ity between the couple. But the act had been Mamá's famous bloodless coup
for her personal freedom. Papá was the benevolent dictator of her body and
her life who had had to be banished from her bed so that Mamá could better
serve her family. Before the telling, we had to agree that the old man—
whom we all recognize in the family as an *alma de Dios,* a saintly, soft-spoken
presence whose main pleasures in life, such as writing poetry and reading the
Spanish large-type editions of *Reader's Digest,* always took place outside the
vortex of Mamá's crowded realm—was not to blame. It was not his fault, after
all, that every year or so he planted a baby-seed in Mamá's fertile body, keeping her from leading the active life she needed and desired. He loved her and
the babies. He would compose odes and lyrics to celebrate births and anniver-
saries, and hired musicians to accompany him in singing them to his family
and friends at extravagant pig-roasts he threw yearly. Mamá and the oldest
girls worked for days preparing the food. Papá sat for hours in his painter's

shed, also his study and library, composing the songs. At these celebrations he was also known to give long speeches in praise of God, his fecund wife, and his beloved Island. As a middle child, my mother remembers these occasions as a time when the women sat in the kitchen and lamented their burdens while the men feasted out in the patio, their rum-thickened voices rising in song and praise of each other, *companeros* all.

It was after the birth of her eighth child, after she had lost three at birth   10
or infancy, that Mamá made her decision. They say that Mamá had had a special way of letting her husband know that they were expecting, one that had begun when, at the beginning of their marriage, he had built her a house too confining for her taste. So, when she discovered her first pregnancy, she supposedly drew plans for another room, which he dutifully executed. Every time a child was due, she would demand, *More space, more space.* Papá acceded to her wishes, child after child, since he had learned early that Mamá's renowned temper was a thing that grew like a monster along with a new belly. In this way Mamá got the house that she wanted, but with each child she lost in health and energy. She had knowledge of her body and perceived that if she had any more children, her dreams and her plans would have to be permanently forgotten, because she would be a chronically ill woman, like Flora with her twelve children, asthma, no teeth; in bed more than on her feet.

And so after my youngest uncle was born, she asked Papá to build a large   11
room at the back of the house. He did so in joyful anticipation. Mamá had asked him for special things this time: shelves on the walls, a private entrance. He thought that she meant this room to be a nursery where several children could sleep. He thought it was a wonderful idea. He painted it his favorite color—sky blue—and made large windows looking out over a green hill and the church spires beyond. But nothing happened. Mamá's belly did not grow, yet she seemed in a frenzy of activity over the house. Finally, an anxious Papá approached his wife to tell her that the new room was finished and ready to be occupied. And Mamá, they say, replied: "Good, it's for you."

And so it was that Mamá discovered the only means of birth control   12
available to a Catholic woman of her time: sacrifice. She gave up the comfort of Papá's sexual love for something she deemed greater: the right to own and control her body, so that she might live to meet her grandchildren, me among them, so that she could give more of herself to the ones already there, so that she could be more than a channel for other lives, so that even now that time has robbed her of the elasticity of her body and of her amazing reservoir of energy, she can still emanate the calm joy that can only be achieved by living according to the dictates of one's own heart.

RESPONDING TO READING

What do you think of Mamá's chosen method of birth control? Why do you think Papá agreed to it without resentment?

GAINING WORD POWER

Cofer uses lots of unusual descriptive terms. Here is a list of nine of them.

massive (para. 3)   agonized (para. 6)
steaming (para. 4)   conspicuous (para. 6)
monstrous (para. 5)   benevolent (para. 9)
elegant (para. 5)   frenzy (para. 11)
heartbreaking (para. 5)

Use each of these words in a sentence of your own. If the term is new to you, look it up in your dictionary before writing the sentence, and add it to your vocabulary list after you finish.

CONSIDERING CONTENT

1. What is a chifforobe (para. 5)? Why are the children fascinated by Mamá's? Why is it kept locked, even though the key is in plain sight?
2. How are Mamá's bedroom walls decorated (para. 6)? What do these decorations tell you about her character? Why is the detail about the crucifix especially significant?
3. What is a "benevolent dictator" (para. 9)? What sort of man is Papá? What details let you know what he is like?
4. What is a "bloodless coup" (para. 9)? Explain how Mamá pulls hers off. Why is the nature of Papá's character important in understanding her success?
5. What meaning did you derive from Cofer's narrative?

CONSIDERING METHOD

1. Besides being an **analogy** (see Glossary), the description in the opening sentence of Mamá's house as "like a chambered nautilus" is also a **simile** (see Glossary). Can you find other similes in paragraphs 2 and 3? Explain why they are effective.
2. What do you call the figure of speech in the first sentence of paragraph 3: "Her own room is the heart of the house"? What does that description tell you, in a word, about Mamá?

3. Papá is referred to as a "benevolent dictator," but Cofer lets us know that Mamá also wields power in the family. What details convey this information?

4. What is the function of the single short sentence punctuated as a paragraph (para. 8)? Why does Cofer divide the essay with a space break following that sentence?

5. How does the concluding paragraph clarify the meaning of the whole piece?

WRITING STEP BY STEP

Write an essay in which you explain how you brought off some "blood-less coup" of your very own. In other words, tell how you managed to get your way in some matter (large or small) by outmaneuvering a person who had authority over you—a parent, teacher, older sibling, boss, coach, or law enforcement officer. Or maybe in an equal relationship with your spouse or roommate, you managed to slither out of some obligation that you felt justified in dodging, as Mamá does in Cofer's essay.

A. Tell your story, as Cofer does, in the **first person,** using *I* and *me, we, us,* and *our.*

B. Begin by setting the scene—the when and where. If your story happened in the past, let your readers know in a phrase how long ago, like Cofer's "I remember how in my childhood . . ." (para. 2). Describe, with plenty of visual details (the way Cofer presents Mamá's room), where you were—at home, in a car, a classroom, an office, on a football field—when you encountered the problem, disagreement, or conflict that you eventually resolved to your satisfaction.

C. Then, briefly explain the situation that gave rise to the problem, including only enough background details to let your readers understand how the difficulty arose.

D. Next, describe the personality of the other person involved. Use concrete details, as Cofer does in telling us the sort of man her grandfather was: "a saintly, soft-spoken presence," who enjoyed "the Spanish large-type editions of *Reader's Digest,*" who loved his wife and children, who wrote poetry and sang songs, who threw "extravagant pig-roasts" with hired musicians, and who gave "long speeches in praise of God, his fecund wife, and his beloved Island" (para. 9).

E. Compose a short transitional sentence (like Cofer's single sentence in para. 8) saying that you are now going to let your readers know the way you resolved your difficulty. Make the sentence a complete paragraph.

F. Finally, present the clever strategy you used in pulling off your "bloodless coup." If you achieved some resulting benefit (as Mamá does in Cofer's final paragraph), you could mention that in your conclusion.

OTHER WRITING IDEAS

1. Tell the story of an episode that allowed you to see another side of a person you thought you knew quite well. Begin by describing the person's character as you first observed it. Then narrate the incident that changed your perception. Conclude by describing briefly how you saw the person's character afterward.

2. Discuss with a group of friends or classmates whether the familiar saying "Sports build character" is true or not. After you decide how you feel about the matter, think of an incident that illustrates your belief, and use the story to make your point in a narrative essay.

3. In Cofer's essay, Mamá regains "the right to own and control her body" (para. 12). Write a narrative telling how you discovered the need to gain control of something in your life—your living expenses; your calorie intake; your large, unruly Dalmatian; your wedding plans; your TV watching. Conclude by letting your readers know whether or not you were successful.

EDITING SKILLS: USING COORDINATION

Experienced writers vary their sentence types and lengths to make their writing more interesting. Even Ernest Hemingway, who was noted for his lean, simple sentences, often put two or more together to make longer ones, as Cofer does in the following example:

In this way Mamá got the house that she wanted, but with each child she lost in health and energy.

These are the sentences that are put together:

In this way Mamá got the house that she wanted.
With each child she lost in health and energy.

To make short sentences into one longer sentence, you splice them together with coordinating conjunctions. There are only seven of them: *and, but, for, or, nor, yet, so.* Put a comma after each short sentence you are combining, but put a period at the very end, as in these examples:

Mamá's belly did not grow, yet she seemed in a frenzy of activity over the house.

[The house] has many rooms, yet it is not a mansion.

If you are dissatisfied with your writing because it sounds choppy, this method will help you achieve longer sentences.

EXERCISE

Using a comma and a suitable coordinating conjunction, combine the following pairs of sentences into compound sentences.

1. Laser videodiscs have superior picture quality.
   Videotape remains the mass-market leader.
2. Laser technology provides a much sharper image.
   It can pick up greater detail and more contrast from the original print.
3. Manufacturers must keep up consumer demand.
   They will never claim the market from videotapes.
4. Panasonic continues to lead the field.
   Sony has just come out with a new laserdisc player.
5. Consumers want more sophisticated equipment.
   Some companies are building compact disc players into their videodisc machines.

Now go back to your essay and combine two sentences into one long one using a coordinating conjunction. Read the new sentence out loud. If you like the effect, leave it in your essay.

WEB SITE

http://parallel.park.uga.edu/~jcofer/home.html
On Judith Cofer's home page, you will find a photo of the author; a short biography; and links to interviews, reviews of her books, and other sites about her.

Student Essay Using Description and Narration

Domestic Abuse

Kelly Berlin

It was the summer of my freshman year, and I had   1
been baby-sitting my two-year-old niece, Briana, at my
sister's house every weekday for the past couple of
months. It was late in the afternoon on a Friday, so
I couldn't wait for my sister Kim to come home from
work. Since she was already a half an hour late, I
decided to take a shower so I wouldn't be late for my
date later that evening. I was in the bathroom blow-
drying my hair when my sister and her boyfriend Scott
came home.

My sister and Scott had been dating a couple of   2
years, despite the disapproval of my family. Scott,
even though he had a child, was not a good "father
figure" for my niece. Scott was a regular drinker and
smoker, and his appearance did nothing for him. He
was over six-feet tall with big, bulging muscles; he
wore tight clothes; and he had long, shaggy hair. My
sister, on the other hand, standing only five-feet-
five-inches tall, was slender with long, curly brown
hair and a beautiful white smile.

I finished blow-drying my hair and was going to   3
ask my sister to take me home, but I heard her and
Scott fighting in the bedroom. I went into the living
room to watch television with my niece and to keep her
mind off the shouting. I started to become worried
because the yelling became more intense. All of a
sudden, I heard a loud noise--not a boom, but more like
a crack, a board breaking. The shouting stopped.

"Briana, stay here!" I left my niece in the   4
living room and ran into the bedroom. "Scott, what in
the hell did you do to her? Get away from her!" My
sister was lying limp on her bed with her face down.

"It's none of your business. Get out of here," he   5
yelled at me with a fierce look in his eyes.

I was shaking but yelled back at him with just as   6
much determination and strength. "Bullshit, if it's

not my business. She's my sister. Don't think I'm
just going to sit here while you push her around!" I
turned, looked at my sister, and asked gently, "Kim,
are you all right?"

"Yeah," Kim told me in a shaky voice. "I'll be   7
all right. But my legs hurt because I hit the foot
board when he pushed me down."

"Scott, leave NOW!" I said with all the authority   8
I could manage.

"Shut up, Kelly. This isn't your house, and I'll   9
leave whenever I please."

My sister pleaded with him. "Scott, please leave   10
me alone. Just leave me alone."

He stormed out of the bedroom and out of the   11
house like a raging bull. I helped my sister sit up
and looked at her legs. She had two long, wide
bruises forming across her upper thighs from where
they hit the foot board. I told her to stay on her
bed while I checked on Briana and called my mom
for help.

My mom arrived about ten minutes later, and I   12
told her what had happened. She was furious and was
determined to do something about it. We called the
police to report the incident and file charges. When
the police arrived at the house, I described the
scene and signed my name to the papers to file
charges. Then, they took photographs of my sister's
bruises and recorded her statement. But she wouldn't
sign the papers. She had decided not to press
charges. Well, I was confused, but I thought I could
still press charges against him. I was wrong. I
hadn't actually seen Scott push my sister. I had
only heard them fighting and had found her lying on
the bed. We tried to convince my sister to press
charges against Scott, but she refused. She believed
that he'd just gotten carried away, that he wouldn't
do it again. We tried to make her realize that he
could very well do it again, but she wouldn't
believe us.

As it turned out, my sister was mistaken. Scott   13
continued to beat her and control her life, and she

continued to refuse to press charges. Finally, she realized he was not going to stop, so she left Scott. At one time, she put a restraining order on him, which kept him away temporarily. And fortunately, he lost his license due to DUIs, so he had no legal transportation to get to her house. Now, the only time he harasses her is when he's high on drugs. But as time and experience have taught my sister, she now calls the police herself.

$$Chapter$$

4

STRATEGIES FOR MAKING A POINT

Example and Illustration

There's an old saying that a picture is worth a thousand words. It may be true. But we can't always communicate with pictures. Most of the time we have to convey our ideas with words—often with written words. You will find that your skills in describing and narrating can be put to good use in providing examples and illustrations to make a point.

Did you ever read a passage that seemed hard to get the meaning of— that remained fuzzy in your mind no matter how many times you plowed through it? Here's an example of the kind of writing we mean:

A democratic plan of education includes more than the mere transmission of the social heritage and an attempt to reproduce existing institutions in a static form. The democratic school is also required to indoctrinate individuals with the democratic tradition, which, in turn, is based on the agitative liberties of the individual and the needs of society.

If a person spoke those words to you, you could say, "What was that again?" or "Could you give me an example, please?" or "What do you mean by *agitative liberties?*" But you can't question the written page, so the meaning of whatever that writer had in mind is lost.

The difference between an **illustration** and an **example** is not clear-cut. Some people use the terms to mean the same thing; some people use illustration to mean several short examples or a fairly long example, such as a brief narrative used within an essay. We don't think it makes a whole lot of difference what you call them—just be sure to use them.

THE POINT OF EXAMPLE AND ILLUSTRATION

Good writers use examples or illustrations to make their writing clear and to make it convincing. As a bonus, concrete examples make writing interesting.

Using Examples to Explain and Clarify

The paragraph about democratic education shows how vague writing is that uses only general statements. Here's another illustration to let you see how examples help in explaining ideas. We have deliberately taken the examples out of the following paragraph. See how much you can get out of it:

> You should define what you mean when any abstract, ambiguous, or controversial terms figure importantly in your writing. Serious miscommunications can occur when audience and writer do not share the same idea about what a word or phrase means, either *connotatively* or *denotatively.*

That's not too clear, is it? But read it now with the examples that were included in the original:

> You should define what you mean when any abstract, ambiguous, or controversial terms figure importantly in your writing. Serious miscommunications can occur when audience and writer do not share the same idea about what a word or phrase means, either *connotatively* (by its associations) or *denotatively* (by its direct meaning). Consider, for instance, the connotations of these words: *daddy, father, old man.* All denote *male parent* but their understood meanings are quite different. Also, the phrase *good writing* seems clear, doesn't it? Yet three English teachers can argue endlessly about what constitutes good writing if teacher A thinks that good writing is honest, direct, and completely clear; if teacher B thinks that good writing is serious, formal, and absolutely correct; and if teacher C thinks that good writing is flashy, spirited, and highly entertaining.

A couple of the examples in that paragraph are definitions; the others explain the need for definitions. All the examples add clarity and meaning to the passage.

Using Examples and Illustrations to Convince

Consider this letter to the editor, published a few years ago in an urban newspaper:

> Liquor is something we can get along without to a very good advantage. The problem of jazz music is a very grave one in this city, also, as it produces an attitude of irresponsibility in the listener.
>
> Let's keep Kansas attractive to God-fearing people. This is the type industry is interested in hiring and this is the type needed in government and the armed forces.

Are you persuaded? Not likely, unless you agreed with the opinions before reading the letter. The writer offers nothing but unsupported personal opinions.

Examples and illustrations are essential in making a point—that is, as evidence to convince your readers that what you say is right. If you want to convince readers that they should run out and rent *Batman Forever,* you have to provide examples to explain why. You will need to discuss the thrill-packed plot, the wonderful gizmos and toys (including a Batmobile that climbs walls), the deadpan jokes, the uproarious physical humor of Jim Carrey, and Chris O'Donnell's spirited performance as Robin. The more illustrations of this sort you can provide, the more persuasive your essay will be.

THE PRINCIPLES OF EXAMPLE AND ILLUSTRATION

The success of a piece of writing often depends on how well you choose your supporting evidence.

Select Appropriate Examples

You must be sure, first of all, that the examples actually do illustrate the point you want to make. If, for instance, you are explaining how you feel about people who borrow a book and then write their own comments in the margins, be sure to focus on your feelings—of interest, of outrage, of violation, of loss, or whatever you felt. Do not slide off the subject to discuss the interesting philosophy course you bought the book for and the time you accidentally left the book on a lunchroom counter and were quite sure you had lost it forever only to have the guy who sat behind you in class return it, saying he found it when he happened to stop in for a late lunch in the same greasy spoon that afternoon. When people do that sort of free associating in conversation, we tend to suffer through it, even as our eyes glaze over. But it will not do in writing.

Give Plenty of Examples

Keep in mind, though, that you need to supply enough examples to make your ideas clear and convincing. Say you want to persuade your readers that becoming a vegetarian is the key to a long life in a healthy body. If you offer only the single illustration of your Uncle Seymour who never ate meat, never had a cold, always felt frisky, and ran in the Boston Marathon to celebrate his seventy-ninth birthday, you are not likely to sway many readers. They'll just think, "Well, wasn't he lucky?" You need either to dig up more examples—perhaps even some statistics about low-fat diets and heart disease—or else change your thesis to focus on Uncle Seymour's personal recipe for keeping fit. There's nothing wrong with using one long illustration, if that single illustration really does prove your point.

Include Specific Information

Finally, you need to develop your examples and illustrations with plenty of specific, graphic **details.** If you say that riding motorcycles is dangerous, you need to follow up with examples more specific than "Every year many people are injured in motorcycle accidents" and "The person on the motorcycle can't always tell what motorists are going to do." Instead, describe what happens when an automobile unexpectedly turns left in front of a motorcyclist traveling forty miles an hour. Mention the crushed noses, the dislocated limbs, the fractured femurs, the broken teeth, and the shattered skulls that such accidents cause. As a general rule, if you use an **abstract word,** like *dangerous,* follow it soon with a specific example, like "His splintered kneecap never did heal properly."

THE PITFALLS OF EXAMPLE AND ILLUSTRATION

If you are writing an essay developed almost entirely through the use of examples, you need to make sure those examples are connected smoothly when you furnish several in a row. Notice how the italicized **transitions** introduce the examples in this paragraph defining a psychological term:

> People who use reaction formation avoid facing an unpleasant truth by acting exactly opposite from the way they truly feel. *For example,* you may have known somebody who acts like the life of the party, always laughing and making jokes, but who you suspect is trying to fool everybody—including herself—into missing the fact that she is sad and lonely.

Another example of reaction formation involves the person who goes overboard to be open-minded, insisting, "I'm not prejudiced! Why some of my best friends are _____!"

—Ronald Adler and Neil Towne, "Defense Mechanisms"

Here are some other transitional expressions that you may find useful:

such as	that is	in the following way
namely	in this case	as an illustration
for instance	in addition	at the same time

It's quite possible to use too many transitions. Ask the friend or classmate who helps you edit your first draft to let you know if you've put in more than you need.

As you prepare to revise your essay, ask yourself (and your editorial helper) the following questions:

1. Does each of my examples really illustrate the point I'm trying to make?
2. Have I included enough examples to be convincing?
3. If I'm using a single illustration in some paragraphs, is that convincing?
4. Do any of my illustrations begin to prove the point and then stray from it?
5. Are any of my examples too short or my illustrations too long?
6. Have I used enough specific details?

WHAT TO LOOK FOR IN EXAMPLE AND ILLUSTRATION

As you study the essays in this chapter, focus on the way examples and illustrations are used.

1. In the paragraphs that have a **topic sentence** (the sentence that tells what the paragraph is about), look at the examples or illustrations and decide how convincing they are—that is, how well they explain, support, or enlarge on that idea.
2. Look for concrete, specific, sometimes visual details in the examples and illustrations themselves. Ask yourself what would be lost if these were omitted.
3. Underline the transitional terms used to introduce the examples and illustrations, and keep a list of them in your journal.

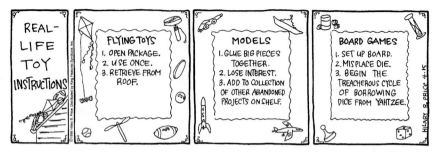

Source: Copyright © 1998 by Hillary Price. Reprinted with special permission of King Features Syndicate Inc.

This cartoon uses three general examples of "Real-Life Toy Instructions": flying toys, models, and board games.

Can you think of other kinds of toys that would fit this cartoon?

Can you think of specific examples for each of the general categories? (The drawings around the boxed-in instructions will give you some ideas.)

Can you think of an experience you had that would illustrate the point of this cartoon?

PREPARING TO READ

When you snatch a tissue, grab a paper towel, toss out a diaper, or pitch a paper napkin, do you ever give a thought to the tree that had to die for that convenience?

Down with Forests

CHARLES KURALT

Born in Wilmington, North Carolina, Charles Kuralt (1934–1997) was one of America's most respected broadcasters. He charmed millions with his "On the Road" TV programs presenting human interest stories found while traveling in a lumbering recreational vehicle to remote corners of America. The piece reprinted here is the text from one of his *Dateline America* series that appeared on the CBS evening news.

TERMS TO RECOGNIZE

habitat *(para. 3)*   the place or region where a plant, animal, or person lives

colleagues *(para. 4)*   people working in the same profession

b altimore, Maryland. I was waiting for breakfast in a coffee shop the 1
other morning and reading the paper. The paper had sixty-six pages.
The waitress brought a paper place mat and a paper napkin and took
my order, and I paged through the paper.

I put the paper napkin in my lap, spread the paper out on the paper place 2
mat, and read on: "The House Agriculture Committee," it said, "is looking over legislation that would once again open national forests to the clear-cutting of trees by private companies under government permits."

The waitress brought the coffee. I opened a paper sugar envelope and 3
tore open a little paper cup of cream and went on reading the paper: "The Senate voted without dissent yesterday to allow clear-cutting," the paper said. "Critics have said clear-cutting in the national forests can lead to erosion and destruction of wildlife habitats. Forest Service and industry spokesmen said a flat ban on clear-cutting would bring paralysis to the lumber industry." And to the paper industry, I thought. Clear-cutting is one way to get a lot of paper, and we sure seem to need a lot of paper.

The waitress brought the toast. I looked for the butter. It came on a little   4
paper tray with a covering of paper. I opened a paper package of marmalade
and read on, "Senator Jennings Randolph, Democrat of West Virginia, urged
his colleagues to take a more restrictive view and permit clear-cutting only
under specific guidelines for certain types of forest. But neither he nor anyone
else voted against the bill, which was sent to the House on a 90 to 0 vote."

The eggs came, with little paper packages of salt and pepper. I finished   5
breakfast, put the paper under my arm, and left the table with its used and
useless paper napkin, paper place mat, paper salt and pepper packages, paper
butter and marmalade wrappings, paper sugar envelope, and paper cream
holder, and I walked out into the morning wondering how our national
forests can ever survive our breakfasts.

RESPONDING TO READING

What do you, your family, or friends do (if anything) to preserve our
natural environment? Is organized recycling done in your community? If
so, is it voluntary or required?

GAINING WORD POWER

Sometimes little words can mean a lot. What, for instance, does the word
flat mean in this sentence:

> Forest Service and industry spokesmen said a *flat* ban on clear-cutting
> would bring paralysis to the lumber industry.

Get together with several of your classmates and see how many other
meanings of the word the group can come up with. Then look it up in a
dictionary. Did you think of most of them?

Now, think about the word *set*. See how many sentences the group can
write using *set* with a different meaning in each one. Do at least five. Then
check the dictionary to see how many there are. Surprising, isn't it, how
much meaning can be packed into such a simple little word?

CONSIDERING CONTENT

1. How many times does the word *paper* appear in this brief piece?
2. Make a list of paper products that might have been used if the writer
   had been eating a fast-food lunch instead of breakfast.
3. Do you think the critics of clear-cutting who are quoted by Kuralt
   in paragraph 3 are right about what happens as a result of that kind
   of logging?

4. Why do you think the senators voted so overwhelmingly to allow clear-cutting again in our national forests?
5. How would you have voted? How do you think Kuralt would have voted?
6. What is the point of the essay? How do you know? Can you find a thesis statement?

CONSIDERING METHOD

1. How does the writer get our interest in the opening paragraph?
2. Besides the timber industry and the paper industry, who else shares responsibility for the destruction of forests? Point out specific sentences that let you know this.
3. The examples Kuralt selected to describe his breakfast are carefully chosen to illustrate what point?
4. Why do you think he decided not to tell us the name of the cafe, what it looked like, whether the service was fast or slow, or any of the dozens of other details he could have included?
5. In virtually every paragraph, he begins with details about his breakfast and then shifts to examples quoted from the morning paper. Would the piece have been as effective if he had reversed the order—quoted first and then supplied examples about his breakfast?
6. What makes the conclusion effective?

WRITING STEP BY STEP

Perhaps you noticed that Kuralt's essay is a short, simple narrative—the story of someone's breakfast one morning. Not exactly an exciting, action-packed adventure, is it? So what makes the piece effective? Probably its success lies in the skillful way Kuralt arranged the examples to prove his point, without ever having to tell us directly what the point was.

Write a brief essay, or perhaps just one well-developed paragraph, using Kuralt's technique.

A. Think of something you do often that has become a nuisance (like prying open safety seals on food) or that serves as a convenience (like tossing out disposable food containers).
B. Then think of a little story that will allow you to use five or six examples to illustrate either the nuisance (of having to peel off all those pesky pieces of plastic in the middle of getting lunch) or the convenience (of just throwing all the mess out when cleaning up after a party).

C. Make a list of examples to use. Trade lists with a classmate and help each other add to the lists.
D. Begin your piece, as Kuralt does, by establishing the setting ("I was trying to fix lunch in a hurry before my one o'clock appointment when I reached for the mustard. . . ." or "I was still half asleep when I faced up to clearing out the remains of the party. . . .").
E. Present your examples, as concretely as possible ("Circling the top of the mustard container was a tight band of clear plastic, impossible to break with mere fingers" or "Into the trash went the revolting remains of the onion dip in its plastic container").
F. Close by making some observation about your story to make a point about the nuisance ("I think it's grossly unfair that we all have to struggle to open even a jar of mayonnaise just because years ago some crazy person poisoned the Tylenol") or the convenience ("Cleaning up was a breeze, but what's going to happen when all the landfills are full of plastic pop bottles and sour cream cartons?").

OTHER WRITING IDEAS

1. Would you be willing to give up using some paper products in order to slow the destruction of our forests? If so, write an essay telling which ones you could do without and what you would use instead, guessing how much time and effort the change would cost you, then figuring how much money you could save in a year. Conclude by urging your readers to do the same.
2. Discuss the problem of excessive packaging of products in our society, offering specific examples and posing possible solutions, if you have any.
3. Write an essay explaining a good, easy method of recycling some product, such as paper, aluminum cans, plastic bottles, or glass containers.

EDITING SKILLS: USING COMMAS IN SERIES

Notice where the commas are placed in the following examples containing items in series. (The strings of **ellipsis** dots tell you that we have left some words out—that is, we quote only part of Kuralt's sentence.)

I put the paper napkin in my lap, spread the paper out on the paper place mat, and read on. . . .

I finished breakfast, put the paper under my arm, and left the table with its used and useless paper napkin, paper place mat, paper salt and pepper packages, paper butter and marmalade wrappings, paper sugar envelope, and paper cream holder. . . .

The commas are necessary to let you know when one item ends and another begins. Try making sense of those words without the commas to see what a hopeless task reading would be without commas:

> the table with its used and useless paper napkin paper place mat paper salt and pepper packages paper butter and marmalade wrappings paper sugar envelope and paper cream holder. . . .

Notice that in all of the series we quoted, Kuralt places a comma before the *and* attaching the last item but not before the *and* in *paper salt and pepper packages* or *paper butter and marmalade wrappings.* The comma used before the *and* connecting the last item in a series is optional these days. But we recommend using it to avoid confusing items like *salt and pepper* with the final item in the list.

EXERCISE

Write a sentence describing a scene you know well or specially observe for this exercise. It could be, like Kuralt's sentences, a restaurant table, or you might choose your own room or a scene from nature or a social event. Try to string the descriptive details in a series using Kuralt's sentence as a model:

> I finished breakfast, put the paper under my arm, and left the table with its used and useless paper napkin, paper place mat, paper salt and pepper packages, paper butter and marmalade wrappings, paper sugar envelope, and paper cream holder, and I walked out into the morning wondering how our national forests can ever survive our breakfasts.

For an extra challenge, try to close your long descriptive sentence with a reflection on the scene, as Kuralt does. Here are some possibilities to jump-start your imagination.

> and I walked out into the morning wondering . . .
> and I looked at the scene and thought about . . .
> and I considered what my mother would say about . . .

🌏 WEB SITE

www.afandpa.org/recycling/Rec-introduction.html
Facts and resources for recycling paper from the American Forest & Paper Association.

PREPARING TO READ

Do you feel safe when you go out alone at night? Are there certain sections of town that you would refuse to enter alone after dark? Does the fear, or lack of fear, in any way relate to your gender, your age, or the color of your skin?

"Just Walk On By": A Black Man Ponders His Power to Alter Public Space

BRENT STAPLES

Born in 1951 in Chester, Pennsylvania, Brent Staples is a journalist who also holds a Ph.D. in psychology from the University of Chicago. His memoir, *Parallel Time: Growing Up in Black and White* (1994), tells the story of his childhood in Chester, a mixed-race, economically declining town. He is currently on the editorial board of the *New York Times*. The selection reprinted here was first published in *Ms.* magazine in September 1986.

TERMS TO RECOGNIZE

uninflammatory *(para. 1)*	not likely to cause violence or excitement
unwieldy *(para. 2)*	hard to manage or to deal with
indistinguishable *(para. 2)*	not clearly different from
elicit *(para. 3)*	draw forth
warrenlike *(para. 5)*	narrow and crowded like a rabbit hutch
bandolier *(para. 5)*	a belt holding bullets, draped across the chest
lethality *(para. 6)*	being lethal or deadly
bravado *(para. 6)*	pretended courage or false confidence
ad hoc *(para. 7)*	for this case only
labyrinthine *(para. 7)*	like the winding, confusing passages in a maze
berth *(para. 9)*	a safe distance
skittish *(para. 9)*	jumpy, easily frightened
constitutionals *(para. 10)*	walks to improve one's health

m y first victim was a woman—white, well dressed, probably in her early 20s. I came upon her late one evening on a deserted street in Hyde Park, a relatively affluent neighborhood in an otherwise mean, impoverished section of Chicago. As I swung onto the avenue behind her, there seemed to be a discreet, uninflammatory distance between us. Not so. She cast back a worried glance. To her, the youngish black man—a broad six feet two inches with a beard and billowing hair, both hands shoved into the pockets of a bulky military jacket—seemed menacingly close. She picked up her pace and was soon running in earnest. Within seconds she disappeared into a cross street. 1

That was more than a decade ago. I was 22 years old, a graduate student newly arrived at the University of Chicago. It was in the echo of that terrified woman's footfalls that I first began to know the unwieldy inheritance I'd come into—the ability to alter public space in ugly ways. It was clear that she thought of herself as the quarry of a mugger, a rapist, or worse. Suffering a bout of insomnia, however, I was stalking sleep, not defenseless wayfarers. As a softy who is scarcely able to take a knife to a raw chicken— let alone hold one to a person's throat—I was surprised, embarrassed, and dismayed all at once. Her flight made me feel like an accomplice in tyranny. It also made it clear that I was indistinguishable from the muggers who occasionally seeped into the area from the surrounding ghetto. I soon gathered that being perceived as dangerous is a hazard in itself: Where fear and weapons meet—as they often do in urban America—there is always the possibility of death. 2

In that first year, my first away from my hometown, I was to become thoroughly familiar with the language of fear. At dark, shadowy intersections, I could cross in front of a car stopped at a traffic light and elicit the *thunk, thunk, thunk, thunk* of the driver—black, white, male, female—hammering down the door locks. On less traveled streets after dark, I grew accustomed to but never comfortable with people crossing to the other side of the street rather than pass me. Then there were the standard unpleasantries with policemen, doormen, bouncers, cabdrivers, and others whose business it is to screen out troublesome individuals *before* there is any nastiness. 3

I moved to New York nearly two years ago and I have remained an avid night walker. In central Manhattan, the near-constant crowd covers the tense one-on-one street encounters. Elsewhere, things can get very taut indeed. 4

After dark, on the warrenlike streets of Brooklyn where I live, I often see women who fear the worst from me. They seem to have set their faces on neutral, and with their purse straps strung across their chests bandolier-style, they forge ahead as though bracing themselves against being tackled. 5

I understand, of course, that the danger they perceive is not a hallucination. Women are particularly vulnerable to street violence, and young black males are drastically overrepresented among the perpetrators of that violence. Yet these truths are no solace against the alienation that comes of being ever the suspect, an entity with whom pedestrians avoid making eye contact.

It is not altogether clear to me how I reached the ripe old age of 22   6 without being conscious of the lethality nighttime pedestrians attributed to me. Perhaps it was because in Chester, Pa., the small, angry industrial town where I came of age in the 1960s, I was scarcely noticeable against a backdrop of gang warfare, street knifings, and murders. I grew up one of the good boys, had perhaps a half-dozen fistfights. In retrospect, my shyness of combat has clear sources. As a boy, I saw countless tough guys locked away; I have since buried several, too. They were babies, really—a teen-age cousin, a brother of 22, a childhood friend in his mid-20s—all gone down in episodes of bravado played out in the streets. I chose, perhaps unconsciously, to remain a shadow—timid, but a survivor.

The fearsomeness mistakenly attributed to me in public places often has a   7 perilous flavor. The most frightening of these confusions occurred in the late 1970s and early 1980s, when I worked as a journalist in Chicago. One day, rushing into the office of a magazine I was writing for with a deadline story in hand, I was mistaken for a burglar. The office manager called security, and with the speed of an ad hoc posse, pursued me through the labyrinthine halls, nearly to my editor's door. I had no way of proving who I was. I could only move briskly toward the company of someone who knew me.

Relatively speaking, however, I never fared as badly as another black male   8 journalist. He went to nearby Waukegan, Ill., a couple of summers ago to work on a story about a murderer who was born there. Mistaking the reporter for the killer, police officers hauled him from his car at gunpoint and but for his press credentials would probably have tried to book him. Such episodes are not uncommon. Black men trade tales like this all the time.

Over the years, I learned to smother the rage I felt at so often being   9 mistaken for a criminal. Not to do so would surely have led to madness. I now take precautions to make myself less threatening. I move about with care, particularly late in the evening. I give a wide berth to nervous people on subway platforms during the wee hours. If I happen to be entering a building behind some people who appear skittish, I may walk by, letting them clear the lobby before I return, so as not to seem to be following them. I have been calm and extremely congenial on those rare occasions when I've been pulled over by the police.

And on late-evening constitutionals I employ what has proved to be an   10 excellent tension-reducing measure: I whistle melodies from Beethoven and Vivaldi and the more popular classical composers. Even steely New Yorkers hunching toward nighttime destinations seem to relax, and occasionally they even join in the tune. Virtually everybody seems to sense that a mugger wouldn't be warbling bright, sunny selections from Vivaldi's "Four Seasons." It is my equivalent of the cowbell that hikers wear when they are in bear country.

RESPONDING TO READING

Why don't we expect muggers to be whistling melodies from Beethoven and Vivaldi? In your journal, write a brief explanation of the possible reasons.

GAINING WORD POWER

The following words appear in the reading but are not included in the Terms to Recognize. Look up each one in your dictionary and use it in a sentence of your own.

1. affluent (para. 1)
2. menacingly (para. 1)
3. dismayed (para. 2)
4. taut (para. 4)
5. vulnerable (para. 5)
6. solace (para. 5)
7. entity (para. 5)
8. attributed (para. 7)
9. precautions (para. 9)
10. congenial (para. 9)

CONSIDERING CONTENT

1. How does the author describe his physical appearance in the opening paragraph?
2. Why does the woman take him for "a mugger, a rapist, or worse"?
3. What does the writer mean when he says "that being perceived as dangerous is a hazard in itself"? What illustrations does he offer to prove his point?
4. What kind of hometown background did Brent Staples have? What kind of person did he turn out to be?
5. At the end of paragraph 6, he speaks of three young men he was close to—"all gone down in episodes of bravado played out in the streets." Although he doesn't tell us how any of them died, can you

guess? Give examples of the kind of "episodes of bravado" that may have cost them their lives.

6. How did Staples learn to deal with the problem of being a large, young black man in the city?

7. Why would hikers in bear country wear cowbells? Explain how that wilderness situation is similar to Staples's urban situation.

CONSIDERING METHOD

1. Explain how the brief narrative in the opening paragraph catches our interest.

2. The thesis of this selection is implied, not directly stated. Write out in your own words a statement of the author's main point.

3. In the first paragraph, Staples uses a two-word sentence fragment, "Not so." Turn those two words into a complete sentence, and then comment on why you think he chose the fragment.

4. How does description help to make Staples's illustrations interesting and convincing in paragraphs 1 and 5?

5. Using words that sound like the noise they describe is called **onomatopoeia** (for example, the *thunk, thunk, thunk, thunk* of the car door locks in para. 3). Explain why that word choice is effective. Can you think of other examples of words that sound like what they mean?

6. This essay is developed through example and illustration, yet Staples does not tell us how the three young men died in paragraph 6. Why does he leave out these details?

7. Explain what makes the conclusion particularly satisfying.

WRITING STEP BY STEP

Stereotypes are oversimplified groupings of people by race, gender, politics, athletic ability, ethnic origin, and so on. Staples was stereotyped because he was a young black male, and as Staples says, "young black males are drastically overrepresented among the perpetrators of . . . violence." There is usually some grain of truth behind stereotypes, but, nonetheless, they tend to be negative and unfair. Women, for instance, are stereotyped as weak, passive, fickle, timid, scatterbrained, and indecisive. Men, on the other hand, are supposed to be strong minded and assertive, but dense and unfeeling. Stereotypes are unfair because they lump lots of people into a category whether or not the characteristics fit every individual.

A. Think of a stereotype that includes you. Choose one that you think is unfair to you; your essay will explain how you are different.

B. Begin, as Staples does, with a brief narrative, a story that illustrates how you *seem* to fit the type although you actually do not.
C. In the next paragraph, define the stereotype by giving examples of several characteristics people expect you to have—or not to have.
D. Next, explain why people would tend to place you in this stereotype. For instance, if you are a male football player, people may take you for a clumsy hulk who can barely read and write.
E. Then, explain why you don't fit the stereotype, and tell about some influence while you were growing up that helped you to avoid the typical pattern of behavior. Provide concrete examples, as Staples does in paragraph 6 when he tells about his childhood among the gangs in Chester, Pennsylvania.
F. In conclusion, explain how you felt about being stereotyped, and tell how you have learned to cope with the mistaken views of strangers—perhaps even relatives and friends—who took you for a different kind of person than you truly are.

OTHER WRITING IDEAS

1. Write the paper outlined in the previous section, but instead, illustrate how you are the perfect example of a stereotype. You may want to think of a positive stereotype—or else make your essay humorous.
2. Write an essay about frustrations at work (or in some other area of your life). What frustrations do you have? How do you deal with them? Do you think you handle them well or poorly? If poorly, what could you do to improve? Give plenty of specific examples to explain and support your general points.
3. With a small group of classmates, discuss phobias, those irrational fears that most of us have—fears of spiders, of snakes, of high places, of flying, of closed spaces. Which ones do you have? Choose your worst or your most embarrassing phobia and tell in an essay how it limits your activities, how it makes you feel, how you think you got it, and what you do to control it.

EDITING SKILLS: COMMAS AROUND INTERRUPTERS

An **interrupter** is just what it sounds like—a word or group of words that interrupts or breaks into the flow of a sentence, like the italicized words do here:

I understand, *of course,* that the danger they perceive is not a hallucination.

You need a comma before and after the interrupter as a signal to your readers that the interrupter is an addition that can be removed without changing the meaning of the sentence. The first comma signals the start of the interruption; the second comma signals the end of the interruption. It would be quite misleading in that sentence, with its flow interrupted, to use only one comma. But if you move the *of course* to the beginning or to the end of the sentence so that it no longer interrupts the flow, then a single comma is fine:

> *Of course,* I understand that the danger they perceive is not a hallucination.
> I understand that the danger they perceive is not a hallucination, *of course.*

The principle remains the same, even when the interrupter is longer:

> One day, *rushing into the office of a magazine I was writing for with a deadline story in hand,* I was mistaken for a burglar.

Remember: put commas *around* interrupters—one before and one after.

EXERCISE

We've omitted the commas from around the interrupters in the following sentences. Figure out where they belong, and put them back in.

1. Suffering a bout of insomnia however I was stalking sleep, not defenseless wayfarers.
2. After dark on the warrenlike streets of Brooklyn where I live I often see women who fear the worst from me.
3. I chose perhaps unconsciously to remain a shadow—timid, but a survivor.
4. The office manager called security and with the speed of an ad hoc posse pursued me through the labyrinthine halls, nearly to my editor's door.
5. Relatively speaking however I never fared as badly as another black male journalist.

Now check the essay you've just written to be sure that you have punctuated interrupters correctly. Did you always remember to include the second comma?

WEB SITE
www.pbs.org/blackpress/modern_journalist/staples.html
This site, maintained by the Public Broadcasting System, offers video and audio clips of Brent Staples.

PREPARING TO READ

Do men or women make better schoolteachers? Or does gender matter? Does the age of the students make any difference?

One Man's Kids

DANIEL R. MEIER

Daniel Meier received a master's degree in education from the Harvard Graduate School in 1984. He taught first grade at schools in Brookline and Boston, Massachusetts, before getting his Ph.D. at the University of California at Berkeley. He now teaches early childhood education at San Francisco State University. His articles about teaching and his reviews of children's books have appeared in a number of educational journals. The essay reprinted here appeared in 1987 in the "About Men" series of the *New York Times Magazine*.

TERMS TO RECOGNIZE

complying *(para. 4)*	agreeing to someone else's request or command
singular *(para. 5)*	exceptional, unusual, distinguished by superiority
consoling *(para. 6)*	offering comfort and advice
intellectual *(para. 7)*	guided chiefly by knowledge or reason rather than by emotion or experience
hilarity *(para. 7)*	spirited merriment, cheerfulness
complimentary *(para. 12)*	given free as a courtesy or a favor

1   I teach first graders. I live in a world of skinned knees, double-knotted shoelaces, riddles that I've heard a dozen times, stale birthday cakes, hurt feelings, wandering stories, and one lost shoe ("and if you don't find it my mother'll kill me"). My work is dominated by 6-year-olds.

2   It's 10:45, the middle of snack, and I'm helping Emily open her milk carton. She has already tried the other end without success, and now there's so much paint and ink on the carton from her fingers that I'm not sure she should drink it at all. But I open it. Then I turn to help Scott clean up some milk he has just spilled onto Rebecca's whale crossword puzzle.

While I wipe my milk- and paint-covered hands, Jenny wants to know   3
if I've seen that funny book about penguins that I read in class. As I hunt
for it in a messy pile of books, Jason wants to know if there is a new seat-
ing arrangement for lunch tables. I find the book, turn to answer Jason, then
face Maya, who is fast approaching with a new knock-knock joke. After
what seems like the 10th "Who's there?" I laugh and Maya is pleased.

Then Andrew wants to know how to spell "flukes" for his crossword. As   4
I get to "u," I give a hand signal for Sarah to take away the snack. But just
as Sarah is almost out the door, two children complain that "we haven't
even had ours yet." I stop the snack mid-flight, complying with their
request for graham crackers. I then return to Andrew, noticing that he has
put "flu" for 9 Down, rather than 9 Across. It's now 10:50.

My work is not traditional male work. It's not a singular pursuit. There   5
is not a large pile of paper to get through or one deal to transact. I don't
have one area of expertise or knowledge. I don't have the singular power
over language of a lawyer, the physical force of a construction worker, the
command over fellow workers of a surgeon, the wheeling and dealing trans-
actions of a businessman. My energy is not spent in pursuing, climbing,
achieving, conquering, or cornering some goal or object.

My energy is spent in encouraging, supporting, consoling, and prais-   6
ing my children. In teaching, the inner rewards come from without. On
any given day, quite apart from teaching reading and spelling, I bandage
a cut, dry a tear, erase a frown, tape a torn doll, and locate a long-lost
boot. The day is really won through matters of the heart. As my students
groan, laugh, shudder, cry, exult, and wonder, I do too. I have to be soft
around the edges.

A few years ago, when I was interviewing for an elementary-school   7
teaching position, every principal told me with confidence that, as a male,
I had an advantage over female applicants because of the lack of male teachers. But in the next breath, they asked with a hint of suspicion why I chose
to work with young children. I told them that I wanted to observe and
contribute to the intellectual growth of a maturing mind. What I really felt
like saying, but didn't, was that I loved helping a child learn to write her
name for the first time, finding someone a new friend, or sharing in the
hilarity of reading about Winnie the Pooh getting so stuck in a hole that
only his head and rear show.

I gave that answer to those principals, who were mostly male, because I   8
thought they wanted a "male" response. This meant talking about intellectual matters. If I had taken a different course and talked about my interest
in helping children in their emotional development, it would have been
seen as closer to a "female" answer. I even altered my language, not once

mentioning the word "love" to describe what I do indeed love about teaching. My answer worked; every principal nodded approvingly.

Some of the principals also asked what I saw myself doing later in my 9
career. They wanted to know if I eventually wanted to go into educational administration. Becoming a dean of students or a principal has never been one of my goals, but they seemed to expect me, as a male, to want to climb higher on the career stepladder. So I mentioned that, at some point, I would be interested in working with teachers as a curriculum coordinator. Again, they nodded approvingly.

If those principals had been female instead of male, I wonder whether 10
their questions, and my answers, would have been different. My guess is that they would have been.

At other times, when I'm at a party or a dinner and tell someone that I 11
teach young children, I've found that men and women respond differently. Most men ask about the subjects I teach and the courses I took in my training. Then, unless they bring up an issue such as merit pay, the conversation stops. Most women, on the other hand, begin the conversation on a more immediate and personal level. They say things like "those kids must love having a male teacher" or "that age is just wonderful, you must love it." Then, more often than not, they'll talk about their own kids or ask me specific questions about what I do. We're then off and talking shop.

Possibly, men would have more to say to me, and I to them, if my job 12
had more of the trappings and benefits of more traditional male jobs. But my job has no bonuses or promotions. No complimentary box seats at the ball park. No cab fare home. No drinking buddies after work. No briefcase. No suit. (Ties get stuck in paint jars.) No power lunches. (I eat peanut butter and jelly, chips, milk, and cookies with the kids.) No taking clients out for cocktails. The only place I take my kids is to the playground.

Although I could have pursued a career in law or business, as several of 13
my friends did, I chose teaching instead. My job has benefits all its own. I'm able to bake cookies without getting them stuck together as they cool, buy cheap sewing materials, take out splinters, and search just the right trash cans for useful odds and ends. I'm sometimes called "Daddy" and even "Mommy" by my students, and if there's ever a lull in the conversation at a dinner party, I can always ask those assembled if they've heard the latest riddle about why the turkey crossed the road. (He thought he was a chicken.)

RESPONDING TO READING

What do you think about Meier's choice of career? Do you think it's reasonable and appropriate? Why or why not?

GAINING WORD POWER

In paragraph 12, Meier uses the word *complimentary*. There is a word that's pronounced the same but has a different spelling and a different meaning—*complementary*. Do you know what each word means? English has many of these sound-alike words, and it's important to know the differences among them. They won't cause you any trouble in speaking, but they will change the meaning of your writing if you choose the wrong one.

Here is a list of words from Meier's essay. Using your dictionary, find a sound-alike word for each item in the list and write down its meaning. Then use the word you found in a sentence.

fare	right	male
new	won	course
principal	seen	whether
through	two	hole

CONSIDERING CONTENT

1. Why did Meier write this essay? What point do you think he wanted to make?
2. Meier says, "My work is not traditional male work" (para. 5). What does he mean by that statement? Do you agree?
3. What is a "singular pursuit"? Why does the author use that phrase to describe "male work"?
4. Why did the principals who interviewed Meier have "a hint of suspicion" about him (para. 7)?
5. What kind of answers did Meier give in his job interviews (para. 8)? What kind of answers did he avoid? Why didn't he mention the word "love"?
6. The author says that men and women respond differently to him when he talks about his job (para. 11). What are the differences?
7. How does Meier feel about his job? Do you think he is being defensive or apologetic about it?

CONSIDERING METHOD

1. In the first paragraph, the author says, "My work is dominated by 6-year-olds." What examples does he give to explain and support this general statement?
2. Why does Meier open his essay the way he does? Why doesn't he state his thesis until paragraph 5?

3. Find the series of words that Meier uses to describe "male work" (end of para. 5) and the words he uses to describe what he does (beginning of para. 6). What is he saying about the difference between his work and "male work"?

4. What does the author mean when he says, "In teaching, the inner rewards come from without" (para. 6)? What examples does he give to make his meaning clear?

5. What is the effect of the series of phrases that begin with "No" in paragraph 12? Why are the positive comments in parentheses? Why is the last sentence in the paragraph not in parentheses?

WRITING STEP BY STEP

Think of a workplace that you know well—a place where you have a job now or had one in the past. If your primary work is being a student, then school is your workplace.

A. First identify and briefly explain your role at the workplace ("I am a cashier, salesperson, and general troubleshooter at Posh Pups, a pet-grooming and pet supply store").

B. Then name three or four personal qualities that make for success in that job. ("To work at Posh Pups, you need to be loyal and good at math and to like people as much as you like animals.")

C. Think about the order in which you want to present these qualities. You might start with a less important quality and build up to the most important one. Or you may see that two of them are related and need to be placed in back-to-back paragraphs. Make a scratch outline to help you decide how to arrange your main points and examples.

D. For each quality you name, give at least one example of how it is important in the job. Think of a specific time when each quality was needed. Tell the story of how you or your co-workers showed the quality (or, unfortunately, showed a lack of it).

E. If an example is long and detailed, give it its own paragraph, as Meier does in paragraphs 2, 3, and 4 of his essay. If some of your examples are only a sentence or two, try to expand them with more details that will give your readers the sights, sounds, and feel of your work.

F. Close with a summarizing statement of how you feel about this job. Or offer a recommendation to anyone who might consider going into this line of work. Try to reinforce your thesis idea without simply repeating it.

G. When you revise, look at the transitions between your paragraphs. Try to fill in any gaps between your main points. Also check to see that you used transitions to lead into your examples. Ask your instructor or your classmates to help you improve the flow of your ideas.

OTHER WRITING IDEAS

1. Select one of the following general statements, or compose one of your own. Make it the central idea of an essay full of examples and illustrations. Draw examples from your reading, your conversation, your observations, and your own experience.

   a. Action heroes in the movies today are pretty much alike.

   b. Being a good parent is probably the hardest job there is.

   c. The stereotypical female (or male) is not easy to find in our society anymore.

   d. Being a teenager can be difficult (or easy or perplexing or a lot of fun).

   e. Jealousy is a destructive emotion.

2. Discuss with your classmates some superstitions that you or members of your family or community have held. Frequently, these superstitions have to do with success or bad luck in sports, performances, weather, or work. Do they have any validity? How did they develop? Write an essay of example about the role that superstition plays in your life or in the life of someone you know.

EDITING SKILLS: USING SUBORDINATION

Writers often combine two or more ideas in a sentence by using **subordination.** When one idea is subordinate to or dependent on another, it is less important. Take a look at these sentences from Meier's essay to see how the subordinate ideas are introduced by words that make them sound less important:

Although I could have pursued a career in law or business, I chose teaching instead.

Then, *unless* they bring up an issue such as merit pay, the conversation stops.

If I had taken a different course and talked about my interest in helping children in their emotional development, it would have been seen as close to a "female" answer.

As you can see, each of these sentences has two parts. Notice that the second part, after the comma, can stand alone as a sentence: that part is called **independent.** If you read the first part alone, it does not sound complete. The first part is called **dependent** for this reason. The opening words—*Although, unless,* and *If*—make the first statement of each sentence dependent. These words are called *subordinating conjunctions;* they indicate that the first idea is not as important as the rest of the sentence. (You will also notice that when the dependent part comes first, a comma separates it from the independent part.)

Subordinating conjunctions are familiar words; we use them a lot. Here are some of the most common ones: *since, because, if, even if, unless, although, even though, though, as long as, after, before, when, whenever, while, until,* and *wherever.* Skillful writers use subordination to give variety to their sentences and to keep readers' attention focused on the main ideas.

EXERCISE

Imitate the following sentences. Each one begins with a dependent statement followed by an independent one. You don't have to imitate each sentence exactly; just follow the dependent–independent pattern and use the same subordinating conjunction as the model sentence. Put in the commas, too.

Model: If we want clean air, then we will have to drive more fuel-
            efficient cars.
Imitation: If you like lasagna, then you should try the new Italian
            restaurant on Division Street.

1. While I was eating my lunch, a friend walked in.
2. Wherever I go in this city, I run into old friends.
3. Before you gather up your books, be sure your notes are complete.
4. Although Selma is a good athlete, she sometimes swears at the umpire.
5. Unless she sees the error of her ways, Selma may get tossed off the team.

Write at least one more imitation of each of the preceding sentences.

Go back to your example essay to see how many sentences like these you've written. What subordinating conjunctions did you use? Did you include the commas? Now combine some more of your sentences by using subordinating conjunctions and the dependent–independent pattern. If they sound sensible, keep them in your essay.

✈ WEB SITES

http://userwww.sfsu.edu/~dmeier/welcome.htm

On Daniel Meier's home page, you will find more information about his life, his research interests, and his teaching.

www.ume.maine.edu/ECEOL-L

The Early Childhood Education Online site provides a wealth of information about teaching young children.

PREPARING TO PEAD

Do you consider yourself a conformist or a nonconformist? What would your friends and family say about the matter? Do you ever wish that you behaved in a more or less conforming way?

Genius or Madness?

LYNN COADY

Lynn Coady lives in Vancouver and writes fiction and essays. Early in her career, she won several prestigious awards and nominations for her first novel, titled *Strange Heaven* (1998). She completed this novel while earning a master's in fine arts at the University of British Columbia. In 2000, Doubleday Canada published her book of short stories, *Play the Monster Blind*. A second novel will appear in 2002.

TERMS TO RECOGNIZE

faux *(para. 2)*	artificial; fake
proclivities *(para. 2)*	natural inclination
interim *(para. 3)*	an interval of time between one event and another
bejeezus *(para. 5)*	slang alteration of "by Jesus"
tenets *(para. 5)*	doctrines

In my hometown, perhaps small towns in general, it's easy to be crazy. As an adolescent, I didn't talk much and liked to read books in my room. That was all it took. Other people were crazy for different reasons. There were a couple of other kids who stayed in their rooms and played guitar (or oboe, or drums . . .). Someone else was a vegetarian and an environmentalist—this in a town whose lifeblood consisted of the pulp of razed forests. Then there was the elementary school art teacher who wore high-heels, chunky jewelry, and low-cut tops. He also had a big, fluffy white mat he liked to lounge on during class, making us kids fidget uncomfortably on the minuscule carpet samples he provided for us. 1

In the glare of small-town scrutiny, any deviation from the norm stands out wildly. The art teacher, because he was an adult, and well-established in the community, was treated with a faux-friendly indulgence that in any modern city would instantly be recognized for the covert bigotry it was. In 2 our town it passed for tolerance. Weirdo adolescents, however, were less kindly indulged—the assumption always being that teenagers exist in a developmental limbo with no solid values or proclivities of their own, and can, therefore, with firm guidance, easily be molded into well-adjusted citizens.

As it turned out, the conformity expected in my hometown actually served 3 as a handy preview of what was to come—the larger-scale conformity that defines the urban adult. Like many a small-town girl, I lived in the hope of getting out and going where not talking much and reading books was even a marginally acceptable pastime and I wouldn't be considered crazy anymore. Off I went to the big city. All I've learned in the ten-year interim since is that reading books is *okay,* in moderation, but not wanting to talk remains a no-no. Small town hicks and urban sophisticates alike can't help but take it personally. People harangue me for never answering my phone, for example. But I don't like answering my phone. "But it's *anti-social,*" they warn, ominously.

This is the crux of crazy, apparently. *Anti-social behavior* is our euphemism 4 for everything from the dabblings of people like the Unabomber, to that hairy street-wanderer who talks and titters to himself as he makes ready to pee on the sidewalk, to Emily Dickinson, in near-obscurity, penning some of the most shattering verse ever written. If you believe what people tell you, it's all the same, and it's all bad. There was probably much concern and consternation over Emily's doings at the time, existing in a cocoon of grief and isolation, only rousing herself to scribble her terse, morbid observations of the world. Anti-social? Definitely. Crazy? According to some, yes. There's one important thing to keep in mind, however. She was also ground-breaking.

Society is not so much afraid of full-blown chemically imbalanced madness 5 as it is of non-conformity. To not conform to societal norms is to insult the painstaking codes of conduct enshrined by our ancestors so that we could live in civilization. The dilemma has always been that a civilization can never move forward until some nut-job flouts one or two of its standards, with the ultimate aim of toppling them. This scares the bejeezus out of people, particularly those who may have spent their lives upholding such precarious tenets. Thus when Socrates starts advising the youth of Athens to question everything around them, the citizens get a bit squirrelly. When Hamlet expresses his rampant disgust at the world and humanity, Elizabethans pop a collective garter. When the young Holden Caulfield denounces his clean-cut compatriots as phonies and whores, post-war America recoils.

You would think by now that we would see the need for this kind of 6 crazy, after centuries of conformity and blind obedience leading us over cliffs. Yet even today, we dare not step out of line. Try not answering your phone for an afternoon.

RESPONDING TO READING

In your experience, which group is more alarmed by nonconformity among its members, adults or adolescents? Why do you think this is so?

GAINING WORD POWER

Coady uses the word *crazy* to mean several different things, including *insane* and *nonconformist*. Brainstorm with classmates to write a list of words that could be substituted for *crazy* in different contexts. Do any of these words have positive connotations? Consult a thesaurus to see how complete your list is.

CONSIDERING CONTENT

1. Why were teens treated less indulgently in Coady's hometown than odd adults were?
2. What is "covert bigotry" (para. 2)? Can you think of another example of it?
3. Why do people hate Coady's not answering her telephone?
4. According to Coady, what is the need for "craziness" in society?
5. Write a definition of "crazy" that would fit Coady's admiring stance toward it.

CONSIDERING METHOD

1. How many examples of crazy people does Coady use? Be sure that you understand the references by looking up any unfamiliar names in a biographical dictionary or encyclopedia.
2. Compare the examples in paragraph 1 to the examples in paragraph 5. What is the main difference? What would be the effect if the examples were switched in placement?
3. In paragraph 4, Coady provides three examples and comments, "it's all the same, and it's all bad." Does she mean for you to take this comment seriously? How do you know what her tone is?
4. Look back at the essay and find the place where you first understood what Coady's purpose is in writing about nonconformity. Is this the same place where your classmates understood the purpose? Where is the thesis most directly stated?

WRITING STEP BY STEP

A. Think of two to four people in your life who are nonconformists. These could be people from school, your hometown, your ethnic subculture, your family, or your social group.

B. Introduce your essay by giving an overview of things that might be considered nonconformist in your setting (school, hometown, and so on), as Coady does in paragraph 1.

C. Develop a paragraph or two about each of your examples. Be sure to provide vivid details. Try to put a picture of each person into your reader's mind.

D. Include an explanation about why each is considered nonconformist (in contrast with most people). If you can, use comparisons with famous people or characters.

E. Reread Coady's paragraph 5. Write a paragraph that pulls all your examples together. Are they all rebelling against "painstaking codes of conduct"? Are they all creative? Are they crazy? Wise? Find some common thread that relates them to each other.

OTHER WRITING IDEAS

1. In paragraph 2, Coady suggests that maybe all small towns are sensitive to deviation from the norms. Certainly, her small town bothered her by the prevailing attitudes toward nonconformists as "crazy." Think about your own hometown, large or small. Is there any prevailing attitude or condition there that bothers you? Write an essay giving examples and explanations for the circumstances that bother you in your hometown.

2. Coady describes how, as an adolescent, she longed to move to a big city, where she expected to see more tolerance of nonconformity. However, the reality turned out to be "larger-scale conformity." Have you ever expected that something would be different as you got older or moved to a new setting, and found that nothing really changed? Write about the experience, providing examples of what you experienced as a younger person, what you expected from a change, and what you got.

3. Coady refers to "codes of conduct enshrined by our ancestors so that we could live in civilization." Write an essay using examples to demonstrate that some measure of conformity is a good practice.

EDITING SKILLS: SEMICOLONS
BETWEEN SENTENCES

If you tend to write mainly short, simple sentences, you may need to add some variety. If you have two sentences *that are closely related in meaning,* you can put them together—separated by a semicolon. For example, Coady could have written sentences in paragraph 3 like this:

Small-town hicks and urban sophisticates alike can't help but take it personally; people harangue me for never answering my phone, for example.

She also could have used a semicolon instead of the coordinating conjunction *and* in this case (again from para. 3):

I lived in the hope of getting out and going where not talking much and reading books was even a marginally acceptable pastime; I wouldn't be considered crazy anymore.

Remember that the semicolon indicates a close relationship in meaning; it can't just go between any two sentences. Also, each of the sentences must be complete in most standard English writing for a semicolon to work between them. When you read older material, like novels by Jane Austen or Charles Dickens, you may see a fragment on one side of a semicolon and a complete sentence on the other, but that is not usually done these days.

EXERCISE

Dave Barry, a popular humorist, once described the new Jolly Green Giant this way: "He no longer looks like the 'Ho, Ho, Ho' guy; he now looks like Paul McCartney on steroids." Why do you think Barry chose a semicolon between his two sentences?

Go through the essay you just wrote to see whether you have any short, closely related sentences that come one right after the other. If so, try taking out the period, putting in a semicolon, and making the second sentence's capital letter lowercase.

A word of caution: be sure to use a *semicolon* in joining sentences. A comma definitely will not do in most cases.

WEB SITES

www.quoteland.com

You can look up quotations by topic—for example, see the topic of "Sanity and Insanity" in relation to Coady's essay. This site is handy when you need a quotation for an essay or speech.

www.nwpassages.com/Profile_book.asp?ISBN=0864922302

You can read a profile of Lynn Coady's *Strange Heaven* at the Northwest Passage site.

Student Essay Using Examples

My Key Chain

David C. Lair

During my four years of army service, I led a   1
very transient life. I moved from Illinois to
Missouri to California to Texas to Massachusetts to
Germany and back to Illinois again, never staying in
one place for very long. Consequently, I had to live
a very sparse lifestyle with few possessions, and
those that I did try to keep fared poorly through all
my relocation. (In the army it is said that two or
three moves have the same effect on one's belongings
as does a house fire.) Therefore, when trying to
think of a possession that has been significant to me
personally, my choices are narrowed to only those
items that I have been able to carry on my person. Of
these items, I believe that my key chain says more
about myself and my life than anything else does.

Upon entering the service I soon learned that my   2
eventual duty station, after I completed training at
various posts in the states, would be somewhere in
Germany. At this time I bought a key chain decorated
with an Imperial Eagle and the inscription
"Deutschland" (which means Germany); it also came
equipped with a handy bottle opener. This key chain
was important because it came at a time when I was
looking forward to being stationed in Germany. My
training was long and mentally arduous, and the key
chain served as a reminder of my goal. Whenever I
felt discouraged, I pulled out my key chain and
thought of traveling around Germany, learning the
language, meeting the people, and drinking the beer,
which I had heard great things about. I already had
big plans for the bottle opener.

When I finally arrived in Germany, my outlook on   3
life changed, and so did the "function" of my key
chain. Now I lived life for the present. I traveled,
learned the language, absorbed the culture, and
sampled as many brands of beer as I could find. Along

with this transition, the duties of my key chain became more based in the present. Now the keys on the chain represented my "home" in the city of Fulda as I wandered around the continent; now the inscription "Deutschland" made sense to me linguistically; and now the bottle opener was my most important tool. I will always look back on this time as a very happy period in my life.

My tour in Germany ended last December, and I returned to the states to begin my new life as a student. But the transition wasn't easy. I found that my mind often dwelled on my former lifestyle; I also found myself missing Germany. Once again, my key chain mirrored my state of mind. By this time the metal around the opener was rusted, the "Deutschland" insignia was scratched, and cracks had begun to form along the entire length of the chain. I frequently looked at my beloved belonging and remembered the fun I had had. As I sprung another cap from an imported beer, I realized that I was now living in the past.   4

Recently, while opening a beer, my key chain broke in half. The stress of opening all the beers finally drove the cracks completely through the key chain. This development caused me to reflect on my present situation. I decided that it was time to stop living in the past, and to start looking toward my future once again.   5

Over Christmas break my girlfriend and I will travel to Brazil to visit her parents, who live in Rio de Janiero. I am very excited about the trip. I am looking forward to exploring a new country once again and to meeting new people. When she heard that my key chain had broken, my girlfriend gave me a small present: a key chain with the Brazilian flag and the inscription "Brazil." Sure, there's no bottle opener, but we have "twist-tops" in the United States anyway. Now I can once again take my key chain out of my pocket and anticipate the future, while at the same time enjoying the present.   6

C h a p t e r

STRATEGIES FOR CLARIFYING MEANING

Definition and Explanation

"PowerTalk gives you a single mailbox icon for all incoming and outgoing mail—including fax, voice, electronic mail, and documents. Communication from on-line services and electronic mail from various sources are routed to your desktop mailbox when you install mail gateways supplied by the vendor," the manual for our new computer operating system cheerfully brags. Sounds great, but we have only the vaguest idea what PowerTalk *is!* How many of the terms in those two sentences would *you* need to have defined or explained? Moreover, how many terms would need definition and explanation for a reader in the 1970s?

THE POINT OF DEFINITION AND EXPLANATION

As suggested by the quotation from the computer manual and by the cartoon following this chapter introduction, the whole point of **definition** and explanation is to clarify things for people. Words are worse than unhelpful when they don't convey meaning but instead create confusion.

The special vocabulary of any group needs explanation when used to communicate with people outside that group. Some groups develop languages that are incredibly mysterious to outsiders. If you've ever been the outsider listening to a bunch of bridge players, computer gamers, or aerobic class addicts, you know the feeling of bafflement that grows quickly into boredom because you have no idea what they're discussing so enthusiastically. The same thing can happen when you read or write essays that don't define or explain as much material as necessary.

Some words can be defined briefly in parentheses, but complex ideas and terms need more than a phrase or sentence of explanation. In this chapter, you will read whole essays whose main purpose is to define and explain difficult or controversial concepts.

THE PRINCIPLES OF DEFINITION AND EXPLANATION

Definitions and explanations make use of a few basic techniques that can be found in almost all writing.

DESCRIPTIVE DETAILS

Can you imagine explaining anything without using descriptive details? "Why are you afraid you'll become a slave to your new silk shirt?" a friend might ask you. To explain, you would naturally give the **details** of caring for it: you must wash it in cold water by hand; then, instead of wringing it, you should wrap it in a clean towel to blot excess water; then it needs to hang dry on a padded hanger away from the sun or electric light; when dry, it will be crinkled and must be ironed with a very cool iron; finally, on the day of wearing, it should be steamed while you shower and lightly re-ironed. In other words, you think you will be a slave to it.

Examples

Concepts are frequently defined or explained through examples. The classic Type A personality can be defined through examples of behavior: if Jake is Type A, he is extremely impatient in a long grocery line, he cannot find the time to go to a film starring his favorite actor, and he considers getting a promotion at work a life-or-death issue. He is likely to slam doors and throw books when angry.

In an essay in this chapter, Isaac Asimov uses himself and his garage mechanic as examples to show how subjective people's definitions of intelligence are.

Narration

Aesop's fables, which you probably remember from childhood, make use of narrative, or story, to explain a basic truth about humans. A "sour grapes" attitude is explained by the story of the fox who sees a bunch of delicious-looking grapes but can't reach them; the fox, therefore, comforts itself by deciding that they were probably sour anyway. A writer might define an abstract quality, such as heroism or courage, by telling a story with a hero who acts out the virtue.

In his essay in this chapter, Wayson Choy uses brief narratives to illustrate the "ugly, unjust" prejudice endured by his parents when they immigrated to British Columbia from China in 1918.

Comparison

Sometimes we define a word by emphasizing its likeness to something else. A **fable** is a kind of story, for example. Writers use imaginative comparison to clarify meaning, too: "A true friend is a port in a storm" and "A true friend is as comfortable as an old shoe."

A comparison may be used for surprising effect. Barbara Ehrenreich, in this chapter, shows how a "cultural heritage" may really be "cultural baggage."

Contrast

Sometimes the best way to define something is to contrast it with something different. This technique can be quite simple: *dearth* is the opposite of *plenty.* Or the definition can consist of a comparison spiked with a contrast. As our friend heard her five-year-old explain to her four-year-old, "Death is like going to Omaha, only longer."

In some cases, contrast is needed to correct a common misconception about a term. *Schizophrenia,* contrary to popular belief, does not involve having more than one personality. And being *educated,* according to Asimov's garage mechanic, doesn't mean being "smart."

THE PITFALLS OF DEFINITION AND EXPLANATION

When you write a definition or explanation, you risk making certain characteristic mistakes.

Missing Your Audience

Would you explain what a control key is to a computer whiz? We hope not. But if you were writing directions for a beginning word processing course, you'd be a fool *not* to define what a control key is. Analyzing your intended **audience** is important in all writing. If you misjudge what your audience needs to have defined or explained, you will either insult or confuse them.

Going in Circles

Some definitions are called circular because they don't go anywhere. They restate rather than explain. "A *smooth operator* is a person who functions without roughness," for example, tells you nothing. The second part of that definition only rewords the first part. The definition must lead some-where, like this: "a *smooth operator* is a person who takes advantage of others by using charm and persuasion."

Abstraction

The previous circular definition also demonstrates the flaw of abstrac-tion. It has no **concrete words** to hang onto. A high-flown sentence like "Our ideal leader is the hope of the future" provides no helpful terms about qualities we can actually identify.

Leaving Information Out

To say merely that a fable is a story doesn't get across the whole idea; it conveys only part of it: a fable has special features, like talking animals and a moral lesson. Incompleteness is a pitfall especially of short definitions, such as "Love is never having to say you're sorry." In this chapter, the essay "Mommy, What Does 'Nigger' Mean?" shows that a sentence like "*Nigger* is a degrading label for an African American" is not a full definition.

Of course, an explanation is incomplete when your reader needs to ask for clarification. Sometimes it's hard to see the holes in what you have written yourself because you already know what you're trying to say. You need to enlist a good peer editor to point out whether you have omitted important information.

WHAT TO LOOK FOR IN DEFINITIONS AND EXPLANATIONS

Here are some guidelines to follow as you study the selections in this chapter.

1. *Focus on which term or concept is being defined or explained.* This focus will help you evaluate the essay's effectiveness.
2. *Identify the ways in which the writer develops the idea,* especially details, narration, example, comparison, and contrast.
3. *Figure out who the intended audience is.* Then think about how the essay would be different if written for a different audience. What definitions and explanations would be added or deleted?
4. *Ask yourself whether the definition or explanation is complete.* If it is not complete, does the writer tell you why?

THE FAR SIDE® By GARY LARSON

"Hang him, you idiots! Hang him! . . . 'String-him-up' is a figure of speech!"

What is a **figure of speech?**

Why do the hapless cowboys misunderstand their instructions?

Can you think of other figures of speech that would be humorous or absurd if taken literally?

PREPARING TO READ

What word could be used to label you? Consider even labels that *you* do not think accurate. Might someone call you a jock? a nerd? an egghead? a bimbo? a tramp? a hero? a male chauvinist? a rabid feminist? a spoiled brat? a bully? a heartbreaker?

"Mommy, What Does 'Nigger' Mean?"

GLORIA NAYLOR

Gloria Naylor came from a rural, working-class southern background and did not enter college until she was twenty-five, after working as a missionary and a telephone operator. Naylor graduated from Brooklyn College in 1981, and in 1983 she won the American Book Award for best first novel for *The Women of Brewster Place*. In this excerpt from an article first published in the *New York Times* on February 20, 1986, Naylor discusses the ways a word's meaning changes according to the context in which it is used.

TERMS TO RECOGNIZE

necrophiliac *(para. 1)*	someone sexually attracted to corpses
verified *(para. 1)*	proven true
gravitated *(para. 2)*	moved toward
mecca *(para. 2)*	a place regarded as the center of interest or activity
inflections *(para. 3)*	tones of voice
trifling *(para. 8)*	shallow, unimportant
connotation *(para. 9)*	the idea suggested by a word or phrase, in addition to its surface meaning
stratum *(para. 12)*	level
internalization *(para. 12)*	making other people's attitudes a part of your own way of thinking

I remember the first time I heard the word "nigger." In my third-grade class, our math tests were being passed down the rows, and as I handed the papers to a little boy in back of me, I remarked that once again he had received a much lower mark than I did. He snatched his test from me and spit out that word. Had he called me a nymphomaniac or a necrophiliac, I couldn't have been more puzzled. I didn't know what a nigger was, but I knew that whatever it meant, it was something he shouldn't have called me. This was verified when I raised my hand, and in a loud voice repeated what he had said and watched the teacher scold him for using a "bad" word. I was later to go home and ask the inevitable question that every black parent must face—"Mommy, what does 'nigger' mean?"

And what exactly did it mean? Thinking back, I realize that this could   2
not have been the first time the word was used in my presence. I was part of a large extended family that had migrated from the rural South after World War II and formed a close-knit network that gravitated around my maternal grandparents. Their ground-floor apartment in one of the buildings they owned in Harlem was a weekend mecca for my immediate family, along with countless aunts, uncles, and cousins who brought along assorted friends. It was a bustling and open house with assorted neighbors and tenants popping in and out to exchange bits of gossip, pick up an old quarrel, or referee the ongoing checkers game in which my grandmother cheated shamelessly. They were all there to let down their hair and put up their feet after a week of labor in the factories, laundries, and shipyards of New York.

Amid the clamor, which could reach deafening proportions—two or   3
three conversations going on simultaneously, punctuated by the sound of a baby's crying somewhere in the back rooms or out on the street— there was still a rigid set of rules about what was said and how. Older children were sent out of the living room when it was time to get into the juicy details about "you-know-who" up on the third floor who had gone and gotten herself "p-r-e-g-n-a-n-t!" But my parents, knowing that I could spell well beyond my years, always demanded that I follow the others out to play. Beyond sexual misconduct and death, everything else was considered harmless for our young ears. And so among the anecdotes of the triumphs and disappointments in the various workings of their lives, the word "nigger" was used in my presence, but it was set within contexts and inflections, that caused it to register in my mind as something else.

In the singular, the word was always applied to a man who had distin-   4
guished himself in some situation that brought their approval for his strength, intelligence, or drive:

"Did Johnny really do that?"   5

"I'm telling you, that nigger pulled in $6,000 of overtime last year. Said   6
he got enough for a down payment on a house."

When used with a possessive adjective by a woman—"my nigger"—it became a term of endearment for husband or boyfriend. But it could be more than just a term applied to a man. In their mouths it became the pure essence of manhood—a disembodied force that channeled their past history of struggle and present survival against the odds into a victorious statement of being: "Yeah, that old foreman found out quick enough—you don't mess with a nigger." 7

In the plural, it became a description of some group within the community that had overstepped the bounds of decency as my family defined it. Parents who neglected their children, a drunken couple who fought in public, people who simply refused to look for work, those with excessively dirty mouths or unkempt households were all "trifling niggers." This particular circle could forgive hard times, unemployment, the occasional bout of depression—they had gone through all of that themselves—but the unforgivable sin was lack of self-respect. 8

A woman could never be a "nigger" in the singular, with its connotation of confirming worth. The noun "girl" was its closest equivalent in that sense, but only when used in direct address and regardless of the gender doing the addressing. "Girl" was a token of respect for a woman. The one-syllable word was drawn out to sound like three in recognition of the extra ounce of wit, nerve, or daring that the woman had shown in the situation under discussion. 9

"G-i-r-l, stop. You mean you said that to his face?" 10

But if the word was used in a third-person reference or shortened so that it almost snapped out of the mouth, it always involved some element of communal disapproval. And age became an important factor in these exchanges. It was only between individuals of the same generation, or from an older person to a younger (but never the other way around), that "girl" would be considered a compliment. 11

I don't agree with the argument that use of the word "nigger" at this social stratum of the black community was an internalization of racism. The dynamics were the exact opposite: the people in my grandmother's living room took a word that whites used to signify worthlessness or degradation and rendered it impotent. Gathering there together, they transformed "nigger" to signify the varied and complex human beings they knew themselves to be. If the word was to disappear totally from the mouths of even the most liberal of white society, no one in that room was naïve enough to believe it would disappear from white minds. Meeting the word head-on, they proved it had absolutely nothing to do with the way they were determined to live their lives. 12

So there must have been dozens of times that the word "nigger" was   13
spoken in front of me before I reached the third grade. But I didn't "hear"
it until it was said by a small pair of lips that had already learned it could
be a way to humiliate me. That was the word I went home and asked my
mother about. And since she knew that I had to grow up in America, she
took me in her lap and explained.

RESPONDING TO READING

Do you agree that Naylor's relatives used the word *nigger* in a nonracist
or counterracist way? Use your own reactions to the word to explain
your answer.

GAINING WORD POWER

The following words appear in Gloria Naylor's essay. They have an ending,
-tion, in common. This ending occurs frequently in our language, making
nouns out of verbs: for example, the noun *conversation* comes from the verb
converse, which means "to talk." Use your dictionary to find the verb behind
each of the nouns in the following list, and give a brief definition of the verb.
Begin each brief definition with the word *to.* The first one is done.

	VERB	**DEFINITION**
connotation	connote	to imply or suggest
conversation		
degradation		
description		
generation		
inflection		
internalization		
recognition		
situation		

Now see how it works the other way around. Here is a list of verbs that
are used in Naylor's essay. Find the *-tion* noun that comes from each verb
(some are obvious, but for others in the list you will need the dictionary).
Be sure to copy the spelling of the noun exactly: sometimes the first part
of the word will change. Then write a brief definition of the noun you have
written. We did the first one for you.

NOUN	DEFINITION
apply	application	a form to be filled out
consider		
determine		
explain		
gravitate		
humiliate		
migrate		
punctuate		
realize		
receive		
repeat		
transform		
verify		

CONSIDERING CONTENT

1. What are Naylor's background and social class? How do you know? Why are they significant to the main point of the essay?
2. Why was the child puzzled when the boy called her *nigger,* even though she had heard the word before?
3. List the definitions of the word *nigger* that were used in the author's grandparents' apartment.
4. Reread paragraph 12. How did the African American community's uses of *nigger* make it not racist, according to Naylor?
5. What does the last sentence suggest about the author's mother? What does it suggest about America?

CONSIDERING METHOD

1. What kind of a little third-grader was Gloria Naylor? Why do you think she presents her childhood self as no angel? What effect does this early presentation of self have on the reader?
2. Reread the description of the author's grandparents' apartment. List at least seven words or phrases that appeal to your senses.
3. How is paragraph 12 different from the rest of the essay? How does the appearance of the page prepare you for this difference?
4. The central part of the essay includes many direct quotations. Why do you think Naylor used people's exact words so often?

WRITING STEP BY STEP

Following Gloria Naylor's essay as an example, write a paper discussing a term that has various—even contradictory—meanings, depending on context: who says it, when it is used, and whether it is applied to men or women, young or old, individual or group, for example. Like Naylor, you might think of a term, such as *wife, macho, liberal, success, feminist, jock,* or *marriage,* that holds more meaning than you once thought.

A. Before you start your essay, brainstorm and jot down the various ways you have heard your term used. Ask friends and classmates for help if you need it.

B. See whether your definitions fall into groups. For example, can you separate the negative meanings from the positive ones? Or do different meanings belong to different social, racial, or ethnic groups? Try at least to decide on a reasonable order in which to present your definitions. For example, the most widely used meanings might come first, with rarer and rarer meanings following it until the last one is the rarest.

C. Begin your essay with an **anecdote,** as Naylor does.

D. Launch into the body of your essay by looking back into your past. Write about how you used to think of the term, perhaps as a child.

E. Develop each meaning of the term with an explanation and examples of direct quotations using it. Keep looking at how Naylor develops her meanings.

F. Close the body of your essay with a speculation about why the term has such a variety of meanings. Look at Naylor's paragraph 12 for ideas about how to present your thoughts.

G. Use the last paragraph to reflect on the anecdote you used in the opening of your essay. This is how Naylor concludes her piece. Your discussion of the term has, by now, added a new dimension to the anecdote.

OTHER WRITING IDEAS

1. What is the first memory you have of someone saying something purposely to hurt you? Or a memory of your saying something purposely to hurt someone else? Write an essay about your own and others' response to the harsh words.

2. In paragraphs 2 and 3, Gloria Naylor describes the lively atmosphere in her grandparents' apartment. Write a description of the atmosphere in some family or social setting that you remember from childhood. Were there unwritten rules about conversation or about

the roles of adults and children, as there were in Naylor's setting? Try to capture the scene vividly.

3. Think of a phrase or word that seems to be plain but is actually used to mean many different things; for example, "Just a minute," "Well," "I'm ready," and "I'll call you," are more slippery than they seem. A group of students in your class can have some fun discussing such sayings, developing ideas for your individual essays.

EDITING SKILLS: HYPHENS

Consider the use of the hyphen—the short dash—in these phrases from Gloria Naylor's essay:

third-grade class   one-syllable word
close-knit network   third-person reference
ground-floor apartment

The hyphenated adjectives, which modify the nouns that come after them, are called *temporary compounds*. They are compound because they consist of two words; they are temporary because the two words usually exist separately. They are hyphenated because they make up a unit that seems more like one adjective than two. Sometimes you need to hyphenate in order to make your meaning clear. Think about these examples:

an Italian art specialist   an Italian-art specialist
a small auto dealer   a small-auto dealer
a comic book approach   a comic-book approach

In the second list, the hyphen shows which words go together—the specialist is not Italian, the dealer is not small, and the approach is not comic.

Sometimes, it is difficult to decide whether to hyphenate two words that frequently occur together (back-seat driver), whether to run them together as a compound word (backseat driver), or whether to leave them separate (back seat driver). There is not wide agreement even among professional writers about some of these blends. You will see "Thank you" and "Thank-you" about equally often. Your dictionary should be your guide to making the decision.

EXERCISE

Look up the following combinations to see whether words are hyphenated, compound, or separate. Write out the form your dictionary endorses.

back seat driver	open and shut case
happily married couple	least restrictive environment
girl friend problems	part way finished
back door business deals	part time worker
child like expression	better fitting word
an easy pick up	half baked plan

Look back on the essay you have just written. Did you use any compound words that needed hyphens? Did you leave out any hyphens? Check a dictionary or with your instructor before making any corrections.

☜ WEB SITES

http://voices.cla.umn.edu/authors/GloriaNaylor.html

Voices from the Gap—a site maintained by the University of Minnesota—provides a biography and other information on Gloria Naylor.

www.poynter.org

The Poynter Institute provides an article "Nigger: A Case Study in Using a Racial Epithet."

PREPARING TO READ

If you took an intelligence test and scored low, how would you feel? What might you say that the test failed to measure about you?

What Is Intelligence, Anyway?

ISAAC ASIMOV

Isaac Asimov (1923–1992) was an American, born in Russia, who wrote more than 200 books, including children's stories, popular science, science fiction, fantasy, and scholarly science. With so many intellectual accomplishments, he was well qualified to wonder just what intelligence is—and is not.

TERMS TO RECOGNIZE

KP *(para. 1)*	kitchen patrol (working in the kitchen)
complacent *(para. 2)*	self-satisfied
bents *(para. 2)*	interests, tendencies
oracles *(para. 3)*	divine communications
devised *(para. 4)*	made up
foist *(para. 4)*	impose
arbiter *(para. 4)*	judge
indulgently *(para. 6)*	as if doing a favor
raucously *(para. 6)*	loudly, in a disorderly way
smugly *(para. 6)*	in a self-satisfied way

What is intelligence, anyway? When I was in the Army, I received a kind of aptitude test that all soldiers took and, against a normal of 100, scored 160. No one at the base had ever seen a figure like that, and for two hours they made a big fuss over me. (It didn't mean anything. The next day I was still a buck private with KP as my highest duty.)   1

All my life I've been registering scores like that, so that I have the complacent feeling that I'm highly intelligent, and I expect other people to think so, too. Actually, though, don't such scores simply mean that I am very good at answering the type of academic questions that are considered worthy of answers by the people who make up the intelligence tests—people with intellectual bents similar to mine?   2

For instance, I had an auto repairman once, who, on these intelligence   3
tests, could not possibly have scored more than 80, by my estimate. I always
took it for granted that I was far more intelligent than he was. Yet, when
anything went wrong with my car, I hastened to him with it, watched him
anxiously as he explored its vitals, and listened to his pronouncements as
though they were divine oracles—and he always fixed my car.

Well then, suppose my auto repairman devised questions for an intelligence   4
test. Or suppose a carpenter did, or a farmer, or, indeed, almost anyone but
an academician. By every one of those tests, I'd prove myself a moron. And
I'd *be* a moron, too. In a world where I could not use my academic training
and my verbal talents but had to do something intricate or hard, working
with my hands, I would do poorly. My intelligence, then, is not absolute but
is a function of the society I live in and of the fact that a small subsection of
that society has managed to foist itself on the rest as an arbiter of such matters.

Consider my auto repairman, again. He had a habit of telling me jokes   5
whenever he saw me. One time he raised his head from under the automobile hood to say, "Doc, a deaf-and-dumb guy went into a hardware store
to ask for some nails. He put two fingers together on the counter and
made hammering motions with the other hand. The clerk brought him a
hammer. He shook his head and pointed to the two fingers he was
hammering. The clerk brought him nails. He picked out the sizes he
wanted, and left. Well, doc, the next guy who came in was a blind man.
He wanted scissors. How do you suppose he asked for them?"

Indulgently, I lifted my right hand and made scissoring motions with my   6
first two fingers. Whereupon my auto repairman laughed raucously and
said, "Why, you dumb jerk, he used his *voice* and asked for them." Then he
said, smugly, "I've been trying that on all my customers today." "Did you
catch many?" I asked. "Quite a few," he said, "but I knew for sure I'd catch
you." "Why is that?" I asked. "Because you're so goddamned educated, doc,
I *knew* you couldn't be very smart."

And I have an uneasy feeling he had something there.   7

———————————

RESPONDING TO READING

Do you think that people who are academically intelligent are often
poor at nonacademic things? Why or why not?

GAINING WORD POWER

Complete these sentences in a reasonable way, showing that you understand the vocabulary words included.

1. Troy indulgently promised to take Rachel _____

   _____.

2. Because he had a mechanical bent, Mark specialized in _____

   _____.

3. _____, the crowd cheered raucously.

4. Dr. Morse foisted his ideas on us when he _____

   _____.

5. By setting himself up as the arbiter of good taste in clothes, Sheldon

   _____.

CONSIDERING CONTENT

1. Why do you think that Asimov's high intelligence score "didn't mean anything" in the army?
2. What is the basic conflict discussed in this essay?
3. Why was the repairman sure he would catch "Doc" Asimov with the joke? Was the repairman stereotyping college professors?
4. What might be on an intelligence test written by auto mechanics? carpenters? farmers? mothers of preschoolers? portrait painters? What point is Asimov making with this type of suggestion?
5. Which "small subsection" (para. 4) of society has set itself up as the definers of intelligence?
6. What do you think about Asimov's "uneasy feeling"? Do you think the mechanic "had something there"? Or do you think the nature of the joke would fool most people, intelligent or not?

CONSIDERING METHOD

1. Asimov's essay contains two anecdotes (look up the word **anecdote** if you have not already done so). How do the anecdotes help you understand the conflict the writer is discussing?
2. In a fitting reflection of the content of the essay, Asimov uses both highly academic words (*oracles, bents, arbiter*) and common, informal words. Point out some of the informal words.
3. Count the number of words in each of the six sentences that make up paragraph 4. Notice the variety in the sentences' lengths. This variety in length is a factor that makes writing lively to read instead of plodding. When you think your own writing sounds plodding, check to see whether you have a good range of sentence lengths. If they are too much alike, try to combine some of the shorter sentences into longer ones or divide long ones into shorter ones.

4. The last paragraph consists of only one sentence. What difference do you see between placing it in this position and simply adding it as a closing sentence to the preceding paragraph?

WRITING STEP BY STEP

Write an essay that investigates the meaning of an **abstract** term—an idea that cannot be directly observed, such as intelligence. You can use some of Asimov's techniques. We also suggest some other techniques for developing an extended definition. Use any combination of techniques to develop your definition. To get your thinking started, consider these abstractions:

common sense	humility	educated
optimism	professionalism	cool
courage	resourcefulness	simplicity
generosity	street smart	beauty
laziness	foolish	stubbornness

Choose your own term, but be sure your choice is an abstraction (not something **concrete,** such as *submarine, pizza,* or *tennis*).

A. Begin with the question "What is _____, anyway?"
B. If you have an anecdote that will serve as an extended investigation of the term, include the story, as Asimov did.
C. Use examples of people you know who demonstrate the abstraction you are defining. Show how they behave or think, with specific details.
D. Use description. For example, an abstract feeling may have a counterpart in a certain type of landscape or weather that you could describe.
E. Point out differences. A good definition will make clear the difference between the word you are explaining and other words with similar meanings. You might tell how feeling peaceful is different from feeling happy or calm.
F. Provide a contrast. We often explain words by clarifying what they are *not.* For example, you could point out that laziness does not merely include lying around doing nothing, which could be depression instead.
G. In your closing, let the reader know how the abstraction is important in your own life.

OTHER WRITING IDEAS

1. Write an essay similar to Asimov's on questioning the usual definition of a term. Challenge the term's usefulness or its usual interpretation or its everyday misuse.

2. Make up a word for a concept or item that doesn't have a name, as far as you know. These new words, called *sniglets,* are sometimes collected in humorous books. Here are some examples:

   BEAVO (n.): a pencil with teeth marks all over it.

   FICTATE (v.): to inform a television or screen character of impending danger under the assumption that he or she can hear you.

   OPUP (v.): to push one's glasses back up on the nose.

   You may need to make up a related group of words and explain how you came up with them in order to write a whole essay.

3. Instead of presenting a unified definition of a concept, try to write an essay presenting all the different, even contradictory, meanings a certain term could have. For example, if you asked a group of people to explain what *sex appeal* means to them, you would probably get some widely varying answers. You may call on a group of classmates to help you come up with meanings.

EDITING SKILLS: USING THE RIGHT TENSE

One of the trickiest skills we learn as we grow up is using the correct tense for verbs. If you have ever learned a foreign language, you are fully aware of the complications of verb tense. In your native language, as you speak, you almost always choose the right tense, but in writing you can get in a snarl.

Asimov's essay shows a combination of tenses. For things that occur in the present or are true in the present, he uses plain old present tense: "I have the complacent feeling that I'm highly intelligent, and I expect other people to think so, too" (para. 2). For the story about the mechanic, which happened in the past, Asimov uses past tense: "Indulgently, I lifted my right hand and made scissoring motions with my first two fingers" (para. 6).

In telling stories, speakers and writers sometimes get confused as they go along, and they switch from past to present and back within the same anecdote. Haven't you heard someone tell a story this way:

You know, if you wait too long, you have to go in person to deal with the licensing bureau. Well, yesterday I went to get my driver's license renewed. So I have to wait in line for an hour. I finally get to the front, and the guy tells me I should have brought my form that I got in the mail. So now I had to go home, and it took my whole lunch hour. When I get back, I tell the guy that if I starve to death, it's his fault. I hate these heartless bureaucracies.

The speaker gives you a sense of being there by switching to present tense; however, in academic writing you have to stick to the past tense for everything that happened in the past. (When writing about what happened in a piece of literature or a film, though, you can summarize plot in the present tense.)

EXERCISE

To make sure you get the idea, rewrite the preceding anecdote, correcting it so that everything in the past is written in past tense, and anything that is currently in force is in present tense.

Now look at the verb tenses in the essay you wrote in response to the Asimov article. Which tenses did you use? Are they consistent and logical? Check over your writing, and make any needed corrections in the verb tenses.

WEB SITE

http://perso.wanadoo.fr/nicolas-elena/Nicolas-Elena/

Intelligence Tests: six IQ tests and three aptitude tests that you can take to see where your "intelligence" ranks in the general population.

PREPARING TO READ

Do you have an ethnic heritage? Are you proud of your cultural roots? If so, why? If you don't know where your ancestors came from, do you feel somehow left out in today's multiethnic society? If so, how do you compensate for the lack?

I'm a Banana and Proud of It

WAYSON CHOY

Born in 1939 and raised in British Columbia, Wayson Choy is best known for his award-winning novel *The Jade Peony,* in which he focuses on his cultural heritage in Vancouver's Chinatown during the first half of this century. A winner of the prestigious Governor General's Literary Award for Non-Fiction, he presently teaches English at Humber College in Toronto. This essay first appeared in the Facts and Arguments column of the *Toronto Globe and Mail.*

TERMS TO RECOGNIZE

alien *(para. 2)*	a foreigner, an outsider
concubine *(para. 3)*	a woman belonging sexually to a man not her husband
Taoist *(para. 7)*	pertaining to a Chinese religion that teaches simplicity and selflessness
assimilation *(para. 12)*	cultural absorption of a minority into the main society
paradox *(para. 13)*	an apparent contradiction that turns out to be true

because both my parents came from China, I took Chinese. But I cannot read or write Chinese and barely speak it. I love my North American citizenship. I don't mind being called a "banana," yellow on the outside and white inside. I'm proud I'm a banana. After all, in Canada and the United States, native Indians are "apples" (red outside, white inside); blacks are "Oreo cookies" (black and white); and Chinese are "bananas." These metaphors assume, both rightly and wrongly, that the culture here has been primarily anglo-white. Cultural history made me a banana.

History: My father and mother arrived separately to the British Colum-   2
bia coast in the early part of the century. They came as unwanted "aliens."
Better to be an alien here than to be dead of starvation in China. But after
the Chinese Exclusion laws were passed in North America (late 1800s,
early 1900s), no Chinese immigrants were granted citizenship in either
Canada or the United States.

Like those Old China village men from *Toi San* who, in the 1850s, laid   3
down cliff-edge train tracks through the Rockies and the Sierras, or like
those first women who came as mail-order wives or concubines and who
as bond-slaves were turned into cheaper laborers or even prostitutes—like
many of those men and women, my father and mother survived ugly, unjust
times. In 1918, two hours after he got off the boat from Hong Kong, my
father was called "chink" and told to go back to China. "Chink" is a hate-
ful racist term, stereotyping the shape of Asian eyes: "a chink in the armor,"
an undesirable slit. For the Elders, the past was humiliating. Eventually, the
Second World War changed hostile attitudes toward the Chinese.

During the war, Chinese men volunteered and lost their lives as   4
members of the American and Canadian military. When hostilities ended,
many more were proudly in uniform waiting to go overseas. Record
Chinatown dollars were raised to buy War Bonds. After 1945, challenged
by such money and ultimate sacrifices, the Exclusion laws in both Canada
and the United States were revoked. Chinatown residents claimed their
citizenship and sent for their families. By 1949, after the Communists took
over China, those of us who arrived here as young children, or were born
here, stayed. No longer "aliens," we became legal citizens of North America. Many of us also became "bananas."

Historically, "banana" is not a racist term. Although it clumsily stereo-   5
types many of the children and grandchildren of the Old Chinatowns, the
term actually follows the old Chinese tendency to assign endearing nicknames to replace formal names, semicomic names to keep one humble.
Thus, "banana" describes the generations who assimilated so well into
North American life. In fact, our families encouraged members of my
generation in the 1950s and sixties to "get ahead," to get an English education, to get a job with good pay and prestige. "Don't work like me," Chinatown parents said. "Work in an office!" The *lao wahkiu* (the Chinatown
old-timers) also warned, "Never forget—you still be Chinese!"

None of us ever forgot. The mirror never lied.   6

Many Chinatown teenagers felt we didn't quite belong in any one   7
world. We looked Chinese, but thought and behaved North American.
Impatient Chinatown parents wanted the best of both worlds for us, but
they bluntly labeled their children and grandchildren *"juk-sing"* or even

"mo no." Not that we were totally "shallow bamboo butt-ends" or entirely "no brain," but we had less and less understanding of Old China traditions, and less and less interest in their village histories. Father used to say we lacked Taoist ritual, Taoist manners. We were, he said, *"mo li."*

This was true. Chinatown's younger brains, like everyone else's of whatever race, were being colonized by "white bread" U.S. family television programs. We began to feel Chinese home life was inferior. We co-operated with English-language magazines that showed us how to act and what to buy. Seductive Hollywood movies made some of us secretly weep that we did not have movie-star faces. American music made Chinese music sound like noise. By the 1970s and eighties, many of us had consciously or unconsciously distanced ourselves from our Chinatown histories. We became bananas.   8

Finally, for me, in my 40s or 50s, with the death first of my mother, then my father, I realized I did not belong anywhere unless I could understand the past. I needed to find the foundation of my Chinese-ness. I needed roots.   9

I spent my college holidays researching the past. I read Chinatown oral histories, located documents, searched out early articles. Those early citizens came back to life for me. Their long toil and blood sacrifices, the proud record of their patient, legal challenges, gave us all our present rights as citizens. Canadian and American Chinatowns set aside their family tongue differences and encouraged each other to fight injustice. There were no borders. "After all," they affirmed, *"Daaih ga tohng yahn . . .* We are all Chinese!"   10

In my book, *The Jade Peony,* I tried to recreate this past, to explore the beginnings of the conflicts trapped within myself, the struggle between being Chinese and being North American. I discovered a truth: These "between world" struggles are universal. In every human being, there is "the Other"—something that makes each of us feel how different we are to everyone else, even to family members. Yet, ironically, we are all the same, wanting the same security and happiness. I know this now.   11

I think the early Chinese pioneers actually started "going bananas" from the moment they first settled upon the West Coast. They had no choice. They adapted. They initiated assimilation. If they had not, they and their family would have starved to death. I might even suggest that all surviving Chinatown citizens eventually became bananas. Only some, of course, were more ripe than others.   12

That's why I'm proudly a banana: I accept the paradox of being both Chinese and not Chinese. Now at last, whenever I look in the mirror or hear ghost voices shouting, "You still Chinese!" I smile. I know another truth: In immigrant North America, we are all Chinese.   13

RESPONDING TO READING

Do you agree with Choy that "In every human being, there is 'the Other'—something that makes each of us feel how different we are to everyone else, even to family members" (para. 11)? For Choy, that "something" was being Chinese in a "white bread" culture. What in your experience makes you feel like "the Other"?

GAINING WORD POWER

Wayson Choy uses a number of -*ly* adverbs in his essay: *barely, primarily, separately, eventually, proudly, clumsily, actually, bluntly, totally, entirely, secretly, consciously or unconsciously, ironically, actually, eventually, proudly.* If you look carefully at how these words are used, you will notice that they occur in a number of different places in the sentence. Adverbs are often movable; you can put them at the beginning of the sentence or at the end, before the verb or after—in any number of spots.

Go back to Choy's essay and find six of the -*ly* words just listed. Rewrite two or three of these sentences to illustrate how the -*ly* adverb can be used in several different places. Here's an example:

Choy's sentence:	I might even suggest that all surviving Chinatown citizens *eventually* became bananas.
Rewrites:	I might even suggest that *eventually* all surviving Chinatown citizens became bananas.
	I might even suggest that all surviving Chinatown citizens became bananas *eventually.*

Now use five of the -*ly* adverbs in sentences of your own. Experiment with several different versions to see where the adverb can be placed.

CONSIDERING CONTENT

1. What does Choy mean when he says he is a "banana"?
2. Why does he think "banana" is not a racist term? Do you agree? What about "apples" and "Oreos" and "white bread"?
3. What were the Chinese Exclusion laws and why were they eventually repealed?
4. What is the origin of the offensive term "chink"?
5. Why did Chinese parents want their children to get "English" educations?
6. What do you think is the main idea of this essay? Where is the thesis stated?

CONSIDERING METHOD

1. How do the first two introductory paragraphs prepare the readers for the rest of the essay?
2. In paragraph 1, Choy uses a **paradox** ("both rightly and wrongly") to explain the metaphors underlying the terms *bananas, apples,* and *Oreos.* Explain how these words can be both right and wrong at the same time.
3. Choy uses a number of short-short sentences: "I'm proud I'm a banana" (para. 1), "They came as unwanted 'aliens'" (para. 2), "None of us ever forgot. The mirror never lied" (para. 6), "We became bananas" (para. 8), "I needed roots" (para. 9), "I know this now" (para. 11), "They had no choice. They adapted. They initiated assimilation" (para. 12). What does he achieve with this rhetorical technique?
4. Why is the phrase "going bananas" in quotation marks in paragraph 12?
5. How do the last three sentences serve to reinforce the theme and also to unify the essay?

WRITING STEP BY STEP

In his essay, Wayson Choy focuses his essay on defining a word. For your essay, think of some words or expressions that need defining because they are misleading, unclear, or too indirect, and define them accurately. You might choose words used in TV commercials, personal ads, real estate descriptions, fast-food restaurants, or menu language. You can focus on a single expression (like "family values") or a group of related terms (like the names for sandwiches or sizes of soft drinks or the names of real estate subdivisions or the language of the funeral business).

A. Begin by telling how the word or name came to your attention.
B. Offer the accurate or dictionary meaning.
C. Then explain what the advertiser, salespeople, or promoters of the terminology want it to mean.
D. As you explain the true meaning, explain why the contrived expression was chosen. If the word or name caught on with the public, such as "lite" or "share" (for "tell" or "discuss") or "senior citizen," speculate as to why it became so popular.
E. Conclude by calling for action from your readers—perhaps to protest this transparent attempt to manipulate the public through the misuse of language.

OTHER WRITING IDEAS

1. Choy says the word "banana" is to him an "endearing nickname." Does your family have an affectionate nickname for you that captures your personality? Perhaps the family pets have nicknames that characterize their behavior. Or maybe you have a friend or relative who has an apt nickname. Write an essay explaining how the nicknames define people or pets.
2. Think of all the words used to describe fat people: large, chubby, full-figured, overweight, big-boned, portly, beefy, stout, heavyset, fleshy, chunky, burly, rotund. Write an essay explaining why there are so many of these terms.
3. Interview several foreign students on your campus, and ask for examples of expressions (such as "cramp my style" or "hit the hay") that surprised or confused them. How did they find out what the expressions really meant? Write up the results of your interviews.

EDITING SKILLS: CAPITALIZATION

Choy's essay illustrates many of the conventions for using capital letters in English. The author, of course, capitalizes the first word in every sentence. He also capitalizes the pronoun *I* every time he uses it. Here are some of the other capitalization rules he follows:

1. *Capitalize the names of nationalities, races, tribes, and languages:* Chinese, North American, Canadian, English, American.
2. *Capitalize the names of political, ethnic, and religious groups:* Communists, Old China traditions, Taoist.
3. *Capitalize brand names of products:* Oreos.
4. *Capitalize names of geographical locations such as cities, states, countries, and regions:* China, B.C., North America, Chinatown, U.S., West Coast.
5. *Capitalize the first and last words and all other words in titles, except articles, prepositions, and coordinating conjunctions* (a, an, the, in, into, at, to, by, and, but, or, nor, for, but, so, etc.): *The Jade Peony.*
6. *Capitalize the names of important government documents:* Chinese Exclusion laws, War Bonds.

Look over the essay you have just written, and check your use of capital letters. A college dictionary will give you a list of capitalization rules along with examples. Entries for specific words will also tell you when to use capitals.

EXERCISE

Supply capital letters where needed in the following sentences:

1. For years women lobbied in washington, d.c., for passage of the equal rights amendment.
2. At present, mexican americans are the fastest-growing minority in the united states.
3. The asian american population is growing rapidly, too, especially in california.
4. People of the muslim faith, adherents of islam, are also a fast-growing group in large cities like chicago and new york.
5. Our book club is reading ann tyler's dinner at the homesick restaurant.

❦ WEB SITES

**www.infoculture.cbc.ca/archives/bookswr/bookswr_10211999_choy
.phtml**

An interview and reading by the author from his new novel *Paper Shadows.*

cbc.ca/millennium/authors/choy.html

A brief essay on the new millennium as part of the Canadian Broadcasting Corporation's Canadian Writers on 2000 series.

PREPARING TO READ

What do you know about your ethnic heritage? Is your ethnic heritage reflected in your everyday life or your family traditions?

Cultural Baggage

BARBARA EHRENREICH

Barbara Ehrenreich is an outspoken leftist political leader whose writings are usually controversial. She regularly contributes to the magazines *Ms.* and *Mother Jones,* as well as to many other periodicals. In the piece we reprint here, first published in the *New York Times Magazine* in 1992, Ehrenreich reconsiders the meaning of cultural heritage.

TERMS TO RECOGNIZE

chauvinism *(para. 2)*	unreasoning, boastful devotion to one's own kind
venerable *(para. 3)*	impressive and respectable
ecumenism *(para. 4)*	the practice of promoting understanding among all religions
sweetbreads *(para. 4)*	animal thymus or pancreas eaten as food
seder *(para. 7)*	a feast on the first day of Passover
secular *(para. 8)*	worldly rather than spiritual
progenitors *(para. 9)*	ancestors
epiphany *(para. 10)*	a flash of insight
spewed *(para. 11)*	gushed forth
maxim *(para. 11)*	a short statement of a general principle
inverted *(para. 11)*	turned upside down

an acquaintance was telling me about the joys of rediscovering her ethnic and religious heritage. "I know exactly what my ancestors were doing 2,000 years ago," she said, eyes gleaming with enthusiasm, "and *I can do the same things now.*" Then she leaned forward and inquired politely, "And what is your ethnic background, if I may ask?"   1

"None," I said, that being the first word in line to get out of my mouth.   2
Well, not "none," I backtracked. Scottish, English, Irish—that was something, I supposed. Too much Irish to qualify as a WASP; too much of the

hated English to warrant a "Kiss Me, I'm Irish" button; plus there are a number of dead ends in the family tree due to adoptions, missing records, failing memories and the like. I was blushing by this time. Did "none" mean I was rejecting my heritage out of Anglo-Celtic self-hate? Or was I revealing a hidden ethnic chauvinism in which the Britannically derived served as a kind of neutral standard compared with the ethnic "others"?

Throughout the 60's and 70's, I watched one group after another—   3
African-Americans, Latinos, Native Americans—stand up and proudly reclaim their roots while I just sank back ever deeper into my seat. All this excitement over ethnicity stemmed, I uneasily sensed, from a past in which *their* ancestors had been trampled upon by *my* ancestors, or at least by people who looked very much like them. In addition, it had begun to seem almost un-American not to have some sort of hyphen at hand, linking one to more venerable times and locales.

But the truth is, I was raised with none. We'd eaten ethnic foods in my   4
childhood home, but these were all borrowed, like the pasties, or Cornish meat pies, my father had picked up from his fellow miners in Butte, Montana. If my mother had one rule, it was militant ecumenism in all matters of food and experience. "Try new things," she would say, meaning anything from sweetbreads to clams, with an emphasis on the "new."

As a child, I briefly nourished a craving for tradition and roots. I   5
immersed myself in the works of Sir Walter Scott. I pretended to believe that the bagpipe was a musical instrument. I was fascinated to learn from a grandmother that we were descended from certain Highland clans and longed for a pleated skirt in one of their distinctive tartans.

But in *Ivanhoe,* it was the dark-eyed "Jewess" Rebecca I identified with,   6
not the flaxen-haired bimbo Rowena. As for clans: Why not call them "tribes," those bands of half-clad peasants and warriors whose idea of cuisine was stuffed sheep gut washed down with whisky? And then there was the sting of Disraeli's remark—which I came across in my early teens— to the effect that his ancestors had been leading orderly, literate lives when my ancestors were still rampaging through the Highlands daubing them- selves with blue paint.

Motherhood put the screws on me, ethnicity-wise. I had hoped that by   7
marrying a man of Eastern European-Jewish ancestry I would acquire for my descendants the ethnic genes that my own forebears so sadly lacked. At one point, I even subjected the children to a seder of my own design, including a little talk about the flight from Egypt and its relevance to modern social issues. But the kids insisted on buttering their matzohs and snickering through my talk. "Give me a break, Mom," the older one said. "You don't even believe in God."

After the tiny pagans had been put to bed, I sat down to brood over   8
Elijah's wine. What had I been thinking? The kids knew that their Jewish
grandparents were secular folks who didn't hold seders themselves. And
if ethnicity eluded me, how could I expect it to take root in my children, who are not only Scottish-English-Irish, but Hungarian-Polish-
Russian to boot?

But, then, on the fumes of Manischewitz, a great insight took form in   9
my mind. It was true, as the kids said, that I didn't "believe in God." But
this could be taken as something very different from an accusation—a
reminder of a genuine heritage. My parents had not believed in God either,
nor had my grandparents or any other progenitors going back to the great-
great level. They had become disillusioned with Christianity generations
ago—just as, on the in-law side, my children's other ancestors had shaken
off their Orthodox Judaism. This insight did not exactly furnish me with
an "identity," but it was at least something to work with: we are the kind
of people, I realized—whatever our distant ancestors' religions—who do *not*
believe, who do not carry on traditions, who do not do things just because
someone has done them before.

The epiphany went on: I recalled that my mother never introduced   10
a procedure for cooking or cleaning by telling me, "Grandma did it
this way." What did Grandma know, living in the days before vacuum
cleaners and disposable toilet mops? In my parents' general view, new
things were better than old, and the very fact that some ritual had
been performed in the past was a good reason for abandoning it now.
Because what was the past, as our forebears knew it? Nothing but
poverty, superstition and grief. "Think for yourself," Dad used to say.
"Always ask why."

In fact, this may have been the ideal cultural heritage for my particu-   11
lar ethnic strain—bounced as it was from the Highlands of Scotland across
the sea, out to the Rockies, down into the mines and finally spewed out
into high-tech, suburban America. What better philosophy, for a race of
migrants, than "Think for yourself"? What better maxim, for people
whose whole world was rudely inverted every 30 years or so, than "Try
new things"?

The more tradition-minded, the newly enthusiastic celebrants of Purim   12
and Kwanzaa and Solstice, may see little point to survival if the survivors
carry no cultural freight—religion, for example, or ethnic tradition. To
which I would say that skepticism, curiosity and wide-eyed ecumenical
tolerance are also worthy elements of the human tradition and are at least
as old as such notions as "Serbian" or "Croatian," "Scottish" or "Jewish." I
make no claims for my personal line of progenitors except that they

remained loyal to the values that may have induced all of our ancestors, long, long ago, to climb down from the trees and make their way into the open plains.

A few weeks ago, I cleared my throat and asked the children, now   13
mostly grown and fearsomely smart, whether they felt any stirrings of ethnic or religious identity, etc., which might have been, ahem, insufficiently nourished at home. "None," they said, adding firmly, "and the world would be a better place if nobody else did, either." My chest swelled with pride, as would my mother's, to know that the race of "none" marches on.

RESPONDING TO READING

Did you find Ehrenreich's pride in being an atheist shocking or disturbing or delightful? Write in your journal about your initial response; then analyze why you had this response.

GAINING WORD POWER

Proper nouns (and the words related to them) designate specific persons, places, languages, brands, titles, and so forth, rather than the general category. For example, *Episcopalian, Coca-Cola,* and *Othello* are proper nouns, unlike *religion, soda pop,* and *play,* which are the corresponding common nouns. Proper nouns are capitalized, whereas common nouns are not. Much of the reading you do in college will include proper nouns, as in the Ehrenreich article we reprint here. These words pose a special vocabulary-building problem because they may or may not be in your college dictionary. You have to branch out to find some of the definitions. An encyclopedia like *Funk & Wagnall's* or *Encarta* will help you in many cases. Sometimes, you need to go to the library for a more specialized reference book, such as *The Reader's Encyclopedia* (specifically about authors and literary works) or *Webster's Biographical Dictionary* (specifically about notable people). Your librarian can help you look in the appropriate book. When you are really stuck, you may find it advisable to simply ask around among your friends and acquaintances: one of them may steer you to the right source for the definition.

Here, in the order in which they appear, are some proper nouns from Barbara Ehrenreich's essay. They are important if you want to get the full meaning of the reading. Find out what the words mean, and fit the definitions into the context of the essay. Write down your observations as well as the place you found each definition.

Anglo-Celtic

Britannically

Cornish

Sir Walter Scott

Ivanhoe

Rebecca

Rowena

Disraeli

Highlands

Manischewitz

Purim

Kwanzaa

Solstice

CONSIDERING CONTENT

1. Why does Ehrenreich report that she "just sank back ever deeper into [her] seat" when other groups celebrated their ethnicity? What made her feel strange?
2. At what times in life was it important to the author that she have a heritage? What did she do to try to acquire one? How did those efforts turn out?
3. When did Ehrenreich's ideas about heritage change? How did she broaden the definition of *heritage* from what other people were meaning?
4. What are some of the elements of Ehrenreich's cultural heritage?
5. Is tradition always good? What does Ehrenreich think? What are some traditions that are not so good?

CONSIDERING METHOD

1. Look closely at paragraphs 1 through 9, noticing particularly where the paragraphs divide. Can you explain some logic behind each division?
2. Consider the first sentence of each paragraph. What techniques are used to show how this paragraph is related to the paragraph before it?
3. How does the introduction catch the reader's attention? To what senses does it appeal?
4. Although the subject of this essay is quite abstract—the meaning of heritage—the writer works in many vivid specific details. Find at

least three passages that are concrete and specific. What is their contribution to the essay?

5. Did you find any humor in the essay? If so, point out where and tell why you found it funny.

WRITING STEP BY STEP

Barbara Ehrenreich writes about how she sometimes felt awkward and uneasy when everyone around her discussed their ethnic heritage because she was raised without one. Your essay will start from a similar situation: think of something that makes you feel odd or out of place socially at times (or that used to make you feel this way). One of our friends, for example, was brought up without television; now, in conversations as an adult, she sometimes feels that her peer group shares a culture that she lacks. Another friend was brought up in an unusual family: she and her two sisters were raised by her mother and two aunts, and she sometimes feels that everyone else came from more "normal" families. Like Ehrenreich, you will investigate the meaning of the difference you possess.

A. In the first section of your essay, set the scene. Show what situation makes (or made) you feel out of place. Briefly state why you feel (or felt) uneasy. Use first person ("I") because this is a personal essay. Consider starting out with a sample incident, as in Ehrenreich's paragraph 1.

B. In the next section, explain how you have tried to come to terms with your difference. You might consider how you dealt with it as a child, as Ehrenreich does in paragraphs 5 and 6. You might discuss a time when the difference really gained importance, as Ehrenreich does in paragraphs 7 and 8.

C. In the third section of your essay, explain where you stand now on the subject. Perhaps you have had an epiphany, as Ehrenreich did, in which you see your difference as valuable. Maybe there was one experience that changed your thinking about being different. Maybe just writing about it brought you to some new conclusions. If you are still as uneasy as ever, say so. Do you expect any change in the future?

D. Divide each section of your essay into paragraphs. You can divide paragraphs according to a shift in time, a new turn of thought, or a switch of focus, or to introduce a new example.

E. Write a closing sentence that reinforces your current point of view about the difference you have explained.

OTHER WRITING IDEAS

1. Write an essay explaining your own cultural heritage and what it means. Be sure to clarify how you are defining *cultural heritage.*

2. Investigate some "great insight" (para. 9) or "epiphany" (para. 10) in which your thinking on a subject changed significantly. The experience need not concern cultural heritage, as Ehrenreich's did. Your essay will be similar only in that it focuses on a change in your point of view and how that change came to be.

3. Get together with some classmates to brainstorm about traditions that should be eliminated or at least revised. Think about holidays, courtship, campus culture, and political campaigning, to get started. Choose one tradition, explain it, and explain how and why it should be altered.

EDITING SKILLS: USING QUESTIONS

Notice how Barbara Ehrenreich uses questions to help us see the mental processes that went on as she thought about cultural heritage. Here are a few of these questions:

Did "none" mean I was rejecting my heritage out of Anglo-Celtic self-hate? (para. 2)

As for clans: Why not call them "tribes," those bands of half-clad peasants and warriors whose idea of cuisine was stuffed sheep gut washed down with whisky? (para. 6)

What had I been thinking? (para. 8)

What did Grandma know, living in the days before vacuum cleaners and disposable toilet mops? (para. 10)

What better philosophy, for a race of migrants, than "Think for yourself"? (para. 11)

These questions make the readers feel that they are witnessing the writer's mental struggle on the spot. We often pose ourselves questions when we are thinking through an issue. When such musings are written in a personal essay, they are called **rhetorical questions,** because they serve only to achieve the effect of immediacy—no one expects the reader to try to answer them.

EXERCISE

Here are five sentences that could be used in a paper focusing on ways to attack the problem of high school dropouts. For practice, turn them into rhetorical questions.

1. There are many reasons that young people drop out of school before graduation.
2. The social costs of the problem are high.
3. We must somehow convince at-risk students to stay in school.
4. We could offer incentives to convince young people to stay in school.
5. Some may object to these reasonable proposals.

Using these sentences as models, write four rhetorical questions for a paper dealing with the problem of teenage pregnancy.

Now, look at the essay you have written. Add at least one rhetorical question that indicates the direction of your thought. If you like the effect, try using a few more.

WEB SITES

www.genealogy.com

Find out what your cultural baggage might be.

www.aclu.org/about/transcripts/ehrn1011.html

Transcript of an interview with Barbara Ehrenreich, conducted October 11, 1995, on America Online by Phil Gutis of the American Civil Liberties Union.

Student Essay Using Definition

Nothing to Be Scared Of

Kerri Mauger

For most of my life, I remember my mother being   1
in and out of hospitals. No one was sure what was
wrong with her, and it took many years to finally put
a label on her. My mother has been diagnosed with
schizophrenia. I am sorry to think about when my
friends and I have passed a mental hospital on the
street and made rude comments, but we, like most
people, were very ignorant about mental illness.
People may laugh and make jokes about it, but it is a
reality to me. I live with it every day of my life.

It has taken me many years to understand what is   2
wrong with my mother. My dad chose to be very
secretive about anything that had to do with her. I
think he tried to protect my sister and me, but in
the long run ignorance hurt us even more.

Schizophrenia is a mental disorder that makes it   3
hard for people who have it to distinguish between
what is real and what is imagined. Therefore,
schizophrenics also have trouble managing emotions,
thinking clearly, and dealing with other people. They
cannot tell what other people's talk and actions
mean, and they respond strangely. People who have
never encountered someone with schizophrenia may feel
intimidated because of bizarre and socially
unacceptable behavior. My mother may sit and listen
to the voices she hears all day long, ignoring
everything else. She explains that they are
communicating to her through telepathy. She replies to
these voices and denies that there is anything wrong
with her. Some schizophrenics shout angrily at people
on the street, believing that they have been insulted
or threatened when they have not.

Early on the day of my eleventh birthday party,   4
my sister and I were downstairs watching TV. My mom
came down and told us to come up to my room. We
followed her upstairs, where she told us to lie on

the floor. She said that there was a man outside with a gun and we had to hide so he would not come and get us. I was really scared and confused, and we stayed in my room for two hours in almost complete silence. Finally I got up and looked out the window. Our neighbors were outside gardening. When my father got home, he called the hospital, and I saw my mother taken away by force. My birthday party was canceled, and I was crushed. I realize now that my mother was hallucinating, having an experience that seemed real but was only in her imagination. Hallucinations can include all of the senses, and my mother had both seen and heard things that weren't there.

There is no cure for schizophrenia. Medication 5 may help some people with the symptoms, but no medicine has helped my mother yet. Psychotherapy can assist schizophrenics in controlling their thoughts. Along with drugs and therapy, family understanding can help. The person suffering from schizophrenia needs sympathy, compassion, and respect. It is best to stay calm and nonjudgmental. Getting excited or starting to argue with the person can worsen an episode. Schizophrenia is not the person's moral fault or rational choice.

It is sometimes easier to laugh at something we 6 fear and do not understand. But ignorance about something like schizophrenia can be hurtful. I love my mother dearly and after many years of being afraid and uninformed, I can finally say I am not scared of her at all. She still is not a "normal" mother, but I know the facts and can deal with whatever comes my way.

C h a p t e r

STRATEGIES FOR SORTING IDEAS

Classification and Division

The next time you get ready to do your laundry, look on the back of the detergent box. There you will see directions for sorting your clothes according to the temperature of the water that you should use. The directions may read something like this:

FOR BEST CLEANING RESULTS

Sort and select temperature and begin filling washer with water.

Hot	Warm	Cold
White cottons	Bright colors	Dark colors
Colorfast pastels	Permanent press	Colors that could bleed
Diapers	Knits	Delicates
Heavily soiled items		Stains like blood and chocolate

Do you follow a procedure like this when you do your laundry? Why do you suppose the detergent makers put directions such as these on the back of the box?

THE POINT OF CLASSIFICATION AND DIVISION

As the preceding laundry example shows, separating and arranging things helps us to accomplish tasks more efficiently and more effectively. This process of "sorting things out" also helps us to clarify our thinking and understand our feelings.

Many writing tasks lend themselves to grouping information into categories. For example, you might write a paper for psychology class on the various ways people cope with the death of a loved one. For a course in economics, you might write about the three basic types of unemployment (*frictional, structural,* and *cyclical*). This approach—called **classification** and **division**—enables you to present a body of information in an orderly way.

Dividing and classifying also forces you to think clearly about your topic. By breaking a subject down into its distinct parts, or categories, you can look at it more closely and decide what you want to say about each part. For example, if you are writing an essay on effective teaching styles, you might begin by dividing the teachers you have had into the "good" ones and the "bad" ones. Then you could break those broad categories down further into more precise ones: teachers who held your interest, teachers who knew their subjects, teachers who made you do busy work, and so forth. As you develop each category, you have to think about the qualities that impressed you, and this thought process leads you to a better understanding of the topic you are writing about. You may end up writing only about the good teachers, but dividing and classifying the examples will help you to organize your thinking.

THE PRINCIPLES OF CLASSIFICATION AND DIVISION

Most things can be classified or divided in more than one way, depending on the reason for grouping the items. In the laundry example, for instance, you are told to sort the clothes according to the temperature of the water. Putting bright colors with knits doesn't make any sense if you don't know the reason—or basis—for the category: *items to be washed in cold water.* When you divide and classify a topic, be sure to have a sound basis for formulating your categories. The following suggestions will help you develop a useful system of classification.

Give a Purpose to Your Classification

Merely putting facts or ideas into different groups isn't necessarily meaningful. Consider these sentences that classify for no apparent reason:

1. There are five kinds of friends in most of our lives.
2. People deal with their spare money in four basic ways.

How could you give a **purpose** to these ideas? You would have to add a *reason* or declare a *point* for the categories. Here are some revisions that give purpose to these two classifications:

1. a. There are five kinds of friends in most of our lives, and each
        kind is important in its own way.
    b. Most of us have five kinds of friends, and each one drives us
        crazy in a special way.
2. a. People deal with their spare money in four ways that reflect their
        overall attitudes toward life.
    b. People deal with their spare money in four ways, only one of
        which is truly constructive.

Establish a Clear Basis for Your Classification

If you are going to classify items or ideas, you have to decide which
organizing principle you want to use to form your groups. For example, if
you are classifying friends, you could group them according to how close
you are to them, as Judith Viorst does in her essay in this chapter. Or you
could group them according to other principles: how long you have known
them, what you have in common with them, or how much time you spend
with the people in each group. The important thing is to choose a workable principle and stick with it.

Make Your Groups Parallel and Equal

In a classification essay, you usually announce the groups or classes in the
introduction: several ways to handle criticism, four kinds of friends, three
types of stress, three levels of intelligence, and so forth. You then devote one
section to each group of your classification. A section can be one paragraph
or several, but the sections for the major categories should be about equal
in length. In a classification essay about friendship, for instance, if you cover
"childhood pals" in 150 words, then you should use approximately the
same number of words for each of the other kinds of friends.

Experienced writers also present each section in a similar way. For example, in this chapter, psychologist David Elkind classifies the three basic types
of stress that young people experience. He labels each one with a letter,
describes it, and gives examples. He follows the same order—label, description, examples—in covering each type. He also mentions the same two
conditions when explaining each type: whether it's foreseeable and whether
it's avoidable. This parallel development helps the reader to recognize the
similarities and identify the distinctions among the types.

THE PITFALLS OF CLASSIFICATION AND DIVISION

The following advice will help you to avoid some of the problems that
writers sometimes encounter in developing an essay of classification.

1. *Know the difference between useful and useless ways of classifying.* Sorting your clothes by brand name probably won't help you get the best cleaning results when doing the laundry. And dividing teachers into those who wear glasses and those who don't is not a very useful way to organize a paper on effective teaching styles. But classifying teachers into those who lecture, those who use a question–discussion format, and those who run small-group workshops might be significant, mainly because such groupings would allow you to discuss the teachers' philosophies, their attitudes toward students, and their effectiveness in the classroom.

2. *Be sure your classification covers everything you claim it covers.* If, for instance, you know some teachers who sometimes lecture and sometimes use small groups, you can't pretend these people don't exist just to make your classification tidy. At least mention exceptions, even if you don't give them as much space as the major categories.

3. *Don't let the basis of division shift.* If you can see a problem with the following classification system, you already understand this warning:

TYPES OF TEACHERS
a. Teachers who lecture
b. Teachers who lead discussions
c. Teachers who have a sense of humor
d. Teachers who run workshops
e. Teachers who never hold office hours

Notice that three types of teachers (a, b, and d) are grouped according to the way they run their classes, but two types (c and e) are defined by some other standard. You can see the confusion these shifting groups cause: Can teachers who lecture have a sense of humor? Don't those who use workshops hold office hours?

4. *Be sure your groups are parallel or equal in rank.* The following classification illustrates a problem in rank:

KINDS OF POPULAR MUSIC
a. Easy listening
b. Country and western
c. Rock 'n' roll
d. Ice-T

Although Ice-T does represent a type of popular music distinct from easy listening, country, and rock, the category is not parallel with the others—it is far too small. It should be "rap," with Ice-T used as an example.

5. *Avoid stereotypes.* When you write about types of behavior or put people into groups, you run the risk of oversimplifying the material. The best way to avoid this problem is to use plenty of specific examples. You can also point out exceptions and describe variations; such honesty shows that you have been thinking carefully about the topic.

WHAT TO LOOK FOR IN A CLASSIFICATION

As you read the essays in this chapter, pay attention to these points:

1. *Figure out what the author is classifying.* Then identify the basis for making up the groups and the purpose of the classification.
2. *Look for the specific groups or classes* into which the author has sorted the material. Jot down a brief list of the major categories just to see if you can keep track of them.
3. *Ask yourself if the groups are clearly defined.* Do they shift? Do they cover what they claim to cover? Are they parallel?
4. *Be alert for stereotypes.* How does the author handle exceptions and variations?
5. *Identify the audience.* How do you know who the intended readers are?

Hanging Loose   **Hanging Tough**   **Just Hanging In There**

What are the three men in the cartoon doing? What type of jobs do they have? How can you tell?

How does this cartoon classify approaches toward office work? What other labels could you use for the three types? Could you use the same classifications for people in other jobs? Might there be classifications within these groups—for example, could there be different types of workers who are "just hanging in there"?

Stereotypes make broad generalizations about groups; they lump individuals together on the basis of a few examples. What stereotypes do you see depicted in this cartoon?

PREPARING TO READ

List five or ten of the people you call "friends." Are they all friends to an equal degree? Do you have a flexible meaning for the word *friend?*

Friends, Good Friends— And Such Good Friends

JUDITH VIORST

A popular humorist who writes essays and light verse for many well-known magazines, Judith Viorst was born in Newark, New Jersey, in 1931 and attended Rutgers University. She has written numerous children's books, including the enduring favorite *Alexander and the Terrible, Horrible, No Good, Very Bad Day* (1972), as well as several books for adults, including *Imperfect Control* (1998) and *Suddenly 60: And Other Shocks of Late-Life* (2000). The following selection appeared in her regular column in *Redbook* magazine in 1977.

TERMS TO RECOGNIZE

ardor *(para. 1)*	enthusiasm, intensity
nonchalant *(para. 2)*	indifferent, offhand
Tuesday-doubles *(para. 7)*	tennis played by four people, in pairs, on Tuesdays
sibling rivalry *(para. 11)*	competition among children for parental favor
dormant *(para. 13)*	sleeping, inactive
revived *(para. 13)*	brought back to life
calibrated *(para. 21)*	adjusted, determined

Women are friends, I once would have said, when they totally love   1
and support and trust each other, and bare to each other the secrets of their souls, and run—no questions asked—to help each other, and tell harsh truths to each other (no, you can't wear that dress unless you lose ten pounds first) when harsh truths must be told. Women are friends, I once would have said, when they share the same affection for Ingmar Bergman, plus train rides, cats, warm rain, charades, Camus, and hate with equal ardor Newark and Brussels sprouts and Lawrence Welk and camping.

In other words, I once would have said that a friend is a friend all the   2
way, but now I believe that's a narrow point of view. For the friendships I
have and the friendships I see are conducted at many levels of intensity,
serve many different functions, meet different needs and range from those
as all-the-way as the friendship of the soul sisters mentioned above to that
of the most nonchalant and casual playmates.

Consider these varieties of friendship: 3

1. Convenience friends. These are the women with whom, if our paths   4
weren't crossing all the time, we'd have no particular reason to be friends:
a next-door neighbor, a woman in our car pool, the mother of one of our
children's closest friends or maybe some mommy with whom we serve
juice and cookies each week at the Glenwood Co-op Nursery.

Convenience friends are convenient indeed. They'll lend us their cups   5
and silverware for a party. They'll drive our kids to soccer when we're sick.
They'll take us to pick up our car when we need a lift to the garage. They'll
even take our cats when we go on vacation. As we will for them. But we
don't, with convenience friends, ever come too close or tell too much; we
maintain our public face and emotional distance. "Which means," says
Elaine, "that I'll talk about being overweight but not about being depressed.
Which means I'll admit being mad but not blind with rage. Which means
that I might say that we're pinched this month but never that I'm worried
sick over money." But which doesn't mean that there isn't sufficient value
to be found in these friendships of mutual aid, in convenience friends.

2. Special-interest friends. These friendships aren't intimate, and they   6
needn't involve kids or silverware or cats. Their value lies in some interest
jointly shared. And so we may have an office friend or a yoga friend or a
tennis friend or a friend from the Women's Democratic Club.

"I've got one woman friend," says Joyce, "who likes, as I do, to take psychol-   7
ogy courses. Which makes it nice for me—and nice for her. It's fun to go with
someone you know and it's fun to discuss what you've learned, driving back
from the classes." And for the most part, she says, that's all they discuss. "I'd say
that what we're doing is *doing* together, not being together," Suzanne says of
her Tuesday-doubles friends. "It's mainly a tennis relationship, but we play
together well. And I guess we all need to have a couple of playmates." I agree.

My playmate is a shopping friend, a woman of marvelous taste, a woman   8
who knows exactly *where* to buy *what,* and furthermore is a woman who
always knows beyond a doubt what one ought to be buying. I don't have
the time to keep up with what's new in eyeshadow, hemlines and shoes and
whether the smock look is in or finished already. But since (oh, shame!) I
care a lot about eyeshadow, hemlines and shoes, and since I don't *want* to wear
smocks if the smock look is finished, I'm very glad to have a shopping friend.

3. Historical friends. We all have a friend who knew us when . . .   9
maybe way back in Miss Meltzer's second grade, when our family lived
in that three-room flat in Brooklyn, when our dad was out of work for
seven months, when our brother Allie got in that fight where they had
to call the police, when our sister married the endodontist from Yonkers,
and when, the morning after we lost our virginity, she was the first, the
only, friend we told.

The years have gone by and we've gone separate ways and we've little   10
in common now, but we're still an intimate part of each other's past. And
so whenever we go to Detroit we always go to visit this friend of our girlhood. Who knows how we looked before our teeth were straightened.
Who knows how we talked before our voice got unBrooklyned. Who
knows what we ate before we learned about artichokes. And who, by her
presence, puts us in touch with an earlier part of ourself, a part of ourself
it's important never to lose.

"What this friend means to me and what I mean to her," says Grace, "is   11
having a sister without sibling rivalry. We know the texture of each other's
lives. She remembers my grandmother's cabbage soup. I remember the way
her uncle played the piano. There's simply no other friend who remembers those things."

4. Crossroads friends. Like historical friends, our crossroads friends are   12
important for *what was*—for the friendship we shared at a crucial, now past,
time of life. A time, perhaps, when we roomed in college together; or
worked as eager young singles in the Big City together; or went together,
as my friend Elizabeth and I did, through pregnancy, birth and that scary
first year of new motherhood. Crossroads friends forge powerful links, links
strong enough to endure with not much more contact than once-a-year
letters at Christmas. And out of respect for those crossroads years, for those
dramas and dreams we once shared, we will always be friends.

5. Cross-generational friends. Historical friends and crossroads friends   13
seem to maintain a special kind of intimacy—dormant but always ready to
be revived—and though we may rarely meet, whenever we do connect, it's
personal and intense. Another kind of intimacy exists in the friendships
that form across generations in what one woman calls her daughter–mother
and her mother–daughter relationships. Evelyn's friend is her mother's
age—"but I share so much more than I ever could with my mother"—a
woman she talks to of music, of books, and of life. "What I get from her
is the benefit of her experience. What she gets—and enjoys—from me is
a youthful perspective. It's a pleasure for both of us."

I have in my own life a precious friend, a woman of 65 who has lived   14
very hard, who is wise, who listens well; who has been where I am and

can help me understand it; and who represents not only an ultimate ideal
mother to me but also the person I'd like to be when I grow up.

In our daughter role we tend to do more than our share of self-revelation;   15
in our mother role we tend to receive what's revealed. It's another kind of pleasure—playing a wise mother to a questing younger person. It's another very
lovely kind of friendship.

6. Part-of-a-couple friends. Some of the women we call our friends we   16
never see alone—we see them as part of a couple at couples' parties. And
though we share interests in many things and respect each other's views, we
aren't moved to deepen the relationship. Whatever the reason, a lack of time
or—and this is more likely—a lack of chemistry, our friendship remains in
the context of a group. But the fact that our feeling on seeing each other
is always, "I'm *so* glad she's here" and the fact that we spend half the evening
talking together says that this too, in its way, counts as a friendship.

(Other part-of-a-couple friends are the friends that came with the   17
marriage, and some of these are friends we could live without. But sometimes, alas, she married our husband's best friend; and sometimes, alas, she
is our husband's best friend. And so we find ourself dealing with her, some-
what against our will, in a spirit of what I'll call *reluctant* friendship.)

7. Men who are friends. I wanted to write just of women friends, but the   18
women I've talked to won't let me—they say I must mention man–woman
friendships too. For these friendships can be just as close and as dear as those
that we form with women. Listen to Lucy's description of one such friendship: "We've found we have things to talk about that are different from what
he talks about with my husband and different from what I talk about with
his wife. So sometimes we call on the phone or meet for lunch. There are
similar intellectual interests—we always pass on to each other the books that
we love—but there's also something tender and caring too."

In a couple of crises, Lucy says, "he offered himself, for talking and for   19
helping. And when someone died in his family he wanted me there. The
sexual, flirty part of our friendship is very small, but *some*—just enough
to make it fun and different." She thinks—and I agree—that the sexual
part, though small, is always *some,* is always there when a man and a
woman are friends.

It's only in the past few years that I've made friends with men, in the   20
sense of a friendship that's *mine,* not just part of two couples. And achieving with them the ease and the trust I've found with women friends has
value indeed. Under the dryer at home last week, putting on mascara and
rouge, I comfortably sat and talked with a fellow named Peter. Peter, I
finally decided, could handle the shock of me minus mascara under the
dryer. Because we care for each other. Because we're friends.

8. There are medium friends, and pretty good friends, and very good   21
friends indeed, and these friendships are defined by their level of intimacy. And what we'll reveal at each of these levels of intimacy is cali-
brated with care. We might tell a medium friend, for example, that
yesterday we had a fight with our husband. And we might tell a pretty
good friend that this fight with our husband made us so mad that we
slept on the couch. And we might tell a very good friend that the reason
we got so mad in that fight that we slept on the couch had something
to do with that girl who works in his office. But it's only to our very
best friends that we're willing to tell all, to tell what's going on with that
girl in his office.

The best of friends, I still believe, totally love and support and trust each   22
other, and bare to each other the secrets of their souls, and run—no questions asked—to help each other, and tell harsh truths to each other when
they must be told. But we needn't agree about everything (only 12-year-
old girl friends agree about *everything*) to tolerate each other's point of view.
To accept without judgment. To give and to take without ever keeping
score. And to *be* there, as I am for them and as they are for me, to comfort
our sorrows, to celebrate our joys.

RESPONDING TO READING

What do you think about friends of the other sex? Is there always a sexual
spark? Are cross-sex friendships different in quality than same-sex friendships? Would you try to restrict your sweetheart in his or her friendships?

GAINING WORD POWER

The following partial sentences include slightly different forms of the
Terms to Recognize. Complete each sentence in a reasonable way that
shows you understand the word used. Use your dictionary to be sure you
grasp the meaning.

1. Elena is an ardent hockey fan, but _____
_____.

2. Stanley did not understand the fine calibrations of politeness: he
often _____.

3. After _____,
Jean's social life went into a period of dormancy.

4. The writer's nonchalance about spelling was clear when _____
_____.

CONSIDERING CONTENT

1. What ideas is Viorst giving up, according to the beginning of the essay? Why does she begin with what she no longer believes?
2. Make a list of the different kinds of friends discussed in the essay. Which kind is the exception from the others?
3. What kind of person is the author of this essay? What kind of life does she lead? Look at paragraphs 4, 5, and 11 for evidence. How might the writer's **point of view** limit her audience? Did you feel included?
4. What are the functions friends perform, according to the essay? Are there underlying similarities among most of the types?
5. Why do you think the women Viorst interviewed insisted that she discuss man–woman friendships?

CONSIDERING METHOD

1. How do you know when Viorst is beginning a section about a new type of friend? What other method might she use to signal such a shift?
2. What is the relationship between the opening of the essay and the closing?
3. Look at the ways Viorst develops the explanation of each type. She uses narration, definition, example, comparison and contrast, and cause-and-effect reasoning. Identify instances showing at least three of these methods.
4. What do the direct quotations do for the essay? Are they from famous people? Think of at least two reasons why they are included.
5. In paragraph 7, you can see the repetition of similar sentence openings. What words are repeated? Find another example of repetition of phrases or structures. What purpose does this repetition serve?

WRITING STEP BY STEP

Using Viorst's essay for inspiration, write an essay that classifies several different types of intelligence.

A. Brainstorm, with help from friends or classmates if you want it, for ideas about the various kinds of "smart" you see around you. Jot down everything mentioned, even if it sounds silly or overlapping—you can sort it out later.
B. Choose three to six types to discuss in your essay. You might combine several different items from your brainstorming notes to make up one type, when the items seem closely related.

C. Make up a label for each type, as Viorst did in "Friends."

D. Develop a section explaining each type. Use examples of people who show each type of intelligence if you can—either people you know personally or public figures most of your readers will be able to identify. Interview your friends, as Viorst did, and use direct quotations from your interviews.

E. Be sure to show how the types are similar and different from each other by using comparisons and contrasts as you go along. Look at paragraphs 13 and 21 of Viorst's essay for samples of how to do this.

F. Use signals to show when you are shifting from one type to the next. You could use numbers and/or labels. Or you could use transitional words, like "The second type of intelligence is . . ."

G. Write an introduction that discusses a misperception (of your own or of others) about intelligence. See Viorst's introduction for a model.

H. Close your essay with a statement that draws all the kinds of intelligence together, telling what they have in common. Alternatively, you may want to close, as Viorst did, by commenting on what you wrote in the introduction.

OTHER WRITING IDEAS

1. There are probably as many kinds of people you dislike as people you like. Write an essay categorizing the types that drive you crazy.

2. Classify the variations of a single emotion—anxiety, nervousness, love, anger, pleasure, embarrassment, confidence, or excitement, for example.

3. Judith Viorst wrote another essay in which she classifies the lies we tell. For example, she discusses lies we tell to save others' feelings, lies we tell to save our own pride, and so on. Write your own essay on this topic. You might get together with classmates to think of categories and examples.

EDITING SKILLS: PROOFREADING

Proofreading your essay should be a painstaking task. You need to look at every word and every piece of punctuation—and use your dictionary when you are not absolutely certain you have it all right. Remember that your dictionary includes a handbook for editing that gives you rules of punctuation and mechanics. If you are composing on a computer, your spelling checker will catch some of your errors, but not all. For example, if you typed *form* instead of *from,* your spelling checker will not flag it. Words that your checker does not know will also need to be looked up in the dictionary—the computer program is able to recognize only about half as many words as a dictionary holds.

EXERCISE

Here is a paragraph from another essay by Judith Viorst, "The Truth about Lying." We have put in errors for you to find and correct. Retype your corrected version and trade papers with a classmate. Discuss any differences you see, and refer again to your dictionary for points of clarification.

Protective lies are lies folks tell—often quite serious lies–because their convinced that the truth would be to dammaging. They lie because they feel their are certian human values that supercede the wrong of of having lied. They lie, not for personnel gain, but because they believe its for the good of the person they're lying to. They lie to those they love, to those who trust them most of all, on the grounds that braking this trust is justifyed.

If you are interested in how well your computer program does, you can try typing in the uncorrected version of the paragraph and running the spelling checker. You will find that quite a few errors slip right past.

WEB SITE

www.annonline.com/interviews/980112/index.html

An interview with and information about Judith Viorst.

Preparing to Read

For the next twenty-four hours, make a note every time you hear someone describe another person's behavior (or idea or talk) as weird or strange or crazy. Also record your ideas about why the behavior was pointed out as different from normal.

I'm OK; You're a Bit Odd

Paul Chance

Paul Chance, a psychologist and teacher at Salisbury State University in Maryland, sits on the advisory board for the Cambridge Center for Behavioral Studies. He writes frequently about human behavior for various professional and educational journals. In this article, first published in 1988 in *Psychology Today* magazine, Chance investigates the ways we decide whether other people are mentally healthy.

TERMS TO RECOGNIZE

quirk *(para. 1)*	minor oddity
Platonic ideal *(para. 2)*	the perfect form, according to the Greek philosopher Plato
emulate *(para. 2)*	imitate
psychopath *(para. 8)*	seriously disturbed person who has aggressive, criminal tendencies
flimflam *(para. 8)*	swindle
paragon *para. 13)*	ideal example
phobias *(para. 13)*	unreasonable and bothersome fears
benchmark *(para. 14)*	a standard level for judging quality or quantity

the new groom was happy with his bride, and everything, he explained, was fine. There was just this one peculiarity his wife had. During lovemaking she insisted that he wear his motorcycle helmet. He found it uncomfortable, and he felt just a tad foolish. Is it normal to want someone to wear a helmet during amorous activities? Does a quirk of this sort keep one off the rolls of the mentally fit? The answer depends on how you define mental fitness. There are several ways of going about it.

One model calls to mind the Platonic ideal. Somewhere in the heavens   2
there exists a person who is the perfect specimen of psychological health.
(Or maybe there are two of them: the perfect man may be different from
the perfect woman. At least, one would hope so.) We all fall short of this
ideal, of course, but it provides a model that we can emulate. Unfortunately, the Platonic answer merely begs the question, since somebody has
to describe what the ideal is like. And how do we do that?

The everyday way of defining mental health is more subjective: if I do   3
it, it's healthy; if I don't do it, it's sick. Is it crazy to spend Saturdays jumping out of airplanes or canoeing down rapids? Not to skydivers and white-
water canoers. Is it sick to hear voices when no one is there? Not if you're
the one who hears the voices—and you welcome their company.

This commonsense way of defining mental health sets ourselves up as the   4
standard against which to make comparisons. There's nothing wrong with
this, except that it's just possible that some of us—not me, you understand—
are a bit odd ourselves. And you can't measure accurately with a bent ruler.

The psychodynamic model of mental health suggests that psychological   5
fitness is a kind of balancing act. There are, according to this view, impulses
in all of us that society cannot tolerate. The healthy person is not the one
who always keeps these impulses under lock and key but the one who lets
them out once in a while when nobody's looking. If you run around the
house smashing delicate things with a hammer, for example, someone's apt
to object. But if you hammer a nail into a board, and seem to have a good
excuse for it, nobody minds. So the healthy person with violent impulses
builds a deck behind the house.

The chief problem with the psychodynamic model is that it doesn't define   6
the standard by which balance is to be measured. Building a deck may be an
acceptable outlet for violent impulses, but what if every time a person feels
like slugging someone he adds on to the deck until his entire backyard is
covered in redwood? He's directing his impulses constructively, but his family
might find him easier to live with if he just broke something once in a while.

Behaviorists offer a different solution. They focus on behavior, naturally,   7
and decide whether behavior is healthy on the basis of its consequences.
If the results are good, the behavior is good. In this view, there is nothing
nuts about building a two-acre redwood deck so long as the person enjoys
it and it doesn't get him or her into trouble. Normal behavior, then, is
whatever works.

The behavioral approach appears to offer an objective and rational way   8
of defining mental health. Alas, appearances are deceiving. We may agree
that a person enjoys an activity, but is that enough? A sadist and a masochist
may work out a mutually rewarding relationship, but does that make them

healthy? A psychopath may flimflam oldsters out of their life savings and do it with such charm that they love him for it, but should the rest of us emulate the psychopath?

An alternative is to let society decide. What is healthy then becomes 9 what society finds acceptable; what is unhealthy is whatever society dislikes. Thus, aggression is abnormal among the gentle Tasaday of the Philippines but normal among the fierce Yanomamo of Venezuela.

The societal model has a lot of appeal, but it troubles some mental-health 10 workers. There is something about fixing mental health to a mailing address that they find unsettling. They think that there ought to be some sort of universal standard toward which we might all strive. Besides, does it really make sense to say that murder and cannibalism are OK just because some society has approved them? And if it is, then why not apply the same standards to communities within a society? Murder is a popular activity among Baltimore youth. Shall we say that, in that city, murder is healthy?

A similar problem exists with the statistical model of mental health. In 11 this case, being mentally healthy means falling close to average. Take the frequency of sexual activity among married couples, for example. Let's say that, on average, married people your age have intercourse about twice a week. That's the norm. If you indulge more or less often than that, you're abnormal—with or without a helmet.

There's some logic to this view. The further people deviate from the aver- 12 age, the more likely they are to seem strange. You may think, for instance, that limiting sex to two times a week is a bit prudish, but almost everyone is likely to think that once an hour is excessive. Again, however, there are problems.

Does it really make sense to hold up the average person as the paragon 13 of mental health? This logic would have everyone cultivate a few phobias just because they happen to be commonplace, even the best students would strive to earn Cs, and all couples in the country would be frustrated by their inability to have exactly 1.8 children.

We can all agree that there are a lot of weirdos around, but there seems 14 no way for us to agree about who's weird. And so there's no way for us to agree about what mental health is. That's unfortunate, because it gives us no clear goal toward which to strive and no stable benchmark against which to gauge our progress. Even so, I'm damned if I'm gonna wear a helmet to bed.

RESPONDING TO READING

Return to your notes from Preparing to Read. What explanations for branding something as weird are covered in Chance's essay? Does the essay change your perspective on the incidents you noted?

GAINING WORD POWER

Weird is an overused and imprecise word. Some **synonyms** from the thesaurus are *uncanny, puzzling, inexplicable, bizarre, nightmarish, irrational,* and *freakish.* Look up each of these synonyms in the dictionary. Write one sentence for each of the seven words. Make your sentences reflect the differences in meaning among the terms.

CONSIDERING CONTENT

1. Who is the **audience** for this essay? How do you know? Who is *not* the audience for the piece? Why?
2. How many approaches to defining mental health or normality does Chance cover? List them.
3. Give your own examples that fit at least two of the models of mental health.
4. Which model of mental health, in your opinion, would label you and your friends most mentally abnormal? Consider your family: what approach would label your family as strange?
5. In paragraph 2, Chance suggests that the ideal of psychological health would be different for men and women. Do you agree? Why or why not?
6. Where does the title of the essay come from? If you don't know, look up the first two words of the title in your library's online or card catalog. How is the essay related to the original source of the title?

CONSIDERING METHOD

1. Under each approach to defining mental health, how does Chance organize his discussion? As you were reading, when did this organization become clear to you?
2. Does each approach include a specific example? Why are the examples important? Would you have liked another example of one of the points?
3. Count how many questions Chance asks in the essay. Thinking of your other reading, is this a weird number of questions? What purpose do you think they serve?
4. What is the **tone** of the piece? For example, what tone of voice would someone use to read it out loud? Give several words that describe the tone. What clues you in to the tone?
5. Reread the last sentence. What is your reaction to it? What technique does it employ to indicate that the essay is finished?

WRITING STEP BY STEP

When we are faced with one of life's problems, we often find ourselves brainstorming to discover approaches to the problem and then considering the strengths and weaknesses of each approach. We ponder, for example, the problem of how to make housemates or family members share cleaning duties, the problem of how to make scarce money go further, or the problem of how to break unwelcome news to someone. Choose a problem that could be considered in several ways, and write an essay using Chance's discussion of approaches to mental health as a model.

A. Identify three or four approaches to the problem. On a piece of scratch paper or on your computer screen, brainstorm for a few minutes, jotting down ideas about each approach. If you need help, ask your classmates for ideas about your topic.

B. Decide on a reasonable order to present your approaches—from weakest to strongest (or vice versa), from your first hunch to your last solution, from the most ordinary to the most bizarre, or along any range that seems reasonable.

C. Choose a tone that suits your purpose and your audience. In choosing a tone, you might also consider the severity of the problem—a serious treatise concerning approaches to bad-hair days will provide a humorous mismatch, for example. Paul Chance, in a similar way, chose a light tone to discuss a serious topic. However, a match between the topic and the tone is the usual expectation, and you should feel free to align them if you want: a humorous tone for a light topic, and a serious tone for a weighty topic.

D. Begin the essay with a little story that highlights the problem, as Chance does. Lead into a general statement of the problem.

E. Write a one- or two-paragraph discussion of your first approach. Begin with a description of the approach.

F. Give the strengths of the approach and provide an example of how it is (or would be) used.

G. Follow the strengths by discussing the weaknesses of the approach along with an example of its failings. You can, as Chance does, use the same example for both strengths and weaknesses, or if you prefer, you can use different examples to show positive and negative elements.

H. Follow steps E, F, and G for the next two or three approaches you identified in the brainstorming stage.

I. In your closing paragraph, you might follow Chance's model and write about why no approach is perfect. On the other hand, you might explain which approach you think is best, if there is one.

J. Write a closing sentence that relates back to the little story in your introduction.

OTHER WRITING IDEAS

1. Choose either school or a workplace you know well, and write about the different approaches people take toward their work. Consider using specific people you know as examples of the approaches. Be sure to give enough examples and details for your reader to get a clear picture.

2. Think of a quality that many people have but that they use in different ways—for example, power, beauty, charm, intelligence, or wealth. Develop an essay that explains three or four approaches to possessing this quality. "Some people use their power for good causes, some for control over others, and some to amass even more power." Consider evaluating each approach or explaining why people differ along these lines.

3. Classify people according to their attitudes toward their own backgrounds—ethnic, religious, cultural, racial, or class roots. For example, in what ways do people who come from poverty-stricken backgrounds relate to their past? What stances do people raised Catholic take toward the religion in later life? To help you get ideas for your paper, get together with a group of classmates and discuss how each of you views your roots.

**EDITING SKILLS: CHOOSING *THERE, THEIR,*
OR *THEY'RE***

Words that sound alike, called **homophones,** can be treacherous. In speech, we don't think about which one to select, but in writing we have to make a choice. Because homophones are often common words, such as *there, their,* and *they're,* we can't avoid using them. And because the meanings are quite different, we really do have to get them right or our readers will be confused.

First, look at the use of the word *there* in these sentences from "I'm OK; You're a Bit Odd":

There was just this one peculiarity his wife had.

There are, according to this view, impulses in all of us that society cannot tolerate.

In these sentences, *there* is just a fill-in word; it doesn't have much mean-ing. We use *there* to begin sentences like these when we want to say that something or someone exists. The same spelling goes for the use of the word to indicate a place:

Is it sick to hear voices when no one is *there?*

Now look at the use of *their* in these passages from the same essay:

Not if you're the one who hears the voices—and you welcome *their* company.
A psychopath may flimflam oldsters out of *their* life savings . . .

The word *their* is a possessive, showing ownership or belonging. In the first example, it refers to voices; in the second example, it refers to oldsters.
Finally, take a look at this sentence:

Behaviorists would say that if people enjoy an action and it doesn't get them in trouble, *they're* normal.

In this example, *they're* sounds just like the others, but you can substitute the words *they are* for it. *They're* is a contraction, just like *don't* for *do not* and *she's* for *she is*. If you can substitute *they are,* you know you have the right word. If you can't, you need *there* or *their.*
All right, let's review:

There are numerous sound-alike words in English.
You have to know the differences in *their* meanings if you want to use them correctly.
They're often common words that we use a lot.

EXERCISE

Fill the blanks in the following sentences with *there, their,* or *they're.*

1. _____ are no solutions to this problem.
2. Your cousins have arrived, and _____ going to stay for dinner.
3. When George Eliot and Jane Austen wrote _____ great novels, _____ were few creative opportunities for women besides writing.

4. The team members should have known that _____ luck wouldn't hold. But _____ definitely looking forward to next season.

5. Although it wasn't _____ fault, the twins are sure to get blamed, and _____ not happy about it.

Look over the essay you have just written to see if you used *there, their,* or *they're.* Did you choose the right one? Go over some past papers, too, to see how accurate you are in using these three homophones. Copy three to five sentences in which you use one, and justify your choice in each case. (For more about homophones, see Chapter 9, p. 258.)

WEB SITE

www.behavior.org/columns

Read more articles and commentaries by Paul Chance at the Cambridge Center for Behavioral Studies.

PREPARING TO READ

How can you tell when someone has good self-esteem? How do people with good self-esteem handle life's problems?

Types of Stress for Young People

DAVID ELKIND

David Elkind is a psychologist who specializes in child development and has written influential books on the subject. In this reading from his book *All Grown Up and No Place to Go* (1988), he describes three kinds of situations that we all face but that are especially stressful for teenagers.

TERMS TO RECOGNIZE

expenditure *(para. 3)*	cost
potential *(para. 4, 12)*	possible
foreseeable *(para. 4)*	seen ahead of time
transient *(para. 7)*	temporary, passing away with time
jeopardize *(para. 7)*	threaten
incorporates *(para. 10)*	combines
inevitable *(para. 12)*	certain to happen
introverted *(para. 14)*	withdrawn, not sociable
extroverted *(para. 14)*	outgoing
bouts *(para. 15)*	short periods

most situations that produce psychological stress involve some sort of conflict between self and society. So long as we satisfy a social demand at the expense of a personal need, or vice versa, the social or personal demand for action is a psychological stress. If, for example, we stay home from work because of a personal problem, we create a new demand (for an explanation, for made-up time) at our place of work. On the other hand, if we devote too much time to the demands of work, we create new demands on the part of family. If we don't manage our energy budgets well, we create more stress than is necessary. 1

The major task of psychological stress management is to find ways to balance and coordinate the demands that come from within with those that come from without. This is where a healthy sense of self and identity comes in. An 2 integrated sense of identity . . . means bringing together into a working whole a set of attitudes, values, and habits that can serve both self and society. The attainment of such a sense of identity is accompanied by a feeling of self-esteem, of liking and respecting oneself and being liked and respected by others.

More than anything else, the attainment of a healthy sense of identity   3
and a feeling of self-esteem gives young people a perspective, a way of looking at themselves and others, which enables them to manage the majority of stress situations. Young people with high self-esteem look at situations from a single perspective that includes both themselves and others. They look at situations from the standpoint of what it means to their self-respect and to the respect others have for them. This integrated perspective enables them to manage the major types of stress efficiently and with a minimum expenditure of energy and personal distress.

The Three Stress Situations

There are three major types of stress situations that all of us encounter.   4
One of these occurs when the potential stress is both foreseeable and avoidable. This is a *Type A* stress situation. If we are thinking about going on a roller coaster or seeing a horror movie, the stress is both foreseeable and avoidable. We may choose to expose ourselves to the stress if we find such controlled danger situations exciting or stimulating. Likewise if we know that a particular neighborhood or park is dangerous at night, the danger is both foreseeable and avoidable, and we do avoid it, unless we are looking for trouble.

The situation becomes more complicated when the foreseeable and   5
avoidable danger is one for which there is much social approval and support, even though it entails much personal risk. Becoming a soldier in times of war is an example of this more complicated Type A danger. The young person who enlists wins social approval at the risk of personal harm. On the other hand, the young person who refuses to become a soldier protects himself or herself from danger at the cost of social disapproval.

Teenagers are often caught in this more difficult type of situation. If the   6
peer group uses alcohol or drugs, for example, there is considerable pressure on the young person to participate. But such participation often puts teenagers at risk with parents and teachers, and also with respect to themselves. They may not like the image of themselves as drinkers or drug abusers. It is at this point that a sense of identity and a positive feeling of self-esteem stand the teenager in good stead.

A young person with a healthy sense of identity will weigh the danger   7
to his or her hard-won feeling of self-esteem against the feelings associated with the loss of peer approval. When the teenager looks at the situation

from this perspective, the choice is easy to make. By weighing the laboriously arrived-at feeling of self-esteem against the momentary approval of a transient peer group, the teenager with an integrated sense of self is able to avoid potentially stressful situations. It should be said, too, that the young person's ability to foresee and avoid is both an intellectual and an emotional achievement. The teenager must be able to foresee events . . . but also to place sufficient value upon his or her self-esteem and self-respect to avoid situations that would jeopardize these feelings.

A second type of stress situation involves those demands which are   8 neither foreseeable nor avoidable. These are *Type B* stress situations. Accidents are of this type, as when a youngster is hit by a baseball while watching a game, or when a teenager who happens to be at a place in school when a fight breaks out gets hurt even though he was not involved. The sudden, unexpected death of a loved one is another example of a stress that is both unforeseeable and unavoidable. Divorce of parents is unthinkable for many teenagers and therefore also unforeseeable and unavoidable.

Type B stress situations make the greatest demands upon young people. . . .   9 With this type of stress teenagers have to deal with the attitudes of their friends and teachers at the same time that they are struggling with their own feelings. Such stress situations put demands upon young people both from within and from without. A youngster who has been handicapped by an accident, like the teenager who has to deal with divorce, has to adjust to new ways of relating to others as well as new ways of thinking about himself or herself.

Again, the young person with a strong sense of identity and a feeling of   10 self-esteem has the best chance of managing these stress situations as well as they can be managed. In the case of divorce, for example, the teenager who incorporates other people's perspectives with his or her own is able to deal with the situation better than other teenagers who lack this perspective. For example, one young man, who went on to win honors at an Ivy League school, told his father when he and the mother divorced, "You are entitled to live your own life and to find happiness too."

This integrated perspective also helps young people deal with the death   11 of a loved one. If it was an elderly grandparent who had been suffering great pain, the young person can see that from the perspective of the grandparent, dying may have been preferable to living a life of agony with no hope of recovery. As one teenager told me with regard to his grandfather who had just died, "He was in such pain, he was so doped up he couldn't really recognize me. I loved him so much I just couldn't stand to see him that way." By enabling the young person to see death from the perspective of others, including that of the person who is dying, the young person is able to mourn the loss but also to get on with life.

The third type of stress situation is one in which the potential stress is   12
foreseeable but not avoidable. This is a *Type C* stress situation. A teenager
who has stayed out later than he or she was supposed to foresees an
unavoidable storm at home. Likewise, exams are foreseeable but unavoidable stress situations. Being required to spend time with relatives one does
not like is another stress situation that the teenager can foresee but not
avoid. These are but a few examples of situations the teenager might wish
to avoid but must learn to accept as inevitable.

To young people who have attained a solid sense of self and identity,   13
foreseeable and unavoidable stress situations are manageable, again, because
of self-esteem and the integrated perspective. They look at the situation
from the perspective of themselves as well as that of the other people
involved and try to prepare accordingly. They may decide, as one young
man of my acquaintance did, that "with my folks, honesty is the best policy.
I get into less trouble if I tell the truth than if I make up stories." In the
case of visiting relatives they do not like, integrated teenagers see it from
the perspective of what it means to others, such as their parents. And with
respect to stress situations like exams, because they want to maintain their
self-esteem, they prepare for the exam so that they will make a good showing for themselves as well as for others.

It is important to say, too, that integrated teenagers come in any and all   14
personality types. Some are introverted and shy, others are extroverted and
fun-loving. Some are preoccupied with intellectual concerns, others primarily with matters of the heart. Despite this diversity, they all share the prime
characteristics of the integrated teenager: a set of attitudes, values, and habits
that enable the young person to serve self and society, and a strong sense
of self-esteem.

To be sure, life is complex and varied. Even the most integrated teenager,   15
of whatever personality type, may occasionally be so overwhelmed by stress
that he or she loses the integrated perspective and suffers bouts of low self-
esteem. We need to remember that teenagers are new at the game of stress
management and have just acquired the skills they need for this purpose.
Nonetheless, the general principle holds true. The more integrated the
teenager is with respect to self and identity, the better prepared he or she
is to manage the basic stress situations.

RESPONDING TO READING

Identify a source of stress in your own life and see whether you can classify it as Type A, Type B, or Type C. Write in your journal about the stress
and whether self-esteem contributes to how you handle it.

GAINING WORD POWER

Elkind's essay on stress uses several words and their opposites, their **antonyms**, such as *extroverted* and *introverted, inevitable* and *avoidable, foreseeable* and *unforeseeable.* Use your dictionary or a dictionary of **synonyms** and antonyms to find the opposites of the following words from the reading. Be sure to choose opposites that are the same part of speech; in the three preceding examples, all the words can be used as adjectives. You may need to use two or three words instead of one. Your dictionary will help you determine parts of speech.

transient	jeopardize
expenditure	potential
incorporate	

CONSIDERING CONTENT

1. According to Elkind, what overall conflict causes most situations of stress?
2. Give examples of each type of stress from your own or your friends' lives.
3. Which type of stress does Elkind think is most difficult for teens? Why is this type the worst?
4. Elkind concentrates on how a teenager with good self-esteem would deal with stressful situations. How would a teen with low self-esteem deal with some of these situations?
5. What is an "integrated perspective" (paras. 3, 11, 13, and 15)? Give an example. Can you think of a synonym for the term?
6. In paragraph 7, Elkind writes, the "young person's ability to foresee and avoid is both an intellectual and an emotional achievement." Explain this statement.

CONSIDERING METHOD

1. How many times does Elkind repeat his main point? Why might a writer repeat the main point several times?
2. Divide the fifteen paragraphs into five main sections. What label could you put on each section?
3. How does Elkind let you know what to expect when you are reading his essay?
4. How do you know when a new paragraph takes up a new type of stress situation?
5. How does Elkind clarify what each type of stress situation is like?

WRITING STEP BY STEP

Using Elkind's classification of types of stress as a model, write an essay in which you investigate types of social pressure in your world. Think about the influences that cause you to think and behave the way you do. Consider which influences you resist and which you accept.

A. Identify two to four types of social pressure you see at work in your environment.

B. Think of some general strength that people could develop that would help them deal with these types of social pressure. Discuss what you mean by this strength in the introduction to the essay.

C. Write a paragraph briefly presenting the types of social pressure you intend to discuss.

D. Explain each type of social pressure in its own section of the paper. Use examples and details to clarify what you mean.

E. For each type, include an explanation of how the basic strength you discussed early in the essay would apply to this type of social pressure.

F. Put in some kind of transitional material or signal when you switch from one type to another. See the editing section at the end of this selection for help.

G. Point out some circumstances in which the basic strength might fail to help a person deal with social pressure.

H. In your closing (one or two sentences), reaffirm the general principle you have developed.

OTHER WRITING IDEAS

1. Classify and explain the types of stress that distinguish a certain period of life other than the teenage years. Think about the first year of college, marriage, parenthood, or retirement, for example.

2. Instead of focusing on stresses, focus on the types of strength that you believe are especially important to develop in young people today.

3. Consider the types of stress that seem to be assigned by sex. What are the types of stress usually felt most by women? What types of stress are felt most by men? You might get together in a mixed-sex group to brainstorm for ideas before you write your paper. Write on either sex but not both.

EDITING SKILLS: TRANSITIONS

Good writers use **transitions**—words and phrases that help connect ideas—to show how one sentence is related, logically, to the sentence before it. Look at these examples from the Elkind essay.

On the other hand, the young person who refuses to become a soldier protects himself or herself from danger at the cost of social disapproval. [*On the other hand* is a transitional phrase indicating that a contrast is about to be made.]

It should be said, too, that the young person's ability to foresee and avoid is both an intellectual and an emotional achievement. [The word *too* indicates that this sentence adds material consistent with the sentence before it.]

Again, the young person with a strong sense of identity and a feeling of self-esteem has the best chance of managing these stress situations as well as they can be managed. [The word *again* lets you know that this sentence repeats something said earlier.]

Notice that the transitional words are separated from the main sentence with commas.

EXERCISE

Find at least two other sentences in the Elkind essay that include transitional words, and copy them exactly.

Now check your own essay to see whether you can provide more transitional "glue" to hold the thoughts together. Transitions can show several types of movement:

Addition: also, too, moreover, next, furthermore, again
Exemplification: for example, that is, for instance
Emphasis: especially, in fact, primarily, most important
Contrast: but, on the other hand, nevertheless, however
Comparison: likewise, similarly, also, too
Qualification: admittedly, of course, granted that
Causation: so, consequently, therefore, as a result
Conclusion: finally, in conclusion, in short, at last

Add at least one transitional word or phrase to your own essay.

☙ WEB SITE

http://stress.about.com/mbody.htm

A guide to coping strategies, support, and information dealing with the effects of stress on everyday life and health.

PREPARING TO READ

What's your idea of a good love story? Do you think your idea is different from other people's, or pretty much the same? Do you find that romantic films or stories relate realistically to your own life?

Love Stories

LOUIS MENAND

Louis Menand writes on a variety of topics, from the serious (his latest book concerns the philosophical movement called pragmatism) to the lighthearted (as in the piece we reprint here, on love stories). He was born in 1952 and got his Ph.D. from Columbia University. Menand served on the faculty at Princeton and now is in the English department at the City University of New York Graduate Center. He is a contributing editor to the *New York Review of Books* and a staff writer for *The New Yorker,* in which the following essay appeared.

TERMS TO RECOGNIZE

smitten *(para. 1)*	affected with great feeling
denouement *(para. 3)*	outcome of a narrative plot
tripartite *(para. 4)*	three-part
evoke *(para. 5)*	call forth
poignantly *(para. 8)*	with agreeable intensity
acculturate *(para. 9)*	to instill the culture of a particular society
tutelage *(para. 9)*	teaching
learning curve *(para. 9)*	time required for mastery
amatory *(para. 9)*	related to love

all the world loves a lover? Not necessarily. In real life, few emotions are less sociable than romantic passion. A person who has valentines dancing in his eyes is a person generally avoided by those not identically smitten, which is to say, in most cases, by the rest of humanity. Passion of the unrequited sort can be an acceptable subject of conversation if your advice is being sought; but does anyone ever listen? "He's a *complete jerk,*" you say. "Forget about him." "Oh, you're so right," she says. "Thank you for helping me face the truth." Later on, you learn she's marrying the guy.

You can talk with other people about their romantic misery, but there   2
is really no way to have a decent conversation about romantic bliss. Not
that love affairs aren't interesting; on the contrary. It's usually both more
enjoyable and more efficient, though, to learn about them from a third
party. The lover himself has a tendency to ignore the ordinary limits of the
human faculty for paying attention. And he somehow expects you to share
all his feelings for the beloved, although, of course, if you actually did share
them he'd want to murder you. Having a friend who is madly in love is
one of the reasons people get call waiting.

What all the world really loves is not a lover. It's a love story. People can't   3
get enough of love stories. What people flee from in reality (where the
stuff is available for nothing) they flock to bookstores, theatres, and cine-
mas to seek out and pay for. A love story is usually a story not about how
happy two people are but about how unhappy they are. It's about either
the difficulty they are having in getting together or the difficulty they are
having in staying together. End of difficulty, generally speaking, end of story.
The repertoire of denouements is fairly limited: marriage, splitsville, murder,
and mutual annihilation. But audiences keep coming back for more.

There are so many love stories—it's hard to think of a novel or a movie   4
or a play, or even an epic poem, that is *not* in some way a love story—that
categorizing them might seem impossible. One way to do it, though, is to
employ a simple lovability index. It's a straightforward and logical tripar-
tite scale. In the first category are love stories in which you find neither of
the lovers particularly lovable; in the second category are love stories in
which you find one but not both of the lovers lovable; and in the third
category are the stories in which you find the lovers nearly as irresistible
as they find each other—stories that give you a feeling for their feeling.

One surprising thing the lovability index reveals is that the more famous   5
the love story the less lovable the lovers. Who actually cares about Romeo?
Only Juliet. And vice versa. They're so busy being infatuated with each
other that neither has a spare moment to waste on seducing us. Romeo
and Juliet, Tristam and Isolde, Lancelot and Guinevere are world-famous
couples, but they don't evoke the emotion of love; they symbolize it. Their
stories invite us to thrill to the force of a passion we cannot share.

The last question we would ever think of asking about the lovers in a   6
story of this type is: What is the basis of their relationship? These people
don't have "relationships," any more than a magnet has a "relationship"
with the North Pole. They are acting under the compulsion of a blind
fate. They are mutually-attracting force fields, missiles preprogrammed to
collide in midair, effects without causes. In the Hollywood version, if he is
fabulous-looking and she is fabulous-looking, they don't need a better

reason for getting together. And, most of the time, we don't need a better one for watching them get together.

The love stories that make us wonder about "the basis of the relation- 7 ship" are stories of the second type—stories in which our feelings for the lovers are asymmetrical. It's easy to fall in love with Emma Woodhouse; it's hard to feel anything more tender than respect for Mr. Knightley. Anna Karenina is wonderful, but what in the world does she see in Vronsky? Second-category love stories are not force-of-nature stories. They are force-of-circumstance stories. Mr. Knightley just happens to be the best card in the hand society has dealt. In a movie Emma could probably have done better—and in "Clueless," actually, she did do better: Alicia Silverstone's Mr. Knightley turned out to be a sweet college kid named Josh.

Third-category love stories—stories that evoke something that resembles 8 the sensation of romantic love most poignantly—are the rarest. These usually seem to involve odd couples—Leopold Bloom and Molly, Harold and Maude, the Owl and the Pussycat—or just everyday, charismatically challenged people. There is something about the spectacle of two ordinary, slightly mismatched characters ending up together which triggers an involuntary gush of sentiment much more quickly and effectively than does the spectacle of two statuesque godlings who can't keep their hands off each other. "When Harry Met Sally," in which the lovers end by getting married, is more moving than "The English Patient," in which they both so glamorously die.

Is it the purpose of love stories to teach us how to be lovers? This is 9 sometimes suggested, by people who take the view that the essential purpose of culture is to acculturate. That seems implausible. People don't require much tutelage to fall in love; it just happens. And when the attraction is mutual the learning curve is short. Amatory awkwardness is quickly forgiven. Lovers tend to find a way to love. Insofar as the lessons learned from love stories do enter into real life, the results are usually disastrous. Few romantic come-ons backfire more humiliatingly than come-ons picked up from books or movies, including come-ons picked up from books or movies (e.g., "Play It Again, Sam") in which characters successfully employ come-ons picked up from books or movies. Only Bogart could be Bogart, only Garbo Garbo, and only Gable Gable; and even they had better luck in the movies.

Maybe the purpose of culture is not to acculturate. Maybe it's not a stealth 10 indoctrination program at all. Maybe art and literature are just what people take them to be: a means of providing a particular and complex kind of pleasure. Love stories are there to allow us to indulge our instinctive fascination with this most exquisite of human emotions, and to do it in a form that has a beginning, a middle, and, unlike certain phone calls, an end.

RESPONDING TO READING

What do you think of Menand's classification system? Is it one you would have thought of yourself? How much of his own taste is reflected, rather than people's in general, or yours?

GAINING WORD POWER

In paragraph 4, Menand writes about "love stories in which you find neither of the lovers *particularly* lovable." In paragraph 10, we read the phrase "a *particular* and complex kind of pleasure." Both words share the meaning of belonging to a special and distinct type. *Particular* is an adjective, describing the noun *kind*. *Particularly* is the adverb form of the same word; adverbs describe words other than nouns, in this case the adjective *lovable*. Most adverbs are made by adding -*ly* to adjectives; for example, *identically* comes from *identical* (para. 1), *usually* comes from *usual* (para. 2), and *actually* comes from *actual* (para. 2).

This reading includes sixteen other adverbs that end in -*ly*. Find at least five of them. Then write their adjective forms, checking with the dictionary for spelling if necessary. Then express the shared meaning between the two forms, again using the dictionary. Here's an example to get you started:

Adverb: awkwardly

Adjective: awkward

Shared meaning: clumsiness, lacking in skill or grace

CONSIDERING CONTENT

1. In paragraphs 1 and 2, Menand provides several reasons why having a friend who's madly in love is not pleasant. What are some of these reasons? Why do you think they capture the reader's attention?
2. What is the summary of a love story offered in paragraph 3? Can you think of a few examples?
3. In paragraph 4, Menand claims that most of literature and drama consists of love stories. Can you think of an exception?
4. What are the three categories of love stories? What is the basis for this classification, according to Menand?
5. Who are the ten famous couples mentioned in paragraphs 5, 7, and 8? Use a reference book to look them up if you don't know. A literary dictionary or reader's encyclopedia will serve the purpose.
6. In paragraph 8, Menand contrasts "two statuesque godlings" with "two ordinary, slightly mismatched characters." The examples come from *When Harry Met Sally* and *The English Patient*. Which is an example of which?

7. Menand asserts that when "the lessons learned from love stories do enter into real life, the results are usually disastrous" (para. 9). What does he mean by this? Have you ever seen anyone try out, in real life, tactics they learned from movies?

8. Do you agree that we have an "instinctive fascination" with love (para. 10)?

9. This essay concerns three types of love stories. Could you also say that it concerns the relation of fiction to reality? Defend this broader theme.

CONSIDERING METHOD

1. How many examples does Menand use within his classification essay? What purpose do they serve?

2. Notice the presence of balanced images and phrases throughout the essay:

   about their romantic misery . . . about romantic bliss (para. 2)

   What people flee from . . . they flock to (para. 3)

   not force-of-nature stories . . . force-of-circumstance stories (para. 7)

   These often serve to emphasize either a strong similarity or a striking contrast. Find three more examples of balanced phrasing in the essay.

3. Find three **analogies**—that is, comparisons that serve to explain—in paragraph 6. Elaborate on why these analogies help the reader understand the nature of category-one lovers.

4. In what paragraph does Menand introduce the classification topic? What are the advantages and disadvantages of delayed placement of the categorization?

5. The love story is ". . . a form that has a beginning, a middle, and, unlike certain phone calls, an end" (para. 10). What phone calls does the writer refer to? What statement early in the essay is reflected here at the end?

6. Where did Menand's essay originally appear? What type of audience was he writing for? If he had been writing the same essay for your college class, what might he have done differently?

WRITING STEP BY STEP

As you were reading Menand's essay, you may have thought to yourself, "That's not the way I'd classify love stories at all!" Here you will have a chance to write an essay categorizing love stories your own way, or categorizing some other literary or popular art form you know well: horror films, child-and-pet stories, modern poetry, pop song lyrics, buddy movies, science fiction novels, TV reality shows, organ music, 1970s rock groups.

A. Start by brainstorming: on a plain piece of paper, jot down titles, names, quotations from the form you have chosen. These will help you solidify your basis for categorization and give you a pool of examples to use.

B. Think of three or four categories without very much overlap. Give each category a descriptive name.

C. Reread Menand's opening paragraphs. Write an opening for your own essay in which you describe a misconception many people hold about your topic. Explain why they are wrong.

D. Reread Menand's paragraph 4. Introduce your own categories by identifying the basis of your classification (for example, "the lovability index") and then naming and briefly summarizing your categories.

E. Write one or two paragraphs expanding on each category. Use your brainstorming sheet to find examples. Unlike Menand, you will probably need to explain your examples. Remember that your reader may not immediately see the difference between *The Amityville Horror* and *Halloween IV* by title alone.

F. Go back over your paragraphs and try to revise in order to include balanced images and phrases to emphasize similarities or contrasts (see Considering Method, item 2).

G. Reread Menand's paragraphs 9 and 10. Write a closing that speculates about the overall purpose of your genre. If possible, let the final line reflect some image or phrase from earlier in the essay.

OTHER WRITING IDEAS

1. In paragraph 2, Menand writes, "The lover himself has a tendency to ignore the ordinary limits of the human faculty for paying attention." What other kinds of people stretch the limits of others' attention, and why? Classify some types of bores.

2. One focus of Menand's essay concerns the difference between art and reality: love stories are not like real love. Write about another topic whose fictional representation is not like the real thing—for example, war, family, parenthood, the teenage years, or a certain career.

3. Is it the purpose of love stories to teach us how to be lovers? If it were, what kind of lessons would we learn? Classify three or four different types of lessons—about the relations between the sexes, about how to deal with conflict, about what makes a person lovable, or other topics. Use examples from love stories you know.

EDITING SKILLS: USING APOSTROPHES

Using apostrophes makes most writers at least a bit nervous. To get a grip on this slippery punctuation mark, think about these basic rules:

1. Use an apostrophe to indicate that two words have been pushed together to form a contraction. Put the apostrophe where you leave the letters out.

would not = wouldn't	is not = isn't
you are = you're	he is = he's
they will = they'll	we have = we've

2. Use an apostrophe plus *s* with singular nouns to show possession.

   the heat of the sun = the sun's heat

   the rent for one year = one year's rent

   the wig belonging to Judy = Judy's wig

   cards from UNICEF = UNICEF's cards

3. Use an apostrophe after the *s* with plurals to make them possessive.

   papers from three students = three students' papers

   alibis of four criminals = four criminals' alibis

   If the plural does not already end in *s,* add an *s* after the apostrophe.

   games for children = children's games

   poetry by men = men's poetry

EXERCISE

In the Menand essay, there are ten separate words that use apostrophes. Copy the ten words exactly. Don't count repeats. Next to each one, write whether the apostrophe makes the word a contraction or a possessive.

Now return to your classification essay, and make sure that you have used apostrophes correctly.

WEB SITES

www.bartleby.com

Search Brewer's Phrase and Fable to look up literary references like the ones Menand uses.

www.eharlequin.com/harle/books/alcove

Discover the writer's guidelines, author videos, and other behind-the-scenes information about the country's most popular contemporary love stories, Harlequin Romances.

Student Essay Using Division and Classification

Stats on *ER*

Megan Quick

Have you ever wondered why people watch the television shows they do? I decided to find out why people watch the popular weekly television show *ER*. *ER* is a television series that tries to portray a real-life emergency room as well as the personal lives of the doctors and staff. The show is set in Chicago, a city full of action, accidents, and drama, so the emergency room is always busy. People of all ages watch this show, including me. What draws us to the television set every Thursday night at 9:00 P.M.? Some people are so obsessive about not missing one episode that all other activities cease while *ER* is on. In my search for answers, I discovered people have many different reasons for watching *ER*.

I interviewed fourteen people, ranging in age from seventeen to forty-eight. I asked them questions such as, "How often do you watch *ER* and why do you watch it?" I also asked them if they thought the show was true to life. For comparison, I asked if they had seen the live episode of *ER*. So much publicity and hype were put into that episode that I wondered how they compared it to the regular episodes of *ER*. I wanted to know why they thought the show is popular. Finally, I asked them to rate the acting abilities of the actors on *ER*.

Most of the people I interviewed watch *ER* as often as they can, but Courtney, who is twenty years old, is fanatical about seeing the show every week. She's the one extremist in the group. If a patient dies, she cries. I asked her, "How did you react when Dr. Green [a doctor on the show] was beat up by gang members?" "I bawled and bawled," she replied. My best friend, Amanda, said her main reason for watching *ER* is that "George Clooney is cute!" But on a more intellectual note she said, "The show has to be true to life. Everything the actors say has to be what doctors in real life would really say. Or, obviously, the viewers of the show, especially doctors, would know whether the information and terminology was correct or not. If it wasn't, the show would be discredited." A male friend of mine, age nineteen, has similar views. He watches *ER* "because of the drama and simulated real-life events. What they're performing is factual for the most part." He informed me that *ER* has "real doctors on the set to make sure [the actors] are behaving like real-life doctors and nurses. It's almost like a real emergency room." I asked him how he knew this information, and he said, "From watching a show about the production of *ER*."

Continuing on my quest for answers, I interviewed my mother, age forty-eight. She likes it that things happen on *ER* that actually happen in real life: "It's not like a soap opera where the stories are far-fetched." When I asked her how she liked the live show, she said, "It drove me nuts. It was like a bad video." She went on to explain how the camera bounced around from scene to scene, almost making her dizzy. I got the point. However, Angie Mulligan, a twenty-two-year-old senior who watches *ER* because she's fascinated with medicine, liked the live *ER*. She "got to see how the actors perform before everything is perfected." Shelby Bivens, a college sophomore, provided me with a totally different reason for watching *ER*. In high school she wanted to be involved in the conversations around her, so she watched *ER* because that was all anyone talked about. Also, watching *ER* makes her feel smart. She knows what's going on because of what she learned in advanced biology.

One of my good friends, Nathan, has views very similar to mine. When I asked him why he watches *ER*, he replied, "I watch it because I like the intensity, realism, and the acting. Not only does it provide entertainment but also substance." These would be my reasons for watching *ER*. The actors often make jokes and humorous remarks, providing laughter in the face of adversity. It's also interesting to observe how

people react in the most critical situations. Will
the doctors buckle under pressure? Will the patients
be hysterical and threatening? The answers are never
certain. The show is not fake or far-fetched. *ER* has
substance in its plot, intensity in its scenes, and
excellence in its acting. To say the least, I am
never bored while watching *ER*.

   All the people I interviewed said everyone should 6
watch *ER* at least once, and I agree. It's a show all
its own; no other program tries to portray an
emergency room. If you have never seen *ER*, try
watching the show one time. Watch out, though--you
may get hooked.

Chapter 7

STRATEGIES FOR EXAMINING TWO SUBJECTS

Comparison and Contrast

Every day we use **comparison-and-contrast** thinking to make decisions in our personal lives. Should I wear the pink shirt or the teal? Should I take my lunch to work or eat out? Will it be Taco Bell or McDonald's? Should I write a check or use my credit card? Often the factors influencing an everyday decision are weighed so quickly in our minds that we may not be aware of having examined both sides. But when faced with a major decision, we think longer and may even make a list of pros and cons: "Reasons for Getting a New Car" on the left side of the sheet; "Reasons for Keeping Old Blue" on the right side. Intelligent decision making helps keep our lives from lapsing into chaos. Comparing and contrasting serve as useful tools in the struggle.

THE POINT OF COMPARISON AND CONTRAST

Technically, we *compare* things that are similar and *contrast* things that are different. But in order to contrast things, we have to compare them. And a comparison will often point out the differences of items being compared. You can see how fuzzy the distinction gets, so don't worry about it.

Using Comparisons to Explain

Using comparisons is a dandy writing strategy for explaining something your readers don't know much about by comparing it to something they do know about. For instance, geologists like to explain the levels in the earth's crust by comparing them to the layers in an onion. Or if you want to explain something complicated, like the way our eyes work, you could compare the human eye to a camera, which is simpler and more easily understood.

Using Comparisons to Persuade

Comparisons can be an effective technique in persuasive writing to help clarify and convince. People who believe that illegal drugs should be decriminalized often compare the current drug-related gang warfare to the alcohol-related crime wave during prohibition in the 1930s. When alcohol was made legal again, the gangsters were out of business and the violence subsided. The same thing would happen today, the argument goes, if drugs were legalized. Such a comparison, called an **analogy,** can be quite convincing if you can think of one that is sensible and clearly parallel.

Using Contrast to Decide

You can set up a contrast to help clarify differences—if, for instance, you are faced with a choice between products or people or pets or proposals (or whatever). You might want to make this investigation for your own benefit or to convince someone else that one thing is preferable to another. Say your boss asks you to find out which photocopying machine would be the best buy for the office. Because the machines are all fairly similar, your report would focus on the differences in order to determine which one would give the best results for the least money. Or if you are trying to determine whether to borrow money or get a part-time job to help pay next year's tuition, you should consider carefully the advantages and disadvantages of each choice.

THE PRINCIPLES OF COMPARISON AND CONTRAST

Since the purpose of comparing and contrasting is to show similarities or differences, good organization is crucial to success. There are two standard ways of composing this kind of writing: the **block pattern** and the **point-by-point pattern.** These patterns can, of course, be expanded to include consideration of more than two elements.

Using the Block Plan

Particularly useful for responding to comparison or contrast essay examination topics is this simple method of organization:

1. State your purpose.
2. Present key features of the first part of your comparison.

3. Make a transition.
4. Present corresponding features of the second part of your comparison.
5. Draw your conclusions.

This simple plan serves perfectly for showing how something has changed or developed: your earliest views about AIDS compared to the way you think now; Madonna's first album compared to her latest one; Picasso's early work compared to his later paintings; hairstyles ten years ago compared with hairstyles today. You will see how effectively this plan works when you read the first three essays in this chapter.

Using the Point-by-Point Plan

When you have time to carefully organize your ideas, you may want to present the material in a way that highlights individual differences. In other words, you choose the points of comparison that best illustrate the similarities or differences and organize the material to contrast those features. If you want to discuss the differences between married life without children and married life with children, you would think of several important ways that parenthood alters lifestyle. You might come up with an outline something like this:

1. Intro.—having kids makes for major life changes
2. Sleep and lack of
    a. Before kids
    b. After kids
3. Household chores
    a. Before kids
    b. After kids
4. Expenses, present and future
    a. Before kids
    b. After kids
5. Leisure-time activities
    a. Before kids
    b. After kids
6. Romance in the marriage
    a. Before kids
    b. After kids
7. Conclusion—parenthood involves sacrifices as well as joys

You could use exactly the same material in writing a block-style essay as you would with this point-by-point pattern. The differences lie in the way you arrange your material.

THE PITFALLS OF COMPARISON AND CONTRAST

If you are following a block pattern, be sure to follow the same order in making your comparison. If you are writing about the differences between waterbeds and airbeds, you could start by explaining the main features of the waterbed—something like this:

1. fill it with a hose
2. adjusting for comfort tricky
3. needs a heater
4. heavy when full of water
5. reasonable in cost

Then, after switching to your discussion of airbeds, take up the same features in the same order:

1. inflate it with a button
2. adjusting for comfort easy
3. no need for a heater
4. light when full of air
5. expensive to buy

Keep the same order in your point-by-point organization, too. After grouping all of the preceding information under headings something like these,

1. comfort
2. convenience
3. cost

be careful to discuss first waterbeds, then airbeds; waterbeds, then airbeds; waterbeds, then airbeds—in presenting the material in each category. As you read Mark Twain's "Two Views of the Mississippi," notice that in his second viewing, he describes the same details in the same order as he did in his first.

Avoid Using Too Many Transitional Words

True, comparison-and-contrast writing involves making lots of transitions, but you won't necessarily need to signal each one with a transitional word. In the block pattern, you will need an obvious transition to let your readers know that you're going to shift to the second item or idea. You'll write a sentence such as, "Airbeds, *on the other hand,* are an excellent buy for several reasons," or "*On the contrary,* waterbeds can sometimes prove troublesome to maintain."

But when you follow the point-by-point pattern, you will probably not want to signal every shift back and forth with a transitional term. (Did you notice that the term *but* in the previous sentence provided a transition between paragraphs?) With the point-by-point method of organization, you will be making contrasts under each point. If you try to signal each one, your prose may get clunky. Once you have established the shifts back and forth, let your readers be guided by the pattern—and stick to it.

Avoid Repetition in Concluding

In a brief comparison or contrast essay, you need not summarize all your points at the end. Your readers can remember what you've said. Instead, draw a meaningful conclusion about the material. Maybe you'll want to assert that two apparently different religions are basically the same. Or, you might stress that the differences are so crucial that conflict will always exist. If you are comparing products, come out in favor of one over the other— or else declare that neither amounts to a hill of beans—or perhaps invite your readers to judge for themselves. Just be sure to make a point of some sort at the end.

WHAT TO LOOK FOR IN COMPARISON AND CONTRAST

As you study the essays in this chapter, pay particular attention to the organization and the *continuity*—what makes it flow.

1. Look for a pattern (or maybe a combination of patterns) that each writer uses in presenting the material. Decide whether you think the method of organization is effective or whether there might be a better way.
2. Underline the transitional terms (such as *on the other hand, but, still, yet, on the contrary, nevertheless, however, contrary to, conversely, consequently, then, in other words, therefore, hence, thus, granted that, after all*). Notice what sort of links are provided between paragraphs when no purely transitional terms appear.
3. Look at the introductions and conclusions to see what strategies are used to set up the comparison or contrast at the beginning and to reinforce the writer's point at the end.

©King Features Syndicate. Reprinted with special permission of King Features Syndicate.

What contrast is presented in this cartoon?

Do you agree with the way the cartoon depicts women and men? Why or why not?

Why is the cartoon called "chromosome planets"? What does the name imply about the behavior that's illustrated?

PREPARING TO READ

Do you think it's possible for two people to look at the same thing and see it quite differently? Consider how a loving owner might view an overweight, bowlegged dog and how a neighbor might view the same animal. Can you think of other examples?

Two Views of the Mississippi

M ARK T WAIN

Before becoming Mark Twain, America's most beloved humorist, Samuel Clemens (1830–1910) was a riverboat pilot, a journalist, and an unsuccessful gold miner. He said late in his life that those days on the river were the happiest he ever spent. In *Life on the Mississippi,* he explains in detail how he became a pilot—how he learned to "read" the river. In the following slightly edited passage, Twain tells of one drawback to that otherwise rewarding experience.

TERMS TO RECOGNIZE

trifling *(para. 1)*	small, a tiny detail
acquisition *(para. 1)*	something gained or acquired
solitary *(para. 2)*	all alone
conspicuous *(para. 2)*	obvious
opal *(para. 2)*	a gemstone showing many shades of pink, blue, lavender, and gold
radiating *(para. 2)*	spreading
somber *(para. 2)*	dark
unobstructed *(para. 2)*	not hidden or blocked to view
rapture *(para. 3)*	joy, delight
wrought *(para. 3)*	brought about, caused
bluff reef *(para. 3)*	steep ridge of sand just beneath the surface of the water
shoaling *(para. 3)*	building up mud and sand
compassing *(para. 4)*	guiding (as with a compass)

ow when I had mastered the language of this water, and had come to   1
know every trifling feature that bordered the great river as familiarly as I knew the letters of the alphabet, I had made a valuable acquisition. But

I had lost something, too. I had lost something which could never be restored to me while I lived. All the grace, the beauty, the poetry had gone out of the majestic river!

I still keep in mind a certain wonderful sunset which I witnessed when   2 steamboating was new to me. A broad expanse of the river was turned to blood; in the middle distance the red hue brightened into gold, through which a solitary log came floating black and conspicuous; in one place a long, slanting mark lay sparkling upon the water; in another the surface was broken by boiling, tumbling rings, that were as many-tinted as an opal; where the ruddy flush was faintest was a smooth spot that was covered with graceful circles and radiating lines, ever so delicately traced; the shore on our left was densely wooded, and the somber shadow that fell from this forest was broken in one place by a long, ruffled trail that shone like silver; and high above the forest wall a clean-stemmed dead tree waved a single leafy bough that glowed like a flame in the unobstructed splendor that was flowing in the sun. There were graceful curves, reflected images, woody heights, soft distances; and over the whole scene, far and near, the dissolving lights drifted steadily, enriching it every passing moment with new marvels of coloring.

I stood like one bewitched. I drank it in, in a speechless rapture. The   3 world was new to me, and I had never seen anything like this at home. But as I have said, a day came when I began to cease from noting the glories and charms which the moon and sun and the twilight wrought upon the river's face; another day came when I ceased altogether to note them. Then, if that sunset scene had been repeated, I should have looked upon it without rapture, and should have commented upon it, inwardly, after this fashion: "This sun means that we are going to have wind to-morrow; that floating log means that the river is rising, small thanks to it; that slanting mark on the water refers to a bluff reef which is going to kill somebody's steamboat one of these nights, if it keeps on stretching out like that; those tumbling 'boils' show a dissolving bar and a changing channel there; the lines and circles in the slick water over yonder are a warning that that troublesome place is shoaling up dangerously; that silver streak in the shadow of the forest is the 'break' from a new snag, and he has located himself in the very best place he could have found to fish for steamboats; that tall dead tree, with a single living branch, is not going to last long, and then how is a body ever going to get through this blind place at night without the friendly old landmark?"

No, the romance and beauty were all gone from the river. All the value   4 any feature of it had for me now was the amount of usefulness it could furnish toward compassing the safe piloting of a steamboat.

RESPONDING TO READING

Do you agree with Twain that gaining knowledge can take some of the "romance" out of life? Have you ever had a similar experience—perhaps learning something that robbed you of a childish illusion or learning something that caused you to question your former understanding of history? If you have, tell briefly in your journal how the change occurred.

GAINING WORD POWER

Twain says the sunset put him in a state of "speechless rapture." The **suffix** -*less* means "without," "lacking," or "not able to." So, speechless means "without speech" or "unable to speak."

For the following list of words, write out brief definitions that show what the **root** word means with the suffix added. If you don't know the meaning of the root word, look it up in your trusty dictionary.

1. clueless
2. ruthless
3. mirthless
4. dauntless
5. meaningless
6. peerless

Now, use each word in a sentence that conveys the meaning—something beyond "I am clueless" or "She is clueless" or "Clyde is clueless."

CONSIDERING CONTENT

1. What two modes of writing does Twain use in this selection?
2. In the opening sentence, what does he mean by the "language" of the river?
3. What did he lose by learning to be a riverboat pilot? What did he gain?
4. What contrast does he present in paragraphs 2 and 3?
5. At the beginning of his description in the second paragraph, he says, "A broad expanse of the river was turned to blood. . . ." What does that mean? Do you know what that figure of speech is called?
6. Can you find a **thesis** statement? If so, where?

CONSIDERING METHOD

1. Point out two **similes** (comparisons using *like* or *as*) in paragraph 2.
2. The second sentence in paragraph 2 is extremely long. Reread this complicated sentence and carefully decide where you would put in periods to create several shorter sentences.
3. What major transitions does Twain use—first in setting up the contrast, then in shifting from the before to the after?

4. In paragraph 3, Twain personifies the river—that is, he gives it human characteristics. Point out three examples of this technique of **personification.** Why do you think he used this figure of speech?
5. Does the contrast follow a point-by-point or a block pattern of organization? Make a brief outline of the way the comparison is arranged.

WRITING STEP BY STEP

Many times we feel nostalgic (warm and sentimental) about the past— about favorite former recording groups, TV programs, friends, cars, houses, articles of clothing, and so forth. Get together with several friends or classmates and talk about what you liked best in "the good old days." Take notes when meaningful memories from your past come to mind.

Choose something long gone that you still feel a fondness for—something now replaced by something newer, but not necessarily better. Then, using a block pattern, write an essay contrasting your lost prize with today's version.

A. Begin by letting your readers know that you have a fine, new whatever—fancy bicycle, designer jeans, sports car, neighborhood bakery, favorite restaurant, TV series, or rock group—but that the new version can't measure up to what you enjoyed before.
B. Then, describe your former favorite. Use plenty of precise descriptive details, as Mark Twain does in his opening paragraph. Show your reader what makes you feel the way you do about this treasure from the past.
C. Next, make a transition similar to Twain's: "But as I have said, . . ." Or write your own: "Then, after old Shep died, I bought an unbelievably dumb purebred Russian wolfhound," or "Finally, I sent my faithful Ford to the junkyard and spent a fortune on a classic MG that gives me nothing but trouble."
D. Now describe your replacement, focusing on its shortcomings—the many ways in which it doesn't measure up to the one you loved. Follow the same order here in presenting the failings that you followed in describing the virtues. (Notice that Twain uses exactly the same order in telling the two ways he saw the river. In his third paragraph, he begins with the sunset, then mentions the log, then the slanting mark on the water, then the "tumbling 'boils,'" then the lines and circles, then the streak in the shadow, and finally the dead tree—just as he did in his second paragraph.)
E. In your final paragraph, express again the sorrow you feel at having to make do with this unsatisfactory replacement and your longing to have the old something back.

OTHER WRITING IDEAS

1. Write an essay following the preceding step-by-step instructions, but choose instead a thing that you replaced with something new that you think is a great deal better.

2. People of different ages sometimes see things differently. Write about an attitude (toward work, religion, education, sports, television, the law, and so forth) that you think is different for people who are older or younger than you are. If you can, interview your peers as well as people from the other generation to see if your understanding of this difference is accurate.

3. Using a block-type organization, first describe a place you knew as a child. Then describe how the place looks to you as an adult. In your conclusion, discuss whether the changes are real or only in your way of seeing.

EDITING SKILLS: QUOTATION MARKS INSIDE QUOTATIONS

Once in a while, when you have enclosed conversation or quoted material in quotation marks, you may need quotation marks around a word or phrase within the passage. You can't use regular quotation marks inside quotation marks because your reader would never be able to tell what ended where. So inside regular double quotation marks, you use single quotation marks around any words that also need quotation marks.

Notice that in his third paragraph, Twain puts a passage in quotation marks because, as he describes his second way of looking at the river, he is giving us a "conversation" with himself. Within that pretended speech, the word "boils" also needs quotation marks because it has an unusual meaning (as did the word "conversation" in the previous sentence). So, he puts "boils" in single quotation marks because it is already inside double marks. Here is another example:

Mr. Blackwell observed, "Baggy clothes are definitely 'in' this season."

On your keyboard, you may have an opening single quotation mark. Check the keys beside the numbers at the top. The closing mark is one you use all the time: the apostrophe. It will also serve as the left-hand quotation mark if you don't have a special key.

Here are some other uses of quotation marks that sometimes end up with single marks inside double ones:

1. To enclose words used as words:

    It's all right to begin a sentence with "and" as long as you don't do it too often.

    (You can use italics or underlining to indicate words used as words, if you prefer.)
2. To enclose titles of short works—short stories, poems, essays, chapters of books, or song titles, for example:

    Edgar Allan Poe's story "The Pit and the Pendulum"

    Robert Frost's poem "The Road Not Taken"

    Richard Selzer's essay "The Discus Thrower"

    Bob Dylan's song "Mr. Tambourine Man"

    But underline or put in italics the titles of longer, separately published works:

    Alice Walker's novel <u>The Color Purple</u>

    Arthur Miller's play <u>Death of a Salesman</u>

    Steven Spielberg's movie <u>Jurassic Park</u>

    Georges Bizet's opera <u>Carmen</u>
3. To enclose quoted material within a quotation:

    "What did your instructor do when you didn't turn in your term paper?"

    "I went into her office with my paper in my hand, and she said, 'I hope you just got out of the hospital; otherwise, you just failed the course.'"

EXERCISE

In the following sentences, insert double quotation marks and single quotation marks where needed. You may use italics in some cases if you prefer.

1. Proofread carefully to be sure you have not confused its and it's.
2. Reggie said to me, You be there on time or I'm leaving without you, Squirt.
3. Then I said to Reggie, You call me Squirt again and I'm not going anywhere with you ever again!
4. Serena wrote an analysis of Sandra Cisneros's short story Woman Hollering Creek.
5. I liked this poem, Kesha observed, but when Frost says The woods are lovely, dark, and deep, what does deep mean?

Now go through your writing for this class (your essays and your jour-nal entries), and see whether you've been using quotation marks correctly. Then make up a sentence of your own using single quotation marks inside double quotation marks.

☙ WEB SITE

www.greatriver.com/

The Mississippi River Home Page provides information about riverboats and an interview with a modern riverboat pilot.

PREPARING TO READ

Are you the kind of person who gets fidgety if the socks aren't tidily arranged by color in your drawer? Or are you a casual type who seldom manages to get the socks from the laundry basket into the drawer? Have you tried to change? Or do you not feel any need to?

Neat People vs. Sloppy People

SUZANNE BRITT

Suzanne Britt is a freelance journalist who teaches English at Meredith College in Raleigh, North Carolina. She has written for the *New York Times,* the *Baltimore Sun,* and *Newsday.* In her collection of witty essays *Skinny People Are Dull and Crunchy like Carrots* (1982), Britt clearly favors fat folks. In the following essay, which comes from her book *Show and Tell* (1983), she sides solidly with slobs, demonstrating that taking an unusual stand—even a not very reasonable stand—can be an effective strategy for humorous writing.

TERMS TO RECOGNIZE

vs. *(title)*	abbreviation of *versus,* meaning in contrast with or against
rectitude *(para. 2)*	uprightness, correctness
metier *(para. 3)*	a person's area of strength or expertise
excavation *(para. 5)*	digging out, uncovering and removing
meticulously *(para. 5)*	giving great attention to details
scrupulously *(para. 5)*	carefully doing the right thing
cavalier *(para. 6)*	free and easy
vicious *(para. 9)*	hateful, spiteful
salvaging *(para. 9)*	saving from destruction, rescuing
swath *(para. 12)*	a long strip
organic *(para. 12)*	having to do with living things

1   I've finally figured out the difference between neat people and sloppy people. The distinction is, as always, moral. Neat people are lazier and meaner than sloppy people.

2   Sloppy people, you see, are not really sloppy. Their sloppiness is merely the unfortunate consequence of their extreme moral rectitude. Sloppy

people carry in their mind's eye a heavenly vision, a precise plan, that is so stupendous, so perfect, it can't be achieved in this world or the next.

Sloppy people live in Never-Never Land. Someday is their metier. Someday they are planning to alphabetize all their books and set up home catalogues. Someday they will go through their wardrobes and mark certain items for tentative mending and certain items for passing on to relatives of similar shape and size. Someday sloppy people will make family scrapbooks into which they will put newspaper clippings, postcards, locks of hair, and the dried corsage from their senior prom. Someday they will file everything on the surface of their desks, including the cash receipts from coffee purchases at the snack shop. Someday they will sit down and read all the back issues of *The New Yorker.* 3

For all these noble reasons and more, sloppy people never get neat. They aim too high and wide. They save everything, planning someday to file, order, and straighten out the world. But while these ambitious plans take clearer and clearer shape in their heads, the books spill from the shelves onto the floor, the clothes pile up in the hamper and closet, the family mementos accumulate in every drawer, the surface of the desk is buried under mounds of paper, and the unread magazines threaten to reach the ceiling. 4

Sloppy people can't bear to part with anything. They give loving attention to every detail. When sloppy people say they're going to tackle the surface of the desk, they really mean it. Not a paper will go unturned; not a rubber band will go unboxed. Four hours or two weeks into the excavation, the desk looks exactly the same, primarily because the sloppy person is meticulously creating new piles of papers with new headings and scrupulously stopping to read all the old book catalogues before he throws them away. A neat person would just bulldoze the desk. 5

Neat people are bums and clods at heart. They have cavalier attitudes toward possessions, including family heirlooms. Everything is just another dust-catcher to them. If anything collects dust, it's got to go and that's that. Neat people will toy with the idea of throwing the children out of the house just to cut down the clutter. 6

Neat people don't care about process. They like results. What they want to do is get the whole thing over with so they can sit down and watch the rasslin' on TV. Neat people operate on two unvarying principles: Never handle any item twice, and throw everything away. 7

The only thing messy in a neat person's house is the trash can. The minute something comes to a neat person's hand, he will look at it, try to decide if it has immediate use and, finding none, throw it in the trash. 8

Neat people are especially vicious with mail. They never go through their mail unless they are standing directly over a trash can. If the trash can 9 is beside the mailbox, even better. All ads, catalogues, pleas for charitable contributions, church bulletins, and money-saving coupons go straight into the trash can without being opened. All letters from home, postcards from Europe, bills and paychecks are opened, immediately responded to, then dropped in the trash can. Neat people keep their receipts only for tax purposes. That's it. No sentimental salvaging of birthday cards or the last letter a dying relative ever wrote. Into the trash it goes.

Neat people place neatness above everything, even economics. They are incredibly wasteful. Neat people throw away several toys every time they walk through the den. I knew a neat person once who threw away a perfectly good dish drainer because it had mold on it. The drainer was too much trouble to wash. And neat people sell their furniture when they move. They will sell a La-Z-Boy recliner while you are reclining in it.   10

Neat people are no good to borrow from. Neat people buy everything in expensive little single portions. They get their flour and sugar in two-pound bags. They wouldn't consider clipping a coupon, saving a leftover, reusing plastic non-dairy whipped cream containers, or rinsing off tin foil and draping it over the unmoldy dish drainer. You can never borrow a neat person's newspaper to see what's playing at the movies. Neat people have the paper all wadded up and in the trash by 7:05 A.M.

Neat people cut a clean swath through the organic as well as the inor-   11
ganic world. People, animals, and things are all one to them. They are so insensitive. After they've finished with the pantry, the medicine cabinet, and the attic, they will throw out the red geranium (too many leaves), sell the dog (too many fleas), and send the children off to boarding school (too many scuff marks on the hardwood floors).

RESPONDING TO READING

Do you think that Britt is right in preferring sloppy people? In your journal, make a list of some advantages of being neat; then make a list of some disadvantages of being sloppy.

GAINING WORD POWER

In her last paragraph, Britt writes of the "*organic* as well as the *inorganic* world." You know from the Terms to Recognize that *organic* means "having to do with living things." So what does the same word mean when you add the **prefix** *in-?* That prefix commonly means "no," "not," or "without." Thus, in her sentence, *inorganic* means "not organic"—having to do with things that are *not* living.

This prefix is quite common, partly because it has several different meanings. Besides making a word negative, *in-* often means "in," "into," "within," or "toward," as in a baseball *infield,* an *inboard* motor, or to *instill* values.

Knowing these two meanings of this prefix can help you make sense of new words. For each of the following terms, write out the meaning of the prefix *in-,* followed by the meaning of the **root** word, as in this example using *indefinite:*

in- = not   *definite* = certain, precise, clear

Get help from your dictionary if you need it.

inhale	inhuman	insomnia
injustice	inland	inability
inroad	invisible	indigestion
indirect	inlay	insane

CONSIDERING CONTENT

1. In the first paragraph, what is the moral difference that Britt finds between neat and sloppy people? Is this the difference you would give? Is she serious about this moral difference? How can you tell?
2. Does the essay have a **thesis** statement? If so, where does it appear?
3. What is "Never-Never Land," mentioned at the beginning of paragraph 3? Do you know where the term comes from?
4. What kinds of things does Britt say messy people are always planning to do? Point out her exact details.
5. What faults does she find with neat people? Again, point out details from every paragraph.
6. Is she being fair? If not, can you explain why not?

CONSIDERING METHOD

1. How does Britt let you know in her opening paragraphs that she isn't entirely serious?
2. What pattern of organization does she use in presenting her contrast?
3. What other writing strategies does Britt use in developing her contrast?
4. Can you find a transitional sentence that leads smoothly into the second part of the contrast?
5. Point out several words that Britt uses for humorous exaggeration. Point out several humorous examples.

6. You probably noticed that this essay has no **conclusion.** Would it be more effective if it had one? Try writing a brief concluding sentence and see whether it adds or detracts.

WRITING STEP BY STEP

Get together with a few friends or classmates to discuss various kinds of people who can be classified into types the way Britt does with neat versus sloppy (such as *plump vs. thin, fun-loving vs. serious, perky vs. droopy,* or *exercise nuts vs. couch potatoes*). In this brainstorming session, jot down any details that might be useful to include in an essay comparing the two types you choose. You can make your contrast either humorous or serious. If you decide to be humorous, you will probably also decide to defend the less positive group—praising fat folks instead of thin people, for instance. Or you may decide to make fun of both sides by contrasting two negative types, such as *eggheads vs. airheads.*

A. Begin with a two- or three-sentence introduction letting your readers know that you'll be contrasting two types of people and favoring one group (as Britt puts it, "Neat people are lazier and meaner than sloppy people").

B. Organize your contrast in a block pattern, first discussing the important characteristics of one type, then the same or similar characteristics of the other type.

C. Be sure to include plenty of examples that will show your readers the behavior you're explaining. Take another look at Britt's essay, and notice the kinds of details she uses—how many of them and how specific: not just *a corsage* but *the dried corsage from their senior prom,* not just *a recliner* but a *La-Z-Boy recliner,* not just *the geranium* but *the red geranium.*

D. In the body of your essay, begin every paragraph (as Britt does) with the name of your type—*plump people,* for instance. Vary this system of deliberate repetition once or twice by adding a transition, like the one Britt adds at the start of her fourth paragraph: "*For all these noble reasons and more,* sloppy people never get neat." (Leave out the *noble* part unless you're being funny.) Consider transitions like these:

   —*Besides all these features,* plump people . . .

   —*In addition to these troubles,* plump people . . .

   —*Furthermore,* plump people . . .

   —*As a matter of fact,* plump people . . .

   —*Without question,* plump people . . .

E. When you finish discussing your first type, include a transitional sentence. Britt shifts smoothly from praising sloppy people to criticizing neat ones with this sentence: "A neat person would just bulldoze the desk" (end of para. 5).

If you can't come up with a similar sentence that supplies a bridge from one type to the next, it's just fine to begin the second half of the contrast with a transitional term like one of these:

Thin people, *on the other hand,* . . .

Contrary to popular belief, thin people . . .

Conversely, thin people . . .

Thin people, *however,* . . .

On the contrary, thin people . . .

Yet thin people . . .

By contrast, thin people . . .

F. If you can think of some insight concerning your contrast, offer it as a conclusion. But don't simply tack on something obvious. That's worse than no conclusion at all. Be sure to end your last paragraph with an impressive sentence—either a short, forceful one or a nicely balanced one, like Britt's:

After they've finished with the pantry, the medicine cabinet, and the attic, they will throw out the red geranium (too many leaves), sell the dog (too many fleas), and send the children off to boarding school (too many scuff marks on the hardwood floors).

Work on that final sentence. Make it one you're proud of. Make it one that leaves your readers feeling satisfied.

OTHER WRITING IDEAS

1. Starting with the lists you made in responding to Britt's essay, write one of your own organized like hers (but probably serious) showing how neatness makes life easier and sloppiness leads to problems. Include plenty of details and examples to show the advantages of being tidy and the folly of being a slob.

2. Using the block pattern, contrast two types of players in a sport or game such as basketball, tennis, poker, chess, or a video game. In your conclusion, tell what you think causes the differences between the two types.

3. Get together with some friends or classmates, and discuss major life changes that you and they have experienced. Talk about what your

lives were like before and after the changes occurred. Consider situations such as life before marriage and life after; life before parenthood and life after; life in your folks' home and life in the dorm or your own apartment; life at your previous job and life at your new one.

Then write an essay about one of your life changes, telling first what your life was like before, then how things were after. Focus on one factor of your experience that changed greatly, like the amount of freedom you had or the amount of responsibility.

EDITING SKILLS: USING APOSTROPHES

Apostrophes probably cause more problems than other marks of punctuation. Even experienced writers feel shaky about using them. If you study the following rules about using apostrophes, you should be able to use them more confidently.

1. *Use an apostrophe to indicate that a noun is possessive.* Possessive nouns usually indicate ownership, as in *Miguel's hat* or *the lawyer's briefcase.* But sometimes the ownership is only loosely suggested, as in *the rope's length* or *a week's wages.* If you are not sure whether a noun is possessive, try turning it into an *of* phrase: *the length of the rope, the wages of a week.*

   A. If the noun does not end in *s,* add *'s.*

   > Rita climbed into the driver's seat.

   > The women's lounge is being redecorated.

   B. If the noun is singular and ends in *s,* add *'s.*

   > The boss's car is still in the parking lot.

   > Have you met Lois's sister?

   C. If the noun is plural and ends in *s,* add only an apostrophe.

   > The workers' lockers have been moved.

   > A good doctor always listens to patients' complaints.

2. *Use an apostrophe with contractions.* Contractions are two-word combinations formed by omitting certain letters. The apostrophe goes where the letters are left out, not where the two words are joined.

does not = doesn't	he is or he has = he's
would not = wouldn't	let us = let's
you are = you're	I am = I'm

3. *Do not use an apostrophe to form the plural of a noun.* The letter *s* gets pressed into service in a number of ways; its most common use is

to show that a noun is plural (more than one of whatever the noun names). No apostrophe is needed with a simple plural:

Two *members* of the starting team are suspended for the next three *games* for repeated curfew *violations*.

EXERCISE

1. Examine this sentence from paragraph 11 in Suzanne Britt's essay: "You can never borrow a neat person's newspaper to see what's playing at the movies." Two words in this sentence end in *'s;* one is possessive and one is a contraction. Do you see the difference? Explain how you can tell.
2. Find two other possessive nouns in Britt's essay, and explain what they mean by turning each into an *of* phrase.
3. Find two other contractions that end in *'s* in Britt's essay. What do these contractions stand for?
4. Find six other contractions in Britt's essay, and explain their meaning.
5. Find several examples of plural nouns that end in *s* (without an apostrophe).

Now go back over the essay you have just written, and check your use of apostrophes. Have you left an apostrophe out of a possessive? Have you put an unneeded apostrophe in a plural noun? Have you misplaced any apostrophes in contractions?

🌐 WEB SITE

http://owl.english.purdue.edu/handouts/grammar/g_apost.html
The Purdue University Online Writing Lab's handout on using the apostrophe. You can print it out and use it when writing and editing your papers.

Do you think men have life better than women? Or do women have life better than men? What makes you think so?

Women and Men

S COTT R USSELL S ANDERS

Scott Russell Sanders was born in Memphis, Tennessee, in 1945 and graduated from Brown University. He teaches writing at Indiana University at Bloomington and is the author of several books, including *Staying Put* (1993) and *Hunting for Hope* (1998). In the following passage, taken from his essay collection *The Paradise of Bombs* (1987), Sanders explains his surprise upon reaching college to find women who felt discriminated against. He eventually discovered that living the good life has a lot to do with expectations and social class as well as gender.

TERMS TO RECOGNIZE

grievances *(para. 1)*	resentments; complaints of injustices
fretted *(para. 1)*	worried
baffled *(para. 2)*	puzzled
cornered *(para. 2)*	grabbed more than a fair share of
barrios *(para. 2)*	Hispanic neighborhoods
Third World *(para. 2)*	poor, nonindustrial countries
tedium *(para. 2)*	boredom
ally *(para. 4)*	someone who sides with you in a disagreement

I was slow to understand the deep grievances of women. This was because, as a boy, I had envied them. Before college, the only people I had known who were interested in art or music or literature, the only ones who read books, the only ones who ever seemed to enjoy a sense of ease and grace were the mothers and daughters. Like the menfolk, they fretted about money, they scrimped and made-do. But when the pay stopped coming in, they were not the ones who had failed. Nor did they have to go to war, and that seemed to me a blessed fact. By comparison with the narrow, ironclad days of fathers, there was an expansiveness, I thought, in the days of mothers. They went to see neighbors, to shop in town, to run errands at school, at the library, at church.

No doubt, had I looked harder at their lives, I would have envied them less. It was not my fate to become a woman, so it was easier for me to see the graces. Few of them held jobs outside the home, and those who did filled thankless roles as clerks and waitresses. I didn't see, then, what a prison a house could be, since houses seemed to me brighter, handsomer places than any factory. I did not realize—because such things were never spoken of—how often women suffered from men's bullying. I did learn about the wretchedness of abandoned wives, single mothers, widows; but I also learned about the wretchedness of lone men. Even then I could see how exhausting it was for a mother to cater all day to the needs of young children. But if I had been asked, as a boy, to choose between tending a baby and tending a machine, I think I would have chosen the baby. (Having now tended both, I know I would choose the baby.)

So I was baffled when the women at college accused me and my sex of   2 having cornered the world's pleasures. I think something like my bafflement has been felt by other boys (and by girls as well) who grew up in dirt-poor farm country, in mining country, in black ghettos, in Hispanic barrios, in the shadows of factories, in Third World nations—any place where the fate of men is as grim and bleak as the fate of women. Toilers and warriors. I realize now how ancient these identities are, how deep the tug they exert on men, the undertow of a thousand generations. The miseries I saw, as a boy, in the lives of nearly all men I continue to see in the lives of many— the body-breaking toil, the tedium, the call to be tough, the humiliating powerlessness, the battle for a living and for territory.

When the women I met at college thought about the joys and privi-   3 leges of men, they did not carry in their minds the sort of men I had known in my childhood. They thought of their fathers, who were bankers, physicians, architects, stockbrokers, the big wheels of the big cities. These fathers rode the train to work or drove cars that cost more than any of my childhood houses. They were attended from morning to night by female helpers, wives and nurses and secretaries. They were never laid off, never short of cash at the month's end, never lined up for welfare. The fathers made decisions that mattered. They ran the world.

The daughters of such men wanted to share in this power, this glory. So   4 did I. They yearned for a say over their future, for jobs worthy of their abilities, for the right to live at peace, unmolested, whole. Yes, I thought, yes yes. The difference between me and these daughters was that they saw me, because of my sex, as destined from birth to become like their fathers, and therefore as an enemy to their desires. But I knew better. I wasn't an enemy, in fact or in feeling. I was an ally. If I had known, then, how to tell them so, would they have believed me? Would they now?

RESPONDING TO READING

If you could choose your gender, which would you be—male or female? In your journal, explain the reasons for your choice.

GAINING WORD POWER

Decide whether the italicized words in the following list are used correctly. Then, write *yes* or *no* beside each sentence. After you finish, look back at the Terms to Recognize definitions to check your work.

_____ 1. When the chips were down, my *ally* betrayed me.

_____ 2. At the funeral, the mourners expressed their *grievances* with tears and moaning.

_____ 3. In the late 1970s, a crooked stockbroker *cornered* the silver market.

_____ 4. The police were *baffled* by what seemed to be a clueless crime.

_____ 5. The soccer game was held in the new sports *tedium*.

CONSIDERING CONTENT

1. What were the lives of the men Sanders grew up with like? And the lives of the women?
2. About the women, Sanders admits, "No doubt, had I looked harder at their lives, I would have envied them less." What sort of hardships had he overlooked?
3. Would you rather tend a baby or a machine? How stressful is caring for young children?
4. What other groups besides factory workers does Sanders say suffer lives that are equally grim for men and women?
5. What is being contrasted in this essay besides the roles of women and men?
6. Sanders wonders at the end of his essay whether women would consider him an ally, even though he considers himself on their side. What **details** does he use that show he is sympathetic to their cause?
7. Respond to his final question: would they accept him now?

CONSIDERING METHOD

1. Because this selection is an excerpt from a longer essay, it plunges right into the topic. Did you find it difficult to get interested in the material as a result? Why or why not?

2. How is the comparison between women and men organized? Does the author tell first about women's roles and then about men's? Or does he shift back and forth, point by point?
3. Does he mention any similarities shared by men and women?
4. Does he give equal space to both genders?
5. In the first paragraph, Sanders speaks of "the narrow, ironclad days of fathers." Write out the same idea in your own words. Which version do you like better? Which is clearer?
6. Does he ever state his **thesis?** If so, where? If not, what is the implied thesis—the main idea of the piece?

WRITING STEP BY STEP

Think of a situation, place, object, or person *then* and *now.* Choose something that has changed a lot: wedding receptions years ago and today, your desk before and after cleaning, your clunky typewriter and your smart computer, your childhood tennis shoes and your new athletic shoes, your granny then and now.

Write a comparison focusing mainly on the *now,* but mentioning the *then* occasionally to show the contrast. If you can get your friends to help, brainstorm with them to think of good points you can use in drawing the comparison. You need qualities that fit both *then* and *now,* but think of a lot more details about the *now.*

A. Begin by giving the subject of your comparison in a sentence or two. Don't state it directly but imply it: "I had no idea that wedding receptions were not always elaborate productions until my mom told me about her wedding thirty years ago," or "I was slow to appreciate the benefits of my new computer because it took so much effort to learn to use it. My trusty typewriter was easy by comparison."
B. As you discuss the *now,* remind your readers, whenever you take up a new point, how it was *then.* Use transitional words when you need them: *by comparison, on the other hand, on the contrary, but, still, after all, like, nevertheless, contrary to, however, granted that.*
C. Mention at least one similarity. For instance, while discussing women's behavior, Sanders mentions a trait they share with males: "Like the menfolk, they fretted about money, they scrimped and made-do."
D. In your last paragraph, tell how you feel about the change. Would you rather have the *then* instead of the *now*—or do you find the *now* a great improvement?

E. If you're stuck for an ending, try concluding with a question and then answering it: "If I had known then how much easier my computer would make writing, would I have complained so loudly? Maybe not," or "If I could go back to planning a reception that cost less than $10,000, would I? You bet I would!"

OTHER WRITING IDEAS

1. In a small group, discuss gender stereotypes—the way society expects women and men to behave. From the notes you take, choose three or four categories—such as manner of speaking, walking, dressing, and showing emotion; or typical careers, leisure activities, and taste in movies. Organize your essay using the point-by-point method, first doing the women's role, then the men's (or the reverse). At the end, draw a conclusion about how society treats people who do not conform to these roles and expectations.

2. Think of two possible views on one of these aspects of life: work, family, or sports. Write a paper comparing and contrasting two people who represent the two views.

3. Compare or contrast your mother's or father's life with your own— or the way you want your own life to turn out, once you get it under control.

EDITING SKILLS: USING PARENTHESES

When you want to include an idea that is interesting but not crucial to your discussion, put it in parentheses. Here's an example from the end of Sanders' first paragraph:

> But if I had been asked, as a boy, to choose between tending a baby and tending a machine, I think I would have chosen the baby. (Having now tended both, I know I would choose the baby.)

His statement about preferring baby tending (stereotypically women's work) to machine tending (stereotypically men's work) is quite to the point. But when, in the next sentence, he comments on that statement, the parentheses tell the reader that the remark is added reinforcement of the same idea.

Parentheses are also used in these ways:

1. To enclose brief definitions within a sentence (like the examples in the previous paragraph):

   machine-tending (stereotypically men's work)

   Writers use transitions to improve *continuity* (the flow of their ideas).

Notice that the period goes after the parenthesis at the end of a sentence.

2. To enclose examples and brief explanations (like the one in item 1 and this one you are presently reading).

3. To enclose dates within a sentence:

John Stuart Mill (1806–1873) favored women's equality with men.

EXERCISE

Find five examples of parentheses in this chapter, and explain which of the uses discussed applies to each example.

Then look at the essay you just finished. Is there any material that should be enclosed in parentheses? Consider adding a definition, a date, a comment, or a brief explanation within parentheses that would add to the reader's understanding of your ideas.

WEB SITES

www.kenyonreview.org/interviews/perryzade-sanders.phtml

An interview with Scott Russell Sanders about his childhood and his writing.

www.previewport.com/Home/sanders-newsletter.html

On Sanders's home page you can find biographical information, read an excerpt from one of his most recent books, and sign up to receive his newsletter by e-mail.

PREPARING TO READ

Before looking at the following essay, consider whether you think children are born smart or whether they get smart by studying hard in school. Jot down your thoughts in your journal.

The Trouble with Talent: Are We Born Smart or Do We Get Smart?

KATHY SEAL

A California-based freelance journalist, Kathy Seal frequently writes about children and education in such popular magazines as *Parents* and *Family Circle*. In the essay we reprint here, first published in *Lear's* magazine in July 1993, she examines an attitude that may help to explain why math scores of American children have fallen far behind those of children in Japan.

TERMS TO RECOGNIZE

rote *(para. 4)*	routine, mechanical repetition
efficacy *(para. 12)*	ability to bring about an effect
rampant *(para. 12)*	widespread, out of control
per se *(para. 16)*	in and of itself
mammoth *(para. 19)*	huge
conviction *(para. 19)*	firmly held belief

Jim Stigler was in an awkward position. Fascinated by the fact that Asian   1
students routinely do better than American kids at elementary math, the
UCLA psychologist wanted to test whether persistence might be the key
factor. So he designed and administered an experiment in which he gave
the same insolvable math problem to separate small groups of Japanese and
American children.

Sure enough, most American kids attacked the problem, struggled   2
briefly—then gave up. The Japanese kids, however, worked on and on
and on. Eventually, Stigler stopped the experiment when it began to feel

inhumane: If the Japanese kids were uninterrupted, they seemed willing
to plow on indefinitely.

"The Japanese kids assumed that if they kept working, they'd eventually get 3
it," Stigler recalls. "The Americans thought 'Either you get it or you don't.'"

Stigler's work, detailed in his 1992 book *The Learning Gap,* shatters our 4
stereotypical notion that Asian education relies on rote and drill. In fact,
Japanese and Chinese elementary schoolteachers believe that their chief
task is to stimulate thinking. They tell their students that anyone who thinks
long enough about a problem can move toward its solution.

Stigler concludes that the Asian belief in hard work as the key to success 5
is one reason why Asians outperform us academically. Americans are
persuaded that success in school requires inborn talent. "If you believe that
achievement is mostly caused by ability," Stigler says, "at some fundamental level you don't believe in education. You believe education is sorting
kids, and that kids in some categories can't learn. The Japanese believe *everybody* can master the curriculum if you give them the time."

Stigler and his coauthor, Harold W. Stevenson of the University of 6
Michigan, are among a growing number of educational psychologists who
argue that the American fixation on innate ability causes us to waste the
potential of many of our children. He says that this national focus on the
importance of natural talent is producing kids who give up easily and artful
dodgers who would rather look smart than actually learn something.

Cross-cultural achievement tests show how wide the gap is: In a series 7
of studies spanning a ten-year period, Stigler and Stevenson compared math-
test scores at more than 75 elementary schools in Sendai, Japan; T'aipei,
Taiwan; Beijing, China; Minneapolis; and Chicago. In each study, the scores
of fifth graders in the best-performing American school were lower than the
scores of their counterparts in the worst-performing Asian school. In other
studies, Stigler and Stevenson found significant gaps in reading tests as well.

Respect for hard work pervades Asian culture. Many folk tales make the 8
point that diligence can achieve any goal—for example, the poet Li Po's
story of the woman who grinds a piece of iron into a needle, and Mao Tse-
tung's recounting of an old man who removes a mountain with just a hoe.
The accent on academic effort in Asian countries demonstrates how expectations for children are both higher and more democratic there than in
America. "If learning is gradual and proceeds step by step," says Stigler,
"anyone can gain knowledge."

To illustrate this emphasis, Stigler videotaped a Japanese teacher at work. 9
The first image on screen is that of a young woman standing in front of a
class of fifth graders. She bows quickly. "Today," she says, "we will be studying triangles." The teacher reminds the children that they already know

how to find the area of a rectangle. Then she distributes a quantity of large paper triangles—some equilateral, others right or isosceles—and asks the class to think about "the best way to find the area of a triangle." For the next 14½ minutes, 44 children cut, paste, fold, draw, and talk to each other. Eventually nine kids come to the blackboard and take turns explaining how they have arranged the triangles into shapes for which they can find the areas. Finally, the teacher helps the children to see that all nine solutions boil down to the same formula: a = (b × h) ÷ 2 (the area equals the product of the base multiplied by the height, divided by two).

Stigler says that the snaillike pace of the lesson—52 minutes from start   10 to finish—allows the brighter students enough time to understand the concept in depth, as they think through nine different ways to find the areas of the three kinds of triangles. Meanwhile, slower students—even learning-disabled students—benefit from hearing one concept explained in many different ways. Thus children of varied abilities have the same learning opportunity; and the result is that a large number of Japanese children advance relatively far in math.

Americans, on the other hand, group children by ability throughout   11 their school careers. Assigning students to curricular tracks according to ability is common, but it happens even in schools where formal tracking is not practiced.

So kids always know who the teacher thinks is "very smart, sorta smart,   12 and kinda dumb," says social psychologist Jeff Howard, president of the Effi-cacy Institute, a nonprofit consulting firm in Lexington, Massachusetts, that specializes in education issues. "The idea of genetic intellectual inferiority is rampant in [American] society, especially as applied to African-American kids."

A consequence is that many kids face lower expectations and a watered-   13 down curriculum. "A student who is bright is expected just to 'get it,'" Stigler says. "Duller kids are assumed to lack the necessary ability for ever learning certain material."

Our national mania for positive self-esteem too often leads us to puff up   14 kids' confidence, and we may forget to tell them that genius is 98 percent perspiration. In fact, our reverence for innate intelligence has gone so far that many Americans believe people who work hard in school must lack abil-ity. "Our idealization of a gifted person is someone so smart they don't have to try," says Sandra Graham of UCLA's Graduate School of Education.

Columbia University psychologist Carol Dweck has conducted a fasci-   15 nating series of studies over the past decade documenting the dangers of believing that geniuses are born rather than made. In one study, Dweck and UCLA researcher Valanne Henderson asked 229 seventh graders whether people are "born smart" or "get smart" by working hard. Then they compared the students' sixth and seventh grade achievement scores. The scores of kids with the get-smart beliefs stayed high or improved, and those of the kids subscribing to the born-smart assumption stayed low or declined. Surprisingly, even kids who believed in working hard but who had low confidence in their abilities did very well. And the kids whose scores dropped the most were the born-smart believers with high confidence.

Dweck's conclusion: "If we want our kids to succeed, we should empha-   16
size effort and steer away from praising or blaming intelligence per se."

Psychologist Ellen Leggett, a former student of Dweck's at Harvard, has   17
found that bright girls are more likely than boys to believe that people are born smart. That finding could help to explain why many American girls stop taking high school math and science before boys do.

Seeing intelligence as an inborn trait also turns children into quitters,   18
says Dweck. "Kids who believe you're born smart or not are always worried about their intelligence, so they're afraid to take risks," Dweck explains. "But kids who think you can get smart aren't threatened by a difficult task or by failures, and find it kind of exciting to figure out what went wrong and to keep at it." Or, in Jeff Howard's words, "If I know I'm too stupid to learn, why should I bang my head against the wall trying to learn?"

Getting Americans to give up their worship of natural ability and to   19
replace it with the Asian belief in effort seems a mammoth undertaking. But Dweck maintains that it's possible to train kids to believe in hard work. The key to bringing kids around, says Dweck, is for the adults close to them to talk and act upon a conviction that effort is what counts.

The Efficacy Institute is working on exactly that. The institute's work is   20
based on theories that Howard developed as a doctoral candidate at Harvard, as he investigated why black students weren't performing in school as well as whites and Asians. Using the slogan "Think you can; work hard; get smart," the institute conducts a seminar for teachers that weans them from the born-smart belief system.

"We tell teachers to talk to kids with the presumption that they can all   21
get As in their tests," explains project specialist Kim Taylor. Most kids respond immediately to their teachers' changed expectations, Howard says. As proof, he cites achievement-test scores of 137 third grade students from six Detroit public schools who were enrolled in the Efficacy Institute program during 1989 and 1990. The students' scores rose 2.4 grade levels (from 2.8 to 5.2) in one year, compared with a control group of peers whose scores only went up by less than half a grade level.

Institute trainers now work in approximately 55 school districts, from   22
Baltimore to St. Louis to Sacramento. In five cities, they're working to train every teacher and administrator in the school district.

While current efforts for change are modest, no less a force than the   23
Clinton administration is weaving this new thinking into its education
agenda. During a talk this past spring to the California Teachers Association, U.S. Secretary of Education Richard Riley pledged to work on setting
national standards in education. "These standards," he says, "must be for all
of our young people, regardless of their economic background. We must
convince people that children aren't born smart. They get smart."

RESPONDING TO READING

Did reading the essay change your mind about kids being born smart
or getting smart through hard work? In your journal, explain how you
think the problem or Americans' attitudes on the subject could be changed,
especially if the government or the National Education Association decided
to spend money on the effort.

GAINING WORD POWER

In paragraph 10, Kathy Seal uses the interesting word *snaillike* to
describe the slow pace of the Japanese teacher's math instruction. The
term *-like* is a combining form meaning "resembling or characteristic of."
By adding *-like* to other words (many of them names for animals), you can
produce useful new descriptive terms. You could write, for instance, of a
child's shell-like ear, and your readers would be able to picture the delicate curve of the ear. Notice that you hyphenate *shell-like,* when there are
three *l*s together, but not *snaillike,* when there are only two.

1. Add *-like* to the end of each word listed below.
   war   child   bird   barn   ostrich
   bell   lady   cat   flower   cow
2. Then write a definition that includes the characteristic conveyed
   by that new word: *slow as a snail, curved like a shell.*
3. Finally, write a sentence for each new word that makes use of the
   descriptive characteristic: The *snaillike* traffic on the freeway resulted
   from an accident.

CONSIDERING CONTENT

1. According to researchers, what happened when groups of American kids and groups of Japanese kids were given insolvable math
   problems to work on?

2. How do most Americans think Asian students are taught? According to researchers quoted by Seal, is this impression true?

3. How did the Japanese instructor teach about triangles in the example given in paragraph 9? What are the advantages of this method of teaching?

4. What is the typical American attitude about learning—that kids are born smart or that they get smart by working hard? What is the Japanese attitude?

5. Do you know what Seal means by "our national mania for positive self-esteem" (para. 14)? What problems do researchers think it causes?

6. How is the Efficacy Institute trying to change the American attitude and instead "train kids to believe in hard work" (para. 19)?

CONSIDERING METHOD

1. How does Seal's opening sentence help get you interested in her material?

2. Find two specific examples that help readers understand why the Japanese kids beat the American kids on achievement tests. How helpful are these examples?

3. What other method of providing evidence and explaining ideas does the author use in the second part of her article about Americans' attitudes?

4. Seal employs the block organization for her contrast. Find the sentence in which she makes the transition from explaining how Japanese kids learn to considering how American kids learn. What transitional term does she use?

5. The essay has a brief concluding section following the contrast of the two educational systems. What is the purpose of these final paragraphs (19–22)?

6. The essay concludes with a direct quotation (para. 23). What makes this ending effective?

WRITING STEP BY STEP

Think of an issue on which you and your parents—or you and your spouse—strongly disagree. With your parents, for instance, you might differ in your attitudes toward premarital sex; or they might disapprove of your taste in music, clothing, or hairstyles. With your spouse, you might disagree about household chores, child care, financial matters, or vacation plans. Choose an issue that you feel confident you are right about, but be sure that you are also quite familiar with the evidence for the opposing point of view.

A. Begin your essay by presenting the problem, as Kathy Seal does in her introduction when she states "the fact that Asian students routinely do better than American kids at elementary math" (para. 1).You can start by admitting that you have this heated disagreement in your immediate family about whatever it is.

B. Next explain how your parents or spouse views this matter, just as Seal explains how Japanese schoolchildren are taught math (paras. 2–10). Try to include brief specific examples as Seal does in paragraphs 8 and 9. And be fair. Give as much space to presenting this opposing view as you will give to your own viewpoint in the second part of the essay.

C. Write a transitional sentence similar to the one that Seal uses at the start of paragraph 11: "Americans, on the other hand, group children by ability throughout their school careers."

D. Now, present your side of the issue. Offer plenty of specific examples. The evidence that Seal uses in analyzing the attitudes of Americans about how children learn are mainly quotations from researchers, but these quotations are full of specifics—problems, beliefs, research studies, testing results.

E. If possible, include a final section similar to Seal's paragraphs 20 to 22 in which she tells what the Efficacy Institute is doing to encourage American kids to work harder in school. Try to think of a way of resolving the problem you described in your essay. It's possible that focusing on the opposing viewpoint (as you did in the first part of your essay) may reveal a middle ground. Look for a compromise. If you find a solution that stops short of involving the law and justice system, present it here.

F. If you can think of no way of resolving the problem, conclude by admitting that you and your family will simply have to agree to disagree. But consider the final quotation in Seal's essay. Modeling the deliberate repetition of a word, try to end with two forceful sentences similar to these: "We must convince people that children aren't born smart. They get smart" (para. 23).

OTHER WRITING IDEAS

1. Using a block pattern of organization, write a comparison for your classmates of two sports. At the end, explain which one is easier to play or more fun to watch, and tell why you think so.

2. Contrast two movies that present a decidedly different treatment of similar subject matter, such as *The Green Berets* with *Saving Private Ryan; Titanic* and *A Night to Remember; Scream* and *Psycho; Buffy the Vampire Slayer* and *Dracula; Unforgiven* and *She Wore a Yellow Ribbon.*

3. Compare a novel and the film made from it—*Pride and Prejudice, The Scarlet Letter, The Great Gatsby, The Color Purple, To Kill a Mockingbird, North Dallas Forty, Like Water for Chocolate, The Joy Luck Club, The Bridges of Madison County, Midnight in the Garden of Good and Evil, The Horse Whisperer, Bridget Jones's Diary, Misery, The Rainmaker, Get Shorty, Interview with the Vampire, The Talented Mr. Ripley, The Shipping News.*

EDITING SKILLS: USING DASHES

The dash is a handy mark of punctuation that will give **emphasis** to whatever follows it—as long as you don't use it too often. Notice how the dash works in this sentence from Seal's essay:

Sure enough, most American kids attacked the problem, struggled briefly—then gave up.

Seal could have used a comma after *briefly*, but she chose the dash because readers pay more attention to what follows a dash than to what follows a comma. Using the dash is unusual, unexpected—thus emphatic.

You can also use two dashes to set off a few words in the middle of a sentence if you want to emphasize them, as Seal does here:

Meanwhile, slower students—even learning-disabled students—benefit from hearing one concept explained in many different ways.

Commas would be quite correct there, but dashes give emphasis to the words enclosed.

There's another handy use for the dash—to avoid comma clutter. Look at this sentence from Seal's essay:

Then she distributes a quantity of large paper triangles—some equilateral, others right or isosceles—and asks the class to think about "the best way to find the area of a triangle."

Again, commas would be correct before and after that phrase, but when the group of words set off contains one or more commas, putting dashes around it makes the whole sentence easier to read.

Finally, you can use a dash instead of a colon to introduce an example, as Seal does here:

Many folk tales make the point that diligence can achieve any goal—for example, the poet Li Po's story of . . . and Mao Tse-tung's recounting of. . . .

When typing, use two hyphens to form a dash (--); but if you are writing on a word processor, you may find that it has a separate key for the dash. In either case, don't put a space before or after the dash. And remember not to use dashes too often, or they will lose their good effect.

EXERCISE

Put in a dash or replace a comma with a dash whenever you think it would improve the sentence.

1. My friend Yolanda said she just turned twenty-nine for the third time.
2. It's time I started saving for a Florida vacation, for a cruise to the Bahamas, for a new Lexus, for my retirement.
3. All kinds of spices, even pepper, garlic, and onion, give Eddie indigestion.
4. Madonna's costume, what there was of it, shocked even broad-minded me.
5. Marvin had only one chance and a slim one at that.

Now examine the sentences in the essay you just wrote. Can you improve any of them by inserting dashes? Try to revise at least two of your sentences using dashes.

WEB SITE

http://content.health.msn.com/content/article/1700.51386

Interview: Kathy Seal discusses the latest research on what motivates children to learn.

Student Essay Using Comparison and Contrast

Shopping Online

Dana Webb

Do you ever stand in front of your closet and   1
think you don't have anything to wear? Then you look
outside and see it's snowing and too cold to go out
of the house for a trip to the mall. Maybe you live
an hour from the closest mall and don't have time to
make the trip. You might even hate trying on clothes
in the tiny dressing rooms while being annoyed by the
salesclerks bringing five more shirts in your size
that you don't even like. Whatever the case, there is
an available alternative. With only a computer and a
credit card, you can shop online from your very own
home. Two of my favorite shopping Web sites, Gap.com
and Abercrombie.com, offer fun and easy ways to view
and buy merchandise online, but they're set up
differently and appeal to different kinds of shoppers.

Just as the home says much about the family, the   2
homepage says much about the Web site. Since the
homepage is the first thing you see, it's the key to
whether you're going to continue shopping. The
homepage should tell you what the Web site is all
about but also be interesting enough to draw you in.
Gap definitely has a more user-friendly homepage than
Abercrombie. Gap has all the clothing options clearly
displayed so you can go to the type you're interested
in straight from the homepage. It has links for men,
women, kids, baby, and maternity clothing, making it
easy to find what you're looking for. Abercrombie's
homepage goes more for style and looks. It opens with
just a picture of one of the striking models
Abercrombie is famous for. You click on the model to
start shopping. It also contains links to a number of
other features: Lifestyle, A&FTV, music, info,
ANFMail, and A&Fquarterly. There's only one link to
shopping. Abercrombie's homepage is made to get
viewers involved; Gap's homepage is designed to let
shoppers shop.

You may be hesitant to shop online because you   3
think it's too complicated. Actually, both Web sites
are easy to use. They both list and describe all
types of clothes with pictures. It is easy to find
sizes and colors. The process for finding the type of
clothes you're looking for is similar on both sites:
once you're inside the section you want (such as
men's or women's), you're given a list of types of
clothing, such as pants, sweaters, and so on. If you
click on sweaters, you then see a list of all the
sweaters to look at. On both sites, you can put
everything into a shopping bag, so that all your
purchases are together when you are ready to check
out. Even though the process of shopping is basically
the same for the two Web sites, there are some
important differences.

In order for one Web site to be more successful   4
than another, it has to have something unique. That
is exactly what Abercrombie.com has. It has something
called "the dressing room." Once inside the dressing
room, you can click on pictures to mix and match any
top you want with any bottom article of clothing to
see how they look together. This is an enjoyable way
to shop online, and it helps you decide what you
want. Abercrombie also has a special deal running
during the Christmas season called the Wishlist. You
can make a list of things you would like, and e-mail
this list to a family member or friend--an effective
way to get the word out about Abercrombie.

Gap.com also has some unique links that   5
Abercrombie does not have. The Gap homepage has an
easy return policy, which gives you assurance about
purchasing merchandise online. Gap.com also has links
to Old Navy and Banana Republic on the homepage,
which are under the same line as Gap. These are the
only links Gap.com has other than for shopping.

By contrast, Abercrombie.com has a variety of   6
things to do other than shop. You can apply for an
Abercrombie credit card. You can sign up for an
e-mail account to receive news about the latest
styles; you can also e-mail Abercrombie and tell them

what you think about the Web site. Since the models are such a big draw for Abercrombie, you can, of course, download pictures of models and make them desktop backgrounds and screen savers. There is even information about how to apply to be a model. Abercrombie.com also has media links to MTV.com, ComedyCentral.com, Nintendo.com, and SportsIllustrated.com.

The options available on Abercrombie.com reflect its customer base. Abercrombie is a store with a distinctive style of merchandise marketed for teenagers, so its Web site appeals to the hip, energetic lifestyle of young people. Gap, on the other hand, has clothing for infants, children, teens, mom, and dads. Its Web site appeals to people who want to buy clothes, not party on the Internet. The two Web sites accurately represent the two different stores.

C h a p t e r

STRATEGIES FOR EXPLAINING HOW THINGS WORK

Process and Directions

Listen to our rural relatives explaining how to get to the family reunion: "Just follow the hard road down to where the Snivelys' cow barn used to stand before the fire; then turn off on the gravel track and go a piece until you get to the top of the second big rise after the creek. Look for Rabbithash's old pickup." All eighty-six first cousins find these directions perfectly clear, but anyone from farther away than Clay City is going to have some difficulty getting there before the potato salad goes funny.

THE POINT OF WRITING ABOUT PROCESS AND DIRECTIONS

When you want to include second-cousins-once-removed and even complete strangers in your audience, you will try to write out directions that don't rely on so much in-group information (such as where the Snivelys' barn *used* to be). Communicating directions so that almost anyone can understand them is a difficult task, as you know if you have ever tried to do it. Explaining a process is quite similar: after you've performed a certain job over and over, it's hard to explain to someone else exactly how it's done. And when a child asks, "Where does the rain come from?" most people would rather come up with a cute story than really grapple with the workings of nature.

But sometimes, frequently on the job, you must come up with an orderly, step-by-step explanation of how something is done or how it works. The explanation may be only part of a larger report or essay; for example, proposing a solution to the company's mail problems must include an account of how the current mail system works. This chapter includes models of several types of **process writing.**

THE PRINCIPLES OF PROCESS AND DIRECTIONS

The basic organizing principle behind process and direction writing involves time. You are usually concerned with a series of events, and these events may not float through your mind in the same order they should appear in your written work. Your readers will be frustrated and confused by flashbacks or detours to supply information that you should have covered earlier. Therefore, the scratch outline takes on great importance in this type of writing effort. A blank piece of unlined paper will help you to get started. On this page, you will list the steps, or stages, of the process as you first think of them—only be sure to space the items widely apart. In the spaces, you can add points you forgot the first time through: these can be major steps ("Collect the dog shampoo and old towels before you attempt to collect the dog"), substeps ("Pile up more old towels than you think you will possibly need"), or warnings ("Don't speak to your beast in a tone of panicky sweetness; he'll know you're up to something"). Once you consider your notes complete, read through them while visualizing the process to pinpoint anything you have forgotten.

"How to Wash Your Dog" doesn't represent the only angle you can take on process writing, although it is a useful one. Garrison Keillor's directions on "How to Write a Personal Letter" combine practical and emotional features of the process—not only showing us how to do it but also persuading us that it is worth doing. And Dave Barry's essay begins with introductory material telling how a Japanese audience views American football before launching into his humorous explanation of the rules of the game. In "The Box That Launched a Thousand Ships," James Surowiecki explains the economic advantages of the revolutionary process of shipping merchandise all over the world in trailer trucks on container ships. "How to Make Your Dendrites Grow and Grow" demonstrates another strategy. It starts from a desirable goal—keeping your brain in top shape—and describes several different methods for reaching that goal (rather than presenting a single process). In your future writing projects, all these techniques for explaining a process and giving directions will be useful.

THE PITFALLS OF PROCESS AND DIRECTIONS

The problems you encounter in process writing usually have their roots in understanding your audience. If you look at the issue from your point of view as a reader, you can see what we mean. Recently, for instance, we joined the Internet, the worldwide communications network that lets us send messages over our computer modems. We were assured that the printed directions we received were quite complete. They began, "Once you are connected to the CCSO Terminal, follow these steps to log on." Once we were *what?* To *what?* Obviously, the directions were written for people much more "connected" than we are. You have no doubt had similar experiences; hundreds of cartoons around Christmastime portray frantic parents trying to follow "easy" assembly instructions for their children's toys.

Reviewing Your Process

When you revise your process writing, think about the people who will be reading it. Ask yourself these questions:

1. Have I chosen the best starting point? Think about how much your audience already knows before you decide where to begin describing the process. Don't assume your readers have background knowledge that they may not have.
2. Have I provided enough definitions of terms? See Chapter 5 for help in writing definitions and deciding when they are needed.
3. Have I been specific enough in the details? "Dig a trench" is more specific than "Dig a hole," but how deep should the trench be? How wide? How long?

Addressing Your Audience

Another decision you will need to face in your process writing concerns not only who your audience is but also how you intend to speak to them. In this book, we address you, our readers, as "you." This straightforward, informal voice is desirable in much writing. Sometimes, you can keep the informality yet leave the "you" out, using **imperative** sentences (or commands) such as "Gather the towels before catching the dog," or "Dig a trench two feet wide." You may also choose to describe a **third person** performing or observing the process: "The experienced water colorist works quickly," or "The first feature a palm reader examines is the life line, running from between the thumb and first finger in a curve down to the wrist." However you decide to deal with addressing your audience, you should be careful not to mix these approaches accidentally.

WHAT TO LOOK FOR IN PROCESS AND DIRECTIONS

The readings in this chapter differ greatly in their treatment of topics, even though they have process and directions in common. As you read, consider these questions:

1. What are the differences among the introductions? Can you account for these differences by looking at the purpose of each author?
2. How does each author signal where a new step, stage, or part begins?
3. How does each author address the readers? Is this way of addressing readers suitable?
4. Are there any points at which you would like further details or explanation? Where, what, and why?
5. What strategies other than process and directions appear within these readings—for example, narration, description, or comparison and contrast?

THE FAR SIDE® By GARY LARSON

"Oh, wait! Wait, Cory! ... Add the cereal *first* and *then* the milk!"

Why is this Gary Larson cartoon humorous?

Do you know anyone who follows directions to a humorous degree of exactness? How about someone who does the opposite, or who doesn't bother with directions at all?

What other kinds of humor have you seen or heard concerning giving and following directions?

PREPARING TO READ

Who is the smartest person you know? What makes this individual smart? List some of the activities that person enjoys.

How to Make Your Dendrites Grow and Grow

DANIEL GOLDEN

Daniel Golden writes on a variety of topics for *Life* magazine. The reading we reprint here accompanied an article about research on what keeps people intellectually active into old age. Although people used to believe that mental powers declined naturally in old age, scientists now think that developing and exercising brain cell connections can keep us sharp. Golden suggests several ways to enrich the connections, which are called dendrites.

TERMS TO RECOGNIZE

UCLA *(para. 1)*	University of California at Los Angeles
computational *(para. 1)*	operating like a computer
reserves *(para. 1)*	supplies kept available for future uses
diverting *(para. 2)*	amusing
neuroscientist *(para. 3)*	scientist specializing in study of the brain
spatial *(para. 3)*	having to do with arrangement in space
cognitive *(para. 7)*	relating to mental processes; intellectual
provocative *(para. 8)*	stimulating, interesting
dendrites *(para. 8)*	the branched parts of brain cells that transmit impulses toward the cell body

What can the average person do to strengthen his or her mind? "The   1
important thing is to be actively involved in areas unfamiliar to you," says Arnold Scheibel, head of UCLA's Brain Research Institute. "Anything that's intellectually challenging can probably serve as a kind of stimulus for dendritic growth, which means it adds to the computational reserves in your brain."

So pick something that's diverting, and most important, unfamiliar. A   2
computer programmer might try sculpture; a ballerina might try marine
navigation. Here are some other stimulating suggestions from brain
researchers:

- Do puzzles. "I can't stand crosswords," says neuroscientist Antonio   3
  Damasio of the University of Iowa, "but they're a good idea." Psychologist Sherry Willis of Pennsylvania State University says, "People who
  do jigsaw puzzles show greater spatial ability, which you use when
  you look at a map."
- Try a musical instrument. "As soon as you decide to take up the violin,   4
  your brain has a whole new group of muscle-control problems to
  solve. But that's nothing compared with what the brain has to do
  before the violinist can begin to read notes on a page and correlate
  them with his or her fingers to create tones. This is a remarkable, high-
  level type of activity," says Scheibel.
- Fix something. Learn to reline your car's brakes or repair a shaver,   5
  suggests Zaven Khachaturian, a brain expert at the National Institute
  of Aging. "My basement is full of electronic gadgets, waiting to be
  repaired. The solution is not the important thing. It's the challenge."
- Try the arts. If your verbal skills are good, buy a set of watercolors   6
  and take a course. If your drawing skills are good, start a journal or
  write poetry.
- Dance. "We keep seeing a relationship between physical activity and   7
  cognitive maintenance," says Harvard brain researcher Marilyn Albert.
  "We suspect that moderately strenuous exercise leads to the development of small blood vessels. Blood carries oxygen, and oxygen
  nourishes the brain." But be sure the activity is new and requires
  thinking. Square dancing, ballet or tap is preferable to twisting the
  night away.
- Date provocative people. Better yet, marry one of them. Willis suggests   8
  that the most pleasant and rewarding way to increase your dendrites
  is to "meet and interact with intelligent, interesting people." Try tournament bridge, chess, even sailboat racing.

And remember, researchers agree that it's never too late. Says Scheibel: 9
"All of life should be a learning experience, not just for the trivial reasons
but because by continuing the learning process, we are challenging our
brain and therefore building brain circuitry. Literally. This is the way the
brain operates."

RESPONDING TO READING

Jot down in your journal the activities that you perform on an average weekday and on an average weekend day. Does one type of activity seem to dominate? For example, are you usually doing something verbal or nonverbal? Passive or active? Solitary or social? Artistic or practical? If you had time to add some activity to help your dendrites grow, what would it be?

GAINING WORD POWER

cognitive   dendritic   provocative
computational   spatial

The preceding words are all used as *adjectives* in the reading. That is, they describe or modify other words (nouns) to make their meaning more specific and vivid. Look back through the reading to find the adjective-plus-noun combinations. We have done the first example for you.

cognitive __maintenance__
computational _____
dendritic _____
provocative _____
spatial _____

The adjective *dendritic* obviously comes from the noun *dendrite,* which is also used in the reading. Using your dictionary, find the nouns that are related to these other four adjectives:

adj.: cognitive   noun: _____
adj.: computational   noun: _____
adj.: provocative   noun: _____
adj.: spatial   noun: _____

Now list one other related word, its meaning, and its part of speech for the five adjectives. Use your dictionary for help. For example, *cognitive* is related to the verb *cogitate,* which means "to think about." Both have to do with mental processes. Choose one set of three related words and try using them in three sentences of your own.

CONSIDERING CONTENT

1. Who is the **audience** for this reading—the "you" that the writer addresses? How do you know?

2. Why is it important that activity to strengthen your brain should be unfamiliar?
3. Why are some dances better than others to develop your dendrites?
4. The closing paragraph says that the brain operates by building "circuitry." What does this statement mean? How is developing your brain comparable to strengthening electrical circuits?
5. How could leisure activities help you with work activities?
6. If the experts quoted here are right, what lifestyle would cause a person's brain to deteriorate rather than grow over time?
7. Where in your own home town could you meet "intelligent, interesting people" (para. 8)? What activities other than bridge, chess, or sailboat racing might such people be doing?

CONSIDERING METHOD

1. How does the introductory paragraph catch the reader's interest?
2. Who are the people quoted in this reading? What do they have in common? Why are they quoted directly?
3. Give another example that could be added to the short paragraph "Try the arts" (para. 6).
4. How is each new suggestion introduced? What other ways could they be introduced?
5. What is the **thesis** of the reading? How does the conclusion reinforce the main point?

WRITING STEP BY STEP

You probably have ideas about how friendships are formed, maintained, and preserved. Write an essay called "How to Make Your Friendships Grow and Grow." You will be following the form of "How to Make Your Dendrites Grow and Grow."

A. Start by asking a question that will catch most readers' interests.
B. Give an overall statement that covers most of the specific points of advice you are going to make. What, in general, do you think makes good friendships?
C. Use the informal "you" to communicate directly to your readers.
D. Give five or six specific suggestions. Include specific details or examples to explain each suggestion.
E. Begin each of the five or six specific suggestions with an imperative sentence. Imperative sentences give commands and begin with a verb, like this: "Do puzzles" and "Try the arts." If you want, use a bullet (a symbol, such as a box or a circle) at the beginning of each suggestion.

F. Interview one or two people whom you consider experts at friend-ship. Use direct quotations from your interview to support one or more of your suggestions or to conclude your essay. Or look up some quotations about friends and friendship in a reference book, such as *Bartlett's Familiar Quotations.*

G. Whether or not you use a quotation, write a closing that reinforces your general statement about friendship.

OTHER WRITING IDEAS

1. Take some of the advice in "How to Make Your Dendrites Grow and Grow." Try an unfamiliar activity one day soon, and write notes about it in your journal directly afterward. Write an essay reporting on the experience.
2. Choose an activity that you do, and explain to your readers how they would benefit from doing it, too.
3. Explain a few basic principles of training a dog or a child to behave.
4. Write a humorous essay on "How to Lose Your Dendrite Power." For fun, before you write, you might brainstorm with a small group of classmates for ideas about how to get mentally duller.

EDITING SKILLS: PUNCTUATING QUOTATIONS

Quotations from experts and from your reading will often enhance your writing. Most people find the punctuation of quotations tricky, though. This exercise will help you put the periods, commas, and quotation marks in the right places. (For advice on using single quotation marks inside regular double quotation marks, see pages 185–187.)

EXERCISE

Copy the following statements from "How to Make Your Dendrites Grow and Grow" *exactly:*

Psychologist Sherry Willis of Pennsylvania State University says, "People who do jigsaw puzzles show greater spatial ability, which you use when you look at a map."

"We keep seeing a relationship between physical activity and cognitive maintenance," says Harvard brain researcher Marilyn Albert.

"I can't stand crosswords," says neuroscientist Antonio Damasio of the University of Iowa, "but they're a good idea."

Notice that you can put the tag line (the part that tells who is being quoted) before the quotation, after the quotation, or in the middle of the quotation. Exchange your copies with a classmate and check each other's writing for exact, accurate placement of all the punctuation. Then look at your essay on "How to Make Your Friendships Grow and Grow" to make sure that you have punctuated the quotations correctly.

WEB SITES

www.neurobics.com/

www.mentalagility.com/

These sites contain additional information about techniques and exercises for brain development and health, as well as the latest news about brain research.

PREPARING TO READ

How do you feel when you receive a letter? Does anyone regularly write to you? To whom do you write, and why? Did you ever read letters written long ago?

How to Write a Personal Letter

GARRISON KEILLOR

Garrison Keillor is a famous radio program host. His show, *A Prairie Home Companion,* is especially popular because of Keillor's spoken essays about the Minnesota town of Lake Wobegon, a make-believe place where "all the men are strong, all the women are good-looking, and all the children are above average." Listeners are delighted by the charming quirkiness of Lake Wobegon citizens and their everyday lives. In the essay reprinted here from *We Are Still Married* (1989), Keillor's neighborly style comes through as he gives advice and support to letter writers.

TERMS TO RECOGNIZE

wahoo *(para. 2)*	probably a type of *yahoo,* which is a coarse, crude person
anonymity *(para. 4)*	namelessness, being unknown
obligatory *(para. 6)*	required by custom or etiquette
sensate *(para. 6)*	filled with feelings
sensuous *(para. 8)*	pleasing to the senses
salutation *(para. 10)*	the greeting that opens a letter
declarative *(para. 10)*	making a statement
episode *(para. 13)*	an incident or event, a unit of a longer story
urinary tract *(para. 13)*	the system relating to the kidneys and their function
means *(para. 14)*	mode or process

We shy persons need to write a letter now and then, or else we'll dry   1
up and blow away. It's true. And I speak as one who loves to reach for the phone, dial the number, and talk. The telephone is to shyness what Hawaii is to February; it's a way out of the woods. *And yet:* a letter is better.

Such a sweet gift—a piece of handmade writing, in an envelope that is   2
not a bill, sitting in our friend's path when she trudges home from a long day spent among wahoos and savages, a day our words will help repair.

They don't need to be immortal, just sincere. She can read them twice and again tomorrow: *You're someone I care about, Corinne, and think of often, and every time I do, you make me smile.*

We need to write; otherwise nobody will know who we are. They will   3
have only a vague impression of us as A Nice Person, because, frankly, we don't shine at conversation, we lack the confidence to thrust our faces forward and say, "Hi, I'm Heather Hooten; let me tell you about my week." Mostly we say "Uh-huh" and "Oh really." People smile and look over our shoulder, looking for someone else to meet.

So a shy person sits down and writes a letter. To be known by another   4
person—to meet and talk freely on the page—to be close despite distance. To escape from anonymity and be our own sweet selves and express the music of our souls.

Same thing that moves a giant rock star to sing his heart out in front of   5
123,000 people moves us to take ballpoint in hand and write a few lines to our dear Aunt Eleanor. *We want to be known.* We want her to know that we have fallen in love, that we quit our job, that we're moving to New York, and we want to say a few things that might not get said in casual conversation: *Thank you for what you've meant to me. I am very happy right now.*

The first step in writing letters is to get over the guilt of *not* writing. You   6
don't "owe" anybody a letter. Letters are a gift. The burning shame you feel when you see unanswered mail makes it harder to pick up a pen and makes for a cheerless letter when you finally do. *I feel bad about not writing, but I've been so busy,* etc. Skip this. Few letters are obligatory, and they are *Thanks for the wonderful gift* and *I am terribly sorry to hear about George's death* and *Yes, you're welcome to stay with us next month.* Write these promptly if you want to keep your friends. Don't worry about the others, except love letters, of course. When your true love writes *Dear Light of My Life, Joy of My Heart, O Lovely Pulsating Core of My Sensate Life,* some response is called for.

Some of the best letters are tossed off in a burst of inspiration, so keep   7
your writing stuff in one place where you can sit down for a few minutes and—*Dear Roy, I am in the middle of an essay but thought I'd drop you a line. Hi to your sweetie too*—dash off a note to a pal. Envelopes, stamps, address book, everything in a drawer so you can write fast when the pen is hot.

A blank white 8″ × 11″ sheet can look as big as Montana if the pen's   8
not so hot—try a smaller page and write boldly. Get a pen that makes a sensuous line, get a comfortable typewriter, a friendly word processor—whichever feels easy to the hand.

Sit for a few minutes with the blank sheet of paper in front of you, and   9
meditate on the person you will write to, let your friend come to mind until you can almost see her or him in the room with you. Remember the

last time you saw each other and how your friend looked and what you said and what perhaps was unsaid between you, and when your friend becomes real to you, start to write.

Write the salutation—*Dear* You—and take a deep breath and plunge in. A simple declarative sentence will do, followed by another and another. Tell us what you're doing and tell it like you were talking to us. Don't think about grammar, don't think about style, don't try to write dramatically, just give us your news. Where did you go, who did you see, what did they say, what do you think?   10

If you don't know where to begin, start with the present: *I'm sitting at the kitchen table on a rainy Saturday morning. Everyone is gone and the house is quiet.* Let your simple description of the present moment lead to something else; let the letter drift gently along.   11

The toughest letter to crank out is one that is meant to impress, as we all know from writing job applications; if it's hard work to slip off a letter to a friend, maybe you're trying too hard to be terrific. A letter is only a report to someone who already likes you for reasons other than your brilliance. Take it easy.   12

Don't worry about form. It's not a term paper. When you come to the end of one episode, just start a new paragraph. You can go from a few lines about the sad state of pro football to the fight with your mother to your fond memories of Mexico to your cat's urinary-tract infection to a few thoughts on personal indebtedness and on to the kitchen sink and what's in it. The more you write, the easier it gets, and when you have a True True Friend to write to, a *compadre,* a soul sibling, then it's like driving a car; you just press on the gas.   13

Don't tear up the page and start over when you write a bad line—try to write your way out of it. Make mistakes and plunge on. Let the letter cook along and let yourself be bold. Outrage, confusion, love—whatever is in your mind, let it find a way to the page. Writing is a means of discovery, always, and when you come to the end and write *Yours ever* or *Hugs and Kisses,* you'll know something you didn't when you wrote *Dear Pal.*   14

Probably your friend will put your letter away, and it'll be read again a few years from now—and it will improve with age. And forty years from now, your friend's grandkids will dig it out of the attic and read it, a sweet and precious relic of the ancient Eighties that gives them a sudden clear glimpse of you and her and the world we old-timers knew. You will have then created an object of art. Your simple lines about where you went, who you saw, what they said, will speak to those children, and they will feel in their hearts the humanity of our times.   15

You can't pick up a phone and call the future and tell them about our times. You have to pick up a piece of paper.   16

RESPONDING TO READING

After reading Keillor's essay, are you encouraged to try writing a letter to a friend? Why or why not? Answer these questions in your journal.

GAINING WORD POWER

Add to the following fragments, making them into reasonable sentences. Be sure that your additions show your understanding of the terms from the reading.

1. President Weber began his after-dinner speech with an obligatory
   _____ .
2. To protect her anonymity, the writer _____ .
3. Preparing _____ is more sensuous than
   _____ .
4. Henry sat down and wrote this salutation: _____ .
5. An office memo usually begins with a plain declarative statement, such as "_____ ."

CONSIDERING CONTENT

1. Why are letters preferable to face-to-face communication for shy people? What other reasons might make letters preferable to conversation, according to Keillor?
2. What are some differences between Keillor's advice and other writing instructions or rules you have heard? Why do you think these differences exist?
3. Did you ever have to write a letter or essay "meant to impress" (para. 12)? What was the experience like? How did you feel about the writing you produced?
4. Note two or three spots where Keillor deals with the emotions a letter writer might have. Why is it important to give advice about these?
5. What does Keillor mean by "an object of art" in paragraph 15? What has changed the ordinary letter into art? Do you think this claim makes sense or exaggerates?
6. What about writing letters electronically, using media such as e-mail? Does Keillor's essay have any relevance to electronic letters? Do you think he would see them as similar to or different from postal letters?

CONSIDERING METHOD

1. Make a brief list of Keillor's pieces of advice. What is the reasoning behind the order he uses?

2. Who is the "we" Keillor refers to in the essay? Who is the "you"? What kinds of people might think the essay does not appeal to them?
3. Does this writing strike you as formal or **informal?** Point out words and phrases that influenced your decision. Why do you think Keillor made this choice about level of formality?
4. What are the lines and phrases printed in italics? Can you identify their purpose?

WRITING STEP BY STEP

In the reading, Keillor advocates writing a letter, even when a phone call is possible. Write an essay in which you promote doing something in the old-fashioned way even though new ways are available. For possible inspiration, think about writing by hand rather than on a word processor, baking bread, sewing clothes, building furniture, doing math without a calculator, reading a novel rather than watching the movie, conducting a courtship, or raising children.

A. In the beginning of your essay, suggest one or two reasons the old way might be better than the new way.
B. Use "I," "we," and "you" to refer to yourself, yourself and your readers, and your readers.
C. Use everyday language and familiar examples to get your points across to a wide audience.
D. Explain why some people feel hesitant about doing things the old way.
E. Suggest ways that the reader can overcome this reluctance. Look at paragraphs 6 through 13 for examples of how Keillor does this.
F. Include, if relevant, some "don'ts" to help your reader avoid problems, as Keillor does in paragraphs 10, 13, and 14.
G. In your closing, reinforce your main point by looking at the positive effect(s) the actions you promote could have. You might look into the future, as Keillor does.

OTHER WRITING IDEAS

1. Try writing a letter to a friend, using Keillor's advice if you want. At the same time, take notes about how you go about performing the task. Record the thoughts and feelings that you experience along the way as well as the techniques you use. Write an essay describing the experience of writing the letter. Use direct quotations from the letter in italics to illustrate your points.
2. Keillor asserts that "writing is a means of discovery" (para. 14). What does this mean? Write an essay about a piece of writing you once

did (or tried to do) that led you to an unexpected discovery. The discovery could be about yourself, about the writing process, about the subject matter, about school, about the intended audience, or about a combination of things.

3. The reading emphasizes writing letters as an outlet for shy people. Another form of communication, public speaking, brings out the shy side of almost everyone. Write an essay modeled on Keillor's in which you give emotional and practical advice to a person who reluctantly must make a speech or give a presentation. To develop ideas, you and a group of classmates may want to brainstorm before you each write.

EDITING SKILLS: BUSINESS LETTERS

Although Keillor gives good advice about writing personal letters, you will also be faced with writing business letters—applications for jobs, requests for action or information from people you don't know personally, or explanations of your proposals or ideas to other people in your workplace. Here is a diagram explaining the format of a business letter.

EXERCISE

After studying the form, type a brief letter from Dr. Fisher to Susan Lee telling her that she is sending the requested bibliography and also another list of books that Susan may find interesting.

```
                                                        Your address: Provide your
      7012 E. Front St.                                 own address in case the
      Bloomington, IL 61701-5413                        letter gets separated from
                                                        the envelope. Use
      December 11, 2001                                 letterhead stationery
                                                        instead if you have it.

                                                        Today's date: Your reader
                                                        will know exactly when
  Dr. Gina Fisher                                       you wrote the letter.
  Department of Communications
  Illinois Valley Community College                     Inside address: Give the
  Oglesby, IL 61348                                     address where you are
                                                        sending the letter. If the
                                                        envelope gets ruined in
                                                        the mail, the letter can still
  Dear Dr. Fisher:                                      be delivered.

                                                        Salutation: Use a colon
  I was your student in a                               after the greeting. If you do
  Communications 211 course two years                   not know the exact name of
  ago, and I am writing to ask you a                    the person you are writing
  favor.                                                to, use a title: Dear
                                                        Director of Admissions.
```

The course was extremely interesting for me, and on the basis of some of the readings you assigned, I decided to major in psychology here at Illinois State.

Since taking your course, I have moved twice and have lost the bibliography about helping behavior that you gave us. This list of articles would be helpful to me again in my present courses. If you still have copies of it, I would greatly appreciate your sending me one.

Thank you for your trouble, and thank you, too, for starting me on a rewarding course of study. I am enclosing an SASE for your reply.

Sincerely,

Susan Lee

Ending: Say something positive if at all possible. "Thank you for your attention" is a good all-purpose ending.

SASE: Stands for self-addressed stamped envelope. Enclosing one of these, addressed to yourself with postage already attached, will increase your chance of a quick reply.

Complimentary close: *Sincerely* is fine for almost any case. Save cute closings for personal friends.

Leave four blank lines for your signature.

Type your full name.

WEB SITE

www.webfoot.com/advice/email.top.html

Take a look at this Web site, called A Beginner's Guide to Effective E-mail, and compare the suggestions there with Keillor's.

PREPARING TO READ

Have you ever thought about how your Sony Walkman got from Japan to your local Target store? Did you ever consider that the means of shipping might have something to do with the inexpensive price of a quality product?

The Box That Launched a Thousand Ships

JAMES SUROWIECKI

James Surowiecki has taught at the Carlson School of Management at the University of Minnesota. He writes about business and finance for a number of publications, including *Fortune,* the *Boston Globe, New York* magazine, and *Talk,* as well as online magazines like *Slate* and *Salon.* The following article appeared in December 2000 as one of Surowiecki's regular columns for "The Financial Page" of *The New Yorker.*

TERMS TO RECOGNIZE

plummeted *(para. 3)*	dropped straight down, plunged
landlubbing *(para. 4)*	inexperienced at sea, comfortable on land
meticulously *(para. 5)*	extremely careful about details
choreographed *(para. 5)*	planned and coordinated the movements of, like a dance
gargantuan *(para. 5)*	of immense size, huge

the heart of the global economy is a rectangular metal box, forty feet long, eight feet wide, and eight and a half feet tall. It's called a freight container, and it can hold up to sixty thousand pounds of goods: sneakers, khakis, televisions, DRAM chips, whatever. Two days before Thanksgiving, about two thousand of these containers were piled thirteen across and as many as fourteen deep aboard the *Mette Maersk* as it sat in its slip in Port Elizabeth, New Jersey. The ship's captain, Thomas Hansen, watched from the bridge as giant cranes lifted containers directly from truck to ship and from ship to truck. Hansen, a stocky Dane with a carefully groomed mustache, closely monitored how quickly the cargo was moved on and off the ship. His schedule was tight. This was the *Mette Maersk's* twelfth stop on a voyage that had begun a month before, in Hong Kong. It had arrived that morning from Charleston, South Carolina, and was due to cast off for Le Havre in five hours. Hansen was eager to get going. "The pressure never lets up," he said. "You can never go fast enough."

It wasn't just the caffeine talking. In the information age, the captain of a container ship like the *Mette Maersk* has to do a lot more than steer his vessel clear of icebergs and pirates. He's the point man in a supply-chain network that extends around the world, linking factories in the Far East, manufacturers in the United States, and retail stores all over the globe. If the world has become one big assembly line, the container ship is its conveyor belt.

Back in 1956, when a man named Malcolm McLean loaded fifty-eight truck trailers onto a ship bound from Newark to Houston, few imagined that these clunky boxes would revolutionize world trade. The idea was simple: you can save more shipping time in port than at sea. Before the advent of containers, goods were mostly loaded and unloaded from ship to shore box by box, which was slow, expensive, and unreliable (as in "It fell off the back of a truck"). The container made the process quick and cheap. By the late sixties, container ships were crossing the oceans regularly, and their impact was immediate. Those longshoremen from *On the Waterfront* gradually grew obsolete. Shipping costs plummeted. Asia boomed. Mass production went global.

Sure, Captain Hansen may get short shrift from *Business 2.0*. But if you think globalization is strictly the province of landlubbing, Surge-slurping software engineers, ask yourself when you last had a pair of pants delivered through your T1 line. In recent years, container ships have only become more important. Since the late nineteen-eighties, the cost of shipping has fallen as much as tenfold, to the point where it generally makes up just one per cent of an item's final retail price. A decade or so ago, it cost thirty dollars to ship a high-end VCR. Today, it costs about a buck-fifty. Container ships now carry twice as much cargo as they did then, and handle it with far more speed and precision. It's no longer enough to deliver those cathode-ray tubes to Long Beach by Tuesday. You have to get them there Tuesday at noon, and have them on deck, ready for the cranes, when the trucks pull on to the pier.

Matching your schedule to your customers is the beauty part, of course, but it's the hard part, too. For every container that comes off a ship, another container should come aboard. Those coming off need to be on top, where the cranes can reach them easily, without having to unload half the ship's cargo. The arrival and departure of the trucks must be meticulously choreographed. The task of keeping track of a shipload of containers—not to mention the trucks, the cranes, and the hundreds of other vessels in your fleet—is gargantuan.

It's not a business for slackers, and the shippers that have managed to stay   6
afloat have done so by introducing sophisticated technologies to the brute
simplicity of McLean's metal box. Maersk Sealand, which owns Hansen's
vessel, has invested hundreds of millions in building its own terminals at
most of the ports where its ships dock, so that it has greater control over
the number of container "moves" that take place every hour. It now works
more closely with its biggest clients to cut down on time spent waiting for
trucks, and has invested heavily in technology to solve the mathematical
puzzle of what belongs where when. Each vessel now has a separate control
room where a computer tracks every container on board. The containers,
identified as either "dry" or "reefer" (for "refrigerated"), are color-coded
according to their eventual destination. When everything is where it's
supposed to be, the screen is filled with solid blocks of green, red, and blue.

Time always mattered in shipping, but now it matters more than ever,   7
because American companies increasingly run on just-in-time schedules
and carry very little inventory, relying on outside suppliers to get them
the parts they need when they need them. These days, those suppliers
tend to be across the sea, not down the street. Container ships make a
six-thousand-mile, just-in-time supply chain possible. In a sense, they are
immense floating warehouses; goods can be in transit and in storage at the
same time. "Now no one has money tied up in spare parts, and no one
carries inventory," Hansen said. "This is why. This ship *is* the inventory."

RESPONDING TO READING

What effect did container shipping have on longshoremen? Why did
this happen? Can you think of other computer technologies that have put
people out of work?

GAINING WORD POWER

Surowiecki uses the word *technology,* which is made up of a combining
form and a familiar **suffix.** The combining form *techno-* means practical,
mechanical, or scientific knowledge. The suffix *-logy* means the science or
study of something. So, *technology* means practical or applied science. From
the combining form *techno-,* we also have the terms *technocrat* and *technoc-
racy.* It's easy to make a word for a person or concept associated with technology by adding a suffix, as in *technobabble.* See how many words you can
think of—or make up—beginning with *techno-.* Think about computers.
Consult your dictionary if you draw a blank.

CONSIDERING CONTENT

1. What idea revolutionized global shipping?
2. What is a supply-chain network?
3. Why is speed so important in shipping today?
4. What does *reefer* mean in container ship lingo?
5. Why do container boxes need to be color-coded according to destination?

CONSIDERING METHOD

1. Do you recognize the **allusion** in the title "The Box That Launched a Thousand Ships"?
2. Why does Surowiecki introduce Captain Hansen and his ship into this account of global shipping?
3. What **figure of speech** is used in the last sentence of paragraph 2? Can you find other figurative language in the same paragraph?
4. What does the author achieve with the three short-short sentences at the end of paragraph 3?
5. How do the opening and closing paragraphs serve to unify the essay?

WRITING STEP BY STEP

Choose a process similar to the one you just read explaining the supply-chain network of global shipping, but think of something a bit less complicated. You might explain to someone who has never flown before the process of selecting a flight, making a reservation, and going through all the checkpoints at the airport before boarding the plane. Or you could tell a teenager how to go about getting a driver's license or explain for a prospective student the process of registration at your college.

A. Direct your writing to people who would be unfamiliar with the process—like someone who has never flown before, someone applying for a first driver's license, or someone planning to enroll in your college next fall.
B. Begin, as Surowiecki does, by identifying the process you're going to explain. To make your writing more interesting, consider using a person—real or fictional—whose progress you can follow through the various steps (someone like Captain Hansen, the "stocky Dane with a carefully groomed mustache").
C. As you present the various steps, warn your readers of possibly stressful situations, such as long lines and rude clerks. Unless it's obvious, explain the purpose of each step.

D. Conclude your essay by offering encouragement and a reminder of the rewards of completing the process successfully.

OTHER WRITING IDEAS

1. Using Surowiecki's article as a model, write an essay that follows the domestic delivery of a single package via FedEx or UPS from sender to receiver. Your purpose is to explain how the company's distribution hub functions. Go to the library or on the Web to gather information on this process.
2. Identify and explain the stages of an emotional process, such as falling in love (or falling out of love). You might want to work in a group to come up with emotional processes and ideas about their stages before you write your individual essay.
3. Find a complicated set of instructions, like those for programming a VCR. Study them until you figure them out. Then write a new set of instructions that a beginner would find easy to follow.

EDITING SKILLS: CHOOSING *ITS* OR *IT'S*

Look at the uses of the italicized words—*it's* and *its*—in these sentences from Surowiecki's essay:

It's called a freight container.

It's no longer enough to deliver those cathode-ray tubes to Long Beach by Tuesday.

[A]bout two thousand of these containers were piled . . . aboard the *Mette Maersk* as it sat in *its* slip in Port Elizabeth, New Jersey.

If the world has become one big assembly line, the container ship is *its* conveyer belt.

Notice that in the first two sentences, the words *it is* can be substituted for *it's*. This substitution would not work in the last two sentences. Sometimes *it's* stands for *it has:*

It's been an exciting trip.

You can use the substitution test to see whether you have used the right form. If you have written *it's*, you should be able to read the sentence with *it is* or *it has* instead. *It's* is a contraction, like *don't* for *do not* and *there's* for *there is.*

Its, however, is a possessive, carrying a sense of ownership or belonging:

The whale made *its* weird noises.
The plan failed because of *its* flaws.
I like the new sitcom in spite of *its* dysfunctional main characters.

Many writers are tempted to put an apostrophe in the possessive *its* because so many other possessives require apostrophes: the *whale's* noises, the *plan's* flaws, the *sitcom's* characters. No wonder it's confusing. Try to put the possessive *its* in a mental list with the other possessives—*his, hers, ours, theirs*—which also have no apostrophes. This mental grouping will help you choose the correct form.

EXERCISE

Fill the blanks in the following sentences with *its* or *it's.* Be prepared to explain your choices.

1. Your proposal has much in _____ favor, but _____ unlikely that the committee will vote for it.
2. _____ an old car, but _____ paint job is new.
3. The dog bit _____ own tail; _____ not an exceptionally smart dog.
4. _____ important that a company give _____ employees a sense of security.

Go back over your past writings and check to see whether you have used the correct form, *its* or *it's.*

WEB SITES

www.filmsite.org/onth.html.
You can find a detailed review of the 1954 Oscar-winning movie *On the Waterfront,* which is mentioned in Surowiecki's article.

http://ilaunion.org/home.asp?h=1/
The home page for the International Longshoremen's Association will direct you to current news, history, and other information about longshoremen.

PREPARING TO READ

Did you ever watch a sporting event (such as rugby, curling, cricket, squash, or soccer) without knowing the rules of the game? How did you figure out what was going on? Do you think you would have enjoyed it more if you had known the rules?

There Are Rules, You Know

DAVE BARRY

Dave Barry, who was born in 1947 in Armonk, New York, is one of America's most popular humorists. A graduate of Haverford College, Barry began his career as a reporter for the Associated Press in Philadelphia. He is now a syndicated columnist for the *Miami Herald* and the author of more than twenty humorous books. He won the Pulitzer prize for commentary in 1988. In the following essay, which appeared on January 30, 2000, Barry focuses his usual wit and irreverent humor on the subject of one of our national obsessions—the Super Bowl.

TERMS TO RECOGNIZE

blitzkrieg *(para. 1)*	a fierce offensive attack
hurling *(para. 3)*	an Irish game resembling field hockey
extraction *(para. 6)*	origin, lineage

We are coming upon the Super Bowl, which is by far the most important sporting event in the world as measured in total tons of free shrimp consumed by sportscasters. This year the Super Bowl will be broadcast to many foreign nations, which, almost by definition, contain numerous foreigners. These people are often puzzled by American football, a highly complex sport that requires a knowledge of many technical terms such as "run," "pass," "cornerbacker," "blitzkrieg," "Texas Leaguer," "ligament," and "Hank Stram." This complexity makes the game difficult for foreigners to grasp. 1

I know this because some years ago, while visiting Japan, I watched the Miami Dolphins and the Oakland Raiders play a demonstration game in a Tokyo stadium where, for a zesty snack, you could buy pieces of fried octopus on a stick. The fans were polite, but they had no clue what was 2 going on. The only thing that aroused their interest was the Dolphin cheer-leaders. The game would stop for a timeout, and the cheerleaders would start jumping around, and immediately the fans would go WILD, cheering and thrusting their octopus nuggets into the air.

I'm not being critical here. I've been on the other side of this coin. While 3 visiting Ireland, I watched an Irish sport called "hurling" (really) in which men who are not wearing helmets basically beat each other senseless with sticks. In terms of violence, this sport makes American football look like "Pat the Bunny." I'd never seen this sport, so I relied on the fans around me to answer my questions ("Is that player dead?" "Did all that blood come out of his EAR?" etc.). So I know how hard it can be to understand a foreign sport, which is why today to help you foreign persons follow the Super Bowl, I am presenting: THE RULES OF AMERICAN PROFESSIONAL FOOTBALL.

Football is played on a field that is 100 yards (374 kilometers) long and 4 is covered with lines called "hash marks" to indicate where players have lost their breakfasts. On either side of the field are the benches, where the 350 players who are not involved in the game sit and wave to their moms. Behind each bench is a big plastic jug of Gatorade. The object of the game is to be the first team to dump this on the "coach," a very angry man who hates everybody.

The game is divided into four 15-minute quarters, each of which lasts 5 a little over three hours. Timeouts may be called by anybody at any time for any reason, including political unrest in Guatemala. Between the second and third quarters, there is a half-time musical extravaganza in which Neil Diamond, Toni Tennille, the Muppets, and the late Al Hirt join with every human being who has ever auditioned for "Star Search" to perform "A Tribute to Medleys."

The game begins when a small man of foreign extraction kicks the 6 pigskin, or "ball," as far as possible, then wisely scuttles off the field. The referee then places the ball on an imaginary "line of scrimmage," which is visible only to the referee and his imaginary friend, Mr. Pootywinkle. On either side of this line, the two teams form "huddles," where they decide who will perform the traditional celebratory dance when the upcoming "play" is over.

The "play" itself happens very quickly so you foreign persons must not 7 blink or you'll miss it. Here's what happens:

1. A large player called the "center" squats over the ball, and then the "quarterdeck" touches him in a way that would get them both executed in the Middle East.
2. All the players run into each other and fall down.

3. Certain players leap to their feet and perform celebratory dances, while referees add to the festivity by hurling brightly colored flags into the air.

Now comes the heart and soul of football: Watching slow-motion replays of the players falling down. You'll see this from every possible point of reference, including the Hubble telescope. You'll see so many replays that at some point you'll swear that, in the background, you can see Mr. Pootywinkle. 8

When the replays are finally over, the referee formally announces that the play does not count. Then it's time for eight commercials featuring sport utility vehicles climbing Mt. Everest, and it's back to the huddles for more non-stop action! 9

Yes, foreign persons, football is a complex sport, but you'll find that if you take the time to watch this year's Super Bowl, you will soon discover why every year so many millions of Americans are glued to their television sets. Watching rental videos. 10

RESPONDING TO READING

Is Barry being fair in his representation of pro football? Do you think he is a dedicated football fan himself? What makes you think so?

GAINING WORD POWER

Barry twice uses the unusual word *celebratory*, which takes the familiar verb *celebrate* and turns it into an adjective (a word describing something) by adding the **suffix** -*ory*. When making adjectives, the suffix means *of, relating to, characterized by, serving for, producing,* or *maintaining*—as in *migratory* (the verb *migrate* plus -*ory*). This same suffix can also turn verbs into nouns (the names of persons, places, or things) as in *observatory* (the verb *observe* plus -*ory*). When forming nouns, the -*ory* means *a place for* or *something that serves for.*

Identify the following words as either adjectives or nouns; then use each one in a sentence. What verbs do they come from? Consult your dictionary if you're unsure of the meaning.

1. crematory
2. sensory
3. oratory
4. laudatory
5. accusatory
6. exploratory

7. obligatory
8. mandatory
9. congratulatory
10. laboratory

CONSIDERING CONTENT

1. What's funny about Barry's list of "technical terms" in the opening paragraph?
2. Why is the Irish game of hurling (as Barry describes it) more violent than American football (para. 3)?
3. What are Barry's criticisms of football referees in paragraph 6? Do you think they are justified?
4. Why does the author describe the coach as "a very angry man who hates everybody" (para. 4)?
5. What does the last line tell you about Barry's attitude toward the Super Bowl?

CONSIDERING METHOD

1. Do you think the "foreign persons" Barry addresses would understand professional football any better after reading his explanation of the rules? Who is the real **audience** for this piece? Why does the author adopt this fictional audience?
2. How does the device of the "foreign persons" serve to unify the essay (paras. 6 and 7)?
3. Where does Barry state his **thesis?** Why do you think he placed it there?
4. Name the figure of speech involving exaggeration that Barry employs for humorous effect (for instance, in para. 4—"the 350 players who are not involved in the game"). Find several other examples in paragraph 5.
5. Why is the last sentence written as a fragment? Would it be more effective if written as a complete sentence?

WRITING STEP BY STEP

Barry's tone is clearly humorous, as he makes fun of professional football and the hoopla that surrounds it. In your essay, think of some sport or cultural practice that involves rituals and present the "rules" that are involved. Consider, for instance, professional wrestling, NASCAR racing, formal weddings, graduation ceremonies, fraternity initiations, or rock concerts. If you have a flair for humorous writing, make fun of the procedure. If not, present the process in a neutral tone to inform someone who might want to know all about it. The effectiveness of your essay in either case will depend on your use of well-chosen, specific details to illustrate each "rule."

A. Begin your essay, as Barry does, with some background on the procedure you're going to explain. Try for an entertaining **anecdote,** like the one in the Tokyo stadium involving cheerleaders and octopus on a stick (para. 2). Work in your thesis gracefully before moving on to the body of your paper.

B. Describe the place in which your chosen ceremony or entertainment event typically takes places (as Barry does in para. 4).

C. Briefly mention the purpose of the event. Barry does so in a single sentence at the end of paragraph 4.

D. Go through the procedure chronologically, providing details. If there are actual rules involved, consider numbering them.

E. Conclude with your positive or negative evaluation of this event.

OTHER WRITING IDEAS

1. Write the paper outlined in the previous section, but instead, describe the steps of something you created that didn't turn out as planned. Then tell the outcome. Perhaps you devised a scheme that backfired or a lab experiment that went wrong. Or maybe you fouled up a project at work, or tried to assemble a bicycle with questionable results, or followed a weight-loss program that didn't work.

2. Write a humorous essay in which you explain how *not* to do something: the wrong way to study for a test, the wrong way to impress a first date, the wrong way to make lasagna, the wrong way to follow a balanced diet, and so on.

3. Get together with a group of classmates, and discuss some procedure or process that you would like to change or do away with, such as courting rituals, the first day of class, applying for credit, shopping for groceries (or some other type of shopping), registering for classes, doing a certain job or chore. Then write an essay explaining the process and giving your objections to it.

EDITING SKILLS: USING COMMAS

Writers put a comma after a word or group of words that comes in front of the main part of the sentence. That main part is called the **independent clause** because it can stand alone as a sentence. Look at these examples from Barry's essay (italics added):

While visiting in Ireland, I watched an Irish sport called "hurling" (really) in which men who are not wearing helmets basically beat each other senseless with sticks.

On either side of this line, the two teams form "huddles," where they decide who will perform the traditional celebratory dance when the upcoming "play" is over.

When the replays are finally over, the referee formally announces that the play does not count.

The italicized words and groups of words that come before the commas are called **dependent elements**: they cannot stand alone as sentences and are not really necessary to the meaning of the sentences.

Writers also put commas before and after dependent elements when they come in the middle of an independent sentence. Here are some examples from Barry's essay:

I know this because some years ago, *while visiting Japan,* I watched the Miami Dolphins and the Oakland Raiders play a demonstration game in a Tokyo stadium where, *for a zesty snack,* you could buy pieces of fried octopus on a stick.

Yes, *foreign persons,* football is a complex sport. . . .

These dependent elements are called **interrupters**: they break up the flow of the sentence and are not really necessary to the meaning of the sentence.

EXERCISE

In Barry's essay, find two more examples of introductory words or groups of words that are separated from the independent clause by a comma. Then find two more examples of interrupters that are set off by commas.

Now copy the following sentences, putting in commas where needed:

1. The rabbit nevertheless does shed fur.
2. Like most people Ralph does not know the name of his congressional representative.
3. Speaking of travel would you like to go to Seattle next week?
4. Jazz some people believe is America's greatest contribution to the arts.
5. The result as we have seen is not a pretty one.

Finally, check the essay you have just written to be sure you have used commas to separate dependent elements from the rest of the sentence.

🌐 WEB SITES

www.herald.com/herald/content/archive/news/barry/archive/ 98jul19.htm

Compare Barry's send-up of soccer with the one you read on pro football.

www.peacefire.org/staff/bennett/autodave/

"The Automated Dave Barry Column Generator" shows how to create your own spoof of Barry's writing.

Student Essay Using Process and Directions

A Graceful Stride

Ann Moroney

A common misconception about hurdle races is that   1
the runner "jumps" over the hurdle. This observation
is completely false. A hurdle runner does just that--
runs. The hurdler takes long steps, or strides, over
the hurdle and sprints on to the next one. As simple
as this process may sound, running hurdles is complicated. For one thing, the hurdle itself is thirty-
three inches high, which comes to about the hip.
"Stepping" over something this high is really quite
difficult, as I found out my freshman year in high
school. I also had to master a number of other skills
to run hurdles efficiently.

The first problem to tackle when it comes to   2
running hurdles is the fear. At every one of my
races, I sat in my blocks looking at the line of
hurdles in front of me with fear in my heart. No
matter how good I became or how long I'd been
running, I always felt *fear:* fear that I'd trip over
the hurdle and fall on the track, fear that I'd knock
the hurdle over in front of everybody, and fear that
I'd actually get over the first hurdle with no
problem and become a hurdler for four years.
Throughout my experience, I found only one way to get
over the fear: stop thinking and start running.

The main thing to concentrate on is form. Form   3
is the way the runner carries himself or herself
over the hurdles. The better the form is, the faster
the run will be. Form includes many elements. The
runner must coordinate legs, arms, torso, and eyes
into a fluid sprint through ten hurdles on 100
meters of track.

The lead leg, the one to go over the hurdle   4
first, should be slightly bent, but more or less
straight in front of the body. The toe should be
pointing toward the sky and the heel should line up
with the middle of the hurdle. (As my former track

coach Ms. Tolefree always said, "Heel to the Gill," referring to the brand name printed directly in the middle of the hurdle.) Just as the body comes over the hurdle, the lead leg should snap down to the ground. The goal is to bring the leg down as close to the back of the hurdle as possible without actually hitting it. The sooner the feet are on the ground, the faster the runner can continue running.

The runner must also concentrate on the trail   5
leg--the one that comes second over the hurdle. The knee should be bent with the leg at the side, the thigh parallel to the hurdle. (Imagine sitting on the ground with one leg bent at the side, mimicking a frog.) As the lead leg snaps down, the trail leg will be following over the hurdle. The hip will rotate so the leg is once again perpendicular to the ground. The knee should snap up to the chest as close as possible, as this will help the runner stretch out the stride. (As Ms. Tolefree was fond of saying, "Your knee is like the scope on a rifle. It directs where your stride will go. If your knee is high, your stride will be long. If it's low, your stride will be short.") After clearing the hurdle, the runner must continue striding through the rest of the hurdles.

Another important part of form is arms; they not   6
only keep balance, but they also keep the form tight. The arm opposite the lead leg is the lead arm. It should be reaching out in front of the body toward the toe of the lead leg. The other arm, the one opposite the trail leg, is the trail arm. It should come back in a biceps-flexing fashion and stay at the side until the body is clear of the hurdle. It's usually a good idea to keep the hands open; a closed fist takes up energy and tenses the muscles in the rest of the body.

The final elements of form have to do with small,   7
yet significant, mechanics. Air time is a major factor when running hurdles. The goal is to remain in the air for as little time as possible; the faster the feet return to the track, the faster the runner

can continue running. So the body should be as low to the hurdle as possible without hitting it. Also, the torso should lean slightly forward--but not be bent, because taking the time to straighten up will slow the runner down. A slight lean forward will get the runner over the hurdle and on to the next one. The final point involves the eyes. Hurdlers should not look at the hurdle they are about to step over. Looking farther down the track instead of directly in front of them keeps runners running.

Running hurdles takes time, practice, and commitment. During the split second it takes to clear a hurdle, the runner must take into account a wide variety of movements to run the race successfully. A good, hard practice schedule is the only way to acquire a productive hurdling technique. And developing a graceful stride is not as easy as it looks.

8

Chapter

STRATEGIES FOR ANALYZING WHY THINGS HAPPEN

Cause and Effect

Human beings are naturally curious. We all want to know why. Why does the car keep stalling? Why are some people better at math than others? Why does a leaf change color? Why did Tom Cruise and Nicole Kidman get divorced? This common human impulse to understand why things happen provides a powerful motive for reading and writing.

THE POINT OF CAUSE-AND-EFFECT WRITING

We study **causes** and their **effects** in order to understand events and solve problems. If we can find out why the car keeps stalling, we can fix it. If we can figure out why some people are good at math, maybe we can help those who aren't. If we know why a leaf changes color, we'll have a greater appreciation for nature and its processes. If we know why Cruise and Kidman broke up, we might get on *Oprah*. A lot of the writing done in college courses requires cause-and-effect thinking; students are frequently asked to explain things like the origins of the Russian Revolution, the roots of prejudice, the causes of volcanic eruptions, the effects of hunger on learning, the reasons for Hamlet's delay. The good news about this kind of writing is that it feeds off the natural curiosity of both reader and writer. Inquiring minds want to know why, and you get to tell them.

When you develop an essay by analyzing causes, you are explaining to your readers *why* something happened. If you go on to explore the effects, you are analyzing *what* happened—the consequences. For example, if your topic is divorce and you write "Why Teenage Marriages Fail," that's primarily a cause paper. But if you write "What Divorce Does to Young Children," that's primarily an effect paper. You will probably stick to one **purpose** in a single essay, but you might take up both causes and effects if you have the time and the assignment allows you to.

THE PRINCIPLES OF CAUSE-AND-EFFECT WRITING

Analyzing cause–effect relationships is one of the primary methods of reasoning. It requires careful thinking and planning.

Types of Causes and Effects

When you think about causes and effects, you need to realize that they can be *immediate* or *remote*. The immediate causes are usually the obvious ones; they occur just before a result appears. An immediate cause for breaking up with your boyfriend might be that he didn't call you last night to tell you he'd be two hours late. But you also know there are deeper, more important reasons for the breakup, for example, his habit of forgetting to call and his general lack of concern for your feelings. These are the remote causes, the ones further removed from the effect they produce. They are also called *underlying causes* because they are often more difficult to see.

Effects can also be immediate or remote. The immediate effect of failing to get gas is that your car stops running. But the remote effects can stretch out for quite a while: you block traffic and cause an accident; you're late for class and miss an important lecture; you do poorly on the next exam and get a lower grade in the class; your car insurance goes up because of the accident; you have to change majors because you don't have the required grade point average to be admitted into advanced courses. Remote effects are also called long-term effects.

Patterns of Cause and Effect

1. If you want to **focus** on causes, begin by describing a condition or problem or result (such as breaking up with your boyfriend), and then fully explain the causes or reasons (for the breakup). With this approach, you may be able to use **chronological order** (according to time) if you can trace the causes from the earliest to the most recent. More likely, though, your organization will fall into some **logical order** that reflects the relative importance of the causes: from the least significant to the most critical or from personal reasons to more general ones.

2. If you want to focus on effects, start with some condition or event and explain the consequences. For example, you might begin by describing the breakup with your girlfriend and then go on to show how it affected you. Again, you can present the effects chronologically: at first you were depressed; then you began to spend more time with your friends; you also had more to time to study, so your grades improved; finally, you began to date again and found a much better girlfriend. Or you can arrange the effects according to importance: from a fairly obvious result to the most subtle, from effects on yourself to effects on other people.

3. Since causes and effects are closely related, you might find that tracing a chain or sequence of events, including both causes and effects, is the best way to approach your topic. In a causal chain, the first cause produces an effect, which becomes the cause of the next effect, and so on. In the example about running out of gas, there were two chains. First, running out of gas caused a blocked intersection, which led to an accident, which resulted (some time later) in higher insurance costs. Also, running out of gas caused you to be late for class and miss an important lecture, which contributed to a lower grade, which affected your grade point average, which prevented you from getting into the program, which caused you to change majors. If you decide to describe a chain of causes and effects, be sure to outline it carefully.

THE PITFALLS OF CAUSE-AND-EFFECT WRITING

An explanation of causes and effects won't be successful if your readers find your thinking fuzzy or flawed. Here are some ways to avoid the most common faults of cause–effect reasoning:

1. Don't mix causes and effects. When talking informally about why things happen, you may shuttle back and forth between causes and their effects. But in writing, you need to follow a clear pattern: focus on causes, focus on effects, or describe an orderly chain of causes and effects.

2. Don't settle for obvious causes and immediate effects. Your explanations will be much more convincing if you look for underlying causes and long-term effects. As Jade Snow Wong shows in her essay in this chapter, her date with a fellow student provided an opportunity to stand up to her parents, but it was not the cause of her rebellion. The "real" causes ran much deeper. It is, of course, possible to go too far back in searching for causes. You'll need to exercise some judgment in deciding which reasons are still valid and relevant.

3. Don't oversimplify. Most conditions and events are complex, involving multiple causes and numerous effects. In a short essay, you may have to concentrate on the primary reasons, but be sure to let your readers know that's what you are doing.

4. Don't omit any key links in a chain of causes and effects. You don't have to spell out every single step in a sequence of events, but be certain that your readers will be able to follow and make all the right connections themselves.

5. Don't worry about absolute proof. In explaining causes and effects, you can't always prove conclusively why something happened. But offer as much evidence as you can to help the reader see the connections that you see. You always need to support your causes and effects with specific details—examples drawn from personal experience, statistics, and statements by experts. You may want to conduct interviews and collect your own information or visit the library to find material on your topic.

WHAT TO LOOK FOR IN CAUSE-AND-EFFECT WRITING

As you read the selections in this chapter, ask yourself these questions:

1. Does the writer focus on causes or effects, or does the essay consider both? Make a list of the causes and the effects as you read.
2. Look for the point, or purpose, of the author's explanation of causes and effects.
3. Decide what kind of causes or effects the author presents—immediate, remote, or both. Does the writer follow a chain of causal relationships?
4. Does the author have a particular audience in mind? How can you tell?
5. What is the tone of the essay? Does the author sound serious, humorous, angry, irritated, sad, regretful, or something else? How does that tone relate to the author's purpose and audience?
6. Notice what writing strategies the author uses to develop the explanations. Take note of examples, descriptions, narratives, comparisons, definitions, and so on.

What appeals of advertising is this cartoon making fun of? Think of some ads that would fit this cartoon.

How is the cartoon making fun of consumers? What do the man's words tell us about him? Do you think you're affected by TV ads the way this cartoon humorously suggests?

PREPARING TO READ

Do you tell your parents and your best friends everything? What do you keep to yourself? Is revealing the truth always the best policy?

Ignorance Is Not Bliss

ERIC MARCUS

A graduate of Vassar College and Columbia University, Eric Marcus works as an associate producer for ABC's *Good Morning America*. He also publishes articles and book reviews and is the coauthor of *Breaking the Surface,* the biography of Olympic diver Greg Louganis. In this selection, which first appeared in the "My Turn" section of *Newsweek* in 1993, Marcus relates the effects of telling his grandmother about his sexual orientation to the "don't ask, don't tell" policy regarding gay people in the U.S. military.

TERMS TO RECOGNIZE

bliss *(title)*	extreme happiness, joy
Sam Nunn *(para. 1)*	former Georgia senator and chair of the Armed Services Committee
policy *(para. 1)*	a plan for making decisions and taking actions
charade *(para. 2)*	a pretense, a disguise, an act
wondrous *(para. 5)*	amazing, astonishing, surprising
exposure *(para. 6)*	the act of being exposed or found out
orientation *(para. 8)*	awareness and adjustment to one's situation or condition
deceit *(para. 10)*	act or practice of lying or misleading

Sam Nunn didn't need to hold Senate hearings to come up with his "don't ask, don't tell" solution for handling gays in the military. If he'd asked me, I could have told him this was exactly the policy some of my relatives suggested years ago when I informed them that I planned to tell my grandmother that I was gay. They said, "She's old, it'll kill her. You'll destroy her image of you. If she doesn't ask, why tell?"

"Don't ask, don't tell" made a lot of sense to these relatives because it sounded like an easy solution. For them, it was. If I didn't say anything to my grandmother, they wouldn't have to deal with her upset over the truth

1

2

about her grandson. But for me, "not telling" was an exhausting nightmare, because it meant withholding everything that could possibly give me away and living in fear of being found out. At the same time, I didn't want to cause Grandma pain by telling her I was gay, so I was easily persuaded to continue the charade.

If I hadn't been close to my grandmother, or saw her only once a year, hiding the truth would have been relatively easy. But we'd had a special relationship since she cared for me as a child when my mother was ill, and we visited often, so lying to her was especially difficult.   3

I started hiding the truth from everyone in 1965, when I had my first crush. That was in second grade and his name was Hugh. No one told me, but I knew I shouldn't tell anyone about it, not even Hugh. I don't know how I knew that liking another boy was something to hide, but I did, so I kept it a secret.   4

I fell in love for the first time when I was 17. It was a wondrous experience, but I didn't dare tell anyone, especially my family, because telling them about Bob would have given me away. I couldn't explain to them that for the first time in my life I felt like a normal human being.   5

By the time I was an adult, I'd stopped lying to my immediate family, with the exception of my grandmother, and told them I was gay. I was a second-rate liar so I was lucky that Grandma was the only person in my life around whom I had to be something I wasn't. I can't imagine what it's like for gays and lesbians in the military to hide the truth from the men and women with whom they serve. The fear of exposure must be extraordinary, especially because exposure would mean the end of their careers. For me, the only risk was losing Grandma's love.   6

Hiding the truth from her grew ever more challenging in the years that followed. I couldn't tell her about the man I then shared my life with. I couldn't talk about my friends who had AIDS because she would have wondered why I knew so many ill men. I couldn't tell her that I volunteered for a gay peer-counseling center. I couldn't talk to her about the political issues that most interested me because she would have wondered why I had such passionate feelings about gay rights. Eventually I couldn't even tell her about all of my work, because some of my writing was on gay issues. In the end, all we had left to talk about was the weather.   7

If being gay were only what I did behind closed doors, there would have been plenty of my life left over to share with my grandmother. But my life as a gay man isn't something that takes place only in the privacy of my bedroom. It affects who my friends are, whom I choose to share my life with, the work I do, the organizations I belong to, the magazines I read, where I vacation and what I talk about. I know it's the same for hetero-   8 sexuals because their sexual orientation affects everything, from a choice of senior-prom date and the finger on which they wear their wedding band to the birth announcements they send and every emotion they feel.

So the reality of the "don't ask, don't tell" solution for dealing with my   9 grandmother and for dealing with gays in the military means having to lie about or hide almost every aspect of your life. It's not nearly as simple as just not saying, "I'm gay."

After years of "protecting" my grandmother I decided it was time to stop   10 lying. In the worst case, I figured she might reject me, although that seemed unlikely. But whatever the outcome, I could not pretend anymore. Some might think that was selfish on my part, but I'd had enough of the "don't tell" policy, which had forced me into a life of deceit. I also hoped that by telling her the truth, we could build a relationship based on honesty, a possibility that was worth the risk.

The actual telling was far less terrifying than all the anticipation. While   11 my grandmother cried plenty, my family was wrong, because the truth didn't kill her. In the five years since, Grandma and I have talked a lot about the realities of my life and the lives of my gay and lesbian friends. She's read many articles and a few books, including mine. She's surprised us by how quickly she's set aside her myths and misconceptions.

Grandma and I are far closer than we ever were. Last fall we even spent   12 a week together in Paris for her birthday. And these days, we have plenty to talk about, including the gays in the military issue.

A few months ago, Grandma traveled with me to Lafayette College, Pa.,   13 where I was invited to give a speech on the history of the gay civil-rights movement. After my talk, several students took us to dinner. As I conversed with the young women across the table from me, I overheard my grandmother talking to the student sitting next to her. She told him he was right to tell his parents he was gay, that with time and his help they would adjust. She said, "Don't underestimate their ability to change."

I wish Sam Nunn had called my grandmother to testify before his Senate   14 committee. He and the other senators, as well as Defense Secretary Les Aspin and the President, could do far worse than listen to her advice.

RESPONDING TO READING

Marcus claims that sexual orientation, whether gay or straight, affects "everything" in a person's life (para. 8). Explore this idea in your journal. Do you think sexual identity influences the choices we make (of friends, work, leisure activities, and so forth)?

GAINING WORD POWER

Marcus uses several words that begin with prefixes. A **prefix** is a syllable or syllables used at the beginning of a word to change or add to the
meaning. For example, *in*complete means "not complete," *re*write means
"write again," *mis*use means "improper or incorrect use," *dis*approve means
"fail or refuse to approve," *mal*adjusted means "poorly or badly adjusted."
Examine the following words that come from Marcus's essay, and explain
how the prefix changes the meaning of the base word. Try to figure out
the meaning on your own first; then look the words up in a dictionary.

*un*likely	*mis*conceptions	*under*estimate
*extra*ordinary	*with*holding	*hetero*sexuals

Now add the indicated prefix to the following words and explain the
change in meaning that occurs. Use your dictionary to help you. Here are
a couple of examples to get you started:

Add ir- to regular.
New word: irregular
New meaning: not regular

Add with- to draw.
New word: withdraw
New meaning: move or draw
back, take back

1. Add non- to sense.
2. Add mis- to understood.
3. Add un- to reliable.
4. Add extra- to sensory.
5. Add dis- to agree.
6. Add under- to rated.
7. Add mal- to practice.
8. Add re- to cycle.

Now try using these eight words in sentences of your own.

CONSIDERING CONTENT

1. Why did the author's relatives want him to hide his sexual identity from his grandmother? Did they really think she would die if he told her?
2. What was the effect on Marcus of having to lie? Why was it exhausting? Why did he find it especially difficult to mislead his grandmother?
3. Marcus says he knew, even in the second grade, that liking another boy was something to hide. How do you suppose he knew that?
4. What does Marcus mean when he says that "for the first time in my life I felt like a normal human being" (para. 5)? How is he using the word *normal?*

5. What reason does Marcus give for finally deciding to tell his grand-mother? What positive effect did he hope for? What effects did his revelation have?
6. Marcus says the "actual telling was far less terrifying than all the anticipation." Explain why.
7. What is Marcus's main **purpose?** Is it to share his personal experience or to comment on the military's "don't ask, don't tell" policy?

CONSIDERING METHOD

1. The title is a variation of the old saying "ignorance is bliss." What does the saying mean? Why does the author change the saying?
2. Why does Marcus include information about his first crush and the first time he fell in love (paras. 4–5)?
3. What details and examples does Marcus include to show the effects of keeping his secret from his grandmother?
4. How many times does Marcus compare his personal dilemma to the situation of gay people in the military? Why does he repeat this comparison?
5. Why does the author include the brief story about his trip to Lafayette College (para. 13)? What is the effect of quoting his grandmother?
6. How does the last paragraph echo the introduction? Would it have been more effective to close with the previous paragraph?

WRITING STEP BY STEP

Write an essay about a time when you were reluctant to reveal something to a family member or a very close friend because you feared a negative reaction. Perhaps it was something you had done, a choice you had made, or an opinion or belief that you felt strongly about.

A. Begin by describing what it is that you were afraid to reveal. Get your readers' attention by including plenty of specific details.
B. Give the reasons for your reluctance to reveal the truth. If other people advised you not to say anything, quote their advice directly, as Marcus does in his opening paragraph.
C. Explain why you wanted to tell this particular person and why you expected a negative response. What effects did you expect your revelation to have? Also describe how you felt about not being able to share your secret with this person.
D. Explain why you decided to reveal your secret, and describe what happened when you did. Was the response what you expected, or did the other person surprise you? Use dialogue to help recreate this scene.

E. Tell how things worked out. Are you still on good terms with this person? Give some supporting evidence, as Marcus does in paragraphs 11 to 13, to show how your relationship was affected by your revelation.

F. Conclude with some comments about how you feel now. Are you glad you revealed your secret? If you had to do it again, would you do the same thing?

OTHER WRITING IDEAS

1. Write an essay about an experience or incident from the past that had a strong effect on you. Perhaps it taught you an important lesson about yourself or changed the way you think about yourself. The experience doesn't have to be a negative one; you can choose an incident that had a positive effect.

2. Think of a prejudice or a belief that offends you. Explain why people think this way and why it offends you.

3. Write an essay about the effects of divorce on children. Gather ideas by talking to friends and classmates who are children of divorced parents.

EDITING SKILLS: DISTINGUISHING BETWEEN HOMOPHONES

Look at these two sentences from Eric Marcus's essay:

I know it's the same for heterosexuals because their sexual orientation affects everything, from a choice of senior-prom date and the finger on which they *wear* their wedding band. . . .

A few months ago, Grandma traveled with me to Lafayette College, Pa., *where* I was invited to give a speech. . . .

Why did Marcus use *wear* in the first sentence but *where* in the second? Words like *wear* and *where,* which have the same pronunciation but different meanings and different spellings, are called **homophones.** There are a lot of these sound-alike words in English, and they cause problems for many writers. The only way to handle homophones is to stay alert for them and double-check their every use when you proofread. It's not just a matter of learning how to spell the words correctly; you also have to match the spelling with the meaning. Keeping a list of the ones that give you trouble will increase your awareness and save you time when you edit. And remember: the spell-checker on your computer won't help you with homophones.

EXERCISE

Each of the following words from Marcus's essay has a common homophone. Identify the homophone, and then write sentences that show the difference in meaning between the word Marcus used and its homophone.

1. weather (para. 7)
2. there (para. 8)
3. right (para. 13)
4. would (paras. 3, 5, 7, etc.)
5. knew (paras. 4, 7)
6. for (paras. 1, 2, 3, etc.)
7. week (para. 12)
8. In paragraph 7, Marcus uses the word *then,* and in paragraphs 11 and 12, he uses the word *than.* What is the difference between these two words? Although there is a slight variation in the way these words are pronounced, their sounds are similar enough to cause confusion. Write sentences that show the difference in meaning.

Compare your sentences with a classmate's. Then proofread the essay you have just written, looking for sound-alike words that you may have used incorrectly. If you have time, look back over previous essays for homophone errors; check to see that you're not still making the same ones.

✤ WEB SITE

http:don't.standford.edu/

The Don't Ask, Don't Tell, Don't Pursue site, a database project of the law library at Stanford University, gives the latest information about the controversy of gays in the military.

PREPARING TO READ

Do you enjoy horror movies? Why do you like to watch them? How do you react when you view them? If you don't enjoy horror movies, can you explain why they do not appeal to you?

Why We Crave Horror Movies

STEPHEN KING

You know Stephen King as the master of terror, the author of a string of best-selling horror novels. And you have probably seen some of the movies made from his novels: *Carrie, Misery, Christine, Pet Sematary,* and *Firestarter* (among others). In the following essay, King offers an entertaining explanation of why people like being scared out of their wits.

TERMS TO RECOGNIZE

grimaces *(para. 1)*	twisted facial expressions
hysterical *(para. 1)*	emotionally uncontrolled
province *(para. 3)*	proper area or sphere
depleted *(para. 3)*	used up, drained, worn out
innately *(para. 4)*	naturally, essentially
reactionary *(para. 4)*	wanting to return to an earlier time
menaced *(para. 6)*	threatened, endangered
voyeur *(para. 6)*	a peeping Tom, someone who enjoys watching something private or forbidden
penchant *(para. 7)*	a strong fondness or inclination
psychic *(para. 7)*	mental, psychological
status quo *(para. 9)*	existing condition or state of affairs
sanctions *(para. 10)*	expressions of disapproval, punishments
anarchistic *(para. 11)*	disorderly, ignoring the rules
morbidity *(para. 12)*	an interest in gruesome and horrible things
subterranean *(para. 12)*	underground

I think we're all mentally ill; those of us outside the asylums only hide it   1
a little better—and maybe not all that much better, after all. We've all known people who talk to themselves, people who sometimes squinch their faces into horrible grimaces when they believe no one is watching,

people who have some hysterical fear—of snakes, the dark, the tight place, the long drop . . . and, of course, those final worms and grubs that are waiting so patiently underground.

When we pay our four or five bucks and seat ourselves at tenth-row center in a theater showing a horror movie, we are daring the nightmare. 2

Why? Some of the reasons are simple and obvious. To show that we can, that we are not afraid, that we can ride this roller coaster. Which is not to say that a really good horror movie may not surprise a scream out of us at some point, the way we may scream when the roller coaster twists through a complete 360 or plows through a lake at the bottom of the drop. And horror movies, like roller coasters, have always been the special province of the young; by the time one turns 40 or 50, one's appetite for double twists or 360-degree loops may be considerably depleted. 3

We also go to re-establish our feelings of essential normality; the horror movie is innately conservative, even reactionary. Freda Jackson as the horrible melting woman in *Die, Monster, Die!* confirms for us that no matter how far we may be removed from the beauty of a Robert Redford or a Diana Ross, we are still light-years from true ugliness. 4

And we go to have fun. 5

Ah, but this is where the ground starts to slope away, isn't it? Because this is a very peculiar sort of fun, indeed. The fun comes from seeing others menaced—sometimes killed. One critic has suggested that if pro football has become the voyeur's version of combat, then the horror film has become the modern version of the public lynching. 6

It is true that the mythic, "fairy-tale" horror film intends to take away the shades of gray. . . . It urges us to put away our more civilized and adult penchant for analysis and to become children again, seeing things in pure blacks and whites. It may be that horror movies provide psychic relief on this level because this invitation to lapse into simplicity, irrationality and even outright madness is extended so rarely. We are told we may allow our emotions a free rein . . . or no rein at all. 7

If we are all insane, then sanity becomes a matter of degree. If your insanity leads you to carve up women like Jack the Ripper or the Cleveland Torso Murderer, we clap you away in the funny farm (but neither of those two amateur-night surgeons was ever caught, heh-heh-heh); if, on the other hand, your insanity leads you only to talk to yourself when you're under stress or to pick your nose on your morning bus, then you are left alone to go about your business . . . though it is doubtful that you will ever be invited to the best parties. 8

The potential lyncher is in almost all of us (excluding saints, past and present; but then, most saints have been crazy in their own ways), and every 9 now and then, he has to be let loose to scream and roll around in the grass. Our emotions and our fears form their own body, and we recognize that it demands its own exercise to maintain proper muscle tone. Certain of these emotional muscles are accepted—even exalted—in civilized society; they are, of course, the emotions that tend to maintain the status quo of civilization itself. Love, friendship, loyalty, kindness—these are all the emotions that we applaud, emotions that have been immortalized in the couplets of Hallmark cards and in the verses (I don't dare call it poetry) of Leonard Nimoy.

When we exhibit these emotions, society showers us with positive rein-   10
forcement; we learn this even before we get out of diapers. When, as children, we hug our rotten little puke of a sister and give her a kiss, all the aunts and uncles smile and twit and cry, "Isn't he the sweetest little thing?" Such coveted treats as chocolate-covered graham crackers often follow. But if we deliberately slam the rotten little puke of a sister's fingers in the door, sanctions follow—angry remonstrance from parents, aunts and uncles; instead of a chocolate-covered graham cracker, a spanking.

But anticivilization emotions don't go away, and they demand periodic   11
exercise. We have such "sick" jokes as, "What's the difference between a truckload of bowling balls and a truckload of dead babies?" (You can't unload a truckload of bowling balls with a pitchfork . . . a joke, by the way, that I heard originally from a ten-year-old). Such a joke may surprise a laugh or a grin out of us even as we recoil, a possibility that confirms the thesis: If we share a brotherhood of man, then we also share an insanity of man. None of which is intended as a defense of either the sick joke or insanity but merely as an explanation of why the best horror films, like the best fairy tales, manage to be reactionary, anarchistic, and revolutionary all at the same time.

The mythic horror movie, like the sick joke, has a dirty job to do. It   12
deliberately appeals to all that is worst in us. It is morbidity unchained, our most base instincts let free, our nastiest fantasies realized . . . and it all happens, fittingly enough, in the dark. For those reasons, good liberals often shy away from horror films. For myself, I like to see the most aggressive of them—*Dawn of the Dead,* for instance—as lifting a trap door in the civilized forebrain and throwing a basket of raw meat to the hungry alligators swimming around in that subterranean river beneath.

Why bother? Because it keeps them from getting out, man. It keeps   13
them down there and me up here. It was Lennon and McCartney who said that all you need is love, and I would agree with that.

As long as you keep the gators fed.   14

RESPONDING TO READING

Do you agree with King that we are all mentally ill and that our "anticivilization emotions don't go away"? Respond to these ideas in your journal.

GAINING WORD POWER

What does it mean to do "a complete 360"? (King uses the expression in para. 3.) You may know that 360 refers to the number of degrees in a circle and that the phrase means to go all the way around to where you started, to travel in a complete circle. One way of expressing the opposite idea is to say you did "an about-face," which is a military command for pivoting around to face in the opposite direction.

Both of these phrases—"a complete 360" and "an about-face"—are figurative expressions; they're supposed to put a picture in our minds by referring to an object (like a circle) or an action (like a military maneuver). **Figurative language** requires interpretation; we have to figure out the references and imagine the picture that the writer wants to put in our minds. Here are some more figurative phrases that Stephen King uses in his essay. Explain what they mean and tell what you see in your mind's eye. If you're not sure of what King means, ask other people for their interpretations.

1. "those final worms and grubs that are waiting so patiently underground"
2. "tenth-row center"
3. "shades of gray"
4. "clap you away in the funny farm"
5. "the couplets of Hallmark cards"
6. "before we get out of diapers"
7. "lifting a trap door in the civilized forebrain and throwing a basket of raw meat to the hungry alligators swimming around in that subterranean river beneath"

CONSIDERING CONTENT

1. What does King mean when he says that we are all mentally ill? What is the nature of the "insanity" that we share?
2. What are the obvious reasons for enjoying horror movies? What are some of the not-so-obvious reasons?
3. King talks about "the mythic, 'fairy-tale' horror film." What does he mean? How are horror movies like fairy tales? Do you think this a good comparison?

4. King refers to our "anticivilization emotions" that occasionally need exercise. What are these emotions? Why do they need to be exercised?
5. According to King, what "dirty job" do sick jokes and horror movies perform? Do you agree with this claim?
6. Do you think Stephen King is biased in his defense of horror movies? Do you think you would respond differently to this essay if it were written by someone you had never heard of?

CONSIDERING METHOD

1. King begins with a startling statement about insanity. What is the effect and point of this opening?
2. How does he maintain the insanity theme throughout the essay? Do you think this is an effective strategy?
3. At what point in the essay does King reveal that he will be dealing with causes?
4. Does King deal with immediate causes or long-term causes or both? In what order does he arrange the causes he discusses?
5. In paragraph 3, King compares watching horror movies to riding a roller coaster. This form of brief comparison is an **analogy.** What other analogies does King use in his essay? What purpose do they serve?
6. Identify comments or passages that you think are humorous. What does the humor contribute to this essay?
7. What is the function of the two one-sentence paragraphs (paras. 5 and 14)?

WRITING STEP BY STEP

Think of another form of entertainment that people seem to crave, and write an essay explaining why. You might write about soap operas, MTV, video games, action movies, reality TV, sports programs, jogging (or other exercise activities), bodybuilding, shopping, online chat rooms, or the like.

A. Begin with a startling statement, as Stephen King does.
B. Give background about the subject by explaining your opening statement.
C. Discuss the obvious or immediate causes first. Identify at least three reasons and explain them.
D. Then examine the long-term or underlying causes. Show how these causes produce the craving that you are writing about.
E. Be sure to name specific programs or games.
F. Use figurative language and analogies to help explain the causes. Even include a little humor the way King does, if you want to.

G. Write a conclusion in which you comment on the behavior you have analyzed. Make your comment an outgrowth of your discussion of underlying causes.

OTHER WRITING IDEAS

1. Interview a variety of people to find out why they like a certain type of entertainment (hospital shows, arcade games, stock car races, line dancing, rock concerts, ballet, situation comedies, or the like). Ask them to give you specific reasons. Then write an essay explaining why this form of entertainment is popular. Use several direct quotations from the people you interview to support your explanations.
2. Conduct an informal survey among your friends and relatives about their favorite junk food: What do they like about it? when do they eat it? how often? Using this information, do some freewriting about why you think people love this kind of food. Then gather your thoughts, and write an essay about either the causes or the effects of eating junk food.
3. Write an essay about the effects of watching too much TV.

EDITING SKILLS: CHECKING PRONOUN REFERENCE

Whenever you use pronouns (words such as *he, she, it, his, her, their,* etc., that stand in for nouns), you must be sure that each has a clear antecedent (the noun that the pronoun stands for). If the antecedents aren't clear, your readers can get lost. Look at this sentence from Stephen King's essay:

> We've all known people *who* talk to *themselves,* people *who* sometimes squinch *their* faces into horrible grimaces when *they* believe no one is watching. . . .

The pronouns *themselves, who, their,* and *they* all clearly refer to the antecedent *people.*

Several pronouns are especially troublesome when they appear without specific antecedents: *this, which,* and *these.* King uses these words eleven times. Sometimes he places them right before the nouns they refer to— "this roller coaster," "this level," "this invitation," "these emotions"—so there is no misunderstanding about what they mean. But in other instances, he uses *this, these,* and *which* as free-standing pronouns. Find these other uses (in paras. 3, 6, 9, 10, and 11), and see if you can name the thing or idea to which these pronouns refer. Do you think King has used these pronouns clearly?

EXERCISE

The following sentences are vague because they contain pronouns without clear antecedents. Rewrite each sentence to make it clear.

Example: Clyde made Gary do his homework.
Revisions: Gary did his homework because Clyde made him.
              Gary did Clyde's homework because Clyde made him.

1. Hampton aced the history test because he made it so easy.
2. Carlo is working on the railroad in Tennessee, which depresses him.
3. Kesha dropped out of school after they took away fall break.
4. Our cat chased the ground squirrel until he got tired.
5. Although Juan's mother is a chemist, Juan hates it.
6. Rosa tried to support herself by painting and acting. This was a mistake.
7. Mel blamed his failure on his choice of occupation, which was unfortunate.
8. Washington wore a sombrero and sequined gloves to the prom. This was a big hit.

Now look at the essay you have just written. Pay particular attention to your use of pronouns. Make sure each has a clear antecedent.

WEB SITE

www.stephenking.com/

Find out more about Stephen King's views on horror stories and other aspects of writing at the official Stephen King Web Presence.

PREPARING TO READ

Did your parents ever forbid you to do something that you went ahead and did anyway? What happened? How did you feel about it later?

Fifth Chinese Daughter

JADE SNOW WONG

Jade Snow Wong grew up in San Francisco, the daughter of immigrant parents who brought with them from China an ancient and rigid set of family traditions. The following excerpt from Wong's autobiography, *Fifth Chinese Daughter*, recounts the inevitable conflict between traditional parents and a young woman who is beginning to discover a different world beyond her home and neighborhood.

TERMS TO RECOGNIZE

oblige *(para. 2)*	accommodate, please
adamant *(para. 3)*	unyielding, inflexible
edict *(para. 3)*	command, rule
incurred *(para. 4)*	acquired, taken on
nepotism *(para. 7)*	favoritism shown to relatives
incredulous *(para. 12)*	unwilling to admit or accept what is heard; unbelieving
unfilial *(para. 12)*	disrespectful to parents
revered *(para. 12)*	honored, respected
innuendos *(para. 14)*	sly suggestions, indirect hints
devastated *(para. 15)*	crushed, overwhelmed
perplexed *(para. 16)*	puzzled, confused

by the time I was graduating from high school, my parents had done their best to produce an intelligent, obedient daughter, who would know more than the average Chinatown girl and should do better than average at a conventional job, her earnings brought home in repayment for their years of child support. Then, they hoped, she would marry a nice Chinese boy and make him a good wife, as well as an above-average mother for his children. Chinese custom used to decree that families should "introduce" chosen partners to each other's children. The groom's family should pay handsomely to the bride's family for rearing a well-bred daughter. They should also pay all bills for a glorious wedding banquet for several hundred guests. Their daughter belonged to the groom's family and must henceforth seek permission from all persons in his home before returning to her parents for a visit.

But having been set upon a new path, I did not oblige my parents with the expected conventional ending. At fifteen, I had moved away from home to work for room and board and a salary of twenty dollars per month. Having found that I could subsist independently, I thought it regrettable to terminate my education. Upon graduating from high school at the age of sixteen, I asked my parents to assist me in college expenses. I pleaded with my father, for his years of encouraging me to be above mediocrity in both Chinese and American studies had made me wish for some undefined but brighter future.   2

My father was briefly adamant. He must conserve his resources for my oldest brother's medical training. Though I desired to continue on an above-average course, his material means were insufficient to support that ambition. He added that if I had the talent, I could provide for my own college education. When he had spoken, no discussion was expected. After this edict, no daughter questioned.   3

But this matter involved my whole future—it was not simply asking for permission to go to a night church meeting (forbidden also). Though for years I had accepted the authority of the one I honored most, his decision that night embittered me as nothing ever had. My oldest brother had so many privileges, had incurred unusual expenses for luxuries which were taken for granted as his birthright, yet these were part of a system I had accepted. Now I suddenly wondered at my father's interpretation of the Christian code: was it intended to discriminate against a girl after all, or was it simply convenient for my father's economics and cultural prejudice? Did a daughter have any right to expect more than a fate of obedience, according to the old Chinese standard? As long as I could remember, I had been told that a female followed three men during her lifetime: as a girl, her father; as a wife, her husband; as an old woman, her son.   4

My indignation mounted against that tradition and I decided then that my past could not determine my future. I knew that more education would prepare me for a different expectation than my other female schoolmates, few of whom were to complete a college degree. I, too, had my father's unshakable faith in the justice of God, and I shared his unconcern with popular opinion.   5

So I decided to enter junior college, now San Francisco's City College, because the fees were lowest. I lived at home and supported myself with an after-school job which required long hours of housework and cooking but   6 paid me twenty dollars per month, of which I saved as much as possible. The thrills derived from reading and learning, in ways ranging from chemistry experiments to English compositions, from considering new ideas of sociology to the logic of Latin, convinced me that I had made a correct choice. I was kept in a state of perpetual mental excitement by new Western subjects and concepts and did not mind long hours of work and study. I also made new friends, which led to another painful incident with my parents, who had heretofore discouraged even girlhood friendships.

The college subject which had the most jolted me was sociology. The   7
instructor fired my mind with his interpretation of family relationships. As he explained to our class, it used to be an economic asset for American farming families to be large, since children were useful to perform agricultural chores. But this situation no longer applied and children should be regarded as individuals with their own rights. Unquestioning obedience should be replaced with parental understanding. So at sixteen, discontented as I was with my parents' apparent indifference to me, those words of my sociology professor gave voice to my sentiments. How old-fashioned was the dead-end attitude of my parents! How ignorant they were of modern thought and progress! The family unit had been China's strength for centuries, but it had also been her weakness, for corruption, nepotism, and greed were all justified in the name of the family's welfare. My new ideas festered; I longed to release them.

One afternoon on a Saturday, which was normally occupied with my   8
housework job, I was unexpectedly released by my employer, who was departing for a country weekend. It was a rare joy to have free time and I wanted to enjoy myself for a change. There had been a Chinese-American boy who shared some classes with me. Sometimes we had found each other walking to the same 8:00 A.M. class. He was not a special boyfriend, but I had enjoyed talking to him and had confided in him some of my problems. Impulsively, I telephoned him. I knew I must be breaking rules, and I felt shy and scared. At the same time, I was excited at this newly found forwardness, with nothing more purposeful than to suggest another walk together.

He understood my awkwardness and shared my anticipation. He asked   9
me to "dress up" for my first movie date. My clothes were limited but I changed to look more graceful in silk stockings and found a bright ribbon for my long black hair. Daddy watched, catching my mood, observing the dashing preparations. He asked me where I was going without his permission and with whom.

I refused to answer him. I thought of my rights! I thought he surely   10
would not try to understand. Thereupon Daddy thundered his displeasure and forbade my departure.

I found a new courage as I heard my voice announce calmly that I was   11
no longer a child, and if I could work my way through college, I would
choose my own friends. It was my right as a person.

My mother had heard the commotion and joined my father to face me;   12
both appeared shocked and incredulous. Daddy at once demanded the source
of this unfilial, non-Chinese theory. And when I quoted my college professor, reminding him that he had always felt teachers should be revered, my
father denounced that professor as a foreigner who was disregarding the superiority of our Chinese culture, with its sound family strength. My father did
not spare me; I was condemned as an ingrate for echoing dishonorable opinions which should only be temporary whims, yet nonetheless inexcusable.

The scene was not yet over. I completed my proclamation to my father,   13
who had never allowed me to learn how to dance, by adding that I was
attending a movie, unchaperoned, with a boy I met at college.

My startled father was sure that my reputation would be subject to whis-   14
pered innuendos. I must be bent on disgracing the family name; I was ruining my future, for surely I would yield to temptation. My mother
underscored him by saying that I hadn't any notion of the problems
endured by parents of a young girl.

I would not give in. I reminded them that they and I were not in China,   15
that I wasn't going out with just anybody but someone I trusted! Daddy
gave a roar that no man could be trusted, but I devastated them in declaring that I wished the freedom to find my own answers.

Both parents were thoroughly angered, scolded me for being shameless,   16
and predicted that I would some day tell them I was wrong. But I dimly
perceived that they were conceding defeat and were perplexed at this breakdown of their training. I was too old to beat and too bold to intimidate.

RESPONDING TO READING

Has college affected you in the same way that it affected Jade Snow
Wong? Write in your journal about the effects college has had on you;
compare your reactions to Wong's.

GAINING WORD POWER

Come up with definitions of your own for the italicized words in the
following sentences. Use the clues from the surrounding words and sentences
to help you. Then check your definition against a dictionary definition.

1. "Chinese custom used to *decree* that families should 'introduce'
   chosen partners to each other's children." (para. 1)

2. "Having found that I could *subsist* independently, I thought it regrettable to *terminate* my education." (para. 2)
3. "I pleaded with my father, for his years of encouraging me to be above *mediocrity* in both Chinese and American studies had made me wish for some undefined but brighter future." (para. 2)
4. "My *indignation* mounted against that tradition and I decided then that my past could not determine my future." (para. 5)
5. "I was kept in a state of *perpetual* mental excitement by new Western subjects and concepts and did not mind long hours of work and study." (para. 6)
6. "My new ideas *festered;* I longed to release them." (para. 7)
7. "He was not a special boyfriend, but I had enjoyed talking to him and had *confided* in him some of my problems. *Impulsively,* I telephoned him. I knew I must be breaking rules, and I felt shy and scared." (para. 8)
8. "I was too old to beat and too bold to *intimidate*." (para. 16)

CONSIDERING CONTENT

1. What did you learn about Wong's parents and their traditional beliefs in the first paragraph?
2. What caused Wong to rebel against her parents? What situations and experiences contributed to her quest for independence?
3. Why was Wong sure that more education would prepare her for a different future from that of her classmates? Did it?
4. Why did the sociology course affect Wong so strongly? What did she learn in that course that changed her views and fed her rebellion?
5. What action did Wong take to demonstrate her independence? Why did she choose this particular way of disobeying her parents? Do her actions seem risky and rebellious to you?
6. In what ways was Wong a lot like her father? Which of his beliefs and attitudes actually contributed to his daughter's rebellion?
7. Wong writes that her parents "were perplexed at this breakdown of their training" (para. 16). What didn't they understand? Did their cultural background cause their lack of understanding, or do all parents face this same problem?

CONSIDERING METHOD

1. Why is the first paragraph important? How does the information in this paragraph prepare you for Wong's actions?
2. What does Wong accomplish by mentioning her oldest brother? What is she trying to show?

3. What is the function of the questions in paragraph 4? Why does Wong express these ideas in questions instead of in statements? (See pages 132–133 for an explanation of rhetorical questions.)

4. How much time passes in this selection? How does Wong indicate the passage of time? Where does she move back in time? Why does she do so?

5. Find sentences or comments that reveal that Wong has positive feelings for her father. Why is it important to include these feelings?

6. Paragraph 8 opens with these words: "One afternoon on a Saturday . . ." What do these words signal? What mode of writing begins at this point?

7. Wong doesn't use direct quotations or quoted conversation. How does she report what she said to her parents and what they said to her? What is the effect of this indirect presentation?

8. How would you describe the **tone** of this selection? Does Wong sound angry, sad, upset, calm, confident, relieved, happy, or what?

WRITING STEP BY STEP

As we grow older, we sometimes change our minds about our parents. We begin to see things more from their point of view. Think of a piece of advice, a household rule, or a parental opinion that you used to hate but now understand. If you don't want to write about your parents, think of another adult, such as a teacher or a coach, who set down rules or gave advice that you once rejected but now think appropriate. Write an essay in which you explain what caused you to change your mind.

A. Begin with a statement of your general point. You might say something like "I used to think my parents' advice was outdated and pointless, but a lot of it makes sense to me today" or "Now that I'm coaching pee-wee soccer, I follow some of the same rules I used to hate when I was a player."

B. Explain the particular rule, opinion, advice, or guideline you used to resist. Re-create specific incidents and arguments you used to have that illustrate your earlier response.

C. Analyze your change in attitude. Cite specific reasons or causes, and explain them.

D. If there was a key incident or turning point in your thinking, focus on that event and describe it in detail.

E. Conclude by revealing how you feel about this change in thinking. Does it mean that you've grown up or that you've sold out?

OTHER WRITING IDEAS

1. Explain why some jobs or professions seem to be done mainly by women (like child care, housework, nursing, elementary school teaching). As you plan your paper, talk to some women who do these jobs or who are preparing to enter one of these professions, and ask their opinions. Also talk to some men, and ask them how they would feel about teaching grade school, being a nurse, cleaning houses, or taking care of children for a living.

2. Write an essay about why adolescents leave home. Or write an essay about the effects of their leaving home.

3. Talk to someone who comes from a cultural background different from yours. If you can, spend some time with this person's friends and family. Then, with your classmates as audience, write an essay explaining what you learned about this culture and how it affected your attitudes toward these people.

EDITING SKILLS: USING PARALLEL STRUCTURE

Look at these last two sentences from paragraph 3 in Wong's essay:

When he had spoken, no discussion was expected.

After his edict, no daughter questioned.

When you look at the sentences in this format, with one on top of the other, you can see how they match up in size and form. This correspondence is called **parallelism,** or parallel structure. Parallel structure often occurs within a sentence, as the following sentences from Wong's essay show. (The parallel parts are italicized for you.)

As long as I could remember, I had been told that a female followed three men during her lifetime: *as a girl, her father; as a wife, her husband; as an old woman, her son.*

I was *too old to beat* and *too bold to intimidate.*

Writers use parallel structure to catch the reader's attention and, as Wong does, to compare or contrast important points. Parallel structures also add **emphasis** and variety to a sentence or paragraph.

EXERCISE

Copy two of the sentences previously quoted; write two or three sentences of your own that imitate Wong's use of parallel structure. Then examine the following sentences, and write your own sentences that imitate the parallel structures.

1. "This freedom, like all freedoms, has its dangers and its responsibilities."—James Baldwin

   Imitation: This new attendance policy, like all school policies, has its supporters and its critics.

2. "We must stop talking about the American dream and start listening to the dreams of Americans."—Reubin Askew

   Imitation: We must stop asking silly questions and start questioning silly policies.

Look over your own essay and revise two or three sentences, using parallel structure. Read the new sentences aloud. If they sound clear and effective, keep them in your essay.

WEB SITE
www.lib.uci.edu/rrsc/asiamer.html
Asian American Studies Resources: an extensive collection of Asian study sites, constructed by the University of California at Irvine Library, that includes bibliographies, magazines, audiovisual materials, research programs, movement groups, gay Asian resources, and more.

PREPARING TO READ

Have you ever had a job where you were unappreciated? If so, write a paragraph in your journal telling how you felt about your employer. If you've never been unhappily employed, write a paragraph telling how you felt about an employer who valued your services and treated you well.

Working: Nobody Talks about the Common Person's Life

STEVE LOPEZ

Steve Lopez grew up in a middle-class neighborhood east of San Francisco. He studied journalism at San José State University and wrote for several newspapers in California before moving to the *Philadelphia Inquirer,* where he was a reporter and columnist for ten years. He returned to California and now writes a column for the *Los Angeles Times.* The following article, syndicated by the Knight-Ridder/Tribune News Service, appeared in a number of newspapers around the country in August 1996. Lopez tells about his father's employment experiences to support his criticism of the way working-class people are treated by the bosses of America.

TERMS TO RECOGNIZE

grievance *(para. 4)*   formal complaint of unfair treatment
ecstasy *(para. 5)*   intense pleasure, delight
CEOs *(para. 9)*   chief executive officers
blather *(para. 13)*   foolish talk, nonsense

the older I get, the more I realize my attitudes about work come from   1
my father. Almost 70 and still working part-time, my father has survived a half-century of being laid off, fired, downsized, taken for granted and blamed for problems that weren't his doing. Through it all, he has put on his pants each morning and found a way to earn a buck.

I've been thinking about this lately because of the presidential campaign   2
and all the stories about the economy, job security, and welfare. I've been thinking about it because my father's experience reminds me how out of touch the average politician is with people who work for a living, or try to.

My father's parents ran a mom-and-pop grocery store in the small town   3
where he grew up, and he spent his childhood working in the store. My
mother did the same at her family's grocery store four blocks away. Tony
Lopez became a star athlete in high school; Grace Costanza Nuzzo was a
cheerleader. Fifty years later, they are still together.

When my older sister was born, my father drove a milk truck. But by   4
the time I came into the world, he had been fired for taking a day off he
had earned with overtime. The Teamsters union stepped in, and my father
eventually won his grievance. But by then, the union had helped him find
another job. Now he drove a truck for Wonder Bread.

As a boy, I thought that was the next-best job to playing centerfield for   5
the Giants. The truck carried more than just bread. My father delivered
Hostess cakes, too. Sometimes he'd come home for lunch and let me inspect
his cargo, but I couldn't touch and I couldn't eat. It was ecstasy and torture,
and to this day, I have a weakness for anything fresh and sweet.

When I was 10 or 11, my father's job was on the line. I didn't know all   6
the details then. I only knew, for the first time in my life, that nothing
could be trusted. If a store wasn't moving bread and cake, the boss said it
was my father's fault. If an order got screwed up at the warehouse, it was
his fault. They were laying everything on him. He was under enormous
pressure and it walked in the door with him each night filling his face with
shadows, and we ate dinner in silence.

One morning he threw his back out and collapsed on the floor, but he   7
was afraid to miss a day of work. He told my mother to run a hot shower
and he dragged himself into it and ran water on his back and put on his
clothes and went to work. In the end, he lost the job. His boss's son wanted
to drive a truck, it turned out; and to clear the way, they fired the man with
the least seniority. They fired my father. The Teamsters took up the grievance and my father won, again. But he knew his bosses would make his
life hell so he took another job, and another, and another. Foster's muffins.
Cloverleaf milk. Blue Seal bread. Dolly Madison cakes.

In the late '60s he caught on with a candy and tobacco distributor. Six   8
years ago sitting on healthy profits, that company won a 28 percent salary
and benefits giveback from the union by spreading fear. They had just
busted another division, turned employees out, and replaced them at lower
salaries. Modern Business 101.

These are the economics I know. The economics of greed at the top and   9
of hard work and lousy pay at the bottom. The economics of million-dollar
bonuses for CEOs who turn employees onto the streets. The rich get richer,
my father always says; the little guys get it in the neck, and the people in
the middle pay.

In some ways, my father was lucky. He had to hustle in his time, but   10
unlike today's market, there were plenty of jobs for unskilled, uneducated
people. The unions were strong and although the pay didn't put you in a
Cadillac, you got by.

Go to college, he always told us. Go to college so you don't end up like   11
your old man. But for all his warnings, I ended up a lot like my father. I
have his contempt for anyone who expects a free pass and his compassion
for anyone who's trying to make it without one. Like him, I trust nobody
associated with money, politics or authority. Week in and week out, some
doofus in a suit and a smile stands up and tells us the economy is in great
shape, and it always raises a question for me. Do they ever get outside?

We have the highest child poverty rate in the industrial world, and the   12
bottom is falling out for people by the millions who came up the way my
family came up. And as it gets harder down there, the talk from on high gets
meaner. They tell you that if you're not working today, you're a louse. Period.

Like my father, I tune out that blather the same way I tune out the notion   13
that the issue of our time is abortion, or terrorism, or taxes. It is none of
those. The challenge of our time, as we head toward the election that takes
us into the next century, isn't even being discussed. No one is talking about
how to educate, train, and employ those who have fallen behind or never
even got started. The issue is the fate of the common, ordinary working
person, who has been written out of the book of American politics.

RESPONDING TO READING

What do you think about the current trend to downsize the workforce
in order to improve corporate profits? Do you know anybody like Lopez's
father who lost a job even though performing well? Do you agree with
Lopez that this practice is wrong? Or do you think employers have the
right to get rid of anybody they choose to fire?

GAINING WORD POWER

Explain as thoroughly as you can what the following phrases mean in
Lopez's essay.

1. mom-and-pop grocery store (para. 3)
2. on the line (para. 6)
3. filling his face with shadows (para. 6)
4. caught on with (para. 8)
5. busted another division (para. 8)

6. put you in a Cadillac (para. 10)
7. a free pass (para. 11)
8. some doofus in a suit (para. 11)
9. the bottom is falling out (para. 12)
10. the book of American politics (para. 13)

CONSIDERING CONTENT

1. Why does Lopez think that the average politician is "out of touch" with working people (para. 2)?
2. What were some of the reasons that Lopez's father repeatedly lost his job?
3. Why did Lopez, as a child, like having his father work for Wonder Bread?
4. Explain as completely as you can the meaning of "Modern Business 101" (para. 8).
5. What advice did Lopez's father always give his children? Do you think it's good advice?
6. What economic problems does Lopez point out in paragraph 12? What does he believe is the cause of these problems?
7. What does Lopez think is the "challenge of our time," a crucial need that "isn't even being discussed" (para. 13)? Why do you suppose politicians are not discussing this issue?

CONSIDERING METHOD

1. Does this article move from causes to effects or from effects to causes? What makes this **structure** more effective than the reverse?
2. Why does Lopez include the details about the early lives of his father and mother in paragraph 3?
3. What is the purpose of the brief narrative in paragraph 7?
4. Why do you think the word "Period" is punctuated as a complete sentence at the end of paragraph 12? What does it mean?
5. What is the author's **tone?** Is it neutral or do you detect an element of resentment or anger? Locate specific details—words and sentences—that convey the tone.

WRITING STEP BY STEP

Think of an event that touched your life forcefully enough that you can describe its effects on you. You need to choose an event with causes you understand well enough to analyze or at least to speculate about. Then write an essay exploring your difficulty, whatever it was or is—a serious accident or illness, your parents' divorce, a date rape, high school drug addiction, an unwanted pregnancy, an incident involving racial prejudice or sexual harassment. (If your life has been blessedly free from trauma and upsets, select a topic from the first item in the following Other Writing Ideas section.)

A. Begin with the effects of this traumatic event on your life, the way Lopez describes in the first half of his essay the effects of his father's employment insecurity. Include specific details when you can (for example, the Hostess cakes, his father's bad back, the hot shower).

B. Make a transition similar to the one Lopez uses in the opening sentence of paragraph 10: "In some ways, my father was lucky."

C. Then discuss the causes, as you understand them, of your problem, the way Lopez presents the underlying economic causes of his father's off-and-on employment.

D. If you can come up with a solution to your problem, present that next, as Lopez does in paragraph 13 when he mentions that "No one is talking about how to educate, train, and employ those who have fallen behind or never even got started."

E. Conclude with a call for action, as Lopez does in his final sentence. By declaring that "the fate of the common, ordinary working person . . . has been written out of the book of American politics," he is, in effect, issuing a challenge to right-minded people to take note of this injustice and to see about correcting it.

OTHER WRITING IDEAS

1. Think of some habit you have or an activity you engage in that you would like to quit, such as smoking cigarettes, being late all the time, eating junk food, watching soap operas, or reading *The National Enquirer*. Following the preceding step-by-step instructions, write an account of how the activity affects you; then discuss the causes of the habit; finally, explain your plan to stop. Your concluding sentence will be your resolution to follow through in beating the habit.

2. Select a magazine advertisement and analyze the causes of its appeal. Submit the ad (or a photocopy) along with your essay.

3. Brainstorm a list of causes for some problem you are facing, such as paying your bills, getting all your work done, dealing with a difficult friend or teacher, sticking to your diet. Organize the list into immediate and long-term causes. Write an essay analyzing the causes of your problem and concluding with your solution.

EDITING SKILLS: ELIMINATING WORDINESS

A good writer would never write only short, simple sentences, but a good clean sentence is better than a wordy, cluttered one. Look at these spare sentences from Lopez's essay:

> Fifty years later, they are still together.
> They fired my father.
> These are the economics I know.
> Go to college, he always told us.

A less skillful writer might have used a lot more words to say the same thing, like this:

> Through thick and thin, through hard times and good times, through better and worse, for half a century they have stayed married to each other.
> With no thought that his self-esteem might be hurt or damaged or that his family might suffer hardship, they ended my father's term of employment.
> These are the unfair and unjust economic realities operating in America as I have been able to observe them so far in my lifetime.
> You can better yourselves financially and intellectually and improve your prospects in life by going to college, he repeatedly advised us.

There's nothing actually wrong with those sentences except what English teachers call *verbiage* and everybody else calls **wordiness.** Be careful not to say the same thing twice ("hurt or damaged," "unfair and unjust," "so far in my lifetime"). And avoid these common expressions:

WORDY	CONCISE
tall in height	tall
past history	history
blue in color	blue
advance forward	advance
expensive in price	expensive
consensus of opinion	consensus
continue to remain	remain
join together	join
few in number	few
positive benefits	benefits
at this point in time	at this time

EXERCISE

If you have trouble saying things succinctly, practice by streamlining the following wordy sentences. Keep the same meaning but eliminate the extra words. Here's an example:

The male-gendered style used online in ListServe communications is, at this point in time, characterized by an adversarial attitude.

(Revised) The male style used in communications on ListServe is adversarial.

1. It is my desire to be called Ishmael.
2. In my opinion there are many diverse elements about this problem that one probably ought to at least think about before arriving at an opinion on the matter.
3. The obnoxious child was seldom corrected or reprimanded because its baffled and adoring parents thought its objectionable behavior was normal and acceptable.
4. There came a time when, based on what I had been reading, I arrived at the feeling that the food we buy at the supermarkets to eat is sometimes, perhaps often, bad for us.
5. By and large, a stitch sewed or basted as soon as a rip is discovered may well save nine times the amount of sewing necessary if the job is put off even for a relatively short time.

Now go through your final draft one more time looking only for verbal clutter. Then, in the words of Mark Twain, "When in doubt, leave it out."

WEB SITE

www.morrill.org/books/lopez.shtml

Biography of Steve Lopez and comments about his writing, with links to his books and recent newspaper columns.

Student Essay Analyzing Causes

Why We Watch Daytime Talk Shows

Tricia Rooney

"Today, learn more than you would ever want to   1
know about fathers who sleep with their daughter's
best friends!" Flip channels. "Up next, we have
people who tip the scales at 500 pounds and wafer-
thin folks under 80 pounds!"

Daytime talk shows have become so daring in the   2
past few years that we are almost numb to the crazy
and sometimes gruesome topics that our friends Jerry
Springer, Gordon Elliot, Geraldo Rivera, and others
present to us. Back in the days of Donahue and early
Oprah, we had our first glimpse of what "other people"
were doing. Even though we got a look at people's
lives, it wasn't as dramatic as today. Donahue would
have, for example, homosexuals who married the
opposite sex to feel normal and fit in, but that was
as far as he would go, and he really did seem to
care. Donahue and early Oprah centered on average
people who had problems or talents, and they showed
compassion and interest. Today's talk show hosts seem
shallow and present their guests as sideshow freaks.

Why have we evolved from interested viewers into   3
sideshow gawkers? One of the reasons is that news
media are more open about covering less pleasant acts
in society. With blood-soaked victims on the six
o'clock news every night, we need something more to
give us chills and make us wonder. Also, more people
are coming out with their personal lifestyles than
ever before. For example, you can catch skinheads
doing something or another on talk shows quite
frequently. Finally, there is the element that we all
need--attention. I firmly believe that some of the
guests on the trashier talk shows are really not all
that they portray themselves to be. Perhaps they had
the chance to go on a talk show and wanted to make
the most of it. Or maybe they were paid to be proud
freaks that we can stare at with a fellow viewer.

Although we are exposed to the oddities and tragedies in society on a regular basis, and have become bored with them, talk shows quench the thirst for our true hunger--curiosity. Part of this curiosity involves the need to hear how crazy someone else's life is so we can feel better about our own. Every day we compare ourselves to others. So-and-so has a better car, but I have a better job, we think. Or maybe we think there is no one worse off than we are. Talk shows give us other people's problems and predicaments to make us feel very normal and well off. Even though talk show topics get radical sometimes, they promote a feeling of well-being within us. When we see shows about battered partners who refuse to leave their abusers, we feel upset and angry, but inside we also feel safe because our situation is not that bad. When we hear about pregnant women who do drugs, we think how foolish and uneducated they must be, and that makes us feel smart.

Our craving for talk shows is like a Brazil nut: dark and distasteful on the outside (like the people on the shows) but pleasant and tasty inside (like us). The nut inside is like us because it's better than the shell in almost every way. And I think we are all a little nuts in some way. Sure, I may have imaginary friends I sometimes talk to, and I hope that Mel Gibson's soul passes through mine when he dies, and I have an irrational fear of dogs, but, hey, I am not as bad off as those people on the talk shows.

Talk shows attract us because they offer far-out topics that shock us, amuse us, or make us wonder. They stimulate us because we talk about the shows with our friends and wonder what those people's lives must be like. All the while, we think how our lives are better and how we could never be that bad. Talk shows are actually healthier than we think because they build our self-esteem and help us feel worthwhile about our own nutty ways.

C h a p t e r

STRATEGIES FOR INFLUENCING OTHERS

Argument and Persuasion

You already know when to use persuasion: when you hope to get your readers to agree with you and maybe, as a result, to take some kind of action—like giving you a refund or picketing city hall. And on essay tests and in classroom assignments, you are often asked to take a stand or support a conclusion.

All the writing strategies that you studied in previous chapters can be used to persuade your readers or to argue a point. You can use comparison/contrast to demonstrate the superiority of whole-wheat over white bread or cause–effect analysis to convince your readers that rap music reinforces violent attitudes toward women or definition to show that computer nerds are more interesting than most people think. In this chapter, you will use all the strategies for organizing your thoughts and ideas as you learn how to influence readers' opinions about controversial or unfamiliar issues.

THE POINT OF ARGUMENT AND PERSUASION

Your purpose in this type of writing is to encourage the readers to accept your point of view, solution, plan, or complaint as their own. Traditionally, the word **persuasion** refers to attempts to sway the readers' emotions, while the word **argument** refers to tactics that address the readers' logic. Most convincing writing today mixes the two types of appeal. A personal testimony from a paraplegic accident victim pleading with readers to use their seat belts persuades through emotional identification. A list of statistics concerning injury rates before and after seat belt laws went into effect argues the point through rationality. A combination of the two tactics would probably be quite effective. In everyday language, *persuasion* means influence over the audience, whether emotional or rational.

THE PRINCIPLES OF ARGUMENT AND PERSUASION

Presenting a conventional persuasive essay involves five tasks.

1. State the **issue** your essay will address, and put it in a context—why is it controversial or problematic? Why do people care about it? Why do people disagree about it?
2. State your main point or thesis. What point of view, solution, or stance do you wish the readers to adopt? This is your **claim.**
3. Provide well-developed **evidence** on your own side of the issue. You can develop your point through facts, statistics, examples, expert testimony, and logical reasoning (cause and effect, analogy), just to name a few strategies. This is the longest part of a conventional argument, and each piece of evidence will probably take a paragraph or more to develop.
4. Respond to opposing viewpoints. This is called the **refutation** section. Especially when arguments against your own are widely known, you need to acknowledge them and counter them or your essay will have obvious holes in it. You might minimize their importance, demonstrate that they are not logical or factual, or offer alternative ways of thinking about them.
5. Close by reminding your reader of your main point and the strength of your evidence. Many persuasive essays include a call to action, encouraging readers to do something in support of your cause.

Writers often alter this conventional plan, especially tasks 3 and 4. For example, in this chapter, "Death Penalty Showdown" focuses on refutation, countering several anti–death penalty arguments, one by one. "The War on Drugs" presents a lengthy indictment of the current drug prosecution policies and ends with the author's proposal, rather than the other way around. "A Crime of Compassion" gives the most space to the moving personal story of an expert on the topic of euthanasia. You can tailor your essay to fit your topic, audience, purpose, and the nature of your evidence.

THE ELEMENTS OF GOOD ARGUMENT

Claims, evidence, and refutation are the basic building blocks of argument. You must understand them in order to write persuasively and effectively.

Claims

The "engine" that propels any argument is its claim. Claims fall into three categories:

1. *Claims of fact* assert that something is true: "Women currently do not receive equal pay for equal work."
2. *Claims of value* support or deny the worth or merit of something: "Getting a college education is more important than playing sports."
3. *Claims of policy* state that certain conditions, courses of action, or practices should be adopted: "A six-month maternity leave policy ought to be required by law."

For any argument to be effective, it must begin with a claim that's significant, reasonable, and supportable by evidence.

Evidence

Some of the most frequently used kinds of evidence are these:

- *Personal observation or experience:* "I came the closest to achieving a decent fit between income and expenses only when I worked seven days a week." This is the least widely accepted form of evidence because it comes from a narrow band of experience and may not be representative. But it can be very persuasive in communicating the human significance of an issue.
- *Facts:* "Rents usually have to be less than 30 percent of one's income to be considered 'affordable.'" Facts are noncontroversial pieces of information that can be confirmed through observation or by generally accepted sources; they are persuasive to the extent that they relate to the statement they support.
- *Relevant examples:* "One waitress shares a room in a boarding house for $250 a week; another lives with her mother; the night cook pays $170 a week for a one-person trailer; the hostess lives in a van parked behind a shopping center at night." Examples are most persuasive when they are objective and clearly relevant.
- *Testimony:* "Maggie Spade of the Economic Policy Institute explains that the low-income housing crisis exists partly because it is not reflected in the official poverty rate, which is based on the cost of food, not shelter." Testimony should come from sources that the readers will accept as credible; it carries its greatest weight when the meaning of the facts or data is not self-evident and some judgment or interpretation is required to reach a conclusion.

- *Data:* "Almost 60 percent of poor renters, amounting to a total of 4.4 million households, spend more than half of their income on shelter." This is probably the most readily accepted form of evidence because of its apparent objectivity and scope.

To be persuasive, all evidence in support of a claim must meet certain standards:

1. It must be reasonably up-to-date.
2. It must be sufficient in scope.
3. It must be relevant to the claim.

Thus, you wouldn't use 1990 unemployment data in support of a 2002 policy decision (recentness). Neither would you rely on unemployment data from only one month to formulate a long-term unemployment policy (scope). Nor would you use employment data from Canada to comment on the American unemployment picture, unless your argument involved an overall comparison of the two countries' economies (relevance).

Refutation

Arguments always assume that other points of view are possible; otherwise, there would be no reason to argue. You may feel so strongly about an issue that you want to attack those who disagree with you and ridicule their opinions, but that strategy can backfire, especially if you're trying to influence readers who are undecided. Your case will be strengthened if you treat opposing views with respect and understanding.

This acknowledgment of and response to the opposing views is called refutation. There is no best place in an argument to refute the opposition. Sometimes you will want to bring up opposing arguments early and deal with them right away. Another approach is to anticipate objections as you develop your own case point by point. Wherever you decide to include your refutation, your goal is to point out problems with the opponents' reasoning and evidence. You can refute opposing arguments by showing that they are unsound, unfair, or flawed in their logic. Frequently, you will present contrasting evidence to reveal the weakness of your opponents' views and to reinforce your own position.

When an opposing argument is so compelling that it cannot be easily countered, you should concede its strength. This approach will establish that you are knowledgeable and fair-minded. You can sometimes accept the opponents' line of thought up to a certain point—but no further. Or you can show that their strong point addresses only *one* part of a complex problem.

A SAMPLE ANNOTATED ARGUMENT

The following selection appeared in *U.S. News & World Report,* December 30, 1996. Although this article is a news report, it also contains an argument. The writer makes a claim of fact: that needle-exchange programs are effective in reducing the rate of HIV infection. He also presents a claim involving policy: that the federal ban on funding these programs should be lifted. The marginal notes identify key features and strategies in building an argument.

Ignoring the Solution

JOSHUA WOLF SHENK

Statement of the problem

AIDS was once the scourge of the gay community. Soon, it will be largely a drug addict's disease. Scientists believe that 50 percent of all new HIV infections occur among intravenous drug users, with an additional 20 percent or so occurring among junkies' sex partners. The syringe is the Typhoid Mary of the 1990s. Yet what worked best in curtailing the spread of HIV among homosexuals—mass education campaigns promoting safe sex—has been ineffective with drug addicts lurking in society's shadows. What does seem to work is giving drug users clean needles.

Primary claim (thesis)

Solution

Since 1986, some 100 small needle-exchange programs have sprouted up around the country, through which used syringes are traded for new, sterile ones—no questions asked. Often run by private groups with limited funds, these experiments have been the object of intense scrutiny by major universities and federal health agencies. The conclusion? The programs work. Studies have shown up to a sevenfold reduction in all blood-borne diseases, a 33 percent projected drop in HIV infections and 25 percent fewer cases of dangerous behavior, such as needle sharing.

Evidence (data)

Claim of fact

Further claim

Besides saving lives, these needle exchanges deliver a huge financial payoff. Consider the case of an HIV-positive addict who infects eight others in a one-year period (a very modest estimate). If

Evidence (example, data)

each turns to Medicaid to pay his or her lifetime medical costs (at an average $119,000 plus), that's about a $1 million burden for taxpayers—money that could have been saved if the one addict had been in a needle-exchange program.

Concession — Evidence for the effectiveness of needle exchanges is not airtight. Drug users who participate in needle exchanges may be more safety conscious and thus at less risk of contracting HIV in the first place. But studies also show that those who participate improve their own behavior over Refutation — time. So evidence that needle exchanges have at | Restatement of claim least some positive effects is strong.

On balance, the studies are persuasive enough that physician Scott Hitt, chairman of President Clinton's Advisory Council on HIV/AIDS, rebuked his own president for banning the use of Evidence (expert testimony) federal AIDS funds for needle exchanges. Hitt is | Implied claim of policy joined in the endorsement of needle exchanges— and the call for more federal involvement—by the National Academy of Sciences, the Centers for Disease Control and Prevention and the General Accounting Office.

The administration worries that needle exchanges might increase drug use. It's a reasonable fear but one not borne out by research, according to the CDC. Only a handful of needle-Refutation of first objection exchange studies have tracked drug use, but their conclusions jibe with anecdotal evidence and common sense: While addicts prefer clean needles, they will eagerly opt for the abundant supply of dirty ones in the face of a monstrous drug craving.

Some worry that needle exchanges are the classic "Band-Aid"—dealing with HIV infection but not the underlying drug addiction. But Refutation of second objection needle exchanges have actually worked as a bridge into real treatment. One program in Tacoma, Wash., made nearly 1,000 referrals to | Evidence (example) drug treatment programs in two years. Others worry that needle exchanges, cheap as they are,

Refutation of third objection	will siphon funds from zero-tolerance treatment efforts. But the real problem is that all anti-addiction programs are woefully underfunded.
	It's hard to avoid the suspicion that these concerns have less to do with science or public health than with politics; specifically, a reluctance to muddy the "just say no" message. But there's another message leaders should heed—that no one
Conclusion	has to die needlessly. Peter Lurie, a leading University of California researcher, estimates that nearly 10,000 lives could have been saved over the past few years by an aggressive expansion of needle-exchange programs. Wasn't the war on drugs supposed to be about saving lives?

The marginal note beside the Conclusion reads: Evidence (expert testimony)

THE PITFALLS OF ARGUMENT AND PERSUASION

If you follow the preceding suggestions, you should be able to write a convincing essay. But there are some risks to be aware of in this kind of writing.

Taking on Too Much

Narrowing your topic is always a good idea, but it's especially important in argumentation. You won't be able to write a sensible essay on "What's Wrong with the American Economy." Select a more manageable problem, such as unemployment or unbridled greed. Even those problems are probably too broad to cover in a short essay. Always consider moving the issue closer to home. For example, if someone in your family has been unemployed, you are probably equipped to write about the psychological effects of unemployment on the individual. If you have found yourself in terrifying and unnecessary credit card debt, you can probably write persuasively about uncontrolled consumerism. In these cases, you have credibility to discuss the issue. Credibility is an important part of your appeal, and you will notice that each author in this chapter establishes the right to claim knowledge about his or her subject, either explicitly or implicitly.

Mistaking the Audience

The readers you most want to reach with a controversial essay are the ones in the middle—those who are undecided and might be swayed by your ideas. People with extreme opinions on either side are likely to be unmovable. Even with persuadable audiences, you must expect some resistance. Be sure your tone does not bolster this resistance by being insulting or condescending. The voice of sweet reason and a "we're in this together" attitude invite your readers to agree with you.

Logical Fallacies

Flaws in reasoning can undermine your cause and harm your credibility. Be sure that you are not guilty of these common logical fallacies:

1. *Overgeneralization.* Recently, a national survey found that the number of unmarried women among highly educated people was much larger than among the less educated. Articles on the alarming shortage of men willing to marry educated females abounded, and solutions to the difficulty were proposed. Actually, most of the single, educated females had chosen their unmarried status. The problem was the false generalization that all unmarried women *wanted* husbands and were seeking them. The shortage of marriage-minded men was not proven.

2. *Either–or thinking.* Be sure that you don't present only two alternatives when more exist. For example, some writers in education want us to believe that either we set national standards for mathematical achievement or our children will continue to fall behind other countries' children in math skills. The fallacy is that national standards are not the only route to high math achievement: smaller classes, better teaching conditions, early intervention policies, and parent involvement are just a few ideas left out of the either–or reasoning. (In fact, the existence of national standards is not correlated with math achievement internationally.)

3. *False analogy.* Analogy is a compelling form of argument, but you must take care that the two cases you compare are really similar. If you argue that your college should imitate a successful general education program used at another university, you must be sure that the two institutions have similar students, faculty, goals, and organizational structures. Otherwise, adopting a plan that works for someone else could be disastrous. Recently, a U.S. congressman claimed that foreign dignitaries, while in our country, should say the Pledge of Allegiance because, similarly, we show respect at the Olympics when other countries' national anthems are played. The analogy falls apart when you consider what the Pledge of Allegiance actually *says.*

4. *Faulty claims about causation.* Remember that two things that occur closely in time or one after the other are not necessarily causally related. In our cities, ice cream sales and murder rates both increase

in the summer; can we say that eating ice cream causes aggression? No, probably it's the heat that encourages both. We say "children who are hugged are more likely to be nice," and "children who are beaten are more likely to be unpleasant." But the causes and effects could be the other way around. Maybe nice children are hugged *because* they're nice, and unpleasant children get beaten *because* they're unpleasant.

WHAT TO LOOK FOR IN ARGUMENT AND PERSUASION

Here are some questions to ask yourself as you study the selections in this chapter.

1. What issue is being addressed? What stance or point of view am I being asked to adopt?
2. What claim or claims does the author make? What kind of claims are they? Are they significant and reasonable?
3. Does the author explain the issue clearly and completely? Are there any holes or gaps in the author's thinking?
4. What evidence does the author use to support the claims? Is this evidence sufficient, relevant, and up-to-date?
5. Does the writer refute possible objections? How effective is this refutation? Has the author ignored any important objections?
6. Is the conclusion satisfactory? Has the author persuaded me?

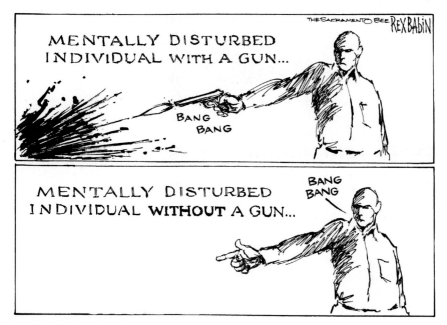

Rex Babin/The Sacramento Bee.

What claim of fact does this cartoon make?

What claim of policy does the cartoon seem to be supporting?

What would you say to refute these claims?

Do you think our society pays too much attention to athletes and athletics? Do you play a sport? If so, what do you think your chances are of becoming a professional?

Send Your Children to the Libraries

ARTHUR ASHE

Arthur Ashe was the first black player to win a major men's tennis tournament: the U.S. Open in 1968 and the Wimbledon championship in 1975. Ashe survived heart surgery in 1979 and announced his retirement from competition in 1980, although he continued to serve as the nonplaying captain of the U.S. Davis Cup team. He became infected with the AIDS virus, probably through a blood transfusion that he received during his second bypass operation in 1983; he died of complications from AIDS in 1993. In this letter, published in the *New York Times* in 1977, Ashe argues that the lure of professional sports is actually harmful to black athletes.

TERMS TO RECOGNIZE

pretentious *(para. 1)*	falsely superior
expends *(para. 1)*	spends, uses up
dubious *(para. 1)*	doubtful, questionable
emulate *(para. 2)*	follow, copy
Forest Hills *(para. 3)*	location of the U.S. Open tennis tournament in 1968
attributing *(para. 4)*	assigning, crediting
viable *(para. 5)*	possible, workable
Wimbledon *(para. 12)*	suburb of London and site of the world-famous tennis tournament

Since my sophomore year at University of California, Los Angeles, I have become convinced that we blacks spend too much time on the playing fields and too little time in the libraries. Please don't think of this attitude as being pretentious just because I am a black, single, professional athlete. I don't have children, but I can make observations. I strongly believe the black culture expends too much time, energy and effort raising, praising and teasing our black children as to the dubious glories of professional sports.

All children need models to emulate—parents, relatives or friends. But when the child starts school, the influence of the parent is shared by teachers and classmates, by the lure of books, movies, ministers and newspapers, but most of all by television.

Which televised events have the greatest number of viewers? Sports— the Olympics, Super Bowl, Masters, World Series, pro basketball playoffs, Forest Hills. ABC-TV even has sports on Monday night prime time from April to December. So your child gets a massive dose of O. J. Simpson, Kareem Abdul-Jabbar, Muhammad Ali, Reggie Jackson, Dr. J. and Lee Elder and other pro athletes. And it is only natural that your child will dream of being a pro athlete himself.

But consider these facts: For the major professional sports of hockey, football, basketball, baseball, golf, tennis and boxing, there are roughly only 3,170 major league positions available (attributing 200 positions to golf, 200 to tennis and 100 to boxing). And the annual turnover is small. We blacks are a subculture of about 28 million. Of the 13½ million men, 5–6 million are under twenty years of age, so your son has less than one chance in a thousand of becoming a pro. Less than one in a thousand. Would you bet your son's future on something with odds of 999 to 1 against you? I wouldn't.

Unless a child is exceptionally gifted, you should know by the time he enters high school whether he has a future as an athlete. But what is more important is what happens if he doesn't graduate or doesn't land a college scholarship and doesn't have a viable alternative job career. Our high school dropout rate is several times the national average, which contributes to our unemployment rate of roughly twice the national average.

And how do you fight the figures in the newspapers every day? Ali has earned more than $30 million boxing, O. J. just signed for $2½ million, Dr. J. for almost $3 million, Reggie Jackson for $2.8 million, Nate Archibald for $400,000 a year. All that money, recognition, attention, free cars, girls, jobs in the off-season—no wonder there is Pop Warner football, Little League baseball, National Junior League tennis, hockey practice at 5 A.M. and pickup basketball games in any center city at any hour.

There must be some way to assure that the 999 who try but don't make it to pro sports don't wind up on the street corners or in the unemployment lines. Unfortunately, our most widely recognized role models are athletes and entertainers—"runnin'" and "jumpin'" and "singin'" and "dancin'." While we are 60 percent of the National Basketball Association, we are less than 4 percent of the doctors and lawyers. While we are about 35 percent of major league baseball, we are less than 2 percent of the engineers. While we are about 40 percent of the National Football League, we are less than 11 percent of construction workers such as carpenters and bricklayers.

Our greatest heroes of the century have been athletes—Jack Johnson, Joe 8
Louis and Muhammad Ali. Racial and economic discrimination forced us to channel our energies into athletics and entertainment. These were the ways out of the ghetto, the ways to that Cadillac, those alligator shoes, that cashmere sport coat. Somehow, parents must instill a desire for learning alongside the desire to be Walt Frazier. Why not start by sending black professional athletes to high schools to explain the facts of life?

I have often addressed high school audiences and my message is always 9
the same. For every hour you spend on the athletic field, spend two in the library. Even if you make it as a pro athlete, your career will be over by the time you are thirty-five. So you will need that diploma. Have these pro athletes explain what happens if you break a leg, get a sore arm, have one bad year or don't make the cut for five or six tournaments. Explain to them the star system, wherein for every O. J. earning millions there are six or seven others making $15,000 or $20,000 or $30,000 a year.

But don't just have Walt Frazier or O. J. or Abdul-Jabbar address your 10
class. Invite a benchwarmer or a guy who didn't make it. Ask him if he sleeps every night. Ask him whether he was graduated. Ask him what he would do if he became disabled tomorrow. Ask him where his old high school athletic buddies are.

We have been on the same roads—sports and entertainment—too long. 11
We need to pull over, fill up at the library and speed away to Congress and the Supreme Court, the unions and the business world. We need more Barbara Jordans, Andrew Youngs, union cardholders, Nikki Giovannis and Earl Graveses. Don't worry: We will still be able to sing and dance and run and jump better than anybody else.

I'll never forget how proud my grandmother was when I graduated 12
from UCLA in 1966. Never mind the Davis Cup in 1968, 1969, and 1970. Never mind the Wimbledon title, Forest Hills, etc. To this day, she still doesn't know what those names mean. What mattered to her was that of her more than thirty children and grandchildren, I was the first to be graduated from college, and a famous college at that. Somehow, that made up for all those floors she scrubbed all those years.

RESPONDING TO READING

Do you think the athletes at your school receive special treatment? Do they spend too much time on their sports and too little time on their studies? In your journal, express your opinion about the place of athletics in colleges and universities.

GAINING WORD POWER

Explain in your own words the meaning of the following phrases. Use clues from surrounding sentences to help you.

1. the lure of books, movies (para. 2)
2. a massive dose (para. 3)
3. blacks are a subculture (para. 4)
4. a child is exceptionally gifted (para. 5)
5. pickup basketball games (para. 6)
6. economic discrimination (para. 8)
7. instill a desire for learning (para. 8)
8. make the cut (para. 9)
9. the star system (para. 9)

CONSIDERING CONTENT

1. What problem is Ashe concerned about? What solution does he propose?
2. Ashe is clearly addressing the parents of black sons. Are his opinions relevant to other races or to parents of girls? Why or why not?
3. In paragraph 8, Ashe says that "economic discrimination" has forced African Americans into sports and entertainment. What does he mean? Do you agree?
4. According to Ashe, why do African American athletes need a diploma? Do these reasons apply to other races and to nonathletes?
5. Who are Barbara Jordan, Andrew Young, Nikki Giovanni, and Earl Graves? Why does Ashe say "We need more" of these people?
6. In paragraph 11, Ashe says that blacks have been "on the same roads—sports and entertainment—too long." Does he want blacks to avoid these careers?
7. This letter was written in 1977, more than twenty-five years ago. Are Ashe's views still relevant?

CONSIDERING METHOD

1. Ashe states the problem in his first sentence. Where does he restate it? Why does he restate the problem several times?
2. What criticisms is Ashe anticipating in his opening paragraph?
3. In his letter, Ashe uses a lot of statistics. How convincing are they?

4. What other kinds of evidence does Ashe use to support his main points?
5. How does Ashe make it clear that he is part of the audience he's addressing? Why does he want his readers to know that he is not an outsider?
6. Notice Ashe's frequent use of parallel structure, items in a series, and intentional repetition. Find several examples of each. What effect is Ashe trying to achieve with these elements?
7. Explain the **metaphor** that Ashe uses in paragraph 11.
8. Why does Ashe conclude with comments about his grandmother? Is this an effective ending?
9. What stereotypes about blacks does Ashe refer to? Why does he use the word *black* and not *African American?*

WRITING STEP BY STEP

Write a letter to a newspaper in which you encourage fellow students or fellow citizens to join you in solving some problem that affects you all. Choose a problem close to home—something on campus or in your community that you want fixed, improved, regulated, legalized, banned, or reorganized.

A. Begin, as Ashe does, with a clear and direct statement of the problem.
B. Explain your interest or involvement in the situation. Make it clear to your readers that you are not an outsider: use the pronouns *we, us, our,* and *ours.*
C. Describe the problem and, if necessary, explain why you think it needs a solution. Your readers may not realize how serious the problem is or how much it affects them.
D. Use actual examples and, if possible, give statistics to support your claims.
E. Emphasize your points and keep your readers' attention by using parallel structure, items in a series, and intentional repetition.
F. State your solution, and explain how it will work.
G. If appropriate, show why other solutions won't work and why your proposal is the best one.
H. Conclude with a personal anecdote or comment, like Ashe's story about his grandmother's pride.

OTHER WRITING IDEAS

1. Is there some rule change that would make your favorite sport safer, fairer, or more interesting to watch? Using a **problem–solution** approach, write a letter to a sports magazine (such as *Sports Illus-*

trated) or to an athletic organization (such as the NCAA), and present your proposal for changing the rules.

2. Write a letter to the Consumer Protection Agency about some problem you have experienced as a consumer. Identify the problem, explain why it needs to be solved, and present your solution.

3. Think of a problem in your life that's bothering you: lack of money, lack of friends, the wrong kind of friends, too much work, too little time. Make sure it is some problem you genuinely need to solve. Write a report or a letter to yourself suggesting at least two reasonable ways to improve the situation.

EDITING SKILLS: AVOIDING SEXIST LANGUAGE

As the opening sentence of paragraph 5, Arthur Ashe writes, "Unless a *child* is exceptionally gifted, you should know by the time *he* enters high school whether *he* has a future as an athlete" (our italics). When this letter was published in 1977, it was acceptable to use masculine pronouns to refer to virtually all living beings as if they were male. And, of course, Ashe is thinking of *sons* as becoming professional athletes—even though he later mentions that we need more "Barbara Jordans" and "Nikki Giovannis" (para. 11).

These days you need to avoid using masculine pronouns to refer to people of both sexes. If Ashe were still alive today, he probably would not write, "And it is only natural that your *child* will dream of being a pro athlete *himself*" (para. 3). More likely he would cast that sentence in the plural this way: "And it is only natural that your *children* will dream of being pro athletes *themselves*." Both sexes are included in all plural pronouns. People don't think either male or female when they read *we, us, our, you, your, they, them, their, ourselves, yourselves, themselves*. So, if you simply write in the plural, the problem disappears.

Occasionally you can revise a sentence to eliminate the pronoun, like this:

(sexist) A tennis player must practice daily to stay at the top of *his* form.

(revised) A tennis player must practice daily to stay in top form.

Or if you find yourself once in a while needing to write a singular sentence for some good reason, it's quite all right to use both male and female pronouns, like this:

Everyone on board must wear a lifejacket for *his or her* own safety.

Just don't do it this way too often, or your writing will get annoyingly cluttered.

EXERCISE

Because your readers may be bothered by **sexist language,** you should write in the plural most of the time. For practice, rewrite the following sentences in the plural to get rid of the italicized masculine pronouns.

1. An Olympic swimmer needs to work out daily to perform at *his* best.
2. But a championship bridge player can take a week off without ruining *his* game.
3. A professional athlete needs to watch *his* diet, as well as exercise *his* body.
4. A chess player is constantly exercising *his* mind, but *he* can eat whatever *he* pleases.
5. Even an amateur golfer gets plenty of exercise when *he* plays eighteen holes, unless *he* rides in a cart.

Now go back over the essay you just wrote and check the personal pronouns. Did you use any (such as *he, his, him* or *she, her, hers*) that unfairly or inaccurately exclude the other sex? Make any necessary changes—such as using *he or she* or rewriting in the plural to allow *they, their,* or *them*.

WEB SITE

http://sportsillustrated.cnn.com/tennis/features/1997/arthurashe
The Arthur Ashe commemorative site presents a comprehensive look at Ashe's life and accomplishments.

PREPARING TO READ

Have you ever been arrested or known anyone who has? Do you think people are ever unfairly punished in this country? Or do you think most people get the sentences they deserve?

The War on Drugs

BILL BRYSON

Having spent two decades living in England, American writer Bill Bryson now lives in New Hampshire. His books include *A Walk in the Woods: Rediscovering America on the Appalachian Trail* (1998) and *In a Sunburned Country* (2000). The following essay was written in 1996 for Bryson's weekly column in a New Hampshire newspaper and appears in his collection *I'm a Stranger Here Myself: Notes on Returning to America after Twenty Years Away* (1999).

TERMS TO RECOGNIZE

extenuating *(para. 1)*	making less serious by providing a partial excuse
ferocity *(para. 2)*	intense fierceness
Newt Gingrich *(para. 2)*	Georgia Republican, Speaker of the House of Representatives from 1995 to 1997
disproportionate *(para. 3)*	unequal, out of proportion in size or amount
affidavit *(para. 7)*	an official statement or legal document
zealous *(para. 9)*	fanatical, passionate
vindictiveness *(para. 9)*	an attitude of revenge, spitefulness

I recently learned from an old friend in Iowa that if you are caught in possession of single dose of LSD you face a mandatory sentence of seven years in prison without possibility of parole. Never mind that you are, say, eighteen years old and of previous good character, that this will ruin your life, that it will cost the state $25,000 a year to keep you incarcerated. Never mind that perhaps you didn't even know you had the LSD—that a friend put it in the glovebox of your car without your knowledge or maybe saw police coming through the door at a party and shoved it into your hand before you could react. Never mind any extenuating circumstances whatever. This is America in the 1990s and there are no exceptions where drugs are concerned. Sorry, but that's the way it is. Next.

It would be nearly impossible to exaggerate the ferocity with which the   2
United States now prosecutes drug offenders. In fifteen states you can be sentenced to life in prison for owning a single marijuana plant. Newt Gingrich, the House Speaker, recently proposed that anyone caught bringing as little as two ounces of marijuana into the United States should be imprisoned for life without possibility of parole. Anyone caught bringing more than two ounces would be executed.

According to a 1990 study, 90 percent of all first-time drug offenders in   3
federal courts were sentenced to an average of five years in prison. Violent first-time offenders, by contrast, were imprisoned less often and received on average just four years in prison. You are, in short, less likely to go to prison for kicking an old lady down the stairs than you are for being caught in possession of a single dose of any illicit drug. Call me soft, but that seems to me a trifle disproportionate.

Please understand it is not remotely my intention here to speak in favor   4
of drugs. I appreciate that drugs can mess you up in a big way. I have an old school friend who made one LSD voyage too many in about 1977 and since that time has sat on a rocker on his parents' front porch examining the backs of his hands and smiling to himself. So I know what drugs can do. I just haven't reached the point where it seems to me appropriate to put someone to death for being an idiot.

Not many of my fellow countrymen would agree with me. It is the   5
clear and fervent wish of most Americans to put drug users behind bars, and they are prepared to pay almost any price to achieve this. The people of Texas recently voted down a $750 million bond proposal to build new schools but overwhelmingly endorsed a $1 billion bond for new prisons mostly to house people convicted of drug offenses.

America's prison population has more than doubled since 1982. There   6
are now 1,630,000 people in prison in the United States. That is more than the populations of all but the three largest cities in the country. Sixty percent of federal prisoners are serving time for nonviolent offenses, mostly to do with drugs. America's prisons are crammed with nonviolent petty criminals whose problem is a weakness for illegal substances. Because most drug offenses carry mandatory sentences and exclude the possibility of parole, other prisoners are having to be released early to make room for all the new drug offenders pouring into the system. In consequence, the average convicted murderer in the United States now serves less than six years, the average rapist just five. Moreover, once he is out, the murderer or rapist

is immediately eligible for welfare, food stamps, and other federal assistance. A convicted drug user, no matter how desperate his circumstances may become, is denied these benefits for the rest of his life.

The persecution doesn't end there. My friend in Iowa once spent four months in a state prison for a drug offense. That was almost twenty years ago. He did his time and since then has been completely clean. Recently, he applied for a temporary job with the U.S. Postal Service as a holiday relief mail sorter. Not only did he not get the job, but a week or so later he received by recorded delivery an affidavit threatening him with prosecution for failing to declare on his application that he had a felony conviction involving drugs. The Postal Service had taken the trouble, you understand, to run a background check for drug convictions on someone applying for a temporary job sorting mail. Apparently it does this as a matter of routine—but only with respect to drugs. Had he killed his grandmother and raped his sister twenty-five years ago, he would in all likelihood have gotten the job. 7

It gets more amazing. The government can seize your property if it was used in connection with a drug offense, even if you did not know it. In Connecticut, according to a recent article in the *Atlantic Monthly* magazine, a federal prosecutor named Leslie C. Ohta made a name for herself by seizing the property of almost anyone even tangentially connected with a drug offense—including a couple in their eighties whose grandson was found to be selling marijuana out of his bedroom. The couple had no idea that their grandson had marijuana in the house (let me repeat: they were in their eighties) and of course had nothing to do with it themselves. They lost the house anyway. 8

The saddest part of this zealous vindictiveness is that it simply does not work. America spends $50 billion a year fighting drugs, and yet drug use goes on and on. Confounded and frustrated, the government enacts increasingly draconian laws until we find ourselves at the ludicrous point where the Speaker of the House can seriously propose to execute people—strap them to a gurney and snuff out their lives—for possessing the botanical equivalent of two bottles of vodka, and no one anywhere seems to question it. 9

My solution to the problem would be twofold. First, I would make it a criminal offense to be Newt Gingrich. This wouldn't do anything to reduce the drug problem, but it would make me feel much better. Then I would take most of that $50 billion and spend it on rehabilitation and prevention. Some of it could be used to take busloads of youngsters to look at that school friend of mine on his Iowa porch. I am sure it would persuade most of them not to try drugs in the first place. It would certainly be less brutal and pointless than trying to lock them all up for the rest of their lives. 10

RESPONDING TO READING

What do you think should be done about the drug problem in this country? Do you agree with Bryson's solution? Why or why not?

GAINING WORD POWER

Look up the following words in a college dictionary. Then write a sentence of your own for each word.

1. mandatory (para. 1)
2. incarcerated (para. 1)
3. illicit (para. 3)
4. fervent (para. 5)
5. petty (para. 6)
6. tangentially (para. 8)
7. draconian (para. 9)
8. ludicrous (para. 9)

CONSIDERING CONTENT

1. What is the point of Bryson's opening example concerning the punishment for possession of LSD in Iowa?
2. Would you agree that the sentences for first-time drug offenders are "disproportionate" when compared to the sentences for violent first-time offenders?
3. In paragraph 4, Bryson says he is not speaking in favor of drugs. What, then, is the purpose of his essay?
4. According to Bryson, in what ways are convicted drug users treated unfairly?
5. Who is Leslie C. Ohta and what did she do? How do you feel about her actions?
6. Bryson says that punishing drug users harshly "simply does not work" (para. 9). What evidence does he give to support this claim? Do you agree?
7. What solution does the author offer? How reasonable is it?

CONSIDERING METHOD

1. Why does Bryson begin by referring to "an old friend in Iowa"? How does he use his friend in Iowa to unify his essay?
2. How does the author establish his credibility on this topic?
3. Bryson uses several contrasts to develop his claim about the unfairness of the war on drugs. Identify four of them. How effective are they in advancing Bryson's claims?

4. What is the point of paragraph 4? Why does Bryson include this paragraph?
5. Find at least four uses of statistics, and discuss their effectiveness.
6. What kind of evidence is used in paragraph 7? How does it differ from the evidence used elsewhere?
7. Identify several examples of humor in this essay. How would you describe that humor? Is it effective?

WRITING STEP BY STEP

Each of us is aware of some system that doesn't (or didn't) work. Think about fads such as miracle weight-loss plans; customs such as dating and marriage; practices such as spanking or social promotion; university or school rules or requirements; local government policies such as curfews; or even national laws such as prohibition. Surely there is somewhere in society that you perceive inadequacy in addressing a real problem. Write an essay based on Bryson's example in which you explain what doesn't work and why.

A. Be sure to establish your credibility for writing about this topic. If your credentials aren't based on personal experience, maybe they are based on some other knowledge or expertise.
B. Write a paragraph telling why the current situation exists. What is the system you're criticizing supposed to do?
C. Write one paragraph explaining that the problem is real but that the present system doesn't address it effectively.
D. Devote two or three paragraphs to evidence for your own claim that the system doesn't work. Each paragraph should develop one point on your side of the matter. Use at least two different types of evidence (facts, statistics, expert testimony, examples, logical reasoning, personal experience).
E. In your closing paragraph, suggest a better approach for efforts to deal with the problem or situation. You don't have to go into detail (Bryson doesn't), but you do need to indicate why you consider this approach more workable.

OTHER WRITING IDEAS

1. Write a response to Bryson's essay. Do you agree with his claims? How would you wage the war on drugs in the United States?
2. Sometimes people cause problems for others without realizing it. Is there something you do that creates a problem for someone else? Describe your behavior and explain how it's a problem. Then indicate what you're going to do about it.

3. Write about a habit (smoking, procrastinating, overeating, or being late, for example) that you broke. To get started, meet with a group of classmates and friends to share stories about bad habits and how to break them. When you write your essay, present the habit as a problem, describe its seriousness, and explain your solution.

EDITING SKILLS: USING COMPOUND VERBS

Look at the verbs in the following sentences from Bill Bryson's essay:

Violent first-time offenders, by contrast, <u>were imprisoned</u> less often and <u>received</u> on average just four years in prison.

The people of Texas recently <u>voted down</u> a $750 million bond proposal to build new schools but overwhelmingly <u>endorsed</u> a $1 billion bond for new prisons.

Because most drug offenses <u>carry</u> mandatory sentences and <u>exclude</u> the possibility of parole, other prisoners are having to be released early.

He <u>did</u> his time and since then <u>has been</u> completely clean.

The verbs that we have highlighted are compound verbs—two verbs that have the same subject and are connected by a coordinating conjunction. With compound verbs you can expand a simple sentence and eliminate wordiness (as we just did in this sentence). Most of the time you will use *and:*

The Internal Revenue Service <u>seized</u> our assets *and* <u>confiscated</u> our computers.

Sometimes you can use *but, or,* and *yet:*

The FBI <u>questioned</u> our neighbors *but* <u>ignored</u> our cleaning crew.
They <u>suspected</u> us of espionage *or* <u>wanted</u> us for tax evasion.

You can also join more than two verbs:

The gymnast <u>leaped</u> up, <u>grabbed</u> the bar, *and* <u>swung</u> into her first maneuver.

EXERCISE

After studying the preceding examples, combine the following groups of simple sentences by using compound verbs.

1. *TV Guide* lists the latest shows. It also describes them briefly.
2. Many people are renting movies. They are playing them on their videocassette recorders.
3. *Frasier* uses recycled plots. This show also features brilliant dialogue.
4. Tillie bakes bread. She talks on the phone. She drinks coffee at the same time.
5. The nurse put down the chart. He grabbed the patient's wrist. He took her temperature.
6. In medieval Europe, the peasants were distracted by war. They were weakened by malnutrition. They were exhausted by the struggle to make a living.

Now check the essay you have just written. See if you can combine a couple of sentences by using a compound verb.

WEB SITES

www.drugsense.org/wodclock.htm
The drug war clock provides a continuously updated count of the money spent on the war on drugs this year, as well as the number of people arrested and incarcerated for drug offenses and the number of HIV infections that could be prevented if the federal ban on needle exchanges were lifted.

www.drcnet.org
The Drug Reform Coordination Network presents the case for the war on drugs.

PREPARING TO READ

If you were dying, slowly and painfully, from an incurable disease, what would you want the hospital staff to do? Should they let you die, or prolong your life (and your pain)?

A Crime of Compassion

BARBARA HUTTMANN

Barbara Huttmann is the associate director of nursing for Children's Hospital in San Francisco. She has written two books about the rights of patients: *The Patient's Advocate* and *Code Blue: A Nurse's True-Life Story.* In the following essay, which originally appeared on the "My Turn" page of *Newsweek* magazine in 1983, Huttmann tells about her decision to let a suffering patient die.

TERMS TO RECOGNIZE

resuscitated *(para. 3)*	revived, brought back to life
haggard *(para. 5)*	worn out
IV solutions *(para. 6)*	liquids given by injection (IV stands for intravenous—"in the vein")
irrigate *(para. 7)*	wash out, flush
lucid *(para. 10)*	aware, clear-minded
impotence *(para. 10)*	powerlessness
imperative *(para. 11)*	command, directive
riddled *(para. 13)*	pierced with numerous holes
pallor *(para. 15)*	paleness, lack of color

"**m**urderer," a man shouted. "God help patients who get *you* for a nurse." 1

"What gives you the right to play God?" another one asked. 2

It was the *Phil Donahue Show* where the guest is a fatted calf and the audience a 220-strong flock of vultures hungering to pick at the bones. I had told them about Mac, one of my favorite cancer patients. "We resuscitated him 52 times in just one month. I refused to resuscitate him again. I simply sat there and held his hand while he died." 3

There wasn't time to explain that Mac was a young, witty, macho cop who walked into the hospital with 32 pounds of attack equipment, look- 4 ing as if he could single-handedly protect the whole city, if not the entire state. "Can't get rid of this cough," he said. Otherwise, he felt great.

Before the day was over, tests confirmed that he had lung cancer. And 5 before the year was over, I loved him, his wife, Maura, and their three kids as if they were my own. All the nurses loved him. And we all battled his disease for six months without ever giving death a second thought. Six months isn't such a long time in the whole scheme of things, but it was long enough to see him lose his youth, his wit, his macho, his hair, his bowel and bladder control, his sense of taste and smell, and his ability to do the slightest thing for himself. It was also long enough to watch Maura's transformation from a young woman into a haggard, beaten old lady.

When Mac had wasted away to a 60-pound skeleton kept alive by liquid 6 food we poured down a tube, IV solutions we dripped into his veins, and oxygen we piped to a mask on his face, he begged us: "Mercy . . . for God's sake, please just let me go."

The first time he stopped breathing, the nurse pushed the button that 7 calls a "code blue" throughout the hospital and sends a team rushing to resuscitate the patient. Each time he stopped breathing, sometimes two or three times in one day, the code team came again. The doctors and technicians worked their miracles and walked away. The nurses stayed to wipe the saliva that drooled from his mouth, irrigate the big craters of bedsores that covered his hips, suction the lung fluids that threatened to drown him, clean the feces that burned his skin like lye, pour the liquid food down the tube attached to his stomach, put pillows between his knees to ease the bone-on-bone pain, turn him every hour to keep the bedsores from getting worse, and change his gown and linen every two hours to keep him from being soaked in perspiration.

At night I went home and tried to scrub away the smell of decaying flesh 8 that seemed woven into the fabric of my uniform. It was in my hair, the upholstery of my car—there was no washing it away. And every night I prayed that Mac would die, that his agonized eyes would never again plead with me to let him die.

Every morning I asked his doctor for a "no-code" order. Without that 9 order, we had to resuscitate every patient who stopped breathing. His doctor was one of several who believe we must extend life as long as we have the means and knowledge to do it. To not do it is to be liable for negligence, at least in the eyes of many people, including some nurses. I thought about what it would be like to stand before a judge, accused of murder, if Mac stopped breathing and I didn't call a code.

And after the fifty-second code, when Mac was still lucid enough to beg 10 for death again, and Maura was crumbled in my arms again, and when no amount of pain medication stilled his moaning and agony, I wondered about a spiritual judge. Was all this misery and suffering supposed to be building character or infusing us all with the sense of humility that comes from impotence?

Had we, the whole medical community, become so arrogant that we 11 believed in the illusion of salvation through science? Had we become so self-righteous that we thought meddling in God's work was our duty, our moral imperative and our legal obligation? Did we really believe that we had the right to force "life" on a suffering man who had begged for the right to die?

Such questions haunted me more than ever early one morning when 12 Maura went home to change her clothes and I was bathing Mac. He had been still for so long, I thought he at last had the blessed relief of coma. Then he opened his eyes and moaned, "Pain . . . no more . . . Barbara . . . do something . . . God, let me go."

The desperation in his eyes and voice riddled me with guilt. "I'll stop," 13 I told him as I injected the pain medication.

I sat on the bed and held Mac's hands in mine. He pressed his bony 14 fingers against my hand and muttered, "Thanks." Then there was one soft sigh and I felt his hands go cold in mine. "Mac?" I whispered, as I waited for his chest to rise and fall again.

A clutch of panic banded my chest, drew my finger to the code button, 15 urged me to do something, anything . . . but sit there alone with death. I kept one finger on the button, without pressing it, as a waxen pallor slowly transformed his face from person to empty shell. Nothing I've ever done in my 47 years has taken so much effort as it took *not* to press that code button.

Eventually, when I was as sure as I could be that the code team would 16 fail to bring him back, I entered the legal twilight zone and pushed the button. The team tried. And while they were trying, Maura walked into the room and shrieked, "No . . . don't let them do this to him . . . for God's sake . . . please, no more."

Cradling her in my arms was like cradling myself, Mac, and all those 17 patients and nurses who had been in this place before, who do the best they can in a death-denying society.

So a TV audience accused me of murder. Perhaps I am guilty. If a doctor 18 had written a no-code order, which is the only *legal* alternative, would he have felt any less guilty? Until there is legislation making it a criminal act to code a patient who has requested the right to die, we will all of us risk the same fate as Mac. For whatever reason, we developed the means to prolong life, and now we are forced to use it. We do not have the right to die.

RESPONDING TO READING

Huttmann says "We do not have the right to die." Should we have this right? In your journal, write down your thoughts and feelings about "the right to die."

GAINING WORD POWER

Writers sometimes make passing references to familiar or significant people, places, objects, or events from history, the Bible, and literature. These references are called **allusions;** they help a writer to set the tone or heighten the meaning without going into a long explanation. Explain the following phrases from Barbara Huttmann's essay. Use a dictionary or other reference works to help you.

1. The "fatted calf" (para. 3) refers to the biblical parable of the Prodigal Son. If you don't remember what happens to the fatted calf, look up the parable (Luke 15:11–32), and explain why Huttmann makes this reference.
2. The *Twilight Zone* (para. 16) was the name of an old TV program. Do you know the show? What quality of that show is Huttmann calling on in this reference? Can you see how it fits her point?
3. "Code blue" is a medical term. You can probably figure out its general meaning from the essay. But why is it a "code," and why is the code "blue" (instead of some other color)?
4. What is the legal definition of "liable" (para. 9)? Do you think Huttmann used the word because of its legal associations?
5. The title of the essay is a variation of the phrase "crime of passion." Do you know what a crime of passion is? How does the meaning of this phrase relate to Huttmann's title?

CONSIDERING CONTENT

1. How does this selection qualify as a **problem–solution** essay? What problem is Huttmann presenting? What is her solution?
2. Explain what a "no code" order is. Why wouldn't Mac's doctor issue one?
3. Huttmann says that Mac's doctor believes "we must extend life as long as we have the means and knowledge to do it." Is that what you believe? What does Huttmann believe?
4. What does the author mean by "a spiritual judge"?
5. Explain the question that ends paragraph 10.

6. Huttmann was accused of "playing God" for letting Mac die. How does she turn the accusation around in paragraph 11? According to Huttmann, who is playing God?
7. Did Huttmann commit a crime? Explain your answer.
8. Do we live in a "death-denying society," as the author claims (para. 17)? What do you think she means by this phrase?
9. Do you think Huttmann feels guilty? Why did she publicly reveal what happened?

CONSIDERING METHOD

1. Why does Huttmann begin by quoting audience members of the *Phil Donahue Show?* Why does she return to the TV audience again in her last paragraph?
2. Why does Huttmann describe Mac on the day he entered the hospital (para. 4)? How does she use a contrast to that description in the next paragraph?
3. What contrast between doctors and nurses does the writer present in paragraph 7? How does this contrast relate to the difference of opinion about the "no-code" order (para. 9)?
4. Why does Huttmann go into so much detail about what the nurses did for Mac (paras. 6 and 7)?
5. How does Huttmann attempt to enlist sympathy for Mac's situation and for hers? Identify specific details that appeal to the readers' emotions.
6. Paragraph 11 is made up entirely of questions. Why does the author use this method of presenting these ideas?
7. What purpose do the quotations from Mac and Maura serve (paras. 6, 12, 14, and 16)?
8. Explain the **irony** in Huttmann's next-to-last sentence. (Irony is the use of language to express an unexpected outcome or to suggest that something is not what it seems to be.)

WRITING STEP BY STEP

Write an essay about a time that you had to make a difficult choice, one that involved a conflict of values. Perhaps a good friend asked you to give her financial and moral support for getting an abortion, and you're opposed to abortion. Or maybe your parents got divorced, and you had to choose which one to live with. Perhaps the decision involved having a beloved pet put to death, standing up for an unpopular opinion, or revealing the dishonesty of someone you liked and admired.

A. Write the essay as a first-person account.

B. Begin with a narrative of the events leading up to the moment of decision. Make the narrative come to life with quotations and concrete details.

C. Tell about making the decision. How did you solve your dilemma? Did you have to compromise?

D. Narrate in detail the sequence of events that followed your decision. Explain how you felt at the time.

E. Discuss the consequences of your decision. How did it affect you? How did it affect others? Did people support you?

F. In your conclusion, express your current feelings about the decision and its consequences. Did things turn out all right? Do you regret your decision? If you had to do it again, would you make the same choice?

OTHER WRITING IDEAS

1. Many topics of public concern are controversial because there are strong arguments on both sides of the issue. Select an important social issue, one that you're familiar with and have mixed feelings about. Write an essay titled "My Uncertainty about _____" or "My Doubts about _____."

2. Write about a time when you performed an act of kindness or helped someone solve a problem.

3. Write an essay about the problems of being in the minority: of being a smoker in an antismoking society, of being left-handed in a world made for right-handers, of being a nondriver in a society dependent on automobiles—or something similar. Talk to other members of the minority to get more information for your essay.

EDITING SKILLS: USING SHORT SENTENCES FOR EMPHASIS

Experienced writers vary their sentences, both in structure and in length. If you look at Barbara Huttmann's sentences, you will see that most of them are at least ten words long and many are more than twenty. But sometimes she throws in a very short sentence for effect:

There wasn't time to explain that Mac was a young, witty, macho cop who walked into the hospital with 32 pounds of attack equipment, looking as if he could single-handedly protect the whole city, if not the entire state [41 words]. "Can't get rid of this cough," he said [8 words]. Otherwise, he felt great [4 words].

Huttmann uses another four-word sentence in the last paragraph—"Perhaps I am guilty"—and a six-word sentence in the third paragraph: "I refused to resuscitate him again." These sentences express very important points; they grab our attention by being noticeably different from the longer sentences around them. The other unusually short sentence in Huttmann's essay is the last one. It contains eight one-syllable words, which drive the final point home: "We do not have the right to die." As you can see, Huttmann doesn't use short sentences very often, but when she does, she creates a strong effect.

EXERCISE

Look through Bill Bryson's essay in this chapter (p. 301), and find the five sentences that contain fewer than eight words. Note where he places them, and describe their effect.

Examine the sentences in your essay. Can you find a place to use a short sentence for **emphasis?** Try to end a paragraph with a short statement. Also take a look at your conclusion; that's another good place to sum up the main point in a short sentence. If you can't think of a new sentence, try shortening one that you've already written.

✪ WEB SITE

www.publicagenda.org/issues/frontdoor.cfm?issue_type=right2die
The Public Agenda guide to the right-to-die issue lays out facts and policy alternatives and offers a detailed profile of public thinking on the issue.

DEBATE: EXAMINING THE DEATH PENALTY

In 1972, the U.S. Supreme Court declared executions unconstitutional. Four years later, the Court approved their resumption. Between 1977 and 2001, 695 prisoners were put to death in the United States. As of January 2002, there were more than 3,700 inmates on death row in this country.

The use of death as a punishment is one of America's most divisive issues. It raises difficult questions: Does it deter violent crime? Is it fair to those who died to let their murderers go on living? Can innocent persons be executed by mistake? Can the death penalty be administered fairly? Here we present two articles that examine these and other questions.

PREPARING TO READ

Does your state sanction capital punishment? If you had to vote in a referendum to legalize or outlaw the death penalty in your state, how would you vote? What reasons would you give for your decision?

Death Penalty Showdown

DAVID LEIBOWITZ

David Leibowitz is a graduate of Florida State University and holds master's degrees from Temple and New York Universities. He worked as a reporter for several newspapers in New Jersey before becoming a regular columnist for the *Arizona Republic* in Phoenix. The following article appeared in the *Arizona Republic* in May 1999.

TERMS TO RECOGNIZE

illusory *(para. 4)*	based on an erroneous belief or perception, unreal
systemic *(para. 4)*	relating to the entire system
dispensed *(para. 9)*	administered or handed down
frivolous *(para. 10)*	trivial, unworthy of serious attention
charade *(para. 13)*	a pretense that is easily perceived
curtailed *(para. 16)*	cut short, stopped

lways, I recall the dead woman's hands. I saw them in a photograph once,   1
not long before I watched her killer die from a dose of poison injected
by the state of Arizona. The woman's name was Amelia Schoville, and in that
picture her hands resembled claws, swollen with blood, thumbs bound by a
shoelace, fingers straining up from the dirty mattress where she died.

I remembered those hands on the night [in April 1998] when Amelia's   2
killer, Jose Roberto Villafuerte, was put to death, 5,540 days after he killed her.
I recalled Amelia's hands again May 5, 1999, when Robert Wayne Vickers
finally got a deadly needle after twenty-one years on Arizona's Death Row.

Imagine those hands, ever-empty, ever-reaching. Now, multiply them by   3
every Death Row convict on every Death Row in each of the thirty-eight
states that uses the death penalty. Think of all those victims, all those empty
hands. All that justice denied.

The Death Penalty Is Just and Legal

Make no mistake: Although foes of capital punishment will try to cloud   4
this issue by injecting religion or by scrambling after some illusory moral
high ground, the death penalty, when imposed and carried out, is justice.
Execution represents a proportional, measured response to mankind's most
barbarous act. It has precedent, it has been ruled legal countless times by
countless courts, and it is supported by an overwhelming majority of Americans. In a nation where justice is often represented by a set of scales, execution as punishment for a depraved murder marks the ultimate—and
only—systemic balance.

Joe Maziarz has spent the past dozen years prosecuting death penalty   5
appeals for the Arizona Attorney General's Office. "If society is not willing
to exact justice, what purpose do we serve for the citizens?" he asks. "If
someone had killed my wife, I can't take the law into my own hands. I rely
on society to do that. For some murders, the only justice, from a societal
perspective, is the death penalty."

Case in point: "Bonzai Bob" Vickers. A one-man crime wave who devel-   6
oped an animal's lust for blood, Vickers first earned a spot on Arizona's
Death Row in 1978, for the jailhouse murder of his cellmate, Frank
Ponciano. Feeling wronged because Ponciano had taken his Kool-Aid and
failed to awaken him for lunch, Vickers stabbed his victim to death, then
carved "Bonzai" into Ponciano's back. Vickers' lone regret, as told to a
prison psychologist? He didn't have time to add a swastika beside the
misspelled Japanese war cry.

Four years later, already a resident of Cellblock Six, Vickers somehow   7
managed to top himself. After fellow killer Buster Holsinger made a sugges-

tive remark about a photo of Vickers' eleven-year-old niece, Vickers fashioned a firebomb using hair gel. He burned Holsinger to death, then tossed in a second firebomb for good measure. "Did I do a good job?" Vickers asked investigators later. "I told them they should have gassed me in December, when they had a chance." Instead, his execution took an additional seventeen years. That was time enough for Vickers to complete his legend: 158 major violations while behind prison walls, including a dozen assaults on corrections officers, twenty attacks on inmates and forty charges of making weapons.

Foes of the death penalty often argue that execution has no deterrent effect. That may well be true for society at-large—especially given the decades between a crime and an execution—but one thing is certain: What happened May 5 in the Florence prison permanently deterred "Bonzai Bob" Vickers, who badly needed deterring. 8

Strengthen the Death Penalty

Another favorite anti–death penalty argument holds at its crux the notion that our justice system is "broken." Death sentences are inconsistently dispensed, say the abolitionists; the decades of appeals represent "cruel and unusual punishment"; the system is not cost-effective. Thus, they say, capital punishment should be abandoned. Wrong. It should be fixed. 9

The Anti-Terrorism and Effective Death Penalty Act, approved in 1996 after nearly twenty years of congressional debate on the subject of federal appeals, was a small step in that direction. The act, with its time limits on filings and judges' decisions, and its limitations on successive federal appeals, has significantly streamlined the judicial process, mostly by cutting down on capital defense lawyers' favorite trick: frivolous claims of mental incompetency. 10

"Usually, it's limited only by the imagination of the defense attorney," Maziarz says. "They shop around for these shrinks that will basically say, based upon these brain scans . . . and looking at this person's background, that they have a 'brain disorder.'. . . It's like trying to grab a hold of Jell-O. There's no way to prove or disprove anything." 11

The Incompetency Charade

Find a sympathetic federal judge, and the process stops cold, even when guilt or innocence is no longer up for contention. As proof, look no further than the case of Michael Poland, convicted in 1979, along with his brother, in the killing of two armored-car guards while stealing $288,000. In October 1998, a federal judge in Hawaii stayed Poland's execution only two 12 hours before its enactment. At the center of his ruling: A defense-team psychologist who claimed the "stress" Poland endured on Death Row left him incompetent for execution.

The amazing thing: Just sixteen days before that psychologist ruled him   13
insane, Michael Poland was sane enough to bribe a prison investigator in a brazen try to escape Death Row. Assistant Attorney General Paul McMurdie has spent years on the Poland case. I spoke with him hours after the stay. "(Mental) incompetence like this isn't all of a sudden just going to happen," he told me. "This is nothing but a charade to make sure the execution didn't take place." And it worked, at least temporarily—Poland comes up for execution again on June 16th, 1999. [He was executed that day.]

Two obvious outcomes of ploys like this: The killer's legal bill soars,   14
while the execution abolitionists rant.

Improve the Appeals Process

"To me, it's like a self-fulfilling prophecy," says McMurdie's colleague,   15
Maziarz. "The anti–death penalty forces try to make it as expensive as possible. They unfortunately convince the courts to spare no expense and no time in allowing all this to keep mushrooming. Then, when they're successful in doing that, they point to that and say, 'Ah ha, look how expensive it is . . . to get someone executed.'" Again, the answer would appear to lie with repairing the process, with making the death penalty a consistent, certain answer to the worst kinds of murder.

Of course, saying the appeals process needs to be fixed isn't saying it   16
needs to be curtailed: In Arizona, there is no time limitation on convicted murderers making claims of actual innocence, nor should there be. Newly discovered evidence and new facts can be brought forth at any time, even if repeated claims of sudden insanity have been limited. "The number one thing is making sure that the guilty are convicted and the innocent are not," Maziarz says. "We don't want to execute innocent people."

What we do want to do, instead, is consistent with the aim of the Amer-   17
ican system of justice: To adequately, proportionally punish those who would violate the code that governs society. The very worst of us, those like "Bonzai Bob" Vickers and Jose Villafuerte, deserve as much as a consequence. And those like Rick Schoville, a man who waited fifteen years to get justice in the murder of his mother, deserve nothing less.

"It brought a closure to it," Schoville says thirteen months after the fact,   18
"and for that I'm really, really happy. . . . Now that I see more of these people getting executed, I personally think it's about time that's actually

taking place. I know how I felt, what a relief it was to finally bring that part of it to an end. I can only imagine how victims of these other people must be feeling. These guys are finally getting what they deserve."

As he speaks, I imagine his mother's hands—now untied, now set free, finally getting to touch what had always been just out of grasp.   19

We, On Death Row

KEN SHULMAN

Ken Shulman (b. 1965) spent fifteen years as a journalist in Italy, covering art and culture for *Newsweek,* the *Times of London,* and the *New York Times.* He publishes widely on sports, film, literature, and music and is a regular contributor to National Public Radio's "Morning Edition." The following article was published by the Benetton Group and distributed as a supplement to the January 2000 edition of *Talk* magazine.

TERMS TO RECOGNIZE

vestige *(para. 2)*	trace or evidence of something that once existed
antithesis *(para. 2)*	direct contrast, opposite
catatonic *(para. 3)*	in a stupor, rigid
thrall *(para. 7)*	servitude, bondage
inebriated *(para. 9)*	exhilarated or stupefied, intoxicated
cynical *(para. 11)*	skeptical, scornful of the motives or virtue of others
cloying *(para. 11)*	overly sweet
placate *(para. 11)*	soothe, lessen the anger of
myriad *(para. 13)*	numerous, countless
squalid *(para. 15)*	filthy, repulsive

ow can you talk to them? How can you take their pictures, make   1
them appear pious, contrite, thoughtful, benign, make them look and sound fully human, as if they were assigned to nothing worse than a third-rate holiday resort, as if the horrible deed that has defined and disfigured them far beyond remedy had never happened, or worse, had simply been forgiven? How can you ignore what they have done?

This project has tried my convictions, and repeatedly. I had always been   2
against the death penalty. From my comfortable perch, from my distance,
I saw capital punishment as a vestige of man's basest instincts. As the brutal
suppression of a human life, helpless before a well-armed, faceless, vindic-
tive state. I thought it the antithesis of justice, of the Christian ethic, of every
noble sentiment that humankind has succeeded in kindling and nurturing
during his brief tenure on earth.

And then I met the murderers. Murderers who were penitent. Murder-   3
ers who were catatonic. Murderers who were arrogant, who proclaimed
their innocence, or had genuinely forgotten just what they had done to land
them on death row. They were as different as their cases, their upbringing,
their race, their intelligence. Yet there was something all of them shared. I
saw it on my first death row, stepping onto an enclosed, three-tiered cell
block, the inmates dressed in hot pink scrub pants and T-shirts, out of their
cells for their two-hour recreation.

It was in the way they noticed us without noticing, making us the   4
intruders. It was in the way they sneered, or hid, or laughed, as if at a joke
we could not possibly understand. It was something in their eyes, a light
that shone neither outward nor inward, but hung suspended, like a bubble
in ice. Something that rendered them diabolic and divine, as if having killed
had lurched them into a new plane of being, a plane where nothing could
embarrass or confuse them again, where they did not need to know
anything they did not already know, where time did not flow but froze,
cracking only when one of them was taken from the block to be executed.

These men, I saw, were different than you and I. Not in what they   5
dreamed of doing, but in what they'd done. Some were pleasant, gangly,
floppy-haired boys wishing they could be out on their mountain bikes,
some fond, regretful men and women wishing they could be with their
children. A few dreamed of taking to the pulpit, where they could preach
the dangers of drugs and alcohol and godlessness to all who would listen.
Some were charming. Some were soulful. Some were philosophical. All of
them, in some ways, inspired pity.

And then I remember their crimes. The sexual assault and cold blooded   6
assassination of a teenage convenience store clerk for a few hundred dollars
and three hundred cartons of cigarettes. The torturing and killing of a
three-year-old girl. Four women kidnapped, raped, and murdered by the
same man over a five year period. A teenage girl and boy clubbed to death
during a robbery. If this had been your daughter, your wife, your brother,
your child . . .

Yes. Yes, I would. More than once, during my interviews, I fantasized   7
about doing them violence. There were times when I thought these inmates

deserved to die. And worse, when I wanted to be their executioner. Yes, I knew, almost all of them were in the thrall of drugs and alcohol, almost all of them could tell stories of childhood abuse and neglect and depravity as unspeakable as the crimes they would later commit. But not every drug addict or childhood victim goes on to take a human life. Many of us have been tempted to cross that ultimate threshold.

And almost all of us have resisted. They broke the rules. They defied the order. What a relief—what a thrill I realized—it was, for me not to have to resist anymore. To act out a script as old as life, to give in to a temptation as great as hunger, love, and power, the ultimate temptation that mankind has gradually and patiently broken in order to be able to live together in a civil manner. It is in our nature to be killers. And we are never far from that most primal region of our nature. 8

No. I was not interested in justice. I wasn't even interested in revenge—how could I be? I didn't know their victims, or the families of their victims. I was just inebriated by the opportunity to kill, freely, without the threat of punishment. 9

I am now more against the death penalty than ever. And not because I have sympathy for the killers. Many of them are likeable. Many of them are changed, especially after having found in prison, ironically and at last, the time and wherewithal to step out of their knotted lives and reflect on every step that has brought them here, to the valley of the shadow of death. Several of them are most likely innocent, although I cannot know which ones. A few might even be capable of leading constructive lives on the outside. Many of them are mentally ill, or deficient. But my sympathy goes to the victims, to their families and friends. These inmates, in most cases born badly, may have had very little control over their destiny. Their victims had none. 10

I am against the death penalty because I believe it gives vent to something very uncivilized within us. Because it makes us, by consensus, a little more like the men I met on death row, more abstract, more cynical, less human. I do not expect those who have lost a loved one to murder to agree with me, that they would want anything other than their pound of flesh—their closure, to use the most cloying, contemporary term. But our justice system does not exist to mete out closure, to placate the bereaved. 11

It bears remembering that the plaintiff in a criminal suit is not the family of the victim, but the people of the commonwealth. Our justice system does not exist to barter revenge or blood lust. It exists to uphold the law, without which our society cannot function. 12

The death penalty subverts that law. And not only in the sanctioning of homicide. Due process is compromised in myriad ways, by elected officials 13 pandering to the voting public with stepped up executions, by prosecutors avid enough to conceal evidence in order to wrest yet one more death conviction from a jury. By altering the severity of punishment to suit the race of the victim, and not the gravity of the crime. By making a community, a state, a nation, an accomplice to homicide. Even if the death penalty could be administered justly—and it cannot—each citizen is cheapened by it. As is our society, and the human race.

It is a strange, out of sorts congregation, this "death community." All who live there forfeit a great part of their lives. It is a place where assistant prosecutors give each other high-fives on the courthouse steps because a jury has just elected to send another poorly represented defendant to the death chamber. Where public defenders and pro bono defense attorneys sacrifice time, sleep, health, career, and in many cases their families in order to win their client's right to spend the rest of his natural life in prison. Where prison guards are forced to participate in the gassing or poisoning or electrocution of men and women with whom they have lived—and in some cases grown fond of—over the ten or twenty year period of incarceration. 14

The death penalty is punishment that contaminates all who come in contact with it. At times, during this long and often fascinating inquiry, it seemed that the inmates were the only balanced elements of this obscene region of the world, and only because their part in this squalid drama has already been spoken. Their role is to wait now, their lives effectively over, even if they should resist for fifty years in prison to die in their sleep as aged, forgotten, useless men. Even if they should, one day, get out. They know that having killed has changed them forever, and for the worst. 15

RESPONDING TO READING

After reading these essays, would you change your vote in the referendum on the death penalty? Explain your response.

GAINING WORD POWER

Because these essays argue for a certain point of view, they use language to undermine opposing ideas. For instance, by saying that the foes of capital punishment are "*scrambling* after some *illusory* moral high ground," David Leibowitz suggests that opponents of the death penalty are struggling to find nonexistent support for their position. Find four words or phrases in each essay that are used to discredit or otherwise undercut the opposition. Briefly explain the negative quality that these words or phrases convey.

CONSIDERING CONTENT

1. Which essay did you find most persuasive, and why?
2. How does Leibowitz refute the claim that execution has no deterrent effect? How effective is his refutation?
3. According to Leibowitz, how should the death penalty process be fixed?
4. According to Shulman, supporting the death penalty makes us, like death row inmates, "more abstract, more cynical" (para. 11). What does he mean? Do you agree with his reasoning on this point?
5. Explain what Shulman means when he says that the death penalty "subverts [the] law" (para. 13). Summarize the ways in which he believes that to be true.

CONSIDERING THE METHOD

1. How do the authors of each essay establish their credentials and credibility on this topic?
2. What types of evidence are used by each author?
3. Look for logical fallacies in each essay. Are there overgeneralizations? Either–or thinking? Jumping to conclusions? Did you notice flaws in the logic while you were reading the first time?
4. Why does Leibowitz begin with the description of Amelia Schoville's hands? Is this an effective opening? Why does he return to this image in the last paragraph?
5. Find at least three examples of **parallelism** in Shulman's essay. What effect does each instance create?
6. Describe the **tone** of each essay.

WRITING STEP BY STEP

Write an essay in which you argue for the best way to punish people convicted of murder: the death penalty or life imprisonment.

A. Before you start writing, make a list of reasons why you support one form of punishment over the other. Next to each reason, try to write a response or a counterargument.
B. Identify at least four major reasons to support your choice. These reasons will be your claims.
C. Start your essay by stating your position and giving a brief overview of your main claims.
D. Take up each of your claims one by one. Explain each reason in a separate paragraph, and provide evidence to demonstrate the validity of that reason.

E. Be sure to consider any objections to your claims that readers might have. If you're not sure what these objections would be, ask classmates, friends, family members, or instructors for their ideas. Refute these objections by minimizing their importance, questioning their factuality, or offering a different point of view. You can include your refutations as part of the argument for each claim, or you can put them in a separate paragraph.

F. Close by summarizing your main ideas. You might end with a rhetorical question, as Joshua Shenk does (p. 290), or with a short, emphatic sentence, like the one Barbara Huttmann uses (p. 310).

OTHER WRITING IDEAS

1. Using a point-by-point refutation format, respond to the four major arguments that David Leibowitz makes in his essay "Death Penalty Showdown." Begin each point of refutation by summarizing Leibowitz's position, and then present your reply to that position.

2. Write an essay in which you respond to Ken Shulman's main arguments. Look at paragraphs 11 to 15 in Shulman's essay to find his major claims about the death penalty.

3. Write an essay about a controversial issue other than capital punishment. Choose a topic about which you have a definite opinion. Write your essay as a guest column for the Op-Ed page of your local or school newspaper. Op-Ed means "opposite the editorial" page; it's the place where professional columnists, as well as local citizens, present their opinions on the issues of the day. Take some time to study the articles that appear on the Op-Ed page of any newspaper; pay attention to length, tone, and approach.

EDITING SKILLS: SUBJECT–VERB AGREEMENT

Look at the verbs in the following sentences:

Execution <u>represents</u> a proportional, measured response to mankind's most barbarous act.
The death penalty <u>subverts</u> that law.
But my sympathy <u>goes</u> to the victims.

The verbs that we have highlighted are in the present tense; they express actions that are happening at the present time or that happen all the time. We also use the present tense to state facts or general truths. You will notice that the verbs end in -*s*. That's because the subject of each verb is singular (execution, penalty, sympathy). When the subject of a present-tense verb is *he, she,* or *it*—or a noun that could be replaced by *he, she,* or *it*—we put an *s* on the end.

This ending is an exception. Present-tense verbs with other subjects do not require the *-s* ending:

> The anti–death penalty foes <u>try</u> to make it as expensive as possible.
>
> Some prosecutors <u>ask</u> for the death penalty in nearly every case involving a capital crime; other prosecutors openly <u>oppose</u> capital punishment and <u>refuse</u> to invoke the death penalty, no matter how heinous the crime.
>
> And then I <u>remember</u> their crimes.
>
> Fifteen counties <u>account</u> for nearly a third of all prisoners sentenced to death.

Because we don't always put an ending on a present-tense verb, some people forget to add it. That causes an error in subject–verb agreement. And sometimes it is difficult to tell what the subject of a verb really is, as in this sentence:

> The <u>death penalty</u>, like the police and the courts, <u>produces</u> little change in the murder rate.

The subject of the verb <u>produces</u> is <u>death penalty</u>, but the words in between might lead a writer to think that <u>the police and the courts</u> is the subject— and to mistakenly leave the *-s* ending off. Now take a look at this example:

> Foes of the death penalty often <u>argue</u> that execution has no deterrent effect.

Can you figure out why there is no *-s* on the verb <u>argue</u>? That's because the subject is <u>foes</u>, a word that does not mean *he, she,* or *it*. When trying to figure out the subject–verb agreement, you just have to forget about the words that come between <u>foes</u> and <u>argue</u>.

EXERCISE

In each of the following sentences, underline the subject and then circle the verb that agrees with it. Example:

> A <u>verb</u> in the present tense take/(takes) an *-s* ending when its subject is *he, she,* or *it*—or a noun that means *he, she,* or *it*.

1. An anthropologist study/studies buildings, tools, and other artifacts of ancient cultures.
2. Anthropologists always look/looks for signs of social change.
3. A box of oranges arrive/arrives at the house every month.
4. An adult student who has children find/finds little time for partying.
5. Low scores on the Scholastic Aptitude Test discourage/discourages students from applying to some colleges.
6. It give/gives me great pleasure to introduce tonight's speaker.
7. The first baseman, along with most of his teammates, refuse/refuses to sign autographs after the game.
8. Bonsai trees require/requires careful pruning.
9. Many movies of the past year contain/contains scenes of violence.

Now check over the essay you have just written. Look at all the verbs, especially those in the present tense. Did you use the -s ending on the appropriate verbs? Edit your writing carefully for subject–verb agreement.

WEB SITES

www.deathpenaltyinfo.org/
Death Penalty Information Center is one of the best sites for anti–death penalty information online.

www.prodeathpenalty.com
This site provides information and resources that support the death penalty.

DEBATE: THE RIGHT TO SAME-SEX MARRIAGE

In 1993, the Hawaii Supreme Court ruled that denying same-sex couples the right to marry violated the state's constitution, and in 1996, a trial judge ruled that the state of Hawaii had failed to show a valid reason for excluding same-sex couples from marriage. These two decisions launched the national debate over the right of gay people to marry.

Eventually, the state of Hawaii amended its constitution to prohibit same-sex marriages. But in 1999, the Vermont Supreme Court ruled that it was unconstitutional for the state to give tax breaks and joint health coverage only to heterosexual couples. Thus, on April 26, 2000, "An Act Related to Civil Unions," which grants same-sex couples the same legal rights as married heterosexuals, was signed into Vermont law. Bills to implement civil unions are pending in Connecticut, New Hampshire, and New York, but it is doubtful that any will succeed.

The following three articles, written in 1996, touch on many of the issues in this ongoing debate.

Preparing to Read

If you were voting in a referendum to legalize same-sex marriage in your state, how would you vote? What reasons would you give for your decision?

When John and Jim Say, "I Do"

CHARLES KRAUTHAMMER

Charles Krauthammer (b. 1950) has enjoyed a varied career beginning with a college major in political science, then attending medical school to become a psychiatrist, and combining his fields of interest as a successful writer. He won a Pulitzer prize in 1987 for his commentary in political and social columns in publications such as *The New Republic* and the *Washington Post*. The column we reprint here first appeared in *Time* on July 22, 1996.

TERMS TO RECOGNIZE

subservience *(para. 3)*	state of being used like a servant
exploitation *(para. 3)*	the using of another person for selfish purposes
riposte *(para. 4)*	pointed response, rebuttal
existential *(para. 4)*	pertaining to or dealing with existence
validity *(para. 5)*	the state of being sound or effective
abhorrent *(para. 7)*	disgusting, repellent

the House of Representatives may have passed legislation last week 1
opposing gay marriage, but the people will soon be trumped by the
courts. In September the judges of the Hawaii Supreme Court are
expected to legalize gay marriage. Once done there, gay marriage—like
quickie Nevada divorces—will have to be recognized "under the full faith
and credit clause of the Constitution" throughout the rest of the U.S. Gay
marriage is coming. Should it?

For the time being, marriage is defined as the union (1) of two people 2
(2) of the opposite sex. Gay-marriage advocates claim that restriction
No. 2 is discriminatory, a product of mere habit or tradition or, worse, prejudice. But what about restriction No. 1? If it is blind tradition or rank
prejudice to insist that those who marry be of the opposite sex, is it not
blind tradition or rank prejudice to insist that those who marry be just
two? In other words, if marriage is redefined to include two men in love,
on what possible principled grounds can it be denied to three men in love?

This is traditionally called the polygamy challenge, but polygamy—one 3
man marrying more than one woman—is the wrong way to pose the question. Polygamy, with its rank inequality and female subservience, is too easy
a target. It invites exploitation of and degrading competition among wives,
with often baleful social and familial consequences. (For those in doubt on
this question, see Genesis: 26–35 on Joseph and his multimothered brothers.) The question is better posed by imagining three people of the same
sex in love with one another and wanting their love to be legally recognized and socially sanctioned by marriage.

Why not? Andrew Sullivan, author of *Virtually Normal: An Argument* 4
about Homosexuality, offers this riposte to what he calls the polygamy
diversion: homosexuality is a "state," while polygamy is merely "an activity." Homosexuality is "morally and psychologically" superior to
polygamy. Thus it deserves the state sanction of marriage, whereas
polygamy does not. But this distinction between state and activity makes
no sense for same-sex love (even if you accept it for opposite-sex love).
If John and Jim love each other, why is this an expression of some kind

of existential state, while if John and Jim and Jack all love each other, this is a mere activity?

And why is the impulse to join with two people "morally and psycho-   5
logically inferior" to the impulse to join with one? Because, insists Sullivan, homosexuality "occupies a deeper level of human consciousness than a polyg-amous impulse." Interesting: this is exactly the kind of moral hierarchy among sexual practices that homosexual advocates decry as arbitrary and prejudiced. Finding, based on little more than "almost everyone seems to accept," the moral and psychological inferiority of polygamy, Sullivan would deny the validity of polygamist marriage. Well, it happens that most Americans, find-ing homosexuality morally and psychologically inferior to heterosexuality, would correspondingly deny the validity of homosexual marriage. Yet when they do, the gay-marriage advocates charge bigotry and discrimination.

Or consider another restriction built into the traditional definition of   6
marriage: that the married couple be unrelated to each other. The Kings and Queens of Europe defied this taboo, merrily marrying their cousins, with tragic genetic consequences for their offspring. For gay marriage there are no such genetic consequences. The child of a gay couple would either be adopted or the biological product of only one parent. Therefore the funda-mental basis for the incest taboo disappears in gay marriage. Do gay-marriage advocates propose to permit the marriage of, say, two brothers, or of a mother and her (adult) daughter? If not, by what reason of logic or morality?

The problem here is not the slippery slope. It is not that if society allows   7
gay marriage, society will then allow polygamy or incest. It won't. The people won't allow polygamy or incest. Even the gay-marriage advocates won't allow it. The point is why they won't allow it. They won't allow it because they think polygamy and incest wrong or unnatural or perhaps harmful. At bottom, because they find these practices psychologically or morally abhorrent, certainly undeserving of society's blessing.

Well, that is how most Americans feel about homosexual marriage,   8
which constitutes the ultimate societal declaration of the moral equality of homosexuality and heterosexuality. They don't feel that way, and they don't want society to say so. They don't want their schools, for example, to teach their daughters that society is entirely indifferent whether they marry a woman or a man. Given the choice between what Sullivan calls the virtu-ally normal (homosexuality) and the normal, they choose for themselves, and hope for their children, the normal. They do so because of various considerations: tradition, utility, religion, moral preference. Not good enough reasons, say the gay activists. No? Then show me yours for oppos-ing polygamy and incest.

Same-Sex Marriage, For Better or Worse?: Readers' Forum

ALEX TRESNIOWSKI

Charles Krauthammer's July 22, 1996, column, which you just read, drew a lot of response from readers of *Time* magazine. Staff writer Alex Tresniowski compiled the following "readers' forum" based on those responses; it was printed in the September 9, 1996, issue of *Time*.

TERMS TO RECOGNIZE

unflinching *(para. 1)*	fearless, decisive
trauma *(para. 2)*	an emotional shock that creates serious and lasting damage
vociferous *(para. 4)*	loud and intense

each week about 1,500 readers provide quick and unflinching feedback to *Time* through letters, faxes, phone calls, E-mails, online postings: everything but carrier pigeon. Such rapid response makes it easy to tell when the magazine has hit a nerve, as it certainly did recently with Charles Krauthammer's piece opposing same-sex marriages. Nearly 500 readers wrote about the Essay. Although some of them strongly supported Krauthammer's position, about 90% of those who wrote criticized—to put it mildly—his arguments, particularly his linking of gay marriages to polygamy and incest.

"I have yet to read a credible study showing a homosexual relationship causes the same level of psychological trauma that incest does," wrote Karyee Wu, 24, a Hong Kong native and second-year medical student at Tufts University in Boston. "Also, I don't remember the last time someone was killed or beaten because he or she was polygamous. I do know that these things happen to homosexuals." Wu, who is straight, says she became more tolerant of people's differences after learning her mother was a lesbian. "It seems hypocritical to be against gay marriages and at the same time in favor of family values," she says. "Gay marriages can and do provide stability for children and for society."

Many readers argued that homosexuality is not a choice. "If Krauthammer believes that one's sexual orientation is chosen, let him say when he chose to find women physically attractive rather than men," wrote Michael Hickey, 45, the executive director of technical services at Paramount Pictures

1

2

3

in Hollywood. Hickey, a homosexual whose partner of 14 years recently died of AIDS, concluded, "Where there is no choice, there can be no moral issue."

Krauthammer's most vociferous critics demanded equal rights for all. 4 "Evidently, gay Americans are to be kept around to work and pay taxes but lack those human qualities that would permit them to marry," wrote Steven M. Ferre, 32, a contract manager for a health-insurance firm in Washington. Ferre, who is gay and currently without a partner, has seen relationships fail because the logical next step—marriage—was not an option. "It's difficult to stay in a relationship if you can't get married," he says. "It becomes very easy to cut your losses and move on."

Luis Torres, 60, a retired editor in San Antonio, Texas, wrote, "I've served 5 in your army, paid taxes like everyone else and tried to live an ethical life, and as a citizen of this country, you can bet your booty that I want the same benefits that others enjoy." Torres also taught college history, served as a German linguist for the U.S. Army Security Agency and worked as a regional editor for *National Geographic Traveler* magazine. He and his partner of 13 years, Don Schechter, 60 (a retired former employee of the National Security Agency), together helped raise two daughters from Schechter's marriage. Like many of those who wrote in, Torres doesn't view the issue of gay marriages as a complex philosophical puzzle; to him it's a life-and-death concern: "Now that my partner and I are approaching old age, I don't want to have to resort to all kinds of legal subterfuge to ensure that what we have built together is not taken away. I want Don to be able to inherit my Social Security benefits if I die before he does. And I want to be covered by his medical retirement benefits. I simply want our waning years to be secure."

No One Has to Send a Gift

DAVID MIXNER

David Mixner (b. 1946) is a writer and political activist who now serves on the editorial staff for Gay.com. His biography, *Stranger among Friends* (1996), tells of his experiences as onetime advisor on gay issues to President Clinton. Mixner's latest book is *Brave Journey: Profiles in Gay and Lesbian Courage* (2000). The following article appeared in the December 16, 1996, issue of *Time* magazine.

TERMS TO RECOGNIZE

demagogues *(para. 1)*	leaders who gain power by appealing to the emotions and prejudices of the populace
jubilation *(para. 2)*	a celebration or other expression of joy
criterion *(para. 3)*	a standard or test on which a judgment or decision can be based

my partner, Patrick Marston, was asked recently why he wanted   1
to marry me. Patrick looked surprised at the question and
replied simply, "Because I love David very much and want to spend the
rest of my life with him." It is hard to imagine that such an honest and
loving statement could be the subject of a bitter national debate. Last
week's Hawaii court ruling has increased the tempo of the morals police,
who are determined to impose their values on our lives. Unfortunately,
there is no shortage of political demagogues willing to build their careers
on the fear of change.

The court ruling has been a cause for jubilation for those who believe   2
in justice. The issue of marriage goes far beyond the commitment of two
people of the same sex. It goes to the civil rights of gay and lesbian Americans. The effort to ban same-sex marriage would deny us the basic rights
accorded to our neighbors and friends. The issue involves immigration,
taxation, family leave, health care, adoption, Medicare, and numerous other
benefits and rights. I don't know one American who would willingly
surrender any of these rights.

Repeatedly I have been told by politicians frantically seeking to avoid   3
leadership that a majority of Americans do not approve of same-sex
unions. Although I am sad that people are so frightened of Patrick's and
my love, I refuse to allow anyone's discomfort to be the reason why we
should be less free than other Americans. I sincerely hope that eventually most of our fellow citizens will be able to understand our love for
each other. But nowhere in the Constitution of the United States does
the word comfortable appear as a criterion for the full enjoyment of the
rights accorded to every American citizen. In fact, this nation's founders
went to great pains to protect an unpopular minority from the tyranny
of a majority.

Let us be clear what this issue does not do. It does not force any reli-   4
gious institution to perform a same-sex marriage. Such institutions are now
free to refuse to marry even heterosexual couples based on certain religious
beliefs. Members of those institutions will continue to have the ability to

chose whom they want to marry. No citizen will be tied to a chair and forced to watch the happy couple dance at a reception. No one is required to send a gift. In fact, if our fellow citizens chose, they can do what they did when many of them disapproved of interracial and interfaith marriages. They can sit at home, loudly condemn us, pray for us and express their disgust. But let us be very clear, their beliefs and disapproval are not grounds to commit a grave injustice to millions of their fellow citizens. Gay and lesbian Americans should be accorded the same rights as other Americans—no more, but certainly no less.

As for Patrick and me, we are going to get married. We both are blessed   5 because our families and many of our straight friends plan to participate in the ceremony and celebrate with us. I guess we could wait until everyone approves and the laws of the land say we can legally get married, but then I guess Rosa Parks could have waited until the laws of Alabama said she could ride in the front of the bus. She refused to give up her dignity in the face of unjust laws—and so do Patrick and I.

RESPONDING TO READING

After reading these essays, would you change your vote in the referendum on same-sex marriage? Explain your response.

GAINING WORD POWER

Make a list of loaded (highly connotative) language used in each article. Which author uses the most emotionally charged words and phrases? What effect does this usage have on you as a reader?

CONSIDERING CONTENT

1. What objections does Charles Krauthammer have to same-sex marriage? Why does he focus on the issues of polygamy and incest?
2. Which of Krauthammer's arguments do the various readers of *Time* try to refute? Which of the readers' responses did you find most persuasive?
3. What is David Mixner's main thesis?
4. What is Mixner's point in bringing up interracial and interfaith marriages (para. 4)? How does that point respond to Krauthammer's argument about how "most Americans" feel toward homosexual marriage?

CONSIDERING METHOD

1. How does Krauthammer use the arguments of Andrew Sullivan? What evidence does he present that Sullivan's views represent those of other gay activists?
2. Krauthammer uses ten questions in his article. How many of them are **rhetorical questions?** Why does he use so many?
3. What organizational strategy does Alex Tresniowski use to present the readers' reactions to Krauthammer?
4. Mixner says in paragraph 4, "Let us be clear what this issue does not do." Why does he include this point?
5. Who is Rosa Parks, and what **analogy** is Mixner making by mentioning her in his conclusion? Is this an appropriate and effective analogy?

WRITING STEP BY STEP

Write an essay in which you argue for or against same-sex marriage.

A. Before you start writing, make a list of reasons why you support or oppose same-sex marriage. Next to each reason, try to write a brief response or a counterargument.
B. Identify at least three major reasons to support your choice. These reasons will be your claims.
C. Start your essay by stating your position and giving a brief overview of your main claims.
D. Take up each of your claims one by one. Explain each reason in a separate paragraph, and provide evidence to demonstrate the validity of that reason.
E. Be sure to consider any objections to your claims that readers might have. If you're not sure what these objections would be, ask classmates, friends, family members, or instructors for their ideas. Refute these objections by minimizing their importance, questioning their factuality, or offering a different point of view. You can include your refutations as part of the argument for each claim, or you can put them in a separate paragraph.
F. Close by summarizing your main ideas. You might end with a challenge, as Charles Krauthammer does (p. 329), or with an analogy, as David Mixner does (p. 333).

OTHER WRITING IDEAS

Write the paper outlined in the previous section, but argue for or against one of the following issues:

1. The use of animals in research should (should not) be allowed.
2. It should (should not) be harder than it is now to get a divorce.
3. Video games do (do not) contribute to violent behavior in young people.
4. Having a working mother does (does not) harm a child's welfare.
5. Laws restricting the use of pesticides should (should not) be repealed.
6. Free speech should (should not) be restricted on the Internet.
7. Sexual harassment is (is not) a serious problem in the workplace.
8. The government should (should not) cut welfare benefits for single parents.

If these topics don't appeal to you, come up with a debatable issue that you would like to write about.

EDITING SKILLS: USING COLONS

Copy the following passages from the articles in this section exactly.

Or consider another restriction built into the traditional definition of marriage: that the married couple be unrelated to each other.

They do so because of various considerations: tradition, utility, religion, moral preference.

Each week about 1,500 readers provide quick and unflinching feedback to *Time* through letters, faxes, phone calls, E-mails, online postings: everything but carrier pigeon.

[T]o him it's a life-and-death concern: "Now that my partner and I are approaching old age, I don't want to have to resort to all kinds of legal subterfuge."

If you copied correctly, you put a colon (:) in each passage. Reread what you copied, and see whether you can come up with a rule about the use of the colon.

If you looked closely, you noticed that a colon comes after a complete sentence. Go back and reread the first portion of each example. The colon then introduces a quotation, a list, or an explanation—something that specifies or expands on the sentence before the colon. If you think of the colon as a verbal equal sign (=), you get the main relationship it suggests between the two parts.

EXERCISE

Complete the following passages that include colons.

1. Sami has already bought her party supplies:
   _____.

2. Beau's next statement gave away his secret plans:
   _____.

3. Marcus acted very strangely toward Doreen:
   _____.

4. _____: a paperback detective novel, a historical romance, and a Far Side cartoon book.

5. _____: Austin only cried a little while.

Now edit the essay you just wrote, looking for places where you could have used a colon instead of a period or a semicolon. After consulting with your instructor, change the punctuation mark to a colon.

✪ WEB SITE

**http://fullcoverage.yahoo.com/Full_Coverage/US/Same_Sex_
Marriage/**

U.S. Full Coverage provides links, updated weekly, to the latest articles and editorials about same-sex marriage and domestic partnerships.

Student Essay Using Argument

Education Interrupted

Steve Dare

You are in your dorm room, enjoying a deep,   1
comfortable sleep after a long, exhausting day of
studying for the third test you have this week. You
are cozy in your warm bed, away from your notes and
your books, fast asleep, and then from a faraway
place you hear the piercing, disturbing sound of an
alarm. Thinking your alarm clock is signaling you to
awake, you groggily rise, but before you are fully
alert, you realize that it is not your alarm clock;
it's the urgent, panicking blare of the fire alarm in
your building. You get up, put on your clothes and
shoes and coat, and go out to the hall to join your
fellow students who must exit the building through
the stairwell. The next two hours are grim: you and
the other students stand in the dorm parking lot,
shivering in the early morning air, as the fire
department arrives and casually runs through its
seemingly routine motions. Soon it becomes clear that
this is a fire drill. As soon as the dorm opens up to
students once more, you trudge back to your room,
where you find you have only a little more than an
hour to sleep before getting up to prepare for
another test.

The events I have just described show a growing   2
problem that students who live in the dorms must
endure. The school's scheduling of fire drills is
inconvenient because these drills almost always occur
in the middle of the night. Students have to get out
of bed and venture down to the dorm parking lot where
they have to wait, in whatever the weather is doing,
until the drill is deemed complete by the fire
department. While the school administration may argue
that these drills are necessary in order to ensure
the safety of the students, I cannot see why the
drills must take place in the middle of the night. A
report issued by the school's fire administration

office last year stated that 95% of actual fires occur between 1 P.M. and 11 P.M. This information leads me to wonder why so many drills take place in the early morning hours, disturbing those students who take their college careers seriously. These students cannot afford to be awakened by a fire drill when they need their sleep. Such a poorly scheduled event can only make more difficult students' attempts to get an education.

Obviously, some students are not serious about their education. But of the thousands who live in the dorms, most work hard at their classwork. They attend, on average, fifteen hours of class per week, and outside the classroom, they are told by professors, they are supposed to spend two hours studying for every hour in class. That means at least thirty hours of studying a week for the serious student. This amount of time demands a lot of energy as well as a lot of sleep to restore that energy. Fire drills that take place in the middle of the night, disrupting sleep, do not help to create a healthy, restful environment for such students.   3

I know that fire drills are indeed necessary. They cannot and should not be ignored or disregarded, no matter when they take place. Even exhausted students must take the alarm seriously and leave the dorm. Fire drills are designed to promote safety by enabling students and dorm staff to practice evacuation procedures in case a real fire breaks out.   4

Yet, the drills do not have to take place in the middle of the night. As the report of the fire administration office makes clear, it would make more sense to have the drills somewhere between 1 P.M. and 11 P.M. when the chance of a real fire is highest. An appropriate time to have a drill might be at 9 P.M. when many students are either studying or lounging in front of the TV or playing cards with their friends. This time in the evening seems more appropriate because students would not be in class then, as they would during a drill at two or three in the afternoon. Granted, a drill that occurs during a   5

student's study time might be seen as counterproductive,
but at least the drill could be completed without
cutting into time for needed sleep.

Another alternative might be to schedule a drill 6
and release the time and date to the students. In
this way, students could plan around the drill. The
obvious drawback of a planned drill is that many
students may choose to be absent, making it useless
as a way of getting students to practice evacuating
the building. But if the planned drill were to take
place in the evening--say nine or ten o'clock--it's
likely that more students would be in the dorm than
for a drill in the afternoon. As long as students are
not roused from their sleep, even a planned drill
could be very effective in the long run.

Many students spend a lot of money to attend this 7
school. They have worked hard at their jobs to pay
for tuition, room and board, and books and supplies.
Many also depend on financial aid, which they will
have to repay, with interest of course, after they
get their degrees. Moreover, they had to work hard at
achieving enough success in their high school classes
to be admitted to this college. Most of them have
come here hoping to continue their achievements by
putting forth even more effort than they did in high
school. It is only fair that the administration meet
them halfway by allowing them uninterrupted sleep--
sleep that they must have in order to maintain an
alert, healthy mind open for learning and achieving.

C h a p t e r

FURTHER READINGS

This chapter provides you with additional reading selections. Although some of these readings are developed by one controlling strategy, most of them illustrate combinations of various strategies. As you read, use the following questions to analyze how a writer combines strategies:

- What are the purpose and thesis of the essay? Who is the intended audience?
- Which strategy controls or dominates the essay?
- How does this strategy help readers to understand the essay's thesis and purpose?
- What other strategies appear in the essay?
- What do these strategies contribute to the readers' understanding of the essay's thesis and purpose?

Also keep in mind our suggestions for being an active reader: preview the selection, make predictions, pay attention to conventions, mark the text, use the dictionary, make inferences and associations, and summarize your reactions on paper. After reading the selection actively, you can then follow the process you've used in earlier chapters: first, reflect on the content; then analyze the writer's techniques; and, finally, write something of your own that relates to the reading. When possible, discuss the readings with your classmates and consult with them about your written responses.

Salvation

L A N G S T O N   H U G H E S

I was saved from sin when I was going on thirteen. But not really saved. 1
It happened like this. There was a big revival at my Auntie Reed's church.
Every night for weeks there had been much preaching, singing, praying,
and shouting, and some very hardened sinners had been brought to Christ,
and the membership of the church had grown by leaps and bounds. Then
just before the revival ended, they held a special meeting for children, "to
bring the young lambs to the fold." My aunt spoke of it for days ahead. That
night I was escorted to the front row and placed on the mourners' bench
with all the other young sinners, who had not yet been brought to Jesus.

My aunt told me that when you were saved you saw a light, and some- 2
thing happened to you inside! And Jesus came into your life! And God
was with you from then on! She said you could see and hear and feel Jesus
in your soul. I believed her. I had heard a great many old people say the
same thing and it seemed to me they ought to know. So I sat there calmly
in the hot crowded church, waiting for Jesus to come to me.

The preacher preached a wonderful rhythmical sermon, all moans and 3
shouts and lonely cries and dire pictures of hell, and then he sang a song
about the ninety and nine safe in the fold, but one little lamb was left in
the cold. Then he said, "Won't you come? Won't you come to Jesus? Young
lambs, won't you come?" And he held out his arms to all us young sinners
there on the mourners' bench. And the little girls cried. And some of them
jumped up and went to Jesus right away. But most of us just sat there.

A great many old people came and knelt around us and prayed, old women 4
with jet-black faces and braided hair, old men with work-gnarled hands. And
the church sang a song about the lower lights are burning, some poor sinners
to be saved. And the whole building rocked with prayer and song.

Still I kept waiting to see Jesus. 5

Finally all the young people had gone to the altar and were saved, but one 6
boy and me. He was a rounder's son named Westley. Westley and I were
surrounded by sisters and deacons praying. It was very hot in the church, and
getting late now. Finally Westley said to me in a whisper: "Goddamn! I'm tired
o' sitting here. Let's get up and be saved." So he got up and was saved.

Then I was left all alone on the mourners' bench. My aunt came and 7
knelt at my knees and cried, while prayers and songs swirled all around me
in the little church. The whole congregation prayed for me alone, in a mighty

wail of moans and voices. And I kept waiting serenely for Jesus, waiting, waiting—but he didn't come. I wanted to see him, but nothing happened to me.
Nothing! I wanted something to happen to me, but nothing happened.

I heard the songs and the minister saying: "Why don't you come? My   8
dear child, why don't you come to Jesus? Jesus is waiting for you. He wants
you. Why don't you come? Sister Reed, what is this child's name?"

"Langston," my aunt sobbed.   9

"Langston, why don't you come? Why don't you come and be saved?   10
Oh, Lamb of God! Why don't you come?"

Now it was really getting late. I began to be ashamed of myself, hold-   11
ing everything up so long. I began to wonder what God thought about
Westley, who certainly hadn't seen Jesus either, but who was now sitting
proudly on the platform, swinging his knickerbockered legs and grinning
down at me, surrounded by deacons and old women on their knees praying. God had not struck Westley dead for taking his name in vain or for
lying in the temple. So I decided that maybe to save further trouble, I'd
better lie, too, and say that Jesus had come, and get up and be saved.

So I got up.   12

Suddenly the whole room broke into a sea of shouting, as they saw me   13
rise. Waves of rejoicing swept the place. Women leaped into the air. My aunt
threw her arms around me. The minister took me by the hand and led me
to the platform.

When things quieted down, in a hushed silence, punctuated by a few   14
ecstatic "Amens," all the new young lambs were blessed in the name of
God. Then joyous singing filled the room.

That night, for the last time in my life but one—for I was a big boy   15
twelve years old—I cried. I cried, in bed alone, and couldn't stop. I buried
my head under the quilts, but my aunt heard me. She woke up and told
my uncle I was crying because the Holy Ghost had come into my life, and
because I had seen Jesus. But I was really crying because I couldn't bear to
tell her that I had lied, that I had deceived everybody in the church, and
I hadn't seen Jesus, and that now I didn't believe there was a Jesus any
more, since he didn't come to help me.

WEB SITE

www.nku.edu/~diesmanj/hughes.html

Contains some of Hughes's poetry as well as links to information about
Hughes's work as a whole and about the Harlem Renaissance, of which
he was an important part.

"I Know What I Can Do"

SHERYL FLATOW

"It was the most exciting moment of my entire life," said Curtis   1
Pride, an outfielder in the Montreal Expos organization. "It was the
middle of a pennant race, and there I was, pinch hitting with runners on
first and second base against the Philadelphia Phillies. I hit the first pitch I
saw for a two-run double. I got my first standing ovation. I was overwhelmed. As I stood on second base and saw all those people cheering, I
reflected back on life, on how I'd come a long way."

Curtis Pride is deaf. He was born with a 95 percent hearing loss. In his   2
left ear he wears a hearing aid that amplifies sound and enables him to hear
voices, though not clearly. But Pride has never allowed his lack of hearing
to deter him from pursuing his dreams. In September 1993, after eight years
in the minor leagues, he made it to Montreal. On Sept. 17, in only his
second at-bat, he got his first major-league hit. It helped spark the second-
place Expos to a come-from-behind victory over the first-place Phillies.

"My parents encouraged me that I could do anything," Pride said. "But   3
I'm also very confident. I know what I'm capable of doing."

How did Pride develop such unshakable confidence? How did the will   4
to succeed evolve into success? Those were the things I set out to discover
when I interviewed Curtis and his parents at the family home in Silver
Spring, Maryland.

Pride, 25, is gracious, good-humored and completely at ease in talking   5
about his deafness. He is a superb lip-reader, and his speech, though not
entirely fluid, is clear. (Last season, he appeared on a radio call-in show in
Montreal. The host lip-synched the questions, and Pride responded without missing a beat.)

Curtis is the only son of Sallie and John Pride, who also have two   6
daughters. The household is further enlivened by a little girl named
Leonda, whom the Prides are adopting. They are a warm, handsome and
determined family. "I knew for a long time that Curt had a special
talent," said his father. "I intended to make sure Curt saw it too, that he
believed in himself."

Curtis was found to be deaf at 6 months. The Prides immediately   7
enrolled him in a special program at the hospital, which he attended once
a week for three years, and after that in a free program offered by the public
school system in Montgomery County, Maryland. The couple also began

to educate themselves on how to create an environment for their son that would enable him to succeed academically and socially. "We read a lot," said Sallie. "We talked a lot, especially to other parents with deaf children. That was really helpful. They tell you the truth."

Sallie, a registered nurse, decided to stay at home with her son. John is a specialist in disabilities with the U.S. Department of Health and Human Services. "I got into disability work as a byproduct of Curt being born deaf," he said. 8

One of the early and most crucial decisions Sallie and John made was to have Curtis not learn sign language. "When you introduce kids to sign language, they tend to rely on it, and it hinders their oral growth," John explained. "We wanted Curt to rely on oral communication." 9

Curtis was fitted with a hearing aid as a baby. He worked with a speech therapist from infancy through high school. His parents also helped teach him to say words and, later, sentences. "There were days my mom would hold up a ball," he recalled, "and she would say the word 'ball' over and over. I would read her lips, and I could sort of 'hear' what it sounded like. I'd put those two things together until I could say the word." 10

Curtis looks back at his first few years in school as the most difficult time of his life. "Kids were always making fun of me," he said, "of the way I talked, of the funny thing in my ear. I had a hard time dealing with it. I used to come home angry, and I would cry all the time." 11

"By the second or third grade, he realized that he had fallen way behind other children in spoken language," said John. "It became apparent to him that he was not going to catch up. That's when he had to come to terms with his deafness." 12

"My parents would reassure me, but they wouldn't let me feel sorry for myself," said Curtis. "They helped me understand that this was the way I was born, and there was nothing I could do about it. So I had to get on with my life." Both Curtis and his parents agreed that this happened in the fourth grade. 13

It helped tremendously that he was already a gifted athlete, excelling in soccer, basketball, baseball, football, and other sports. "People wanted me on their team," said Curtis. 14

Soon, no one was making fun of him. "I never heard any kid make a cruel remark," said John, who took turns with Sallie accompanying their son to practice sessions to make sure Curtis understood whatever instructions he was given. "The coaches would not have tolerated any nonsense. Later on, when he began playing against different kids, his reputation was such that if someone had resorted to making remarks about him, that person would have been ridiculed by his teammates." 15

Curtis also became a top-notch student. Prior to entering the seventh grade, he decided he wanted to be mainstreamed—against the recommendations of the auditory staff of his county. "I wanted to be more independent," he said. "It was a challenge for me. I would be the only deaf person in the whole school." Still, he conceded, "I was nervous and shy. I wondered how people would treat me." 16

But the kids and the teachers were supportive. And though his parents always made sure the teachers knew what he needed, Sallie said, "Curt had an inner drive to succeed. He motivated himself. We never said, 'Now, Curt, you've got to practice, you've got to do your homework.' He did it on his own." 17

Curtis graduated from John F. Kennedy High School with a 3.6 average. He starred in three sports and earned *Parade* all-American honors as a striker for the soccer team. "I've worked hard at everything I've done," he said, "whether it's classwork or sports. I want to be the best at everything I do." 18

After high school, Pride was drafted by the New York Mets. He also had the opportunity to attend the College of William and Mary on a basketball scholarship. "My parents and I agreed it was important for me to get an education," he said. "There's no guarantee of making it in professional sports. So I worked out an agreement with the Mets that allowed me to go to college full-time and play in the minor leagues in the summers." Following his graduation in 1990 with a degree in finance, Pride turned his undivided attention to baseball. 19

Pride was in the Mets organization for seven years but batted just .251. "While I was in college, my playing time was limited," he said. "That hurt my development a lot. But I have no regrets." Pride became a minor-league free agent at the end of the 1992 season, and he signed with the Expos that December. "I needed to get a fresh start," he said. 20

Pride approaches the game much the same as a hearing person. He even joked that his deafness can be an advantage at bat. "The crowd noise won't get to me," he said. "I'm able to maintain my full concentration." When he plays center field, he said, "We have one simple rule: Any time I call for the ball, it's automatically mine. If someone else calls for it, he'll wave me off with a glove." 21

The key for Pride, always, is to keep his eyes on the ball. As a result, he said, he is probably more visually astute than most ballplayers. Prior to the 1993 season, he worked at length with a sports vision trainer, in order to fine-tune his visual skills even further. 22

Despite getting four hits in nine at-bats with the Expos last fall, Pride is now with the Ottawa Lynx, a Montreal farm team. Regardless of how his career turns out, he's already a hero to many people. Pride firmly 23 believes in giving back to others, and these are not just words: Following the '92 season, he worked as an instructional aide in a special-education class. "I helped the children with their schoolwork and tried to build their confidence," said Pride. "I shared my experiences with them. It gave me great satisfaction to see them do well in school, to see them feel good about themselves."

Pride said he wants to inspire as many people as he can—and not just   24
those with disabilities. "I want inner-city children to know they have no excuse for not being successful," said Pride. "They see people like me, and they see that I overcame a handicap. I never let my deafness hold me back. I never feel sorry for myself. Never. I know I have a disability. I've accepted it. I can't worry about it. I want to make the most of my life. And I am."

🌎 WEB SITES

www.nidcd.nih.gov

The National Institute on Deafness and Other Communications Disorders site includes health information, research updates, news and events, and FAQs.

http://baseball.espn.go.com/mlk/players/profile?statsId=5166

Current facts and playing stats about Curtis Pride from ESPN.

Navajo Code Talkers:
The Century's Best Kept Secret

JACK HITT

during World War II, on the dramatic day when Marines raised the American flag to signal a key and decisive victory at Iwo Jima, the first word of this momentous news crackled over the radio in odd guttural noises and complex intonations. Throughout the war, the Japanese were repeatedly baffled and infuriated by these seemingly inhuman sounds. They conformed to no linguistic system known to the Japanese. The curious sounds were the military's one form of conveying tactics and strategy that the master cryptographers in Tokyo were unable to decipher. This perfect code was the language of the Navajo tribe. Its application in World War II as a clandestine system of communication was one of the twentieth century's best-kept secrets.

After a string of cryptographic failures, the military in 1942 was desperate for a way to open clear lines of communication among troops that would not be easily intercepted by the enemy. In the 1940s there was no such thing as a "secure line." All talk had to go out onto the public airwaves. Standard codes were an option, but the cryptographers in Japan could quickly crack them. And there was another problem: the Japanese were proficient at intercepting short-distance communications, on walkie-talkies for example, and then having well-trained English-speaking soldiers either sabotage the message or send out false commands to set up an ambush. That was the situation in 1942 when the Pentagon authorized one of the boldest gambits of the war.

The solution was conceived by the son of missionaries to the Navajos, a former Marine named Philip Johnston. His idea: station a native Navajo speaker at every radio. Since Navajo had never been written down or translated into any other language, it was an entirely self-contained human communication system restricted to Navajos alone; it was virtually indecipherable without Navajo help. Without some key or way into a language, translation is virtually impossible. Not long after the bombing of Pearl Harbor, the military dispatched twenty-nine Navajos to Camp Elliott and Camp Pendleton in California to begin a test program. These first recruits had to develop a Navajo alphabet since none existed. And because Navajo lacked technical terms of military artillery, the men coined a number of neologisms specific to their task and their war.

1

2

3

According to Chester Nez, one of the original code talkers: "Everything   4
we used in the code was what we lived with on the reservation every day,
like the ants, the birds, bears." Thus, the term for a tank was "turtle," a tank
destroyer was "tortoise killer." A battleship was "whale." A hand grenade was
"potato," and plain old bombs were "eggs." A fighter plane was "humming-
bird," and a torpedo plane "swallow." A sniper was "pick 'em off." Pyrotech-
nic was "fancy fire."

It didn't take long for the original twenty-nine recruits to expand to an   5
elite corps of Marines, numbering at its height 425 Navajo Code Talkers,
all from the American Southwest. Each Talker was so valuable, he traveled
everywhere with a personal bodyguard. In the event of capture, the Talkers had solemnly agreed to commit suicide rather than allow America's
most valuable war code fall into the hands of the enemy. If a captured
Navajo did not follow that grim instruction, the bodyguard's instructions
were understood: shoot and kill the Code Talker.

The language of the Code Talkers, their mission, and every detail of   6
their messaging apparatus was a secret they were all ordered to keep, even
from their own families. They did. It wasn't until 1968, when the military
felt convinced that the Code Talkers would not be needed for any future
wars, that America learned of the incredible contribution a handful of
Native Americans made to winning history's biggest war. The Navajo Code
Talkers, sending and receiving as many as 800 errorless messages at fast
speed during "the fog of battle," are widely credited with giving U.S. troops
the decisive edge at Guadalcanal, Tarawa, Saipan, Iwo Jima, and Okinawa.

❧ WEB SITE

www.mgm.com/windtalkers/

The official site for *Windtalkers,* the 2001 movie about the Navajo Code
Talkers, directed by John Woo and starring Nicholas Cage, contains links
to a lot of information about the code talkers and the code they used.

The Discus Thrower

RICHARD SELZER

i spy on my patients. Ought not a doctor to observe his patients by any   1
means and from any stance, that he might the more fully assemble
evidence? So I stand in the doorways of hospital rooms and gaze. Oh, it is
not all that furtive an act. Those in bed need only look up to discover me.
But they never do.

From the doorway of Room 542 the man in the bed seems deeply   2
tanned. Blue eyes and close-cropped white hair give him the appearance
of vigor and good health. But I know that his skin is not brown from the
sun. It is rusted, rather, in the last stage of containing the vile repose within.
And the blue eyes are frosted, looking inward like the windows of a snowbound cottage. This man is blind. This man is also legless—the right leg
missing from midthigh down, the left from just below the knee. It gives him
the look of a bonsai, roots and branches pruned into the dwarfed facsim-
ile of a great tree.

Propped on pillows, he cups his right thigh in both hands. Now and then   3
he shakes his head as though acknowledging the intensity of his suffering.
In all of this he makes no sound. Is he mute as well as blind?

The room in which he dwells is empty of all possessions—no get-well   4
cards, small, private caches of food, day-old flowers, slippers, all the usual
kick-shaws of the sickroom. There is only the bed, a chair, a nightstand, and
a tray on wheels that can be swung across his lap for meals.

"What time is it?" he asks.   5

"Three o'clock."   6

"Morning or afternoon?"   7

"Afternoon."   8

He is silent. There is nothing else he wants to know.   9

"How are you?" I say.   10

"Who is it?" he asks.   11

"It's the doctor. How do you feel?"   12

He does not answer right away.   13

"Feel?" he says.   14

"I hope you feel better," I say.   15

I press the button at the side of the bed.   16

"Down you go," I say.   17

"Yes, down," he says.   18

He falls back upon the bed awkwardly. His stumps, unweighted by legs   19
and feet, rise in the air, presenting themselves. I unwrap the bandages from
the stumps, and begin to cut away the black scabs and the dead, glazed fat
with scissors and forceps. A shard of white bone comes loose. I pick it away.
I wash the wounds with disinfectant and redress the stumps. All this while,
he does not speak. What is he thinking behind those lids that do not blink?
Is he remembering a time when he was whole? Does he dream of feet?
Of when his body was not a rotting log?

He lies solid and inert. In spite of everything, he remains impressive, as   20
though he were a sailor standing athwart a slanting deck.

"Anything more I can do for you?" I ask.   21

For a long moment he is silent.   22

"Yes," he says at last and without the least irony. "You can bring me a   23
pair of shoes."

In the corridor, the head nurse is waiting for me.   24

"We have to do something about him," she says. "Every morning he   25
orders scrambled eggs for breakfast, and, instead of eating them, he picks
up the plate and throws it against the wall."

"Throws his plate?"   26

"Nasty. That's what he is. No wonder his family doesn't come to visit.   27
They probably can't stand him any more than we can."

She is waiting for me to do something.   28

"Well?"   29

"We'll see," I say.   30

The next morning I am waiting in the corridor when the kitchen   31
delivers his breakfast. I watch the aide place the tray on the stand and
swing it across his lap. She presses the button to raise the head of the bed.
Then she leaves.

In time the man reaches to find the rim of the tray, then on to find the   32
dome of the covered dish. He lifts off the cover and places it on the stand.
He fingers across the plate until he probes the eggs. He lifts the plate in
both hands, sets it on the palm of his right hand, centers it, balances it. He
hefts it up and down slightly, getting the feel of it. Abruptly he draws back
his right arm as far as he can.

There is the crack of the plate breaking against the wall at the foot of his   33
bed and the small wet sound of the scrambled eggs dropping to the floor.

And then he laughs. It is a sound you have never heard. It is something   34
new under the sun. It could cure cancer.

Out in the corridor, the eyes of the head nurse narrow.   35

"Laughed, did he?"   36

She writes something down on her clipboard.   37

A second aide arrives, brings a second breakfast tray, puts it on the night-   38
stand, out of his reach. She looks over at me shaking her head and making
her mouth go. I see that we are to be accomplices.

"I've got to feed you," she says to the man.   39

"Oh, no you don't," the man says.   40

"Oh, yes I do," the aide says, "after the way you just did. Nurse says so."   41

"Get me my shoes," the man says.   42

"Here's oatmeal," the aide says. "Open." And she touches the spoon to   43
his lower lip.

"I ordered scrambled eggs," says the man.   44

"That's right," the aide says.   45

I step forward.   46

"Is there anything I can do?" I say.   47

"Who are you?" the man asks.   48

In the evening I go once more to that ward to make my rounds. The   49
head nurse reports to me that Room 542 is deceased. She has discovered
this quite by accident, she says. No, there had been no sound. Nothing. It's
a blessing, she says.

I go into his room, a spy looking for secrets. He is still there in his bed.   50
His face is relaxed, grave, dignified. After a while, I turn to leave. My gaze
sweeps the wall at the foot of the bed, and I see the place where it has been
repeatedly washed, where the wall looks very clean and very white.

WEB SITE

http://endeavor.med.nyu.edu/lit-med-db/webdocs/webauthors/
selzer83-au-.html

Medical Humanities: Literature, Arts, and Medicine, a site maintained by
New York University, summarizes and comments on a number of essays and
stories by Richard Selzer.

CORBIS, Kim Sayer

Volkswagen's Campaign in America

ROY GRACE

Once upon a time, advertising was very different. People lived happily   1
ever after in a world of pure fantasy, where all life's problems were
solved. Cars were glamorous objects, retouched and airbrushed to a fare-
thee-well, often accessorized with mansions and sold by beautiful women
wearing little more than diaphanous gowns and dazzling smiles.

And then onto the scene came an ugly, little car called Volkswagen.   2
Nothing else was ever quite the same. It didn't look like any other car, and
its advertising didn't look or speak like anything that had gone before.

First off, the car didn't have a fancy name. People dubbed it "the Bug"   3
or "the Beetle." And the name stuck. It was shown in simple photos, often
plain black-and-white, without flattering air-brushing. No mansions
hovered in the background; no one gamboled in the foreground. There
was no suave, debonair driver. And no gorgeous female. There the Bug sat
in all its dumb flat-footed homeliness.

Sometimes it was shown upside down, or in pieces, or floating in   4
water, or mired in mud. It was dented, it was battered. It appeared as a
lump of clay, as a hunk of meat. It was shown without wheels, without
a body, even crushed out of shape. It was seen as a police car, as a taxi-
cab, and not quite seen under snow. It was shown wearing giant
sunglasses or covered with psychedelic designs, or with a huge windup
key. It was shown as a single simple line. Sometimes it wasn't even
shown at all.

Volkswagen ads sold the steak instead of the sizzle. They talked about air-   5
cooled engines that never needed antifreeze or water, about how the engine
was mounted over the drive wheels to give better traction, how the car was
inspected thousands of times, how easy it was to replace parts, how
economical it was, and how it sustained its value.

Just as unusual as the way the ads looked was their tone of voice. Early   6
on, the decision was made that this was an honest product, honestly made,
and could be sold no other way but honestly. So these ads would go
where advertising had seldom gone before—right to people's intelligence.
They would appeal to common sense and logic and would never resort
to fluff or hype.

The copy spoke to readers as though they were bright, quick-witted   7
friends. The tone was self-deprecating rather than self-congratulatory. It
was irreverent. The car was never treated as an object of quasi-religious
idolatry. Instead it was . . . well, human, with all of humanity's oddities and
quirks. The overall impression was friendly, straightforward, and plain
spoken. A German car with all-American attributes.

For the first time, advertising talked *to* people and not *at* them. The ads   8
were designed to make people think, to appeal to their intelligence. (And
indeed, research throughout the years showed that VW buyers were better
educated than other car buyers.) People were respected, flattered; their sense
of humor tickled as they read the ads. They felt smart driving the little
Bugs: they had made a thoughtful choice. The advertising became part of
the car—they "drove" the advertising.

The copy in the ads was crafted to leave the reader with a little smile   9
at the end, a smile relevant to the selling message. (Almost fifty years later,
this continues to be the style of copy in "creative" advertising.) The
campaign spoke to Americans' traditional desire to root for the underdog.

And Americans responded. They were entertained by the ads. They found   10
them fresh, endearing, and fun. They talked about them at cocktail parties.
Hundreds wrote their own ads and sent them in. It may have been the first
advertising people looked forward to. In one of those wonderful marriages
of cause and effect, extraordinary sales resulted. In 1968, VW's best year,
423,000 of the little Bugs were sold.

In 1978, twenty years after the campaign began, it ended. The Beetle   11
was killed, a victim of the falling dollar, the surging Deutsche Mark, tough
new EPA standards, and newly savvy competition. As someone once said,
the car ran out of gas before the advertising did. Those of us who were in
on the creation of the campaign ads will never forget the experience.

It was a great ride.   12

🌐 WEB SITES

www.vw.com/commercials/

Information on the latest Volkswagen commercials; you can watch and listen to them, too.

www.geocities.com/MotorCity/4941/vgal.htm

The Volksgallery Page includes memorabilia, VW literature, and all eras of Volkswagen advertising.

Wordstruck

ROBERT MACNEIL

P eople are deeply attached to the language they use, more emotionally 1
involved than they may know. I am easily offended when someone
questions my pronunciation or usage—and broadcasters are constantly
being corrected by the audience. My first emotion is anger, even when it is
immediately apparent that I am wrong, because the correction seems to
imply an attack on more than one innocent word: not a sniper shot out of
the woods but the opening of a siege on my entire education and culture.

In Britain I once interviewed the rightwing politician Enoch Powell, 2
notorious for opposing more black immigration. Powell was a former
schoolmaster. When I asked what he *envisaged* happening, he stopped me
to say, "I think you mean *envisioned*." I didn't but let it go because the
cameras were running. When we stopped, we argued about it. It was humiliating to be corrected in public and infuriating to be told patronizingly that
"*envisage* must be a Canadian usage." In fact it was one of many ancient
usages that persisted in North America and changed in Britain. That
exchange ended up on the cutting-room floor.

As people evolve and do new things, their language will evolve too. 3
They will find ways to describe the new things and their changed perspective will give them new ways of talking about the old things. For example, electric light switches created a brilliant metaphor for the oldest of
human experiences, being *turned on* or *turned off*. To language conservatives
those expressions still have a slangy, low ring to them; to others they are
vivid, fresh-minted currency, very spendable, very *with it*.

That tolerance for change represents not only the dynamism of the 4
English-speaking peoples since the Elizabethans, but their deeply-rooted
ideas of freedom as well. This was the idea of the Danish scholar Otto
Jespersen, one of the great authorities on English. Writing in 1905, Jespersen
said in his *Growth and Structure of the English Language:*

> The French language is like the stiff French garden of Louis XIV, while
> the English is like an English park, which is laid out seemingly without
> any definite plan, and in which you are allowed to walk everywhere
> according to your own fancy without having to fear a stern keeper
> enforcing rigorous regulations. The English language would not have

been what it is if the English had not been for centuries great respecters of the liberties of each individual and if everybody had not been free to strike out new paths for himself.

I like that idea and do not think it just coincidence. Consider that the same cultural soil, the Celtic-Roman-Saxon-Danish-Norman amalgam, which produced the English language also nourished the great principles of freedom and rights of man in the modern world. The first shoots sprang up in England and they grew stronger in America. Churchill called them "the joint inheritance of the English-speaking world." At the very core of those principles are popular consent and resistance to arbitrary authority; both are fundamental characteristics of our language. The English-speaking peoples have defeated all efforts to build fences around their language, to defer to an academy on what was permissible English and what not. They'll decide for themselves, thanks just the same.

Nothing better expresses resistance to arbitrary authority than the persistence of what grammarians have denounced for centuries as "errors." In the common speech of English-speaking people—Americans, Englishmen, Canadians, Australians, New Zealanders, and other—these usages persist, despite rising literacy and wider education. We hear them every day:

Double negative: "I don't want none of that."
Double comparative: "Don't make that any more heavier!"
Wrong verb: "Will you learn me to read?"

These "errors" have been with us for at least four hundred years, because you can find each of them in Shakespeare.

Double negative: In *Hamlet,* the King says:
    Nor what he spake, though it lack'd form a little, Was not like madness.
Double comparative: In *Othello,* the Duke says:
    Yet opinion . . . throws a more safer voice on you.
Wrong verb: In *Othello,* Desdemona says:
    My life and education both do learn me how to respect you.

I find it very interesting that these forms will not go away and lie down. They were vigorous and acceptable in Shakespeare's time; they are far more vigorous today, although not acceptable as standard English. Regarded as error by grammarians, they are nevertheless in daily use all over the world by a hundred times the number of people who lived in Shakespeare's England.

It fascinates me that *axe,* meaning *ask,* so common in black American   9
English, is standard in Chaucer in all forms—*axe, axen, axed:* "and *axed* him
if Troilus were there." Was that transmitted across six hundred years or
simply reinvented?

English grew without a formal grammar. After the enormous creativity of   10
Shakespeare and the other Elizabethans, seventeenth- and eighteenth-century
critics thought the language was a mess, like an overgrown garden. They
weeded it by imposing grammatical rules derived from tidier languages, chiefly
Latin, whose precision and predictability they trusted. For three centuries,
with some slippage here and there, their rules have held. Educators taught
them and written English conformed. Today, English-language newspapers,
magazines, and books everywhere broadly agree that correct English obeys
these rules. Yet the wild varieties continue to threaten the garden of cultivated
English and, by their numbers, actually dominate everyday usage.

Non-standard English formerly knew its place in the social order. Char-   11
acters in fiction were allowed to speak it occasionally. Hemingway believed
that American literature really did not begin until Mark Twain, who
outraged critics by reproducing the vernacular of characters like Huck
Finn. Newspapers still clean up the grammar when they quote the ungram-
matical, including politicians. The printed word, like Victorian morality, has
often constituted a conspiracy of respectability.

People who spoke grammatically could be excused the illusion that their   12
writ held sway, perhaps the way the Normans thought that French had
conquered the language of the vanquished Anglo-Saxons. A generation ago,
people who considered themselves educated and well-spoken might have
had only glancing contact with non-standard English, usually in a well-
understood class, regional, or rural context.

It fascinates me how differently we all speak in different circumstances. We   13
have levels of formality, as in our clothing. There are very formal occasions,
often requiring written English: the job application or the letter to the
editor—the dark-suit, serious-tie language, with everything pressed and the lint
brushed off. There is our less formal out-in-the-world language—a more
comfortable suit, but still respectable. There is language for close friends in the
evenings, on weekends—blue-jeans–and–sweat-shirt language, when it's good
to get the tie off. There is family language, even more relaxed, full of grammatical short cuts, family slang, echoes of old jokes that have become intimate
shorthand—the language of pyjamas and uncombed hair. Finally, there is the
language with no clothes on; the talk of couples—murmurs, sighs, grunts—
language at its least self-conscious, open, vulnerable, and primitive.

Broadcasting has democratized the publication of language, often at its   14
most informal, even undressed. Now the ears of the educated cannot escape

the language of the masses. It surrounds them on the news, weather, sports, commercials, and the ever-proliferating talk and call-in shows.

This wider dissemination of popular speech may easily give purists the   15
idea that the language is suddenly going to hell in this generation, and may explain the new paranoia about it.

It might also be argued that more Americans hear more correct, even   16
beautiful, English on television than was ever heard before. Through television more models of good usage reach more American homes than was ever possible in other times. Television gives them lots of colloquial English, too, some awful, some creative, but that is not new.

Hidden in this is a simple fact: our language is not the special private   17
property of the language police, or grammarians, or teachers, or even great writers. The genius of English is that it has always been the tongue of the common people, literate or not.

English belongs to everybody: the funny turn of phrase that pops into   18
the mind of a farmer telling a story; or the travelling salesman's dirty joke; or the teenager saying, "Gag me with a spoon"; or the pop lyric—all contribute, are all as valid as the tortured image of the academic, or the line the poet sweats over for a week.

Through our collective language sense, some may be thought beautiful   19
and some ugly, some may live and some may die; but it is all English and it belongs to everyone—to those of us who wish to be careful with it and those who don't care.

WEB SITES

www.infoplease.com/ce6/society/A0817376.html

From the Learning Network, an article about the English language, including a brief history and a discussion of various linguistic changes.

www.shared-visions.com/explore/english.html

From the Knowledge Explorer Center, a site that explores "the wonders and quirks of the English Language, including the parts of speech, sentences, style guidelines, usage, punctuation, spelling, and more."

GLOSSARY

Abstract words: language that refers to ideas, conditions, and qualities that cannot be observed directly through the five senses. Words such as *beauty, love, joy, wealth, cruelty, power,* and *justice* are abstract. In his essay (p. 113), Isaac Asimov explores the abstract term "intelligence," offering a series of concrete examples and incidents to make the meaning clearer. *Also see* Concrete words.

Active reader: a reader who gets involved with the reading material by surveying the text, making predictions, writing questions and responses in the margins, rereading difficult passages, and spending time afterward summarizing and reflecting.

Allusion: a passing reference to a person, place, or object in history, myth, or literature. Writers use allusions to enrich or illuminate their ideas. For instance, in her essay on cultural heritage, Barbara Ehrenreich mentions the "flight from Egypt" (p. 127), an allusion to the biblical story of the Israelites' deliverance from slavery in Egypt and their search for the Promised Land. And when Suzanne Britt mentions "Never-Never Land" (p. 189), she alludes to the imaginary land in *Peter Pan*.

Analogy: a comparison that uses a familiar or concrete item to explain an abstract or unfamiliar concept. For example, a geologist may compare the structure of the earth's crust to the layers of an onion, or a biologist may explain the anatomy of the eye by comparing it to a camera.

Anecdote: a brief story about an amusing or interesting event, usually told to illustrate an idea or support a point. Writers also use anecdotes to begin essays, as Barbara Huttmann does in "A Crime of Compassion" (p. 308).

Antonym: a word that has the opposite meaning of another word. For example, *wet* is an antonym of *dry; coarse* is an antonym of *smooth; cowardly* is an antonym of *brave.*

Argument: a type of writing in which the author tries to influence the reader's thinking on a controversial topic. See the introduction to Chapter 10.

Audience: the readers for whom a piece of writing is intended. Many essays are aimed at a general audience, but a writer can focus on a specific group of readers. For example, Arthur Ashe directs his essay "Send Your Children to the Libraries" (p. 294) to the parents of young African American males, while David Mixner in "No One Has to Send a Gift" (p. 331) is primarily addressing people who oppose same-sex marriage.

Block pattern: an organizational pattern used in comparison-and-contrast writing. In this method, a writer presents, in a block, all the important points about the first item to be compared and then presents, in another block, the corresponding points about the second item to be compared.

Brainstorming: a method for generating ideas for writing. In brainstorming, a writer jots down a list of as many details and ideas on a topic as possible without stopping to evaluate or organize them.

Causes: the reasons or explanations for why something happens. Causes can be *immediate* or *remote.* See the introduction to Chapter 9.

Chronological order: the arrangement of events according to time—that is, in the sequence in which they happened.

Claim: a positive statement or assertion that requires support. Claims are the backbone of any argument.

Classification: the process of sorting items or ideas into meaningful groups or categories. See the introduction to Chapter 6.

Cliché: a phrase or expression that has lost its originality or force through overuse. To illustrate, novelist and teacher Janet Burroway writes: "Clichés are *the last word* in bad writing, and it's *a crying shame* to see all you *bright young things* spoiling your *deathless prose* with phrases *as old as the hills.* You must *keep your nose to the grindstone,* because the *sweet smell of success* only comes to those who *march to the tune of a different drummer.*"

Coherence: the logical flow of ideas in a piece of writing. A writer achieves coherence by having a clear thesis and by making sure that all the supporting details relate to that thesis. *Also see* Unity.

Colloquial language: conversational words and expressions that are sometimes used in writing to add color and authenticity. Dave Barry (p. 238) and Mike Royko (p. 41) use colloquial language to good effect in their writing. *Also see* Informal writing.

Comparison and contrast: a pattern of writing in which an author points out the similarities and differences between two or more subjects. See the introduction to Chapter 7.

Conclusion: the sentences and paragraphs that bring an essay to its close. In the conclusion, a writer may restate the thesis, sum up important ideas, emphasize the topic's significance, make a generalization, offer a solution to a problem, or encourage the reader to take some action. Whatever the strategy, a conclusion should end the essay in a firm and definite way.

Concrete words: language that refers to real objects that can be seen, heard, tasted, touched, or smelled. Words such as *tree, desk, car, orange, Chicago, Roseanne,* or *jogging* are concrete. Concrete examples make abstractions easier to understand, as in "Contentment is a well-fed cat asleep in the sun." *Also see* Abstract words.

Connotation and denotation: terms used to describe the different kinds of meaning that words convey. **Denotation** refers to the most specific or direct meaning of a word—the dictionary definition. **Connotations** are the feelings or associations that attach themselves to words. For example, *assertive* and *pushy* share a similar denotation—both mean "strong" or "forceful." But their differing connotations suggest different attitudes: an assertive person is admirable; a pushy person is offensive.

Controlling idea *See* Thesis.

Conventions: customs or generally accepted practices. The conventions of writing an essay require a title, a subject, a thesis, a pattern of organization, transitions, and paragraph breaks.

Definition: a method of explaining a word or term so that the reader understands what the writer means. Writers use a variety of methods for defining words and terms; see the introduction to Chapter 5.

Denotation *See* Connotation and denotation.

Dependent clause: a group of words that contains a subject and verb but does not stand alone as a sentence. For example, *until the game ended* is a dependent clause; its complete meaning depends on being attached to an independent clause: *Few fans stayed until the game ended. Also see* Independent clause.

Derivation: the historical origin and development of a word. For instance, the English word *verbiage* (meaning "too many words") comes from the French word *verbier* meaning "to chatter." *Also see* Root.

Description: writing that uses sensory details to create a word picture for the reader. See the introduction to Chapter 3.

Details: specific pieces of information (examples, incidents, dates, statistics, descriptions, and the like) that explain and support the general ideas in a piece of writing.

Development: the techniques and materials that a writer uses to expand and build on a general idea or topic.

Dialogue: speech or conversation recorded in writing. Dialogue, which is commonly found in narrative writing, reveals character and adds life and authenticity to an essay.

Diction: choice of words in writing or speaking.

Division: the process of breaking a large subject into its components or parts. Division is often used in combination with classification. See the introduction to Chapter 6.

Editing: a step in the writing process that focuses on making small-scale changes to correct mechanics and improve clarity and readability.

Effects: the results or outcomes of certain events. Effects can be *immediate* or *long term*. Writers often combine causes and effects in explaining why something happens. See the introduction to Chapter 9.

Ellipsis: three equally spaced dots that signal an omission of words.

Emphasis: the placement of words and ideas in key positions to give them stress and importance. A writer can emphasize a word or idea by putting it at the beginning or end of a paragraph or essay. Emphasis can also be achieved by using repetition and figurative language to call attention to an idea or term.

Essay: a short prose work on a limited topic. Essays can take many forms, but they usually focus on a central theme or thesis and often convey the writer's personal ideas about the topic.

Evidence *See* Supporting material.

Example: a specific case or instance used to illustrate or explain a general concept. See the introduction to Chapter 4.

Fable: a brief narrative that teaches a lesson or truth.

Figurative language: words that create images or convey symbolic meaning beyond the literal level. Richard Selzer, for example, uses figurative language to portray the dramatic, often agonizing experiences of a practicing surgeon: "And the blue eyes are frosted, looking inward like the windows of a snowbound cottage" (see "The Discus Thrower," p. 349).

Figure of speech: deliberate departure from the ordinary, literal use of words in order to provide fresh perceptions and create lasting impressions. *See* Metaphor, Paradox, Personification, *and* Simile.

First person: the use of *I, me, we,* and *us* in speech and writing to express a personal view or present a firsthand report. *Also see* Point of view.

Focus: the narrowing of a topic to a specific aspect or set of features.

Freewriting: a procedure for exploring a topic that involves writing without stopping for a set period of time.

Generalization: a broad assertion or conclusion based on specific observations. The value of a generalization is determined by the number and quality of the specific instances.

Generic nouns: the name of a class of people, such as *doctor, teacher, student, player, citizen, juror, consumer, reader, author,* and so forth. The use of such nouns in the singular to designate a whole class or group causes problems with pronoun selection. For example, a sentence like "Each applicant is responsible for scheduling his own interview" seems to ignore or exclude female applicants. This same point can be expressed without relying on the masculine pronoun (*his*): "Each applicant is responsible for scheduling his or her own interview" or "Applicants are responsible for scheduling their own interviews."

Homophone: a word that sounds the same as another but is different in spelling and meaning. *Knew* and *new* are homophones of each other.

Hyperbole: a conscious, intentional use of exaggeration, as in "I'm so hungry I could eat a horse" or "All the perfumes of Arabia will not sweeten this little hand." This figure of speech is used to heighten effect, or it may be used for humor, as Dave Barry does in his essay "There Are Rules, You Know" (p. 238).

Illustration: the use of examples, or a single long example, to support or explain an idea. See the introduction to Chapter 4.

Images: descriptions that appeal to our senses of sight, smell, sound, touch, or taste. Images add interest and clarify meaning.

Imperative sentence: a sentence that gives a command or a direction. Imperative sentences usually begin with a verb; they are often used in writing about a process: "Snap the knee up to the chest as close as possible"; "Leave enough space after the complimentary close to sign your name"; "Don't forget to proofread your final copy."

Independent clause: a group of words that contains a subject and verb and can stand alone as a sentence.

Inference: a conclusion drawn by a reader from the hints and suggestions provided by the writer. Writers sometimes express ideas indirectly rather than stating them outright; readers must use their own experience and knowledge to read between the lines and make inferences to gather the full meaning of a selection.

Informal writing: the familiar, everyday level of usage, which includes contractions and perhaps slang but requires standard grammar and punctuation.

Interrupter: a word or phrase that interrupts the normal flow of a sentence without changing the basic meaning. Interrupters are usually set off from the rest of the sentence with commas: "Magnum Oil Company, *our best client,* canceled its account." "Being lucky, *it seems to me,* is better than being smart."

Introduction: the beginning or opening of an essay, which usually presents the topic, arouses interest, and prepares the reader for the development of the thesis.

Irony: the use of verbal clues to express the opposite of what is stated. Writers use irony to expose unpleasant truths or to poke fun at human weakness.

Issue: an important point or problem for discussion or debate, such as the issue of global warming or the issue of same-sex marriage.

Jargon: the specialized or technical language of a trade, profession, or similar group. To readers outside the group, jargon is confusing and meaningless.

Journalistic style: the kind of writing found in newspapers and popular magazines. It normally employs informal diction with relatively simple sentences and unusually short paragraphs.

Logical order: arrangement of points and ideas according to some reasonable principle or scheme (e.g., from least important to most important).

Main idea *See* Thesis.

Metaphor: a figure of speech in which a word or phrase that ordinarily refers to one thing is applied to something else, thus making an implied comparison. For example, Mark Twain writes of "the language of this water" and says the river "turned to blood" ("Two Views of the Mississippi," p. 181). Similarly, Judith Ortiz Cofer refers to Mamá's room as "the heart of the house" (p. 57), and Scott Russell Sanders writes about "the narrow, ironclad days of fathers" and "what a prison a house could be" (pp. 196–97).

A *dead metaphor* is an implied comparison that has become so familiar that we accept it as literal: the arm of a chair, dog tired, or time is running out.

Modes *See* Patterns of organization.

Narration: writing that recounts an event or series of interrelated events; presentation of a story in order to illustrate an idea or make a point. See the introduction to Chapter 3.

Onomatopoeia: the use of words that suggest or echo the sounds they are describing—*hiss, plop, buzz, whir,* or *sizzle,* for example.

Order: the sequence in which the information or ideas in an essay are presented. *Also see* Chronological order *and* Logical order.

Paradox: a seeming contradiction that may nonetheless be true. For example, "Less is more" or "The simplest writing is usually the hardest to do."

Paragraph: a series of two or more related sentences. Paragraphs are units of meaning; they signal a division or shift in thought. In newspapers and magazines, frequent paragraph divisions are used to break up the narrow columns of print and make articles easier to read.

Parallelism: the presentation of two or more equally important ideas in similar grammatical form. In his essay "Send Your Children to the Libraries" (p. 294), Arthur Ashe emphasizes his thesis by using parallel structure: "I have become convinced that we blacks spend *too much time on the playing fields* and *too little time in the libraries.*" He also uses parallelism to make other points forceful and memorable: "Somehow, parents must instill *a desire for learning* alongside *the desire to be Walt Frazier*"; "*While we are about 35 percent of* major league baseball, *we are less than 2 percent of* the engineers. *While we are about 40 percent of* the National Football League, *we are less than 11 percent of* construction workers such as carpenters and bricklayers."

Patterns of development: strategies for presenting and expanding ideas in writing. Some of these patterns relate to basic ways of thinking (classification, cause and effect, argument), whereas others reflect the most common means for presenting material (narration, comparison–contrast, process) or developing ideas (example and illustration, definition, description) in writing.

Person *See* Point of view.

Personification: a figure of speech in which an inanimate object or an abstract concept is given human qualities. For example, "Hunger sat shivering on the road"; "Flowers danced on the lawn." In "Two Views of the Mississippi" (p. 182), Mark Twain refers to the "river's face" and describes the river as a subtle and dangerous enemy.

Persuasion: writing that attempts to move readers to action or to influence them to agree with a position or belief.

Point-by-point pattern: an organizational pattern used in comparison-and-contrast writing. In this method (also called the *alternating method*), the writer moves back and forth between the two subjects, focusing on particular features of each in turn: the first point or feature of subject *A* is followed by the first point or feature of subject *B* and so on.

Point of view: the angle or perspective from which a story or topic is presented. Personal essays often take a first-person (or *I*) point of view and sometimes address the reader as *you* (second person). The more formal third person (*he, she, it, one, they*) is used to create distance and suggest objectivity.

Prefix: a syllable or syllables used at the beginning of a word to change or add to the meaning. For example, prefixes change *mature* to **im**mature and **pre**mature; and *form* can be expanded to **in**form, **re**form, **per**form, **de**form, **trans**form, **uni**form, and **mis**inform. *Also see* Root *and* Suffix.

Previewing: the first step in active reading in which the reader prepares to read by looking over the text, and making preliminary judgments and predictions about what to expect.

Prewriting: the process that writers use to prepare for the actual writing stage by gathering information, considering audience and purpose, developing a provisional thesis, and mapping out a tentative plan.

Problem–solution: a strategy for analyzing and writing about a topic by identifying a problem within the topic and offering a solution or solutions to it.

Process writing: a pattern in which the author explains the step-by-step procedure for doing something. See the introduction to Chapter 8.

Proper noun: a noun that names a single particular person, place, or historical event, and is written with a capital letter: Carlo, Warsaw, Mexico, Garfield, the Holocaust.

Purpose: the writer's reasons for writing; what the writer wants to accomplish in an essay.

Refutation: in argumentation, the process of acknowledging and responding to opposing views. See the introduction to Chapter 10.

Revising: the stage in the writing process during which the author makes changes in focus, organization, development, and style to make the writing more effective.

Rhetorical question: a question that a writer or speaker asks to emphasize or introduce a point and usually goes on to answer. Barbara Ehrenreich uses a number of rhetorical questions in her essay "Cultural Baggage" (p. 126).

Root: the stem or base of a word; the element that carries the primary meaning of a word. The Latin word *videre*, meaning "to see," is the root of such English words as *video, vista, vision, visionary*, and *revision. Also see* Derivation.

Satire: writing that uses wit and irony to attack and expose human folly, weakness, and stupidity. Dave Barry (p. 238) and Suzanne Britt (p. 188) use satire to question human behavior and criticize contemporary values.

Sentence *See* Independent clause.

Sexist language: words and phrases that stereotype or ignore members of either sex. For example, the sentence "A doctor must finish his residency before he can begin to practice" suggests that only men are doctors. Writing in the plural will avoid this exclusion: "Doctors must finish their residencies before they can begin to practice." Terms like *mailman, stewardess, manpower*, and *mothering* are also sexist; try to use gender-neutral terms instead: *mail carrier, flight attendant, workforce, parenting*.

Simile: a figure of speech in which two essentially unlike things are compared, usually in a phrase introduced by *like* or *as*. For example, in "More Room" (p. 56) Judith Ortiz Cofer says the house is "*like* a chambered nautilus" and that "it rested on its perch *like* a great blue bird, more *like* a nesting hen. . . ."

Slang: the informal language of a given group or locale, often characterized by racy, colorful expressions and short-lived usage.

Standard English: the language written or spoken by most educated people.

Structure: the general plan, framework, or pattern of a piece of writing.

Style: individuality of expression, achieved in writing through selection and arrangement of words, sentences, and punctuation.

Subject: what a piece of writing is about.

Subordination: the process of expressing less important ideas in dependent clauses and combining them with independent clauses. For example, the independent statement "Tim heard a noise" can be subordinated and combined with "Tim began to run" by using the subordinator *when:* "Tim began to run *when he heard a noise.*"

Suffix: a syllable or syllables added to the end of a word to change or affect the meaning. For example, suffixes change *love* to *loved, lover, lovable, loveless, loving,* and *lovely. Also see* Prefix *and* Root.

Supporting material: facts, figures, details, examples, reasoning, expert testimony, personal experiences, and the like, which are used to develop and explain the general ideas in a piece of writing.

Symbol: a concrete or material object that suggests or represents an abstract idea, quality, or concept. The lion is a symbol of courage; a voyage or journey can symbolize life; water suggests spirituality; dryness stands for the absence of spirituality. In Richard Selzer's "The Discus Thrower" (p. 349), the stumps of the patient's amputated legs can be seen as symbols of human helplessness and immobility.

Synonym: a word that means the same or nearly the same as another word. *Sad* is a synonym of *unhappy. Also see* Antonym.

Thesis: the main point or proposition that a writer develops and supports in an essay. The thesis is often stated early, normally in the first paragraph, to give the reader a clear indication of the essay's main idea.

Third person: the point of view in which a writer uses *he, she, it, one,* and *they* to give the reader a less-limited and more seemingly objective account than a first-person view would provide. *Also see* Point of view.

Title: the heading a writer gives to an article or essay. The title usually catches the reader's attention and indicates what the selection is about.

Tone: the attitude that a writer conveys toward the subject matter. Tone can be serious or humorous, critical or sympathetic, affectionate or hostile, sarcastic or soothing, passionate or detached—or any of numerous other attitudes.

Topic sentence: the sentence in which the main idea of a paragraph is stated. Writers often state the topic sentence first and develop the rest of the paragraph in support of this main idea. Sometimes a writer will build up to the topic sentence and place it at the end of a paragraph.

Transitions: words and expressions, such as *for example, on the other hand, next,* or *to illustrate,* that help the reader to see the connections between points and ideas.

Unity: the fitting together of all elements in a piece of writing; sticking to the point. *Also see* Coherence.

Usage: the way in which a word or phrase is normally spoken or written.

Voice: the expression of a writer's personality in his or her writing; an author's distinctive style or manner of writing.

Wordiness: the use of roundabout expressions and unnecessary words, such as "majoring in the field of journalism" instead of "majoring in journalism"; or "these socks, which are made of wool" instead of "these wool socks"; or "in this day and age" instead of "today"; or "at this point in time" instead of "now."

Writing process: the series of steps that most writers follow in producing a piece of writing. The five major stages in the writing process are finding a subject (prewriting), focusing on a main idea and mapping out an approach (planning), preparing a rough draft (writing), reworking and improving the draft (revising), and polishing style and correcting errors (editing).

CREDITS

INDEX